THE SEMINAR OF
JACQUES LACAN

BOOK I

THE SEMINAR OF
JACQUES LACAN

Edited by Jacques-Alain Miller

BOOK I

Freud's Papers on Technique 1953–1954

TRANSLATED WITH NOTES BY

John Forrester

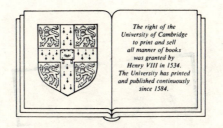

The right of the
University of Cambridge
to print and sell
all manner of books
was granted by
Henry VIII in 1534.
The University has printed
and published continuously
since 1584.

CAMBRIDGE UNIVERSITY PRESS

CAMBRIDGE
NEW YORK   NEW ROCHELLE
MELBOURNE   SYDNEY

Published by the Press Syndicate of the University of Cambridge
The Pitt Building, Trumpington Street, Cambridge CB2 1RP
32 East 57th Street, New York, NY 10022, USA
10 Stamford Road, Oakleigh, Melbourne 3166, Australia

Originally published in French as *Le Séminaire I*
by Les Editions du Seuil, Paris, 1975 and
© Les Editions du Seuil 1975

First published in English by Cambridge University Press 1988 as
The Seminar of Jacques Lacan I
Introduction, notes and English Translation
© Cambridge University Press 1988

Printed in Great Britain at the University Press, Cambridge

British Library cataloguing in publication data

Lacan, Jacques
The seminar of Jacques Lacan.
Bk. 1: Freud's papers on technique 1953–1954
1. Freud, Sigmund 2. Psychoanalysis
I. Title II. Miller, Jacques Alain
III. Le Seminaire. *English*
150.19'52 BF173.F85

ISBN 0 521 26679 3 hard covers
ISBN 0 31800 9 paperback

CONTENTS

MICHAEL BALINT'S BLIND ALLEYS

SPEECH IN THE TRANSFERENCE

TRANSLATORS' NOTE

1. What follows is a complete translation of the seminar that Jacques Lacan gave in the course of a year's teaching within the training programme of the Société Française de Psychanalyse. The French text was prepared by Jacques-Alain Miller in consultation with Jacques Lacan, from the transcriptions of the seminar. Certain minor errors in the text have been corrected in the translation, and will be incorporated in later editions of the French text. All notes are supplied by John Forrester (who also compiled the index), in order to clarify questions of translation and supply limited bibliographical information.

2. We have aimed at an exact translation. This involves, however, finding appropriate colloquial English to correspond to a text which is both informal and complex – a rendition of Lacan's spoken French. The translation aims at being both informal and literary, corresponding as faithfully as possible with the original text.

3. As we needed to pay additional attention to the German background of many psychoanalytic concepts, in many passages the requirements of three languages had to be taken into account. There has been considerable debate in French analytic circles about the translation of Freud's works, in large part stimulated by these seminars of Lacan's, which, until the early 1960's, were advertised as 'Commentaries on the texts of Freud'. In recent years the admirable English edition of Freud prepared by James Strachey has also been the subject of discussion and criticism in the English-language world. Anticipating the decision of the next Freud translators, we have made one decision which follows the French translations of Freud at the expense of Strachey's: where '*investir, investi, investissement*' appears in the French text, corresponding to the German '*besetzen, besetzt, Besetzung*', we have translated this by 'invest, invested, investment', instead of 'cathect, cathected, cathexis'. We have also translated '*pulsion*', corresponding to '*Trieb*', by 'drive' and '*instinct*', corresponding to '*Instinkt*', by 'instinct'; this decision is hardly

vii

controversial. Both of these decisions accord with Schneiderman's practice.[1]
Other decisions are pointed out in the notes.

4. We have paid considerable attention to the practices of previous translators
of Lacan, in particular Anthony Wilden,[2] Alan Sheridan,[3] Stuart
Schneiderman and Jacqueline Rose,[4] in the hope that some consistency in the
English rendition of Lacan can be achieved. This Seminar, together with
Seminar II, which is being published simultaneously, was worked on by both
translators so as to produce uniformity in both terminology and style. In
attempting to follow our predecessors, we came to the conclusion that it was
often more accurate to render one single French term by a variety of English
terms. This was made all the more necessary in view of the fact that Lacan's
'technical' vocabulary was, throughout his life, always tentative and decidedly
in flux. Nonetheless, the translations of the following terms have, or have
acquired, such importance in discussion of Lacan's work that it may be useful
to point them out, together with certain differences between our translation
and that of other Lacan translators.

FRENCH TERM	PREVIOUS TRANSLATORS	THIS TRANSLATION
parole	Word (Wilden)	speech
signification	signification (Sheridan) meaning (Schneiderman) }	signification or significance
sens	sense (Schneiderman) meaning (Sheridan) }	meaning
signifier		to mean or to signify
travail		labour or work

5. In the original text, words in a language other than French were printed in
italics. We have followed this practice, indicating in notes which words in the
original appeared in English. An exception to this rule is made for the terms 'ego'
and 'moi'. Both these terms are translated in this text by 'ego'; when italicized, it
is 'ego' in the French; when it is in roman face, the original word is 'moi'.

JOHN FORRESTER
SYLVANA TOMASELLI
Cambridge, June 1986

---

[1] In *Returning to Freud: Clinical Psychoanalysis in the School of Lacan*, New Haven and London:
Yale University Press, 1980, pp. vii–viii.

[2] Anthony Wilden, trans. and ed., *The Language of the Self: The Function of Language in
Psychoanalysis*, by J. Lacan, Baltimore: Johns Hopkins University Press, 1968.

[3] Jacques Lacan, *Écrits: a Selection*, London: Tavistock Publications, 1977; Jacques Lacan, *The
Four Fundamental Concepts of Psychoanalysis*, London: Hogarth Press and the Institute of Psycho-
analysis, 1977.

[4] Juliet Mitchell and Jacqueline Rose, eds., *Feminine Sexuality. Jacques Lacan and the École
Freudienne*, translated by Jacqueline Rose, London: Macmillan, 1982.

ABBREVIATIONS

E   Lacan, *Écrits*, Paris: Seuil, 1966. Where there are two numbers, separated by /, the first number refers to the page number in the French edition, the second to the page number in *Écrits; a Selection*, translated by Alan Sheridan, London: Tavistock, 1977.

Sem   Lacan, *Le Séminaire*, Paris: Seuil, 1973– (26 volumes).

SE   Freud, *The Standard Edition of the Complete Psychological Works of Sigmund Freud* (24 volumes), edited by James Strachey in collaboration with Anna Freud, assisted by Alix Strachey and Alan Tyson, London: The Hogarth Press and the Institute of Psycho-analysis, 1953–74.

GW   Freud, *Gesammelte Werke* (18 volumes), London: The Hogarth Press, 1940–68.

Stud   Freud, *Studienausgabe* (10 volumes with an unnumbered *Ergänzungsband*, abbreviated as *Erg*), Frankfurt am Main: Fischer Verlag, 1969–75.

Origins Sigmund Freud, *The Origins of Psychoanalysis. Letters to Wilhelm Fliess, Drafts and Notes 1887–1902*, ed. Marie Bonaparte, Anna Freud, Ernst Kris, authorised translation by Eric Mosbacher and James Strachey, introduction by Ernst Kris, London: Imago, 1954.

Robert   Paul Robert, *Dictionnaire Alphabétique & Analogique de la Langue Française*, Paris: S.N.L., 1977.

The interventions of participants in the Seminar have on occasion been abbreviated by Jacques-Alain Miller; these omissions are indicated by dotted lines.

OVERTURE TO THE SEMINAR

The master breaks the silence with anything – with a sarcastic remark, with a kick-start.

That is how a buddhist master conducts his search for meaning, according to the technique of *zen*. It behoves the students to find out for themselves the answer to their own questions. The master does not teach *ex cathedra* a ready made science; he supplies an answer when the students are on the verge of finding it.

This kind of teaching is a refusal of any system. It uncovers a thought in motion – nonetheless vulnerable to systematisation, since it necessarily possesses a dogmatic aspect. Freud's thought is the most perennially open to revision. It is a mistake to reduce it to a collection of hackneyed phrases. Each of his ideas possesses a vitality of its own. That is precisely what one calls the dialectic.

Certain of these ideas were, at a given moment, indispensable to Freud, because they supplied an answer to a question that he had formulated previously, in other terms. Hence one only gains a sense of their value by relocating them in their context.

But it is not enough to do some history, the history of thought, and to say that Freud lived in a scientistic century. Rather, with *The Interpretation of Dreams*, something of a different essence, of a concrete psychological density, is reintroduced, namely, meaning.

From the scientistic point of view, Freud appeared at this point to revert to the most archaic thinking – reading something in dreams. He later returns to causal explanations. But when one interprets a dream, one is always up to one's neck in meaning. What is at issue is the subjectivity of the subject, in his desires, in his relation to his environment, to others, to life itself.

Our task, here, is to reintroduce the register of meaning, a register that must itself be reintegrated on its own level.

Brücke, Ludwig, Helmholtz, Du Bois-Reymond had instituted a kind of

1

pledged faith – everything reduces down to physical forces, those of attraction and repulsion. Once one takes these as premises, there's no reason to go beyond them. If Freud did go beyond them, it is because he also took on others. He dared to attach importance to what was happening to him, to the antinomies of his childhood, to his neurotic problems, to his dreams. That is why Freud is for us all a man beset, like anyone else is, by all the contingencies – death, woman, father.

This represents a return to origins, and barely warrants being called science. What holds good in the art of the expert cook, who knows how to joint a bird, to disjoint it with as little resistance as possible, is also true for psychoanalysis. We know that there is a method of conceptualisation proper to each structure. But since this leads to complications, one prefers to cling to a monistic notion of a deduction of the world. That's how one goes astray.

One has to realise that we do our dissecting with concepts, not with a knife. Concepts have their specific order in reality. They do not emerge out of human experience – if they did, they would be well made. The first appelations arise out of words themselves, they are instruments for delineating things. Hence every science remains in darkness for a long time, entangled in language.

At first there is language, already formed, which we use as we would a very poor instrument. From time to time, reversals occur – from phlogiston to oxygen, for instance. Lavoisier introduces the right concept, oxygen, at the same time as his phlogistic. The root of the difficulty is that you can only introduce symbols, mathematical or otherwise, by using everyday language, since you have, after all, to explain what you are going to do with them. You are then at a certain level of human exchange, the level of healer in this instance. So is Freud, despite his denial. But, as Jones has demonstrated, he imposed upon himself right from the beginning the discipline of not dabbling in the speculation to which his nature inclined him. He submitted himself to the discipline of the facts, of the laboratory. He distanced himself from the wrong language.

Let us now turn to the notion of the subject. When one brings it in, one brings in oneself. The man speaking to you is a man like any other – he makes use of the wrong language. Oneself is then at issue.

Thus, Freud knew, from the beginning, that he would only make progress in the analysis of the neuroses if he analysed himself.

The growing importance attributed today to counter-transference means that it is a recognised fact that in analysis the patient is not alone. There are two of us – and not only two.

Phenomenologically, the analytic situation is a structure, that is to say that it is only through that that certain phenomena are isolable, separable. It is another structure, that of subjectivity, which gives human beings the idea that they are comprehensible to themselves.

Hence being neurotic can help one become a good psychoanalyst, and at the beginning, it helped Freud. Like Monsieur Jordain with his prose,[1] we make sense, nonsense, we misunderstand. But the lines of structure still had to be found there. Jung as well, to his own amazement, rediscovers, in the symbols of dreams and religions, certain archetypes, proper to the human race. This is also a structure – but differing from the analytic structure.

Freud introduced the determinism proper to this structure. Hence the ambiguity that is to be found throughout his corpus. For example, is a dream desire or the recognition of desire? Or, again, the *ego* is on the one hand like an empty egg, differentiated at its surface through contact with the world of perception, but it is also, each time we encounter it, that which says *no* or *me*, *I*, which says *one*, which speaks about others, which expresses itself in different registers.

We are going to employ the techniques of an art of dialogue. Like the good cook, we have to know what joints, what resistances, we will encounter.

The *super-ego* is a law deprived of meaning, but one which nevertheless only sustains itself by language. If I say *you turn to the right*, it's to allow the other to bring his language into line with mine. I think of what goes through his head when I speak to him. This attempt to find an agreement constitutes the communication specific to language. This *you* is so fundamental that it arises before consciousness. Censorship, for example, which is intentional, nevertheless comes into action before consciousness, functioning with vigilance. *You* is not a signal, but a reference to the other – it is order and love.

In the same way, the ego-ideal is an organism of defence established by the ego in order to extend the subject's satisfaction. But it is also the function that depresses most, in the psychiatric meaning of the term.

The *id* is not reducible to a pure and objective given, to the drives of the subject. An analysis never leads to specifying a given quantity of aggressivity or erotism. The point to which analysis leads, the end point of the dialectic of existential recognition, is – *You are this*. In practice this ideal is never reached.

The ideal of analysis is not complete self mastery, the absence of passion. It is to render the subject capable of sustaining the analytic dialogue, to speak neither too early, nor too late. Such is the aim of a training analysis.

The introduction of an order of determinations into human existence, into the domain of meaning, is what we call reason. Freud's discovery is the rediscovery, on fallow ground, of reason.

18 November 1953

The rest of this session is missing, as are all those sessions from the end of 1953.

[1] '*Il y a plus de quarante ans que je dis de la prose sans que j'en susse rien*' ('I have been speaking prose for more than forty years without knowing it') – Molière, *Le Bourgeois Gentilhomme*, M. Jourdain, Act II, Scene IV.

THE MOMENT OF RESISTANCE

I

Introduction to the commentaries on Freud's Papers on Technique

I would very much like to start off this new year, for which I offer you my best wishes, by telling you – *The fun is over!*

Last term you had little else to do but listen to me. I declare that this term now starting, I trust, I hope, I venture to hope that I too will hear from you a bit.

It's actually the law, and tradition, of the seminar that those who participate in it bring more to it than a purely personal effort – a contribution through effective communication. This can only come from those involved in the work in the most direct manner, from those for whom these seminars on texts take on their full meaning, from those who are involved in a variety of capacities in our practice. All this does not exclude your obtaining from me answers that I will be in a position to give you.

It would be particularly appreciated if everyone were to give, according to his or her resources, his or her utmost, in contributing to this new phase of the seminar. Your utmost consists in not replying with a long face, saying it just so happens that this week you are particularly heavily burdened, when I call upon one or other of you and consign a specific segment of our common task to him or her.

I am talking here to those who are part of the psychoanalytic group that we represent. I would like you to realise that if it is constituted as such, as an autonomous group, it is for a task that for each of us brings with it nothing less than the future – the meaning of everything which we do and will have to do for the rest of our lives. If you are not coming to put into question everything you do, I don't see why you're here. Why would those who do not sense the meaning of this task remain tied to us, rather than joining up with some sort of bureaucracy or other?

1

These reflections are particularly pertinent, to my way of thinking, just when we are going to tackle what are commonly called Freud's Papers on Technique.

Papers on Technique is a term that a certain tradition has already fixed upon. During Freud's lifetime, a small octavo volume was published with the title *Zur Technik der Psychoanalyse und zur Metapsychologie*, which brought together a certain number of Freud's writings dating from 1904 to 1919, whose title, presentation, contents indicated that they dealt with psychoanalytic method.

The motivation and justification for this format is that there are good grounds for cautioning an inexperienced practitioner who would like to embark upon analysis, so that he might avoid a certain number of confusions regarding the practice of the method, and also regarding its essence.

There are passages in these writings which are extremely important for understanding the progress that the development of practice has seen over these years. What one sees gradually appearing there are notions fundamental to the mode of operation of the analytic therapy, the notion of resistance and the function of transference, the mode of operation and of intervention in the transference, and even, up to a certain point, the essential role of the transference neurosis. There's no need, then, to underline any further the quite special interest this little collection of writings possesses.

To be sure, this way of bringing them together is not entirely satisfactory, and the term Papers on Technique is perhaps not what gives it its unity. They possess no less of a unity for all that. The whole attests to a stage in the development of Freud's thought. We will study it from this perspective.

There is an intermediary step here. It follows on from the initial development of what someone, an analyst who does not always have a way with words, but who on this occasion made a rather fortunate, even beautiful, find, has called Freud's *seminal experience*. It antedates the elaboration of the structural theory.[1]

The beginnings of this intermediary step should be placed between 1904 and 1909.

The article on the psychoanalytic method appeared in 1904;[2] some say that this is where the word psychoanalysis first appears – which isn't true, since Freud had used it well before, but what matters is that it is there used in a formal manner, in the very title of the article. 1909 – the date of the lectures at Clark University, Freud's journey to America, accompanied by his son, Jung.

If we pick up the thread again in the year 1920, we find the theory of the agencies, the structural, or again the metapsychological theory, as Freud called it. That is another theoretical development which he bequeathed to us out of his experience and his discovery.

As you see, the so-called papers on technique are spread between these two advances. It is what gives them their meaning. It is a mistake to think that they

[1] The structural theory is the shorthand term for Freud's theory of the ego, id and super-ego, introduced with *The Ego and the Id* (1923b).

[2] 'Freud's psycho-analytic procedure' (1904a) GW V 3–10; Stud Erg 101–6; SE VII 249–54.

owe their unity to the fact that Freud discusses technique in them.

In a certain sense, Freud never ceased discussing technique. I only have to remind you of the *Studien über Hysterie*, which is nothing other than one long account of the discovery of the analytic technique. That is where we witness it in the making, and that is what makes these studies priceless. If we wanted to give a complete and systematic account of the development of Freud's technique, we would have to start with them. I have not taken up the *Studien über Hysterie* for the simple reason that they are not easily accessible, since not all of you read German, nor even English – to be sure, there are more reasons than just those of expediency leading me to choose instead the Papers on Technique.

The Interpretation of Dreams is itself always, endlessly, about technique. If we put to one side what he wrote on mythological, anthropological and cultural topics, hardly any of Freud's work fails to tell us something about technique. I do not need to emphasise that an article like 'Analysis terminable and interminable', which appeared around 1934, is one of the most important on technique.

I would now like to stress what in my opinion is the best frame of mind in which to conduct our commentary on these papers this term. This is a matter that should be settled today.

2

If we are under the impression that we are here to stand back in admiration of the Freudian texts and marvel at them, we will certainly be well satisfied.

The freshness and vivacity of these papers is not surpassed by any of Freud's other writings. At times his personality is revealed in them in so direct a manner that one cannot fail to remark it. The simplicity and frankness of tone are in and of themselves a kind of education.

More specifically, the ease with which the question of practical rules to be observed is dealt with shows us the extent to which they were, for Freud, an instrument, in the sense that one says one has a hammer firmly in hand. *Firmly held by this hand of mine*, he says in short, *and this is how I am accustomed to holding it. Others may possibly prefer a marginally different instrument, which sits better in their hand.* You will come across passages that will tell you that far more clearly than I do in this metaphorical way.

So the codification of rules of technique is dealt with in these papers with a freedom which in and of itself might well be a sufficient education, and even on a first reading bears fruit and yields its reward. There is nothing more wholesome and liberating. And nothing demonstrates more clearly that the real issue lies elsewhere.

But that's not all. In the manner in which Freud communicates to us what we could call the paths of the truth of his thought, there is a quite different aspect, to be discovered in those passages which may perhaps appear of secondary importance, but which are nonetheless quite perceptible. It is the long-suffering side of his personality, the feeling he has of the necessity of authority, which in his case is not without a certain fundamental depreciation of what anyone who has something to communicate or teach can expect from those who listen to and follow him. In many a place we come across a measure of profound contempt for the manner in which these things are made use of and understood. As you will see, I even believe that one finds in him a very specific disparagement of the human raw material made available to him by the society in which he lived. Undoubtedly this is what allows us to catch a glimpse of why Freud, in contrast to what happens in his writings, mobilised the full weight of his authority so as to assure, so he believed, the future of analysis. He both excluded all manner of doctrinal dissensions – quite real dissensions – which emerged, and at the same time was quite imperious as to what could be organised around him as the means for the transmission of his teaching.

All this is only a glimpse of what this reading reveals of the historical aspects of Freud's activity and presence. Are we going to restrict ourselves to this level? Certainly not, if only because it would be quite ineffectual, despite the interest, the stimulation, the amusement and relaxation that we might expect from it.

It is always in relation to the question, *what do we do when we do analysis?* that up to now I have offered this commentary of Freud. The scrutiny of these short papers will be undertaken in the same spirit. Hence my starting point is the current state of technique – what is said, written and done concerning analytic technique.

I don't know if most of you – I hope at least some – are fully aware of the following fact. When – I am referring to the present, 1954, this brand new year – we examine now the manner in which the diverse practitioners of analysis think, express, conceive of their technique, we conclude that things have come to such a pass that it would not be an exaggeration to call it the most radical confusion. I can tell you that right now, amongst those who are analysts, and who think – which already limits the field – there isn't perhaps a single one who, deep down, has the same conception as any other of his contemporaries or peers as to what one does, what one aims to do, what one achieves, what is going on in analysis.

It has even got to the point where we could amuse ourselves with the little game of comparing the most extreme conceptions – we would see that they arrive at formulations which are strictly contradictory. Without even seeking out those who cherish paradoxes – anyhow, there aren't that many of them. The question is of such import that the various theoreticians tackle it with no inclination to whimsicality, and humour, in general, is excluded from their laborious pontifications on therapeutic results, their forms, their procedures and the means by which one obtains them. They content themselves with hanging on to a balustrade, to a guard-rail offered by some corner or another of Freud's theoretical system. This alone gives each of them the guarantee that he is still communicating with those who are his fellow-analysts and colleagues. The Freudian language acts as the go-between by which a channel of communication is kept open between practitioners who hold to manifestly different conceptions of their therapeutic activity, and, what is more, of the general form of this interhuman relation called psychoanalysis.

When I say *interhuman relation*, you can already see that I am describing things the way they are today. Indeed, the elaboration of the notion of the relation between analyst and analysand is the path taken by contemporary analytic doctrines in trying to rediscover a firm basis for the realities of that experience. Certainly it represents the most fertile line of thought traced out since Freud's death. Balint calls it a two-body psychology[3] – a term which, in fact, is not his, but which he borrowed from the late Rickman, one of the rare souls to have had a modicum of theoretical originality in analytic circles since Freud's death.[4] Around this formula one may quite easily align all studies on object-relations, on the importance of counter-transference, and on a certain set of related terms, amongst which fantasy stands in the foreground. The imaginary inter-reaction between analysand and analyst is thus something we shall have to take into consideration.

Does this mean that this is the way to locate our problem precisely? On the one hand, yes. On the other, no.

It is very worthwhile to stimulate research of this character in as much as it highlights the originality of what is at stake when compared to a one-body psychology,[5] the conventional constructive psychology. But is it sufficient to say that we are dealing with a relation between two individuals? It is in this way that we are brought to recognise the impasses into which theories of technique are currently led.

I am not in a position to say more to you about this for the moment – even though, as those who are old hands in this seminar know, you are obviously aware that there is no two-body psychology[5] without the intervention of a third element. If, as we must, we take speech as the central feature of our perspective, then it is within a three- rather than two-term relation that we have to formulate the analytic experience in its totality.

---

[3] English in the original.

[4] See John Rickman, *Selected Contributions to Psycho-analysis*, compiled by W. C. M. Scott, with an introductory memoir by S. M. Payne, London: Hogarth Press and the Institute of Psycho-analysis, 1957, in particular 'The factor of number in individual- and group-dynamics' (1950) pp. 165–9; 'Methodology and research in psycho-pathology' (1951), pp. 207–17, esp. pp. 207–10; 'Number and the human sciences' (1951), pp. 218–23. See also Michael Balint, 'On love and hate' (1951) in: *Primary Love and Psycho-analytic Technique*, London: Hogarth Press and the Institute of Psycho-analysis, 1952, pp. 141–56; see p. 146. Balint's phrase is 'two-person psychology'.

[5] English in the original.

Which doesn't mean to say that we cannot express fragments, pieces and tail-ends of it in other registers. In that way you can grasp the kind of obstacles the theoreticians have come up against. It's really very easy to understand – if the foundation of the inter-analytic relation is truly something that we are obliged to represent as being triadic, there are a number of different ways of choosing two elements from out of this triad. You can put the accent on one or other of the three dyadic relations that are set up within it. As you will see, this furnishes a practical means of classifying a certain number of theoretical elaborations concerning technique that have been proposed.

3

All this may appear to you at the moment to be a little abstract, and I want to do my best to tell you something a bit more concrete, to bring you into this discussion.

I am going to remind you quickly of Freud's seminal experience which I mentioned earlier on, since in fact that is what was partly the object of our lectures of last term, totally centred as they were on the notion that the complete reconstitution of the subject's history is the element that is essential, constitutive and structural for analytic progress.

I believe that I have demonstrated that that is where Freud started from. What is at issue for him is the understanding of an individual case. That is what gives each of the five great case-histories their value. The three that we have already looked at, pondered over and worked on together in previous years show you just that. Freud's progress, the discoveries he made, lies in the way he considers the singularity of a case.

Consider it in its singularity, what does that mean? That means essentially that, for him, the interest, the essence, the basis, the dimension proper to analysis is the reintegration by the subject of his history right up to the furthermost perceptible limits, that is to say into a dimension that goes well beyond the limits of the individual. To lay the foundations, deduce it, demonstrate it employing a thousand subtleties in Freud's texts, is what we have accomplished together over the last few years.

What reveals this dimension is the accent that Freud puts in each case on those points that it is essential to overcome by means of the technique and which are what I will call the bearings [*situations*] of the history. Does this amount to placing the accent on the past, as it may appear at first sight? I showed you that it is not as simple as that. History is not the past. History is the past in so far as it is historicised in the present – historicised in the present because it was lived in the past.

The path of restitution of the subject's history takes the form of a quest for the restitution of the past. We should consider this restitution as the butt to be aimed at by the recourses of technique.

Throughout Freud's works, in which, as I have told you, technical suggestions are to be found at every turn, you will discover that the restitution of the past retained its prominent position in his preoccupations right to the end. That is why the very questions which are opened up by Freud's discovery are raised by this restitution of the past, and they turn out to be none other than the questions which up to now have been avoided, skirted round, in analysis I mean, namely those which bear on the function of time in the realisation of the human subject.

When we return to the origin of the Freudian experience – when I say *origin*, I do not mean historical origin but point-source – one realises that this is what has always kept analysis alive, despite the profoundly different garbs it has been given. Again and again, Freud emphasises the restitution of the past, even when, with the conception of the three agencies – you will see that one can even talk of four – he gives a considerable extension to the structural point of view, favouring thereby a certain orientation which will increasingly focus on the analytic relation in the present, on the here and now of the session, between the four walls of analysis.

To back up what I am telling you, all I need do is cite an article he published in 1934, *Konstruktionen in der Analyse*, in which what is at issue, again and as ever, is the reconstruction of the subject's history.[6] You won't find a more characteristic instance of the persistence of this point of view in all of Freud's work. In this article, it is something like a final insistence on this pivotal theme. We have here something like the distilled essence, the point, the last word on what has been at stake all along, in a work as central as the *Wolfman* – what value does the subject's reconstructed past have?

One could say that Freud touches there – though one senses it in many other places in his corpus – on a notion that was emerging in the course of our discussions last term, and which is roughly the following – the fact that the subject relives, comes to remember, in the intuitive sense of the word, the formative events of his existence, is not in itself so very important. What matters is what he reconstructs of it.

On this point, there are some striking turns of phrase. After all, Freud writes, *Träume*, dreams, *sind auch erinnern*, are also a way of remembering.[7] He even goes so far as to say that screen-memories themselves are, after all, an adequate representative of what is at issue.[8] To be sure, in their manifest form as memories, they certainly are not, but if we work on them sufficiently they render up to us the equivalent of what we are looking for.

Can you see where this is all leading to? It leads, within Freud's own conception, to an idea that what is involved is a reading, a qualified and skilled

---

[6] 'Constructions in analysis' (1937d) GW XVI 43–56; Stud Erg 395–406; SE XXIII 257–69.
[7] 'From the history of an infantile neurosis' (1918b[1914]) GW XII 80; Stud VIII 169; SE XVII 51.
[8] *Ibid.* SE XVII 50–1.

translation of the cryptogram representing what the subject is conscious of at the moment – what am I going to say now? of himself? no, not only of himself – of himself and of everything else, that is to say of the whole of his system.

As I told you just a moment ago, the restitution of the subject's wholeness appears in the guise of a restoration of the past. But the stress is always placed more on the side of reconstruction than on that of reliving, in the sense we have grown used to calling *affective*. The precise reliving – that the subject remembers something as truly belonging to him, as having truly been lived through, with which he communicates, and which he adopts – we have the most explicit indication in Freud's writings that that is not what is essential. What is essential is reconstruction, the term he employs right up until the end.

There is something truly remarkable here, which would be paradoxical if we gained access to it without having an awareness of the meaning it may take on in the register of speech, which I am trying here to highlight as being necessary to the understanding of our experience. I would say – when all is said and done, it is less a matter of remembering than of rewriting history.

I tell you what there is in Freud. That doesn't imply that he was right; but this thread is continuous, permanently subjacent to his thought's development. He never abandoned something which can only be put in the way I've found of saying it – *rewriting history* – a formula which allows one to put in perspective the various directions that he gives apropos of little details in the narratives within analysis.

4

To the Freudian conception that I am expounding to you, I could counterpose completely different conceptions of the analytic experience.

Certain authors maintain that analysis is a sort of homeopathic discharge by the subject of his fantasised understanding of the world. In their view, this fantasised understanding should, little by little, within the day-to-day experience taking place in the consulting-room, boil down, transform itself, and achieve a new equilibrium within a given relation to the real. What is emphasised here, as you see, in clear contrast to Freud, is the transformation of the fantasised relation in the course of a relation which one calls, without further ado, *real*.

Certainly one can formulate these matters in a more open fashion, sufficiently nuanced to accommodate the plurality of the expression, as has been done by someone to whom I have already referred here, who has written on technique. None of which, in the end, stops it from coming back to that. Some peculiar repercussions thereby result, which we will be in a position to point to when we come to our commentary on the Freudian texts.

How did the practice that Freud initiated get transformed into a manipulation of the analyst-analysand relationship in the sense that I have just outlined? That's the fundamental question that we will be encountering in the course of the study we are undertaking.

The ideas that Freud introduced in the period immediately after that of the Papers on Technique, namely those of the three agencies, were greeted, employed, and dealt with in such a way as to result in this transformation. Of the three, the ego took on the greatest importance. Since then all subsequent development of analytic technique has revolved around the conception of the *ego*, and that is where we must locate the source of all the difficulties arising out of the theoretical elaboration on this development in practice.

There is, without doubt, a world of difference between what we actually do in this sort of den where the patient talks to us and where, from time to time, we talk to him – and the theoretical account that we give of it. Even in Freud, where the gap is infinitely more narrow, we have the impression that some distance remains.

I am certainly not the only one to have asked myself the question – what was Freud really doing? Bergler asked this question in plain black and white, and answers that we don't really know much, apart from what Freud himself allowed us to see when he himself set down, also in plain black and white, the fruits of certain of his experiences, namely his five great case-histories. They are the best introduction we have to the manner in which Freud behaved. But it really does seem as if the character of this experience cannot be reproduced in its concrete reality. For one very simple reason, on which I have already insisted – the singularity of the analytic experience, when it comes to Freud.

It really was Freud who opened up this path of experience. This in itself gave him an absolutely unique perspective, as his dialogue with the patient demonstrates. As one can sense all the time, the patient is for him only a sort of prop, or question, or sometimes even a check, along the path that he, Freud, took alone. Hence, the drama, in the true sense of the word, of his quest. The drama which, in each of the cases he gave us, ends in failure.

Throughout his life, Freud followed the paths that he opened up in the course of this experience, attaining in the end something that one could call a promised land. One cannot say, however, that he entered into it. You need only read what can be considered to be his testament, 'Analysis terminable and interminable', in order to see that if there was one thing that he was aware of, it was that he hadn't entered into it, into the promised land. This article isn't recommended reading for all and sundry, for anyone who knows how to read – luckily there are not that many people who do know how to read – it is a difficult one to digest if you happen to be an analyst – if you aren't an analyst, you don't give a toss.

Those who find themselves in a position to follow Freud are confronted with the question as to how the paths we inherit were adopted, reapprehended, and rethought through. So, we cannot do anything else but gather together what we will contribute to it under the heading of a *critique*, a critique of analytic technique.

Technique is, and can only be, of any value to the extent that we understand wherein lies the fundamental question for the analyst who adopts it. Well then, we should note first of all that we hear the *ego* spoken of as the ally of the analyst, and not only the ally, but the sole source of knowledge. The only thing we know of is the *ego*, that's the way it is usually put. Anna Freud, Fenichel, nearly all those who have written about analysis since 1920, say it over and over again – *We speak only to the ego, we are in communication with the ego alone, everything is channelled via the ego.*

On the other hand, in contrast, every advance made by this ego psychology can be summed up as follows – the ego is structured exactly like a symptom. At the heart of the subject, it is only a privileged symptom, the human symptom *par excellence*, the mental illness of man.

To translate the analytic ego in this quick and shorthand manner is at best to sum up what emerges from a straightforward reading of Anna Freud's book, *The Ego and the Mechanisms of Defence*. One cannot avoid being struck by the fact that the ego is constructed and is to be located within the subject as a whole, just as a symptom. Nothing differentiates the one from the other. No objection can be made to this quite dazzling argument. No less dazzling is the fact that things have got so confused that the catalogue of defence mechanisms which make up the ego is as heterogeneous a list as one could conceive of. Anna Freud herself underscores this very clearly – to bring repression closer to notions such as the turning of the drive against its object, or the inversion of its aims, is to put side by side elements which are in no respect homogeneous.

Given the point where we still find ourselves, perhaps we cannot do any better now. But we can still highlight the profound ambiguity of the conception analysts entertain of the *ego* – which is the only thing to which one has access, despite also being only another hindrance, a failure [*acte manqué*], a slip.

At the start of his chapters on analytic interpretation, Fenichel speaks of the *ego* as everyone does, and feels the need to say that it plays the essential role of being a function by which the subject learns the meaning of words. So, from the very start, then, Fenichel is at the heart of the matter. Everything is there. The issue is knowing whether the meaning of the *ego* exceeds the self [*moi*].

If this function is a function of the *ego*, everything that follows in Fenichel's account is incomprehensible, and, besides, he doesn't press the point. I say that it is a slip of the pen, since it isn't pursued, and everything that goes on from there amounts to saying the opposite, and leads him to the conclusion that, in the end, the *id* and the *ego* amount to exactly the same thing, which isn't about to clarify matters. But, I repeat, either the subsequent argument is unthinkable or it is not true that the *ego* is the function through which the subject learns the meaning of words.

This *ego*, what is it? What is the subject caught up in, which is, beyond the meaning of words, a completely different matter – language, whose role is formative, quite fundamental in his history. With respect to Freud's Papers on Technique we will have to ask ourselves these questions, which will take us a long way – but only on condition that, it is first of all in relation to each of our experiences.

It will also be incumbent upon us, when we try to engage in discussions taking as our starting point the present state of theory and technique, to ask ourselves what was already implicit in what Freud brought us. What, perhaps, already inclined him towards those formulae to which we are now led in our practices? What constraints might there be in the manner in which we are led to look at things? Or, in what sense does something that has happened since amount to being a development, a more rigorous systematisation which corresponds better to reality? This is the register within which our commentary will take on its meaning.

5

I would like to give you a still clearer sense of how I envisage this seminar.

At the end of the last few lectures I delivered to you, you had a taste of a reading of what can be called the psychoanalytic myth. The direction of this reading is not so much that of criticism as of gauging the reality which confronted it, and to which it offers its mythical reply.

Well, the problem is more restricted, but also much more pressing, where technique is concerned.

Indeed, the scrutiny that we will have to engage in of everything pertaining to our technique falls within the purview of our own discipline. If we have to differentiate the actions and the behaviour of the subject from what he says to us about them in the session, I would say that our actual behaviour in the analytic session is just as far from the theoretical account that we give of it.

But this is only a first truth, which only has significance in so far as it may be reversed, and at the same time mean – *just as close*. The fundamental absurdity of interhuman behaviour can only be comprehended in the light of this *system* – as Melanie Klein so happily called it, not knowing, as usual, what she was saying – called the human ego, namely that set of defences, of denials [*négations*], of dams, of inhibitions, of fundamental fantasies which orient and direct the subject. Well then, the theoretical conception we have of our technique, even if it doesn't coincide exactly with what we are doing, doesn't structure any the less, or motivate any the less, the least of our interventions with the said patients.

And that is precisely what is so serious. Because we have effectively allowed ourselves – in the sense, revealed to us by analysis, in which we allow ourselves things, without knowing it – to bring our *ego* into play in the analysis. Since it is argued that one is trying to bring about the patient's readaptation to the real, one really ought to find out if it is the analyst's *ego* which offers the measure of the real.

To be sure, it isn't enough to have a definite conception of the ego for our ego to come into play like a bull in the china shop of our relation to the patient. But a certain way of conceiving of the function of the *ego* in analysis does have some relation to a certain practice of analysis that we might well call inauspicious.

I am only opening up the question. It is our task to resolve it. The totality of each of our world systems – I am referring to the concrete system which doesn't have to be already spelled out for it to be there, which does not pertain to the order of the unconscious, but which acts in the manner in which we express ourselves in daily life, in the smallest spontaneous detail of our discourse – is that something which must in actual fact, yea or nay, be employed in analysis as the yardstick?

I think I have opened up the question sufficiently for you now to see the point of what we can do together.

Mannoni, will you get together with one of your neighbours, Anzieu for instance, to study the notion of resistance in those of Freud's writings available to you under the title *On Psychoanalytic Technique*, published by Presses Universitaires?[9] Don't overlook the concluding lectures of the *Introductory Lectures*. Will two others, Perrier and Granoff for instance, collaborate on the same topic? Then we will see how to proceed. We will let ourselves be guided by experience itself.

13 January 1954

[9] The French book entitled *De la Technique Psychanalytique*, trans. A. Berman, Paris: Presses Universitaires Françaises, 1953 (reprinted as *La Technique Psychanalytique*, Paris: Presses Universitaires Françaises, 1970), comprises the six papers included in the Papers on Technique in SE XII, together with six others: (1904a), (1905a), (1910d), (1910k), (1914a) and (1919a).

II

Preliminary comments on the problem of resistance

ANALYSIS THE FIRST TIME
MATERIALITY OF DISCOURSE
ANALYSIS OF ANALYSIS
FREUD'S MEGALOMANIA?

1

Following O. Mannoni's presentation.

We should offer our heartiest thanks to Mannoni who has given us a most happy prologue to the resumption of the seminar's dialogue. Nonetheless, he has distinctly phenomenological leanings, and I don't think that the solution has quite the form that he leads us to believe – as he himself has sensed. But it is useful to have framed the question as he has, by speaking of an interpersonal mechanism, although the word 'mechanism' can only be an approximation at this juncture.

2

Interruption in the course of D. Anzieu's presentation.

Freud explains, apropos of Lucy R., that he had recourse to pressure of the hands when he could only obtain partial hypnosis. Later on, he says that he stopped worrying about this, and even renounced seeking an answer from the subject to the question, in accordance with the classical method, *are you asleep?*, since he had had the unpleasant experience of receiving the reply, *no, I am not at all asleep* – which put him in a rather embarrassing position.[1] He recounts in a naive and charming manner that he was obliged to tell the subject that he was not talking about quite the same sort of sleep as that to which the other's reply pertained, and that the latter must, nonetheless, have been a little bit asleep. Within the limits of the most perfect ambiguity, he quite clearly states that all this put him in a most embarrassing position, which only came to an end the day he no longer cared one way or the other.

---

[1] *Studies on Hysteria* (1895d) GW I 165–6; SE II 108–9.

19

But he retained the pressure of hands, either on the forehead or on either side of the head, and at the same time he asked the patient to concentrate upon the cause of the symptom. That was an intermediary stage between dialogue and hypnosis. The symptoms were dealt with one by one, in themselves, tackled directly like so many formal problems. In Freud's hands, the patient was assured that the memories which were going to come forth were the most relevant ones, that all he had to do was trust in that. And Freud added the detail that it would be at the moment when he removed his hands – mimicking the lifting of the barrier – that the patient would be completely aware, and would only have to take hold of what came into his mind in order to be certain of being on the right track.

It is quite remarkable that this method proved itself perfectly effective, for the cases which Freud tells us of. Indeed, the case of Lucy R., which is so elegant, was entirely solved, with an effortlessness which has all the beauty of works by primitives. You'll find happy chance, a benevolent divine conjunction, in everything new that is discovered. In contrast, with Anna O. we find the hard labour of working-through[2] possessing all the animation and density of the most modern analytic cases, despite the method that was used – the whole series of events, the whole history, is relived and re-worked several times. It required work of extended scope, lasting almost a year. In the case of Lucy R., things happened much more quickly, and with an elegance that turns it into something quite striking. Undoubtedly we aren't truly able to see where the mainsprings lie, on account of its being too compressed, but, even so, it is of enormous use. This woman had what one could call olfactory hallucinations, hysterical symptoms, and their signification was detected, with locations and dates, in an altogether happy manner. On this occasion, Freud reveals all the minutiae of his way of working.

3

Idem.

I have already emphasised the uniquely privileged character of the cases which Freud dealt with, on account of the special character of his technique. What that was, we can only guess at on the basis of a number of rules which he has given us, and which have been faithfully applied. As the best authors, and those who knew Freud, have admitted, one cannot gain a complete conception of the way in which he applied the technique.

I must emphasise the fact that Freud progressed on a course of research which is not characterised by the same style as other scientific research. Its domain is that of the truth of the subject. The quest for truth is not entirely

---

[2] English in the original.

reducible to the objective, and objectifying, quest of ordinary scientific method. What is at stake is the realisation of the truth of the subject, like a dimension peculiar to it which must be detached in its distinctiveness [*originalité*] in relation to the very notion of reality – I have emphasised this in all of this year's lectures.

Freud was taken up in the quest for a truth which engaged him totally, including there his own self, and hence also his presence with respect to the patient in his function, let us say, of therapist – even though the term is completely inadequate as a description of his attitude. As Freud himself said, this engagement gave an absolutely unique character to his relations with his patients.

To be sure, analysis as a science is always a science of the particular. The coming to fruition of an analysis is always a unique case, even if these unique cases lend themselves all the same to some generality, since there is more than one analyst. But with Freud the analytic experience represents uniqueness carried to its limit, from the fact that he was in the process of building and verifying analysis itself. We cannot obliterate the fact that it was the first time that an analysis was undertaken. Doubtless the method is derived from it, but it is only method for other people. Freud, for his part, did not apply a method. If we overlook the unique and inaugural character of his endeavour, we will be committing a serious error.

Analysis is an experience of the particular. The very first experience of this particular thus takes on an even more peculiar value. If we do not emphasise the difference between this *first time* and everything that has followed since, we, who are interested not so much in this truth as in the construction of the access roads to this truth, will never be able to grasp the meaning of certain sentences, certain texts, which come into view in Freud's oeuvre, and subsequently take on, in other contexts, a completely different meaning, even though one might consider them to be stencilled one on top of the other.

The interest of these commentaries on the Freudian texts allows us to follow out in detail those questions which – as you will see, as you already see today – have a considerable importance. They are numerous and insidious – strictly speaking the sort of questions that each and everyone of us is careful to avoid, relying instead on a jingle, a formula which is schematic, abbreviated and vivid.

4

D. Anzieu cites a passage from the Studies on Hysteria, *(SE II 287–9). Interruption.*

What's striking about the passage that you refer to is that it takes off from the pseudo-anatomical metaphor called to mind whenever Freud talks about verbal images wandering up and down the nerve fibres. Here, what is stratified around the pathogenic nucleus calls to mind a bundle of papers, a score with several registers. These metaphors overpoweringly tend to suggest the materialisation of speech, not the mythical materialisation of the neurologists, but a concrete materialisation – speech begins to flow in the leaves of a printed manuscript. The metaphor of the blank page, of the palimpsest, is also taken up on another occasion.[3] It has since appeared under the pen of more than one analyst.

Here we come upon the idea of several longitudinal strata, that is to say of several threads of discourse. One may imagine them as rendered material in the text in the form of literally concrete bundles. There is a stream of parallel words, and these broaden out at a certain moment to encompass this famous pathogenic nucleus which itself is also a story, they move away from it in order to include it and join up a little further on.

The phenomenon of resistance is to be located precisely at this point. There are two directions, one longitudinal and one radial. Resistance acts in the radial direction, when one wants to get closer to the threads which lie at the heart of the bundle. It is the result of an attempt to move from the external registers towards the centre. From the repressed nucleus a positive repulsive force is exerted, and when one strives to reach the threads of the discourse which are closest to it, you feel resistance. Freud even goes so far as to write, not in the *Studies*, but in a later text, published under the title *Métapsychologie* that the strength of the resistance is inversely proportional to one's distance from the repressed centre.[4]

I am not sure if this is the exact wording, but it is very striking. It makes manifest the materialisation of resistance acquired in the course of experience, and precisely, as Mannoni put it just now, in the subject's discourse. In order to know where it is happening [*où ça se passe*], what the material, biological foundation is, Freud quite straightforwardly takes the discourse to be a reality in its own right, a reality which is there, a sheaf, a bundle of proofs as one also calls it, a bundle of juxtaposed discourses which overlap, follow on from each other, forming a dimension, a layer, a dossier.

The notion of a material support of speech, singled out as such, was not yet available to Freud. Today, he would have taken the succession of phonemes which make up a part of the subject's discourse as the basis for his metaphor. He would say that one encounters greater and greater resistance the closer the subject comes to a discourse which would be the ultimate one, the right one, but one which he absolutely refuses.

---

[3] GW II/III 140 n1; Stud II 152 n1; SE IV 135 n2.

[4] 'Repression' (1915d) GW X 251; Stud III 110; SE XIV 149. At the time Lacan spoke, the article was to be found in French in *Métapsychologie*, trans. M. Bonaparte and A. Berman, Paris: Gallinard, 1940, pp. 67–90.

In the attempt at synthesis that you are making, what has not perhaps been highlighted is the question which however is in the foreground, where resistance is concerned – the question concerning the relations of the unconscious and the conscious. Is resistance a phenomenon which occurs only in analysis? Or is it something we can talk about when the subject goes about his business outside of analysis, and even before he enters into it, or after he has left it? Does resistance continue to have a meaning outside of analysis?

There is a discussion of resistance in the analysis of dreams, to which neither of you have referred, and which nevertheless constitutes the implicit hypothesis behind some of the problems both of you have raised, since Freud there asks himself about the inaccessible nature of the unconscious.[5] The ideas of resistance are extremely old. And right from the start, from Freud's initial researches, resistance is linked to the idea of the *ego*. But when one reads some startling sentences in the text of the *Studies*, where it is not just a question of the *ego* as such, but of the *ego* as representing the ideational mass, one realises that the notion of the *ego* already foreshadows for Freud all the problems that it now presents for us. I would almost say that it is a notion with retroactive effect. It even seems, from reading these early pieces in the light of what has developed since around the *ego*, that the most recent formulations mask, rather than reveal.

One cannot but see in this phrase, *the ideational mass*,[6] something very close to a formula that I could have given you, namely that the counter-transference is nothing other than the function of the analyst's *ego*, what I have called the sum total of the analyst's prejudices. Thus, one discovers in the patient a whole organisation of certainties, beliefs, of coordinates, of references, which constitute in the strictest sense what Freud right from the beginning called an ideational system, which we can in an abbreviated manner here call *the system*.

Does resistance stem only from that? When, at the limit of this domain of speech which is exactly the ideational mass of the ego, I portrayed for you the sum of silence after which another speech again makes its appearance, that speech which is to be reconquered in the unconscious since it is that part of the subject separated from his history – is that resistance? Is it, yea or nay, purely and simply the ego's organisation which, in and of itself, constitutes resistance? Is this what makes it difficult to gain access to the contents of the unconscious in the radial dimension – to use Freud's term? That is a very simple question, too simple, insoluble as such.

Fortunately, in the first thirty years of this century, analytic technique made sufficient progress, has been through enough experimental phases to distinguish its own questions. As you see, it boils down to this – which as I told you

---

[5] See GW II/III 527–30; Stud II 500–3; SE V 522–5.
[6] *Studies* GW I 174; SE II 116.

will be the model of our quest – we must assume that the evolution, the ups and downs of the analytic experience teach us something concerning the very nature of this experience, in so far as it is also a human experience, masked from itself. That is applying to analysis itself the schema that it has taught us. After all, isn't it itself a roundabout way of having access to the unconscious? It also raises to the second degree the problem that is set for us by neurosis. I am only making a claim for this now, you'll see it demonstrated as we examine it.

What do I want? – if not to get out of this genuine impasse, mental and practical, in which analysis has now ended up. You see that I push what I say quite far – it is incumbent on us to submit even analysis to the operational schema that it has taught us and which consists in reading enough in the different phases of its theoretico-technical development to advance further towards the reconquest of the authentic reality of the unconscious by the subject.

This method will require us to go well beyond the simple formal catalogue of procedures or of conceptual categories. Submitting analysis to an examination which is itself analytic is a step which will reveal its fertility in relation to technique, as fertile as it has already revealed itself in relation to Freud's clinical writings.

5

Interventions in the course of the discussion.

Psychoanalytic writings swarm with improprieties of method. These are difficult themes to deal with, to verbalise, without giving the verb a subject, in addition we are always reading that the *ego* emits the signal of anxiety, handles the life instinct, death instinct – one no longer knows where the switch board, the signalman, the pointer is. All of this is quite improper. We are continually finding Maxwell's little demons making an appearance in analytic writing, possessing foresight, intelligence . . . The annoying thing is that analysts do not have a clear idea of the nature of these demons.

We're here to discover what the evocation of the notion of the *ego* means from one end to the other of Freud's work. It's impossible to understand what this notion represents as it began to emerge with the work of the 1920s, with the studies on the psychology of groups and *Das Ich und das Es*, if one starts by drowning everything in a sum total, under the pretext that what is involved is the apprehension of a certain aspect of the psyche. That's not at all what the *ego* is in Freud's work. It has a functional role, linked to technical necessities.

The triumvirate who work in New York, Hartmann, Loewenstein and Kris, in its current attempt to elaborate a psychology of the *ego*, is always asking itself – what was Freud trying to get at in his last theory of the *ego*? Has anyone up to now really drawn out all the technical implications from it? I am not interpreting, I am only repeating what can be found in Hartmann's two or three most recent articles. In the *Psychoanalytic Quarterly* for 1951, you'll find three articles by Loewenstein, Kris and Hartmann on this topic, which are worth reading. It can't be said that they lead to a fully satisfying formulation, but they are looking in that direction, and propose theoretical principles which have very important technical applications, which according to them have not been noticed. It is very interesting to follow the development of this work in a series of articles we have seen appear over several years, especially since the end of the war. I believe that what has happened there is a very significant failure, one which has to be very instructive for us.

In any case, there is a world of difference between the *ego* as discussed in the *Studies*, the ideational mass, container of ideations, and the final theory of the *ego*, such as it had been wrought by Freud himself from 1920 on, which is still a problem for us. Between the two lies the central field we are in the process of studying.

How did this final theory of the *ego* get to see the light of day? It is the apex of Freud's theoretical elaboration, an extremely original and novel theory. Yet, under Hartmann's pen, it seems as if it strove with all its might to merge once again with classical psychology.

Both of these things are true. This theory, Kris writes, brings psychoanalysis within general psychology, and, at the same time, constitutes an unprecedented innovation. A paradox that we will highlight here, whether we carry on with the technical papers up to the holidays, or tackle the same problem in Schreber's writings.

. . . .

In Bergman's article, *Germinal Cell*, the germinal cell of analytic observations is taken to be the notion of a rediscovery and restitution of the past. He refers to the *Studien über Hysterie* in order to show how, right up to the end of his work, right up the final expressions of his thought, Freud always kept this notion of the past in the foreground, in a thousand forms, and above all in the form of reconstruction. In this article, the experience of resistance is therefore in no way considered as central.

. . . .

M. Hyppolite is alluding to the fact that Freud's anatomical researches can be viewed as successes, and have been recognised as such. In contrast, when he set himself to work at the physiological level, he seems to have shown a certain lack of interest. That is one of the reasons why he didn't recognise the importance of the discovery of cocaine. His physiological research was feeble, because it stuck fast to therapeutics. Freud concerned himself with the use of cocaine as an analgesic, and left to one side its anaesthetic value.

Here we are reminding ourselves of a trait of Freud's personality. Certainly we can ask ourselves if he was, as Z* was saying, keeping himself for a more glorious destiny. But to go so far as to say that turning towards psychopathology was for him a compensation is, I believe, a bit excessive. If one reads the works published under the title *The Origins of Psycho-analysis* and the rediscovered early manuscript in which the theory of the psychic apparatus figures, one realises that he was following the line of contemporary theoretical elaboration of the mechanistic functioning of the nervous apparatus – besides, everyone recognised it.

One shouldn't really be surprised therefore that electrical metaphors are mixed up in it. But nor should you forget that the electric current was experimented with for the first time in the area of nerve conduction, without anyone knowing what the implications would be.

Z*: *I believe that, from the clinical point of view, the notion of resistance clearly represents an experience that we all encounter at some time or another with almost all the patients in our practices – he is resisting and it makes me furious.*

Sorry? What's that?

Z*: *I mean that extremely unpleasant experience when you say to yourself – he was on the point of discovering, he could have discovered himself, he knows it without knowing that he knows it, all he has to do is take the trouble to look up, and this damn idiot, this cretin, all those aggressive and hostile words that leap to mind, doesn't do it. And the temptation that one feels to push him, to compel him, . . .*

Don't get too excited about it.

M. HYPPOLITE: *The only thing that allows the analyst to be intelligent, is when this resistance makes the analysand look like an idiot. It promotes heightened self-esteem.*

All the same, the trap of counter-transference, since we have to to call it that, is more insidious than this first plane.
. . . .

Z*: *For direct power over human beings, Freud substitutes the indirect and more palatable power that science gives over nature. We see here again the mechanism of intellectualisation, understand nature and by that very fact subdue her to oneself, the classical formula of determinism, which allusively refers back to Freud's authoritarian character, which punctuates the whole of his history, particularly in his relations with heretics as much as with his disciples.*

I ought to say that if I do speak in this manner, I stopped short of making it the key to the Freudian discovery.

Z*: *I don't think I'm making it the key either, but it is an interesting point to highlight. In this resistance, Freud's hypersensitivity to the subject's resistance is not unconnected to his own character.*

What allows you to speak of Freud's hypersensitivity?

Z*: *The fact that he, and not Breuer, nor Charcot, nor anyone else, discovered it. After all, it happened to him, because he felt it more keenly, and he accounted for what he had experienced.*

You believe that the fact of bringing out a function like resistance indicates a specific intolerance in the subject to whatever resists him? Isn't it, on the contrary, knowing how to conquer it, how to go elsewhere and well beyond, which allowed Freud to turn it into one of the mainsprings of the therapy, a factor which one can render objective, nameable and manageable? You think that Freud was more authoritarian than Charcot? – whereas Freud, in so far as he could, renounced suggestion so as to let the subject integrate what the resistances separated him from. In other words, are those who fail to recognise [méconnaissent] resistance less authoritarian, or is it the person who recognises it for what it is? I am rather inclined to believe that someone who, in hypnotism, attempts to make an object of the subject, his thing, to make him as supple as a glove so as to give him any form that he chooses, so as to take from him what he wants, is, more so than Freud, driven by a need to dominate and exercise his power. In contrast, Freud seems respectful of what is generally known as the object's resistance.

Z*: *Certainly.*

I believe that one must be extremely careful here. We cannot make use of our technique so importunately. When I talk about analysing Freud's work, it's so as to venture into it with unqualified analytic prudence. One shouldn't make a character trait into a constant of the personality, still less a characteristic of the subject. On this topic, you'll find some very hasty things from Jones's pen, but things which are nonetheless more subtly put than what you have said. To think that Freud's career was a compensation for his desire for power, even for his clearcut megalomania, of which moreover one may find traces in remarks he made, I think that's. . . . Freud's drama, from the moment when he discovers his path, cannot be summarised like that. We have after all learned enough through analysis not to feel ourselves obliged to identify the Freud who dreams of world-domination with the Freud who reveals a new truth. It doesn't seem to me to arise out of the same cupido, if not of the same libido.

M. HYPPOLITE: *Even so, it seems to me – without accepting in their totality the formulations of Z* and the conclusions he draws from them – that, in Charcot's domination through hypnosis, it was only a matter of domination over someone reduced to an object, of the possession of a being no longer master of himself. Whereas in the Freudian domination, it is the vanquishing of a subject, a being who still has self-awareness. Hence there is a stronger will for domination in the domination of the resistance to be conquered than in the simple and straightforward suppression of this* *resistance – without being able to draw from that the conclusion that Freud wanted to dominate the world.*

Is domination really what is at stake in Freud's experience? I always have reservations about lots of things which aren't specified in his way of going about things. His interventionism, in particular, I find surprising, if we compare it to some of the technical principles to which we now grant importance. But you'll find in this interventionism no satisfaction being gained from having won a victory over the patient's consciousness, in contradiction to what Hyppolite says, less, certainly, than in the modern techniques, which put all the emphasis on the resistances. In Freud we find a more nuanced attitude, that's to say, more humane.

He doesn't always define what is now called interpretation of defence, which is not, perhaps, the best way of putting it. But when all is said and done, interpretation of contents has for Freud the role of interpretation of defence.

You're right to allude to this, Z*. That is because that's for you. I will try and show you in what way the danger of a forcing of the subject through the analyst's intervention emerges. It's much more out in the open in so-called modern techniques – as one says in talking about analysis the way one talks about chess – than it ever was in Freud. And I don't believe that the theoretical promulgation of the notion of resistance can be used as a pretext for making this accusation against Freud, an accusation which goes radically against the liberating effect of his work and of his therapeutic activity.

I am not putting your opinions on trial, Z*. For this is well and truly your opinion. Certainly, one should show a spirit of scrutiny, of criticism, with respect to the founding works, but, in this form, it can only serve to increase the mystery, and not at all to throw light on it.

20 and 27 January 1954.

III

Resistance and the defences

MARGARET LITTLE'S TESTIMONY

FROM *EGO* TO *EGO*

REALITY AND FANTASY OF THE TRAUMA

HISTORY, THE LIVED AND THE RELIVED

Let us first congratulate Mannoni and Anzieu on their reports, which have the merit of showing us the controversial aspects of the question we are dealing with. As is appropriate to minds well-educated, but only recently initiated into, if not the application of analysis, at least its practice, there was in their reports something quite sharp, even polemical, which is always of value in revealing the problem's vividness.

A very delicate question has been raised, all the more delicate since, as I pointed out in my interruptions, it is very much a present concern for some of us.

A reproach has implicitly been levelled at Freud, as to his authoritarianism, alleged to be constitutive of his method from the beginning. That is paradoxical. If anything constitutes the originality of the analytic treatment, it is rather to have perceived at the beginning, right from the start, the problematical relation of the subject to himself. The real find, the discovery, in the sense I explained to you at the beginning of this year, is to have conjoined this relation with the meaning of symptoms.

It is the subject's refusal of this meaning that poses a problem for him. This meaning must not be revealed to him, it must be assumed by him. In this respect, psychoanalysis is a technique which respects the person – in the sense in which we understand it today, having realised that it had its price – not only respects it, but cannot function without respecting it. It would thus be paradoxical to place in the foreground the idea that analytical technique has as its aim to break down the subject's resistance. Which isn't to say that the problem doesn't ever arise.

Indeed, aren't we aware these days that an analyst doesn't make a single move in the treatment without teaching his students to be always asking themselves, in relation to the patient, the question – *What defence has he come up with now?*

This isn't really a policeman's approach, in the sense that it involves looking

29

for something hidden – that term should rather be reserved for the suspect phases of analysis in its archaic periods. Rather, they are always trying to find out what posture the subject could possibly take up, what find he could have made, in order to get himself into a position such that everything we might say to him will be ineffective. It would not be fair to say that they impute bad faith to the subject because *bad faith* is too much tied to implications of the order of knowledge, which are totally foreign to this state of mind. That would be too subtle by half. There is in all this the idea of the subject's fundamental ill will. All these features lead me to think that I am being accurate in calling this style of analysis inquisitorial.

1

Before going into my subject, I will take as an example Margaret Little's article on counter-transference, which appeared in the first number of the *International Journal of Psycho-analysis* for 1951.

This article takes its bearings from a manner of orienting technique which is pushed very far by a certain section of the English school. As you know, it leads to the view that the whole of the analysis must unfold in the *hic et nunc*. Everything is supposed to take place through grappling with the subject's intentions, here and now, in the session. That one catches glimpses of bits and pieces of his past is no doubt conceded, but it is thought that in the end it is in the trial – I was about to say the trial of psychological strength – within the treatment that the entire activity of the analyst is deployed.

And that really is the problem – the activity of the analyst. How does he act? What are the implications of what he does?

For the authors in question, for Margaret Little, nothing else matters but the recognition by the subject, *hic et nunc*, of the intentions of his discourse. And his intentions only ever have value in their implications *hic et nunc*, in the immediate exchange. The subject may well describe himself taking on the grocer or the hairdresser – in fact, he is bawling out the person he's talking to, that is to say the analyst.

There is some truth in that. The slightest experience of conjugal life will tell you that there is always an implicit demand of some sort in the fact that one spouse relates to the other what got his goat during the day, rather than the other way round. But it may also stem from a concern to inform the other of some incident worth knowing about. Both are true. It is a question of knowing on which aspect one should throw some light.

As the following story told by Margaret Little shows, things do sometimes go even further. Certain of its features are a bit confused, but everything points to the fact that it is a training analysis, or in any case, the analysis of someone whose area of interest is very close to psychoanalysis.

The analysand had occasion to make a radio broadcast on a topic that intensely interested the analyst himself – these things happen. It so happened that he gave this broadcast a few days after his mother's death. Now everything points to the fact that the mother in question plays an extremely important role in the patient's fixations. He is certainly very affected by this mourning, but he nonetheless fulfils his obligations in a particularly brilliant manner. The next session, he arrives in a state of stupor close to confusion. Not only is it impossible to get anything out of him, but what he does say is surprising in its lack of coordination. The analyst interprets boldly – *You are in this state because you think I greatly begrudge you your success on the radio the other day, with this topic which, as you know, personally interests me in the highest degree.* There we have it!

The rest of the account shows that it took a year for the subject to recover from this shock-interpretation, which hadn't failed to have some effect, since he had instantly recovered his spirits.

This shows you that the fact that the subject comes out of a confused state of mind following an intervention by the analyst by no means proves that it was effective in the strictly therapeutic, structuring sense of the word, namely that it was, in the analysis, true. On the contrary.

Margaret Little brought the subject back to a sense of the unity of his ego. Suddenly he tears himself out of the confusion in which he found himself, saying to himself – *Here is someone who points out to me that indeed everything is much of a muchness and that life goes on.* And he starts off, gets going again – the effect is instantaneous. It is impossible, in the analytic experience, to consider the subject's change of style as being the proof of the correctness of an interpretation. I consider the proof of the correctness of an interpretation to lie in the confirmatory material the subject supplies. And even that needs to be put more subtly.

After a year, the subject realises that his state of confusion was linked to the backlash of his reactions to mourning, which he had only been able to overcome by inverting them. I refer you at this point to the psychology of mourning, whose depressive side some of you are sufficiently familiar with.

Indeed, a radio-talk is produced in accordance with a very specific modality of speech, since it is addressed to a mass of invisible listeners by an invisible speaker. It may be said that, in the imagination of the speaker, it isn't necessarily addressed to those who listen to it, but equally to everyone, the living and the dead. The subject there enters into a relationship of conflict – he might regret that his mother was not able to be a witness to his triumph, but perhaps, at the same time, in the speech which he gave, to his invisible listeners, there was something that was intended for her.

However that may be, the nature of the subject's attitude is then clearly inverted, pseudo-manic, and its strict relation with the recent loss of his mother, privileged object of his bonds of love, is quite clearly the source of the critical state in which he had arrived for the next session, after his exploit, after having accomplished, despite the unpropitious circumstances, and in a brilliant fashion, what he had set himself to do. Thus, Margaret Little, who is however far from having a critical attitude with respect to this style of intervention, herself testifies to the fact that an interpretation based on the intentional signification of the discursive act in the immediate present of the session is subject to all the relativities implied by the possible engagement of the analyst's *ego*.

In a word, the important thing is not that the analyst himself was mistaken and there's nothing in the slightest to indicate that the counter-transference is to be blamed for this interpretation, so clearly refuted by the rest of the treatment. Not only can we concede that the subject had been prey to the feelings that the analyst imputed to him, it is even extremely probable. That they led the analyst into giving the interpretation he did, isn't something dangerous in itself. If the only analysing subject, the analyst, had even felt some jealousy, it is up to him to take it into account in an appropriate manner, to be guided by it as by an extra needle on the dial. No one has ever said that the analyst should never have feelings towards his patient. But he must know not only not to give in to them, to keep them in their place, but how to make adequate use of them in his technique.

In this particular instance, it is because the analyst thought he should look first in the *hic et nunc* for the reason for the patient's attitude that he found it in something which, without a shadow of a doubt, really existed in the intersubjective field shared by the two characters. He was well placed to recognise it, because he felt some hostility, or at the very least irritation in connection with the patient's success. What is serious is to have believed himself authorised by a certain technique to make use of it straightaway and in a direct manner.

What do I contrast this to? I will now try and show you.

The analyst here believes himself authorised to offer what I will call an interpretation from *ego* to *ego*, or from equal to equal – allow me the play on words – in other words, an interpretation whose foundation and mechanism cannot in any way be distinguished from that of projection.

When I say projection, I am not saying erroneous projection. Let there be no mistake about what I'm explaining to you. Before I became an analyst, I had – thanks to what little psychological gifts I have – taken a formula as the principle of the little compass with which I appraised some situations. I was quite happy to say to myself – *Feelings are always reciprocated*. It is absolutely true, appearances notwithstanding. As soon as you put two subjects together – I say two, not three – feelings are always reciprocated.

This explains why the analyst was justified in thinking that given that he had these particular feelings, corresponding feelings could be elicited in the other. The proof of it is in their wholehearted acceptance by the other. All that would be necessary is for the analyst to tell him – *You are hostile, because you think that I am irritated with you* – and the feeling would be elicited. The feeling then was already there, virtually, since all that was required for it to exist was to light the blue touch-paper.

The subject was perfectly justified in accepting Margaret Little's interpretation, for the simple reason that, in a relationship as intimate as that which exists between analysand and analyst, he was sufficiently aware of the analyst's feelings to be induced into something symmetrical.

The question is to know whether this way of understanding the analysis of defences doesn't land us with a technique which almost inevitably generates a specific sort of error, an error which in fact isn't one, something prior to truth and falsity. There are interpretations which are so to the point and so true, so necessarily to the point and true, that one cannot say if they do or do not speak to a truth. Whichever way they will be verified.

It is best to abstain from offering this interpretation of the defence, which I will call from *ego* to *ego*, whatever value it may eventually have. In the interpretation of defences, there should always be at least a third term.

In fact, you need more than that, and I hope to be able to prove it to you. But I am only opening up the problem today.

2

It is late. Which will not allow us to go as far as I would have liked into the problem of the relation between resistance and the defences. Nevertheless I would like to give you some sense of where we're heading.

After having listened to Mannoni's and Anzieu's reports, and after having shown you the risks run by a particular analytic technique, I think it necessary to lay down some guidelines.

It is in *The Interpretation of Dreams* that Freud offered the first definition, in relation to analysis, of the notion of resistance, in Chapter Seven; Section One. There is this decisive sentence – *Was immer die Fortsetzung der Arbeit stört ist ein Widerstand* – which means – *Everything which destroys/suspends/changes the continuation of the work* – symptoms are not at issue here, what is is the analytic work, the cure, the *Behandlung*, as we say when dealing with an object undergoing certain processes – *Everything which destroys the continuation of the work is a resistance.*[1]

This has been unhappily translated into French as – *Tout obstacle à l'interprétation provient de la résistance psychique.*[2] I am pointing this out to you,

[1] SE V 517: 'whatever interrupts the progress of analytic work is a resistance.'
[2] 'Every obstacle to interpretation stems from psychical resistance.'

because it doesn't make life easy for those who can only go by the very congenial translation of the brave M. Meyerson. And the whole of the preceding paragraph is translated in the same vein. This should instil in you a healthy suspicion of a number of translations of Freud. In the German edition a note is added to the sentence quoted, which discusses the following point – if the patient's father dies, is it a resistance? I am not going to tell you what conclusion Freud reaches, but you see that this note shows how broadly the question of resistance is conceived. Well, this note is omitted in the French edition.

Everything which suspends/destroys/interrupts/the continuity – Fortsetzung can even be translated like that – *of the cure is a resistance*. You must start from texts such as these, mull them over a bit, sift them and see where it gets you.

What does all this add up to? What is at issue is the continuation of the treatment, of the work. In order to make it perfectly unambiguous, Freud did not say *Behandlung*, which could mean *the cure*. No, what is at issue is work, *Arbeit*, which can be defined by its form, as the verbal association determined by the rule which he has just mentioned, the fundamental rule of free association. Now, this work, since we are dealing with the analysis of dreams, is quite clearly the revelation of the unconscious.

This will allow us to consider a certain number of problems, in particular the one which Anzieu mentioned just now – this resistance, where does it come from? We've seen that none of the texts in the *Studien über Hysterie* allow one to suppose that, as such, it comes from the ego. Nor does anything in the *Traumdeutung* indicate that it comes from the secondary process – whose introduction is such an important stage in the development of Freud's thought. When we get to the years around 1915 when Freud published *Die Verdrängung*, the first of those studies to appear amongst those which were eventually to be regrouped into the metapsychological writings, resistance is indeed conceived of as something produced on the side of consciousness, but whose identity is essentially determined by its distance, *Entfernung*, from what was originally repressed. The relation then of resistance to the contents of the unconscious itself is in this instance still extremely tangible. It will remain so right up to a period later than that of this article, which belongs to the middle period of Freud's development.

What is it, in the end, which has been primally repressed, from *The Interpretation of Dreams* up to this period which I call intermediary? It is still, as always, the past. A past which must be reinstated, and whose ambiguity we cannot but recall once again, no less than the problems that it raises as to its definition, its nature and its function.

This period is the same as that of the *Wolfman*, in which Freud raises the question, what is a trauma? He realises that trauma is an extremely ambiguous concept, since it would seem that, according to all the clinical evidence, its fantasy-aspect is infinitely more important than its event-aspect. Whence, the event shifts into the background in the order of subjective references. In contrast, the dating of the trauma remains for him a problem that he sees fit to retain quite, if I may put it this way, pig-headedly, as I reminded those of you who followed my course on the subject of the Wolfman. Who will ever know what he saw? But whether he saw it or not, he can only have seen it on a specific date, he cannot have seen it were it only one year later. I don't think I am being unfaithful to Freud's line of thought – all you need is to know how to read him, it's written down in black and white – by saying that it is only the perspective of history and of recognition that allows a definition of what counts for the subject.

For those of you who aren't familiar with this dialectic which I have already developed at great length, I would like to offer a certain number of basic concepts. One should always work at the level of the alphabet. I am therefore going to take an example which will make you understand clearly the questions raised by recognition, and which will keep you from drowning it in notions as confused as those of memory and recollection. If *Erlebnis*, in German, can still have a meaning, the French notion of a memory that is lived or not lived leads to all sorts of ambiguities. I am going to tell you a little story.

I wake up in the morning with my curtain, like Semiramis, and I open one eye. I don't see this curtain every morning because it's the curtain of my house in the country, where I go only every week or so, and among the lines fomented by the fringe of the curtain I notice, once again – I say once again, I have only ever seen it once like that in the past – the silhouette of a face, all at once, sharp-edged, caricatured and old-fashioned, which for me is vaguely like the face of an eighteenth-century marquis. This is one of those completely stupid fabulations to which the mind lends itself when waking, produced as a result of a gestalt-like crystallisation, as one would say these days, in speaking of the recognition of a figure one has known for a long time.

The same thing could have happened with a spot on the wall. That's why I can say that the curtain hasn't moved an inch since precisely eight days before. A week ago, on waking up, I had seen the same thing. I had, of course, completely forgotten it. But it is because of that that I know that the curtain hasn't moved. It is still there, in exactly the same position.

This is only a fable, because it takes place on the imaginary plane, although it wouldn't be difficult to put the symbolic coordinates in place. The bits of nonsense – the eighteenth-century marquis, etc. – play a very important part in it, because if I didn't have a certain number of fantasies on the subject of what the profile represents, I wouldn't have recognised it in the fringe of my curtain. But let's leave that.

Let us see what this implies on the plane of recognition. The fact that it really was like that eight days previously is linked to the phenomenon of recognition in the present.

This is exactly the expression that Freud uses in the *Studien über Hysterie*. He recounts having undertaken, at this period, several studies on memory, and he relates the memory evoked, the recognition, to the actual and present-day force which lends it, not specifically its weight and its density, but quite simply its possibility.[3]

That is how Freud proceeds. When he doesn't know which way to turn to elicit the reconstruction of the subject, he takes hold of him then and there, with the pressure of the hands on the forehead, and enumerates all the years, all the months, all the weeks, even all the days, naming them one by one – Tuesday the 17th, Wednesday the 18th, etc. He trusts sufficiently in the subject's implicit structuration by what has since been defined as *socialised time*, to think that, when his enumeration reaches the point at which the hand of the clock truly intersects with the critical moment of the subject, the latter will say – *Oh, yes, that's right, I do remember something for that day*. Note that I am not saying that it works. It is Freud who assures us that it did work.

Have you got hold of the implication of what I am saying to you? The subject's centre of gravity is this present synthesis of the past which we call history. And it is in that that we trust when it is a matter of keeping the work going. That is what is presupposed by analysis from its beginnings. Henceforth, there are no grounds on which to prove that it is refuted at its end. In truth, if it isn't like that it is absolutely impossible to see anything novel in analysis.

This is a first phase. Is it enough?

No, of course it isn't enough. The subject's resistance is no doubt in action on this plane, but it manifests itself in an odd manner which deserves to be explored and in strictly specific instances.

There is one case in which Freud knew the whole story – the mother had told him it. So he tells it to the subject, by saying to her – *Here is what happened, this is what was done to you*. On each occasion, the patient, a hysteric, responded with a little hysterical crisis, a replica of the characteristic crisis. She listened and replied, in her own way, which was her symptom. Which raises several small problems, and this one in particular – is it a resistance? It is a question that I open up for today.

I would like to conclude with the following remark. At the end of the *Studien über Hysterie*, Freud defines the pathogenic nucleus as what is being sought, but which repels the discourse – what discourse shuns. Resistance is the inflexion the discourse adopts on approaching the nucleus. From then on, we will only be able to resolve the question of resistance by deepening our understanding of what is the meaning of this discourse. We have already said it, it is a historical discourse.

Don't let's forget what analytic technique is in its beginning – a hypnotic

[3] See (1895d) GW I 169–72; SE II 111–14.

technique. In hypnotism, the subject sustains this historical discourse. He even sustains it in a particularly striking, dramatised manner, which implicates the presence of the listener. Once out of this hypnotised state, the subject remembers nothing of this discourse. Why is this precisely the point of entry into the technique of analysis? Because the reviviscence of the trauma is revealed here, in itself, immediately, if not in a permanent, therapeutic manner. It turns out that a discourse held like that, by someone who can say *me* [*moi*], concerns the subject.

It still is ambiguous to speak of the lived, relived character of the trauma in the second, hysterical state. It is not on account of the discourse having been dramatised and presented in a pathetic manner that the word *relived* does the trick. What does it mean to say that the subject assumes his own lived experience?

You see that I am bringing the question to bear at the point where this relived is at its most ambiguous, namely in the subject's second state. But isn't it exactly the same at every level of analytic experience? At every turn we come upon the question – what is the meaning of this discourse which we force the subject to set up within the parenthesis of the fundamental rule. This rule tells him – *When all is said and done, your discourse has no importance.* As long as he surrenders himself to this exercise, he already only half believes in his discourse, since he knows himself to be in the cross-fire of our interpretation at every moment. So the question then becomes – *What is the subject of the discourse?*

That is where we will start off again next time, and we'll try to discuss the meaning and importance of resistance in relation to these fundamental problems.

27 January 1954

IV

The ego and the other

Last time we began to ask ourselves about the nature of resistance.

You did get a sense of the ambiguity, and not only the complexity, in our approach to this phenomenon of resistance. Several of Freud's formulations seem to indicate that resistance stems from what is to be revealed, that is to say from the repressed, from the *verdrängt* or again from the *unterdrückt*.

The early translators rendered *unterdrückt* by *étouffé* [stifled] – that is really feeble. Are *verdrängt* and *unterdrückt* the same thing? We are not going to go into these points of detail. We'll only do that when we have begun to see differences between these phenomena grounded in our experience.

Today I want to lead you, in the Papers on Technique, to one of these points which offers some perspective. Before using the vocabulary, what one has to do is to try to understand, and, to this end, to get oneself into a position in which things fall into place.

At the clinical consultation on Friday, I gave you advance notice of the reading of an important text, and I am going to try to keep to my promise.

Right at the heart of the collection of these so-called technical papers, there is a text which is called 'The dynamics of transference'. Like all the texts in this collection, one cannot say that we have cause to be entirely satisfied with its translation. There are some peculiar inaccuracies, which go right to the limit of impropriety. Some of them are astonishing. They all tend in the same direction, which is to efface the sharp edges of the text. For those who know German, I cannot recommend referring to the original text too much. I warn you of a break in the translation, a full stop inserted in the penultimate line, which separates off a very small sentence which seems to be there for no reason, one knows not why – *For when all is said and done, it is impossible to destroy anyone* in absentia *or* in effigie.[1] In the German text, we find – . . . *because one should recall that no one can be killed* in absentia *or* in effigie. It is linked to the preceding

[1] See GW VIII 374; Stud Erg 167–8; SE XII 108.

38

phrase. Isolated, the phrase cannot be understood, whereas Freud's text is perfectly articulated.

The passage from this article I mentioned to you I'll now read. You'll find it on page fifty-five of the French translation. It is directly linked with this important passage from the *Studien* that I reminded you of, which deals with the resistance met with by approximation[2] in the *radial direction* as Freud puts it, of the subject's discourse, when it finds itself closer to the deep formation which Freud calls the *pathogenic nucleus*.

Let us look[3] *at a pathogenic complex which is sometimes very obvious and sometimes almost imperceptible* . . . I would rather translate – *either apparent as a symptom, or impossible to apprehend, non-manifest* – because it is a question of the way in which the complex is translated, and it is the translation of the complex that is said to be apparent or imperceptible. It isn't the same thing to say that it, the complex, is. In the French translation there's a displacement which is enough to produce a kind of wavering. I'll continue – . . . *from its manifestation in the conscious right down to its roots in the unconscious, we soon reach a region where the resistance makes itself felt so clearly that the association which then emerges bears its mark* – of this resistance – *and appears to us as a compromise between the requirements of this resistance and that of the work of investigation*. It is not quite *the association which emerges*, it is the *nächste Einfall*, the closest, the next association, but in the end the meaning is retained. *Experience* – here's the important point – *shows that it is at this point that transference emerges. When something from amongst the elements of the complex (in the latter's contents) is suitable for being transferred on to the doctor's person, transference takes place, furnishes the next idea and manifests itself in the form of a resistance, in the cessation of associations for example. Similar experiences teach us that the transference-idea is arrived at in preference to all other possible associations capable of sliding into consciousness, precisely because it satisfies the resistance.* The last part of the sentence is underlined by Freud. *A fact of this sort is replicated on an incalculable number of occasions in the course of a psychoanalysis. Every time that one gets close to a pathogenic complex it is first of all the part of the complex capable of transference that finds itself forced towards consciousness and which the patient persists in defending with the greatest tenacity.*

The elements of this paragraph which should be highlighted are the following. First, *we soon reach a region where the resistance makes itself clearly felt.* This resistance stems from the very process of the discourse, from its approximation,[2] if I may say. Secondly, *experience shows that it is at this point that the transference emerges.* Thirdly, transference is produced *precisely because*

---

[2] The sense of approximation Lacan is using here is close to that used in mathematics (e.g. Archimedes) – a method that recursively approximates to its desired end, by repeated application of a rule.

[3] In the passage that follows I give a literal translation of the French translation in order to make clear the conceptual points that Lacan draws out of problems of translation. See GW VIII 368; Stud Erg 163; SE XII 103.

it satisfies the resistance. Fourthly, *a fact of this sort is replicated on an incalculable number of occasions in the course of a psychoanalysis.* It really is a question of a palpable phenomenon in the analysis. And that part of the complex which manifested itself in the form of transference finds itself *forced towards consciousness at this particular instant. The patient persists in defending it with the greatest tenacity.*

There's a note added here which throws the phenomenon in question into relief, a phenomenon which is clearly observable, sometimes in an extraordinary purity. This note intersects with a point emerging from another of Freud's texts – *When the patient is silent, there is every chance that this drying up of his discourse is due to some thought relating to the analyst.*[4]

Employing a not uncommon technical maneouvre, but one which nonetheless we have taught our students to curb, to refrain from, this translates itself as a question of the sort – *Doubtless you are having some thought that relates to me?* Sometimes the patient's discourse is crystallised by this inquiry into some remarks concerning the analyst's style or face, or his furniture, or the way in which the analyst welcomed him that day, etc. This manoeuvre does have a rationale. Something like this can be on the patient's mind at the time and in thus focussing his associations, one can extract a whole variety of things from him. But sometimes one comes across an infinitely purer phenomenon.

Just when he seems ready to come out with something more authentic, more to the point than he has ever managed to come up with up to then, the subject, in some cases, breaks off, and utters a statement, which might be the following – *I am aware all of a sudden of the fact of your presence.*

That is something that has happened to me more than once and which analysts can easily testify to. The phenomenon occurs in connection with the concrete manifestation of resistance as it cuts into the very fabric of our experience in relation to transference. If it takes on a selective value, it's because the subject himself then feels something like a sharp bend, a sudden turn which causes him to pass from one slope of the discourse to the other, from one aspect of the function of speech to another.

I wanted to put this sharply focussed phenomenon before you straightaway, since it clarifies my remarks today. It is the point which will allow us to begin raising our questions again.

Before pursuing this line, I want to stay for a moment with Freud's text so as to show you clearly the extent to which what I am talking about is the same thing as what he is talking about. For a moment, you should stand back from the idea that resistance is all of a piece with the notion that the unconscious is, in a given subject, at a given moment, contained and, as one says, repressed. Whatever the extension that we may eventually give to the term resistance in

---

[4] See GW VIII 367; Stud Erg 161; SE XII 101.

its relation to the totality of the defences, resistance is a phenomenon which Freud localised in the analytic experience.

It is for this reason that the little note appended to the passage that I read to you is important – Freud there spells it out one word at a time.

However, one shouldn't conclude on the pathogenic importance . . . – that's exactly what I am telling you, it is not a question of the conception we construct for ourselves after the event, concerning what motivated, in the deep sense of the term, the stages of the subject's development – . . . *excessively great pathogenic importance of the element chosen with a view to the transference-resistance. If in the course of a battle there is a particularly embittered struggle over the possession of some little church or some individual farm, there is no need to suppose that the church is a national shrine, perhaps, or that the house shelters the army's pay-chest. The value of the object may be a purely tactical one and may perhaps emerge only in this one battle.*

It is within the movement in which the subject acknowledges himself that a phenomenon which is resistance appears. When this resistance becomes too great, the transference emerges.

It's true that the text doesn't say a *transference-phenomenon*. If Freud had wanted to say *a transference-phenomenon appears*, he would have done so. The proof of this distinction's significance is to be found at the end of the article. In the last sentence, the one which starts, *Let us confess that nothing in analysis is more difficult* . . ., the French translation gives *vaincre les résistances* [*conquer the resistances*], whereas the text is *die Bezwingung der Übertragungsphänomene*, that is to say, *the forcing of the transference-phenomena.*[5] I mention this passage to show you that *Übertragungsphänomene* belongs to Freud's vocabulary. Why, however, has it been translated as *resistance*? It isn't a mark of great learning, nor of great understanding.

Freud wrote that it is exactly at that point that something emerges which is not the phenomenon of transference itself, but a phenomenon with an essential relation to it.

As for the rest, what is at issue throughout this article is the dynamics of transference. I am not going to take up in their entirety all the questions it raises, because they touch on the specificity of transference to analysis, on the fact that there the transference isn't like it is everywhere else, but rather *that it there has a quite particular function.* I advise you to read this article. I bring it up here solely as an aid to our study of resistance. Nonetheless, it is, as you'll see, the pivotal point for what's at issue in the dynamics of transference.

What can this teach us about the nature of resistance? It allows us to reply to the question, *who is speaking?* and hence to know what the reconquest, the rediscovery of the unconscious might mean.

[5] GW VIII 374; Stud Erg 167–8; SE XII 108.

We have raised the question as to the meaning of memory [*mémoire*], rememoration, the technique of rememoration, as to the meaning of free association in as much as it allows us to arrive at a formulation of the subject's history. But what does the subject become? In the course of his progress, is it always the same subject at issue?

When confronted by this phenomenon, we get hold of a knot in this progress, a connection, a primary pressure, or rather, strictly speaking, a resistance. At a certain point in this resistance, we see what Freud calls the transference being produced, that is to say in this context the actualisation of the analyst's person. In extracting it from my experience, I told you just now that at the most sensitive and, it seems to me, significant point of the phenomenon, the subject experiences it as an abrupt perception of something which isn't very easy to define – presence.

It isn't a feeling that we have all the time. To be sure, we are influenced by all sorts of presences, and our world only possesses its consistency, its density, its lived stability, because, in some way, we take account of these presences, but we do not realise them as such. You really can sense that it is a feeling which I'd say we are always trying to efface from life. It wouldn't be easy to live if, at every moment, we had the feeling of presence, with all the mystery that that implies. It is a mystery from which we distance ourselves, and to which we are, in a word, inured.

I think that it is something which we cannot dwell on for too long. And we are going to try to find other ways of getting at it, because what Freud teaches us, the trusty analytic method, consists in always rediscovering the same connection, the same relation, the same schema, to be found simultaneously in forms of experience, of behaviour, and for that matter, within the analytic relationship.

Our aim is to establish a perspective, a perception in depth, of several planes. Notions like the id and the ego, which particular techniques have accustomed us to assuming in a wholesale manner, are perhaps not simply a contrasted pair. There we have to set up a stereoscope that is a little more complicated.

For those of you who came to my commentary on the *Wolfman* – already a long time back now, a year and a half ago – I'd like to remind you of certain particularly striking features of this text.

Just as he gets to the question of his patient's castration complex, a question which has an extremely specific function in this subject's structuration, Freud sets out the following problem. As soon as the fear of castration comes up for this subject, symptoms appear, located on a plane we commonly call the anal, since they are intestinal. Now, we interpret all of these symptoms according to the register of the anal conception of sexual intercourse, we regard them as attesting to a certain phase of infantile sexual theory. By what right? Isn't the subject raised to a level of genital structure from the very fact that castration has come into play? What is Freud's explanation?

Even though the subject, Freud says, has arrived at an initial infantile maturation, or pre-maturation, and even though he was mature enough to secure, at least partially, a more specifically genital structuration of his parent's relationship, he had refused the homosexual position allotted to him in this relation, he didn't realise, make real the Oedipal situation, he refused, rejected – the German word is *verwirft* – everything pertaining to the plane of genital realisation. He turned back to his previous version[6] of this affective relation, he retired into the positions of the anal theory of sexuality.

This is not even a repression, in the sense in which an element which would have been realised on a certain plane is repulsed. Repression, he says on page 111,[7] is something else – *Eine Verdrängung ist etwas anderes als eine Verwerfung.* In the French translation, the work of people whom intimacy with Freud should have rendered a little more enlightened – but doubtless it is not enough to have borne the relic of an eminent person to be authorised to become his guardian – the translation is – *a repression is something other than a judgement which rejects and chooses [un refoulement est autre chose qu'un jugement qui rejette et choisit].* Why translate *Verwerfung* thus? I admit that it's difficult, but the French language . . .

M. HYPPOLITE: *Rejection [rejet]?*

Yes, *rejection.* Or, on occasion, *refusal [refus].*[8] Why suddenly introduce *a judgement* into it, in a place where no trace of *Urteil* is to be found? What's there is *Verwerfung.* Three pages further on, on the eleventh line, after elaborating on the consequences of this structure, Freud concludes by saying – *Kein Urteil über seine . . .*[9] It's the first time that he brings in *Urteil*, to round off the passage. But, here, there isn't any. No judgement has been brought to bear on the existence of the problem of castration – *Aber etwas so*, but it was the same, *als ob sie nicht*, as if it didn't exist.

This important articulation shows us that originally, for repression to be possible, there must be a beyond of repression, something final, already primitively constituted, an initial nucleus of the repressed, which not only is unacknowledged, but which, for not being formulated, is literally *as if it didn't exist* – I'm just following what Freud says. And nevertheless, in a certain sense, it is somewhere, since, as Freud everywhere tells us, it is the centre of attraction, calling up all the subsequent repressions.

I'd say that that is the very essence of the Freudian discovery.

---

[6] '*vérification*'.   [7] GW XII 111, Stud VIII 194; SE XVII 79–80.
[8] Lacan's translation of *Verwerfung* here, and throughout Seminar I, is *rejet* or *refus*, the verb form being *rejeté.*
[9] GW XII 115; Stud VIII 198; SE XVII 84.

To explain how a repression of this or that sort is produced, of an hysterical or obsessional type, there is actually no need to have recourse to an innate predisposition. Freud on occasion allows it as a broad general framework, but never as a principle. Read *Bemerkungen über Neurosen*, the second article, from 1896, on the neuroses of defence.[10]

The forms that repression takes on are brought on by this initial nucleus, which Freud then attributes to a certain experience, which he calls the original traumatic experience. In what follows we will take up the question of what *trauma* means, a notion which had to be relativised, but do hang on to the idea that the primitive nucleus is to be found at another level from that of the derivatives of repression.[11] It is their foundation and support.

In the structure of what happened to the Wolfman, the *Verwerfung* of the realisation of genital experience is a quite specific moment, which Freud himself distinguishes from all the others. The strange thing is, what is there, excluded from the subject's history, and which he is incapable of saying, had to be forced out by Freud, in order to see the back of it. It's only then that the repeated experience of his infantile dream took on its meaning, and made possible, not the reliving, but the direct reconstruction of the subject's history.

I'll leave the theme of the *Wolfman* hanging for the moment in order to look at things from another angle. Let's take up Chapter Seven of the *Traumdeutung*, devoted to the dream processes, *Traumvorgänge*.

Freud starts by summarising everything which had been brought out by his argument in the course of his book.

The fifth part of the chapter starts off with this splendid sentence – *Elements in this complicated whole which are in fact simultaneous can only be represented successively in my description of them,* – since he is once again going over everything he has explained about the dream – *while, in putting forward each point, I must avoid appearing to anticipate the grounds on which it is based: difficulties such as these it is beyond my strength to master.*[12]

This sentence shows clearly the very difficulties that I am also having here, in ceaselessly taking up that problem which is always to the forefront in our experience, for one must succeed somehow in a variety of ways in recreating it every time from a new perspective. Freud tells us that one must play dumb each time.

The movement of the argument in this chapter brings us face to face with

---

[10] See '*Weitere Bemerkungen über die Abwehr-Neuropsychosen*' (1896b) GW I 379–403; SE III 162–85.

[11] *Ibid.* SE III 166 n2, 172, 173.

[12] '*Il est bien difficile de rendre par la description d'une succession la simultanéité d'un processus compliqué, et en même temps de paraître aborder chaque nouvel exposé sans idée préconçue.*' – '*Die Gleichzeitigkeit eines so komplizierten Zusammenhangs durch ein Nacheinander in der Beschreibung wiederzugeben und dabei bei jeder Aufstellung voraussetzungslos zu erscheinen will meinen Kräften zu schwer werden.*' – GW II/III 593; Stud II 559. See SE V 588.

something truly very peculiar. Freud lists all the objections one can make as to the validity of the memory of the dream. What is the dream? Is the subject's reconstitution of it accurate? What guarantee do we have that a later verbalisation isn't mixed in with it? Isn't every dream a thing of the moment, to which the subject's speech gives a history? Freud sets aside all these objections, and shows that they are groundless. And he does so by underlining the following, which is quite peculiar, that the more uncertain the text that the subject gives us is, the more it is meaningful. It is in the very doubt that the subject casts on certain bits of the dream that Freud, who listens to it, who expects it, who is there in order to reveal its meaning, clearly recognises what is important. Because the subject doubts, one must be certain.

But as the chapter progresses, the procedure is pared down to a point such that, at the limit, the most significant dream would be the dream that has been completely forgotten, one about which the subject couldn't say anything. That is more or less what Freud writes – *It is often possible by means of analysis to restore all that has been lost by the forgetting of the dream's content; at least, in quite a number of cases one can reconstruct from a single remaining fragment, not, it is true, the dream – which is in any case a matter of no importance – but all the dream-thoughts.*[13] *A single remaining fragment* [*Quelques bribes*] – that's exactly what I've been telling you, there's nothing left of the dream.

What else, besides, interests Freud? Here, we come on *all the dream-thoughts.*

For those who have done psychology, there is nothing more difficult to deal with than the term 'thought'. And as we have done psychology, these thoughts are, for us, as people used to thinking, what we have in our heads all the time.

But we are sufficiently enlightened by the whole of the *Traumdeutung* to realise that these *dream-thoughts* are not perhaps what one thinks they are when one studies the phenomenology of thought, thought without or with images, etc. These aren't what are usually called thoughts, since what is always involved is a desire.

God knows that we have learnt in the course of our research to realise that this desire runs away, appearing and disappearing before our eyes, like the slipper in a game of now you see it, now you don't. In fact, we don't always know if it should be located on the side of the unconscious or on that of the conscious. And whose desire anyway? and above all from what lack?

Freud illustrates what he means with an example, in a little note that he takes from the *Introductory Lectures.*[14]

A woman patient, who is both sceptical about and interested in him, Freud, tells him a fairly long dream, in the course of which, she says, some people told her about his book on *Witz*, and spoke highly of it. All this seems to lead nowhere. Then something else comes up, and the only scrap that remains of the

---

[13] SE V 517.
[14] Lecture XII; see GW II/III 520–1; Stud II 496; SE V 516–7.

dream is this – *channel*. Perhaps some other book where this word occurs, something in which *channel* is involved . . . she doesn't know, it's quite obscure.

So we are left with *channel*, and we don't know what it relates to, nor from whence it came, nor where it is going. Well, this is what is most interesting, he says, this thing which is only a tiny scrap, surrounded by an aura of uncertainty.

And what does it lead to? The next day, not the very same day, she recounts how she has an idea which relates to *channel*. It is a witticism. On a crossing from Dover to Calais, an Englishman and a Frenchman. In the course of conversation, the Englishman quotes the well-known dictum – *De sublime au ridicule, il n'y a qu'un pas*. And the Frenchman, gallantly, replies – *Oui, le Pas-de-Calais*, which is being particularly gracious to his fellow conversationalist. Now, the *Pas-de-Calais* is the channel of *la Manche*, the English Channel. We thus come upon the channel again, and what else, by the same token? Pay strict attention, because this has the same function as the emerging of presence in the moment of resistance. The sceptical patient had previously deliberated at length on the merits of Freud's theory of jokes. After her discussion, at the moment in which her discourse hesitates and is directionless, exactly the same phenomenon appears – just as Mannoni put it the other day, in what seemed to me a most happy way, because he was speaking as a midwife, *resistance makes itself felt in the guise of transference.*

Du sublime au ridicule, il n'y a qu'un pas – that is the point by which the dream hangs on the listener, because that is meant for Freud.

Thus, *channel*, it wasn't a lot, but after the associations, it's indisputable.

I would like to use some other examples.

God knows that Freud is careful in the grouping of facts, and it is not by chance that things are brought together in specific chapters. For example, phenomena which belong very specifically to the order of language appear in the dream just when it takes a certain direction. The subject quite consciously makes a linguistic mistake. In the dream, the subject knows that it's a linguistic mistake since someone intervenes in it to correct it. At a critical point, then, one finds an adaptation which is carried out poorly, and whose function is split before our eyes. But let's leave this to one side for the moment.

Let us turn our attention once again – I picked it out this morning, a little at random – to that celebrated example which Freud published as early as 1898 in his first chapter of *The Psychopathology of Everyday Life*. Regarding the forgetting of names, Freud makes use of the difficulty he once had, during a discussion with a travelling companion, of bringing to mind the name of the author of the celebrated fresco in the cathedral at Orvieto, a vast composition depicting the phenomena expected at the end of the world and centred around the apparition of the Antichrist. The fresco's author is Signorelli, and Freud doesn't manage to recover the name. Others come to mind – it's that one, no it isn't – *Botticelli, Boltraffio . . .*, he doesn't manage to recover *Signorelli*.

He gets to it in the end thanks to an analytic technique. For this little phenomenon doesn't come out of nowhere, it's ensconced in the text of a conversation. At the time they are travelling from Ragusa towards the Dalmation interior, and they are roughly at the limit of the Austrian empire, in Bosnia-Herzegovina. This word *Bosnia* gives rise to a certain number of anecdotes, as does *Herzegovina*. Then some remarks follow about a particularly endearing inclination of the Muslim clientele, which is, from a certain point of view, primitive, and which here attests to an extraordinary sense of propriety. When a doctor brings particularly bad news, of an incurable disease – Freud's interlocutor seems in fact to be a doctor practicing in the area – these people allow themselves to give vent to a certain hostility. So they immediately appeal to him, in saying – *Herr, what is there to be said? If he could be saved, I know you would have saved him.*[15] They are confronted with a fact which has to be accepted, whence their measured, courteous, respectful attitude to the doctor, the *Herr*, as he is called in German. All of this provides the background against which the rest of the conversation proceeds, punctuated by the meaningful forgetting which presents Freud with his problem.

Freud indicates that he did indeed take a full part in the conversation, but at a certain point, his attention wandered away – even while he was speaking, he was thinking of something else, to which this medical story was leading him.

On the one hand, he turned over in his mind the value that patients, especially Muslims, attach to everything concerned with the sexual functions. A patient who consulted him about a disturbance of his sexual potency had quite literally said to him – *If one no longer has that, life isn't worth living.* On the other hand, he remembered having learnt, in one of the places he had stayed, of the death of one of his patients, whom he had cared for for a very long time, something one doesn't come to hear of, he said, without a certain shock. He hadn't wanted to express these thoughts about the high evaluation of sexual activities, because he wasn't very sure of his interlocutor. And then, he wasn't happy to let his thoughts dwell on the subject of this patient's death. But in thinking about all this, he had withdrawn his attention from what he was in the middle of saying.

In his text Freud draws up a very pretty little picture – go look at the German edition – on which he writes all the names – *Botticelli, Boltraffio, Herzegovinia, Signorelli* – and at the bottom the repressed thoughts, the sound *Herr* and the question. The result is what is left. The word *Signor* had been called up by the *Herr* of these ever so polite Muslims, *Traffio* had been called up by the fact that that is where he had received the shock of the bad news about his patient. What he was able to rediscover, at the moment when his discourse was searching out

[15] GW IV 7; SE VI 3.

the author of the Fresco at Orvieto, was what was still available, after a certain number of root elements had been recalled by what he calls *the repressed*, that is to say the ideas concerning the sexual stories of the Muslims, and the theme of death.

What does this mean? The repressed wasn't as repressed as all that, although he hadn't spoken to his travelling companion about it, he presents us with it straightaway in his text. But everything happens, in effect, as if these words – one can properly speak of words even if these vocables are parts of words – were those parts of the discourse that Freud truly had to offer to his interlocutor. He didn't say it, even though he had started to. That[16] is what interested him, that is what he was ready to say, and because he didn't say it, what stayed with him, in the rest of his intercourse with this interlocutor, was the debris, the pieces, the scraps of this speech.

Don't you see here to what extent this phenomenon, which takes place at the level of reality, is complementary to what takes place at the level of the dream? What we are witnessing is the emerging of a veridical speech.

God knows that it can reverberate a great deal, this veridical speech. What is at issue? – if not the absolute, namely death, which is present in it, and which Freud tells us that he preferred, and not only on account of his interlocutor, not to confront too closely. God also knows that the problem of death is experienced by the doctor as a problem of mastery. Now, the doctor in question, Freud, like the other, lost – it's always like that that we feel the loss of a patient, above all when we have cared for him for a long time.

So what beheads *Signorelli*? Everything is indeed focussed on the first part of this name, and on its semantic reverberations. It is in as much as speech, that speech which might reveal the deepest secret of Freud's being, isn't spoken, that all Freud can do is hang on to the other with the scraps of this speech. Only debris is left. That is the phenomenon of forgetting, literally made manifest by the degradation of speech in its relation to the other.

Now – this is what I've been wanting to get at with these examples – it is in so far as the confession of being doesn't come to term that speech runs entirely along the slope by which it hooks on to the other.

Hooking on to the other is not alien, if I can put it this way, to the essence of speech. Without doubt, speech is mediation, mediation between subject and other, and it implicates the coming into being of the other in this very mediation. An essential element of the coming into being of the other is the capacity of speech to unite us to him. This is above all what I have taught you up to now, because this is the dimension within which we are always moving.

But there is another side to speech – revelation.

Revelation, and not expression – the unconscious is not expressed, except by

---

[16] *ça* in the French (play on *ça* = *Es* = *id*).

deformation, *Entstellung*, distortion, transportation. This summer I wrote *The Function and Field of Speech and Language*, intentionally without using the term 'expression', because the whole of Freud's work unfolds in the dimension of revelation, and not of expression. Revelation is the ultimate source of what we are searching for in the analytic experience.

Resistance is produced at the moment when the speech of revelation is not said, when – as Sterba puts it in a most bizarre manner at the end of an atrocious, though entirely honest, article, which focusses the whole of the analytic experience around the dissociation [*dédoublement*] of the *ego*, one half of which must come to our aid against the other – the subject can no longer get himself out of it.[17] He hooks on to the other because what is pressing towards speech cannot attain it. The arrested arrival of speech, in so far as something perhaps renders it fundamentally impossible, that's the pivotal point around which, in analysis, speech entirely seesaws over into its initial aspect and is reduced to its function of relationship to the other. If speech then functions as mediation, it is on account of its revelation not having been accomplished.

The question is always one of knowing at which level hooking on to the other occurs. You have to be made mutton headed by a certain way of theorising, of dogmatising and of regimenting yourself in analytic technique, to be capable of telling us, as someone once did, that one of the preconditions of analytic treatment, is what? – is that the subject has a certain awareness of the other as such. You don't say! But the point is knowing at what level this other is realised, and how, in which function, in which circle of its subjectivity, at what distance, this other is.

In the course of the analytic experience, this distance is continuously changing. How silly can you be to claim that it is a specific stage of the subject!

The same way of thinking leads M. Piaget to talk of the egocentric idea of the infant's world. As if adults had something to teach kids on this subject! And I would really like to know what, in the scales of eternity, has the greater weight when it comes to a better apprehension of the other, that held by M. Piaget, in his professorial position, and at his age, or that of a child! This child, we see that he is prodigiously open to everything concerning the way of the world that the adult brings to him. Doesn't anyone ever reflect on what this prodigious porosity to everything in myth, legend, fairy tales, history, the ease with which he lets himself be invaded by these stories, signifies, as to his sense of the other? Does anyone think that it's compatible with the child playing little games with blocks, thanks to which M. Piaget shows us that he arrives at a Copernican view of the world?

The point is to know how, at a given moment, this quite mysterious feeling of

[17] Richard Sterba 'Das Schicksal des Ichs im therapeutischen Verfahren', International Zeitschrift für Psychoanalysis 20, 1934, 66–73; 'The fate of the ego in analytic therapy', International Journal of Psycho-analysis 15, 1934, 117–26.

presence points to the other. Maybe it is part of what Freud tells us about in 'The dynamics of transference', that is, part of all the preliminary structurations, not only of the love life of the subject, but of his organisation of the world.

If I had to single out the first inflection of speech, the initial moment in which the entire realisation of the truth of the subject is inflected in its trajectory, the initial level on which the captation of the other takes on its function, I would isolate it in a formula given me by someone who is present here and whom I supervise. I was asking him – *Where has he got to, your subject, in relation to you this week?* He then gave me an expression which coincides exactly with what I have tried, in this inflection, to pinpoint – *He called on me to bear witness*. And, indeed, that really is one of the most elevated, although already deflected, functions of speech – the call to bear witness.

A little further and it will be seduction. A little further still, the attempt to inveigle[18] the other into a game in which speech even turns into – as analytic experience has clearly shown us – a more symbolic function, into a deeper instinctive satisfaction. Not to speak of the final stage – the complete disintegration of the speech function in the transference-phenomena, in which the subject, Freud notes, frees himself entirely and does exactly what he pleases.

In the end, doesn't this consideration bring us back to what I started off with in my commentary on the functions of speech? namely, the opposition between empty and full speech, full speech in so far as it realises the truth of the subject, empty speech in relation to what he has to do *hic et nunc* with his analyst, in which the subject loses himself in the machinations of the system of language, in the labyrinth of referential systems made available to him by the state of cultural affairs to which he is a more or less interested party.[19] Between these two extremes, a whole gamut of modes of realisation of speech is deployed.

This perspective brings us exactly to the following consideration – the resistance in question projects its effects on to the system of the ego, in as much as the system of the ego isn't even conceivable without the system, if one can put it this way, of the other. The ego has a reference to the other. The ego is constituted in relation to the other. It is its correlative. The level on which the other is experienced locates exactly the level on which, quite literally, the ego exists for the subject.

For resistance, in fact, is embodied in the system of the ego and the other. It comes into being at this or that moment of the analysis. But it emanates from somewhere else, namely from the subject's impotence to end up in the domain in which his truth is realised. In a way, a way doubtless more or less defined for a given subject by the fixation of his character and his structure, it is always on a specific level, through a specific style of relations with the other, that the act of speech comes to be projected.

[18] *'capter'.*   [19] See E 247-65/40-56.

Look at the paradox of the analyst's position from that moment on. It's just at the moment when the speech of the subject is at its fullest that I, the analyst, can intervene. But I would be intervening in what? – in his discourse. Now, the more intimate the discourse is for the subject, the more I focus on this discourse. But the inverse is equally true. The emptier his discourse is, the more I too am led to catch hold of the other, that is to say, led into doing what one does all the time, in this famous analysis of the resistances, led into seeking out the beyond of his discourse – a beyond, you'll be careful to note, which is nowhere, the beyond that the subject has to realise, but which he hasn't, and that's the point, realised, and which is in consequence made up of my own projection, on the level on which the subject is realising it at that moment.

Last time I showed you the dangers of interpretations or of intentional imputations, which, whether verified or not, susceptible or not to verification, are in fact no more verifiable than any other system of projections. And right there you have the difficulty of analysis.

When we say that we engage in the interpretation of resistances, we are confronting this difficulty – how can one operate at a level of the speech relation which has a lower density? How can one operate within this interpsychology, of *ego* and *alter ego*, to which we are reduced by the very degradation of the process of speech? In other words, what are the possible relations between that intervention of speech which is interpretation, and the level of the *ego*, in so far as this level always mutually involves the analysand and the analyst? When the function of speech has become so firmly inclined in the direction of the other that it is no longer even mediation, but only implicit violence, a reduction of the other to a correlative function of the subject's ego, what can we do so as to still legitimately employ speech in the analytic experience?

You get a sense of the oscillating character of the problem. It brings us back to the question – what meaning does this support taken in the other have? Why does the other become less and less truly other to the extent that it takes on more and more exclusively the function of support?

This is the vicious circle which one has to find a way out of in analysis. Aren't we all the more caught up in it the more the history of technique shows that a stronger emphasis has always been placed on the ego-related aspect of resistances? It is the same problem as is expressed again in the following way – why does the subject alienate himself all the more the more he affirms himself as ego?

We thus come back to last session's question – who, then, is it who, beyond the ego, seeks recognition?

3 February 1954

V

Introduction and reply to Jean Hyppolite's presentation of Freud's *Verneinung*

THE LINGUISTIC CRISS-CROSSING

THE PHILOSOPHICAL DISCIPLINES

STRUCTURE OF HALLUCINATION

IN EVERY RELATION TO THE OTHER, NEGATION

Those who were here last time heard an exposition on the central passage in Freud's paper, 'The dynamics of transference'.

The whole of this exposition consisted in showing you that the principal phenomenon of transference starts with what I could call the basis of the movement of resistance. I isolated that moment, which remains masked in analytic theory, in which resistance, in its most essential aspect, is manifested in a see-saw motion of speech towards the presence of the listener, towards the witness who is the analyst. The moment when the subject interrupts himself is usually the most significant moment in his approach towards the truth. At this point we gain a sense of resistance in its pure state, which culminates in the feeling, often tinged with anxiety, of the analyst's presence.

I also taught you that the analyst's questioning when the subject interrupts himself – a questioning which, because it has been pointed out to you by Freud, has become almost automatic for some people – *Aren't you thinking about something that has to do with me, the analyst?* – is only an activism which crystallises the orienting of the discourse towards the analyst. All this crystallisation shows is the following, that the subject's discourse, in so far as it doesn't attain this full speech in which its base in the unconscious should be revealed, is already addressed to the analyst, is so made as to interest him, and is supported by this alienated form of being that one calls the *ego*.

1

The relation of the *ego* to the other, the relation of the subject to this other himself, to this fellow being in relation to whom he is initially formed, is an essential structure of the human constitution.

It is by taking our cue from this imaginary function that we can conceptualise and explain what the *ego* is in analysis. I am not talking about the *ego* in psychology, where it performs a synthetic function, but the *ego* in analysis, a dynamic function. The *ego* makes itself manifest there as defence, as refusal. Inscribed in it is the entire history of successive oppositions which the subject manifested to the integration of what will subsequently be called within the theory, but only subsequently, his deepest and most misunderstood drives. In other words, in these moments of resistance, so clearly pointed out by Freud, we gain a sense of the means by which the very movement of the analytic experience isolates the fundamental function of the *ego* – misunderstanding [*méconnaissance*].

I showed you the mainspring, the fine point of Freud's investigation, in relation to dream analysis. You there saw, in an almost paradoxical form, the extent to which the Freudian analysis of the dream presupposes a function of speech. This is clinched by the fact that Freud grasps the last trace of a vanishing dream just at the moment when the subject turns completely towards him. It is at the precise moment when the dream is no more than a trace, a fragment of a dream, an isolated vocable, that we rediscover its transferential tip. I have already mentioned this significant, isolated interruption, which may be the turning-point of a phase in the analytic session. The dream is hence modelled on an identical movement.

Similarly, I have shown you the significance of speech that is unspoken because it is refused, because *verworfen*, rejected [*rejetée*] by the subject. I made you realise the specific weight of speech in the forgetting of a word – with an example taken from *The Psychopathology of Everyday Life* – and the extent to which there is, in this instance also, a sizeable difference between what the subject's speech should have proferred, and what is left to him with which to address the other. In the present instance, on account of the effect of the word *Herr*, something is lacking in the subject's speech, the vocable *Signorelli*, which he will no longer be able to bring to mind with the interlocutor, with whom the word *Herr* had, in an implicit manner, been called up a moment earlier, with all of its signification. Revealing as this moment is of the fundamental relation between resistance and the dynamic of the analytic experience, it leads us to a question which can be polarised between these two terms – the *ego*, speech.

This is a question which has been so little explored – although it should be the object of the essential investigation for us – that somewhere, under Mr Fenichel's pen, we find, for example, that the subject indisputably gains access to the meaning of words via the *ego*. Does one have to be an analyst to think that such a view is, at the very least, subject to dispute? Even if we admit that the *ego* is indeed what, as they say, controls our motor activities, and as a consequence the issuing of these vocables known as words, can one claim that, in our discourse, right now, the *ego* is the master of everything that these words harbour?

The symbolic system is extraordinarily intricate, marked as it is by this *Verschlungenheit, property of criss-crossing*, which the translation of the papers on technique has rendered as *complexity*, which is, and how, much too weak. *Verschlungenheit* designates linguistic criss-crossing – every easily isolable linguistic symbol is not only at one with the totality, but is cut across and constituted by a series of overflowings, of oppositional overdeterminations which place it at one and the same time in several registers. This language system, within which our discourse makes its way, isn't it something which goes infinitely beyond every intention that we might put into it, and which, moreover, is only momentary?

It is precisely on these ambiguities, on these riches already involved in the symbolic system as it has been constituted by the tradition in which we as individuals take up our places, far more than we can spell out or learn of it, it is on these functions that the analytic experience plays. At every moment this experience consists in showing the subject that he is saying more than he thinks he is – to take up only this aspect of the question.

We might be led to take up the question from the genetic point of view. But we would then get caught up in an investigation in psychology which would lead us so far away that we can't broach it now. Nevertheless it seems to be indisputable that one cannot make judgements concerning the acquisition as such of language on the basis of the acquisition of the motor mastery revealed by the appearance of the first words. The punching in of words which observers are pleased to record leaves intact the problem of knowing to what extent the words which do indeed emerge in motor representation emerge precisely as a result of an initial appreciation of the totality of the symbolic system as such.

The words that first appear have, as clinical experience shows, an entirely contingent signification. Everyone knows the degree of diversity shown by the first fragments of language as they appear in the child's elocution. And we also know how striking it is to hear the child give expression to adverbs, particles, words, to *perhaps* or *not yet*, before having given expression to a substantive, the minimal naming of an object.

Setting up the problem in this way from the outset seems indispensable to finding a place for any valid observation. If one doesn't manage to grasp clearly the autonomy of the symbolic function in the realising of the human, it is impossible to proceed from the facts without at once committing the crassest of errors in understanding.

Since this isn't a course in general psychology, I will probably not have an opportunity to return to these questions again.

2

Today, I think I will only be able to introduce the problem of the *ego* and of speech, starting, of course, with the way in which it is revealed in our experience.

We can only address this problem in the form which it now has. We cannot pretend that the Freudian theory of the *ego* doesn't exist. Freud opposed the *ego* to the id, and this theory permeates our theoretical and technical conceptions. That's why today I want to draw your attention to a text called *Verneinung*.

Verneinung, as M. Hyppolite pointed out to me just now, is *dénégation* and not *négation*, as it has been translated in French. That is how I myself have always referred to it in my seminars, each time I had occasion to.

The text dates from 1925. It comes after the publication of the articles dealing with the psychology of the ego and its relation to the id. Specifically, it comes after the article *Das Ich und das Es*. In it Freud takes up again this relation, always so alive for him, of the *ego* with the spoken manifestation of the subject in the session.

It seemed to me, for reasons which will become apparent to you, that M. Hyppolite, who by his presence, not to speak of his interventions, does us a great honour in coming here to participate in our work, could make us privy to a critique that is sustained by everything that we know of his previous work.

The problem at issue, as you are going to see, concerns nothing less than the entire theory, if not of knowledge, at least of judgement. That is why I asked him, no doubt a little insistently, to be so good as, not only to stand in for me, but to bring what he alone can bring to a text as rigorous as *Die Verneinung*.

I think that this could present difficulties for any mind not trained in those philosophical disciplines which we could not do without in our present capacity. Our experience is not that of affective smoochy-woochy. We don't have to elicit in the subject the return of more or less evanescent, confused experience, in which would consist all the magic of psychoanalysis. Hence we are plainly doing our duty in listening, when it comes to a text like this, to the expert opinions of someone who is practised in the analysis of language and trained in philosophical disciplines.

This paper shows once more the fundamental value of all of Freud's writings. Every word is worthy of being measured for its precise angle, for its accent, its specific turn, is worthy of being subjected to the most rigorous of logical analyses. It is in that way that it is distinguished from the same terms gathered together more or less hazily by the disciples, for whom the apprehension of the problems was at second-hand, if one may say it, and never in any depth, which resulted in this degradation of analytic theory to which its hesitations so constantly attest.

Before giving the floor to M. Hyppolite, I would like to draw your attention to an intervention that he made in the course of the sort of debate that was instigated by a certain way of putting things concerning Freud and his intentions with respect to the patient. M. Hyppolite had at that time come to Z*'s rescue . . .

M. HYPPOLITE: . . . *for a brief moment.*

. . . yes, for a brief moment of rescue. What was at issue, if you remember, was to find out what was Freud's basic, intentional attitude with respect to the patient, when he claimed to have substituted the analysis of resistances by speech for the subjugation that operates through suggestion or through hypnosis.

I showed myself to be extremely guarded on the question of knowing if there were at this point signs of combativeness in Freud, indeed of domination, vestiges of an ambitious style which we might see betrayed in his youth.

On this point, I think there is a quite decisive text. It is a passage from *Group Psychology and the Analysis of the Ego*. It is in connection with collective psychology, that is to say, relations to the other, that the ego, in so far as it is an autonomous function, is brought into Freud's work for the first time – a simple point, perhaps, but worth making because it justifies the particular manner in which I myself am introducing it to you. This passage comes from chapter four, entitled 'Suggestion and libido'.

We shall therefore be prepared for the statement that suggestion (or more correctly suggestibility) is actually an irreducible, primitive phenomenon, a fundamental fact in the mental life of man. Such, too, was the opinion of Bernheim, of whose astonishing arts I was a witness in the year 1889. But I can remember even then feeling a muffled hostility to this tyranny of suggestion. When a patient who showed himself unamenable was met with the shout: 'What are you doing? Vous vous contre-suggestionez!' I said to myself that this was an evident injustice and an act of violence. For the man certainly had a right to counter-suggestions if people were trying to subdue him with suggestions. Later on my resistance took the direction of protesting against the view that suggestion, which explained everything, was itself to be exempt from explanation. Thinking of it, I repeated the old conundrum:

> Christoph trug Christum,
> Christus trug die ganze Welt,
> Sag' wo hat Christoph
> Damals hin den Fuss gestellt?[1]

So – Freud experienced genuine revulsion on contact with the violence that speech can bring with it. This potential tendency of the analysis of resistances which Z* attested to the other day is precisely the misconstrual to be avoided in putting analysis into practice. I think that in this respect this passage has a very great value, and deserves to be cited.

In thanking him once more for the collaboration that he is willing to give us, I will ask M. Hyppolite who, from what I have gathered, was willing to devote a considerable amount of time to this text, to tell us straightforwardly what he makes of it.

---

[1] (1921c) GW XIII 97; Stud IX 84; SE XVIII 89. 'Christopher bore Christ; Christ bore the whole world; Say where did Christopher then put his foot?'

Jean Hyppolite's contribution to the seminar, 'A spoken commentary on Freud's Verneinung'*, will be found in an Appendix.*

3

We cannot thank M. Hyppolite enough for giving us the opportunity, through a movement coextensive with Freud's thought, to encounter straightaway this beyond of positive psychology, which he has so very remarkably located.

In passing, let me point out to you that in insisting in these seminars on the trans-psychological character of the psychoanalytical domain, we are only rediscovering what is quite evident from our practice, and which the very thought of the person who opened its gates to us constantly manifests in the very slightest of his writings.

There is a great deal to be drawn from a careful reflection on this text. The great concision of M. Hyppolite's presentation is perhaps, in a sense, much more didactic than what I myself, in my own way, tell you, with specific intentions in mind. I will get it duplicated for the benefit of those who come here, because it seems to me that one couldn't have a better preface to this differentiation of levels, to this critique of concepts, which I have myself endeavoured to introduce to you, with the aim of avoiding confusions.

M. Hyppolite's elaborations on Freud's text has shown us the difference between the levels of the *Bejahung*, of affirmation, and of negativity in as much as it sets up at a lower level – I use much more clumsy expressions quite on purpose – the constitution of the subject-object relation. That is exactly what this text, so minimal in appearance, introduces us to from the start, and it clearly links up with some of the most recent philosophical thinking.

By the same token, it allows us to criticise the ambiguity that always dogs us concerning the notorious opposition between the intellectual and the affective – as if the affective were a sort of colouration, a kind of ineffable quality which must be sought out in itself, independently of the eviscerated skin which the purely intellectual realisation of a subject's relationship would consist in. This conception, which urges analysis down strange paths, is puerile. The slightest peculiar, even strange, feeling that the subject professes to in the text of the session is taken to be a spectacular success. That is what follows from this fundamental misunderstanding.

The affective is not like a special density which would escape an intellectual accounting. It is not to be found in a mythical beyond of the production of the symbol which would precede the discursive formulation. Only this can allow us from the start, I won't say to locate, but to apprehend what the full realisation of speech consists in.

There is a little time left. I would like just now to try to indicate with some examples how the question arises. I am going to show it to you from two different angles.

Let us begin by taking a phenomenon whose perspective has been completely transformed by the development of thinking about psychopathology – hallucination.

Up to a certain date, hallucination was considered to be a critical phenomenon around which revolved the question of the discriminating value of consciousness – it couldn't be consciousness which was hallucinated, it had to be something else. In fact, one need only acquaint oneself with the new phenomenology of perception as put forward in M. Merleau-Ponty's book to see that hallucination is on the contrary integrated as being essential to the subject's intentionality.

When it comes to hallucination, one is usually content with a certain number of registers, such as that of the pleasure principle, in order to explain its production. One thus considers it as the initial movement in the order of the subject's satisfaction. We cannot rest content with a theorisation as simple as this.

Recall the example that I mentioned to you last time in the *Wolfman*. The progress of the analysis of the subject in question, the contradictions which are revealed by the traces through which we follow the specification of his position in the human world, point to a *Verwerfung*, a rejection – literally, it has always been for him as if the genital plane did not exist. We have been led to locate this rejection on the level, I would say, of the *non-Bejahung*, because we cannot, in any way, place it on the same level as a negation.

What is striking is what happens next. In the light of the explanations that have been given you today concerning the *Die Verneinung*, it will be much easier to comprehend. In a general way, in fact, the condition such that something exists for a subject is that there be *Bejahung*, this *Bejahung* which isn't a negation of the negation. What happens when this *Bejahung* doesn't happen, in such a way that nothing appears in the symbolic register?

Just let's look at the Wolfman. There was no *Bejahung* for him, no realisation of the genital plane. There is no trace of this plane in the symbolic register. The only trace we have of it is the emergence, not at all in his history, but really in the external world, of a minor hallucination. Castration, which is precisely what didn't exist for him, manifests itself in the form of something he imagines – to have cut his little finger, so deeply that it hangs solely by a little piece of skin. He is then overwhelmed by a feeling of a castastrophe that is so inexpressible that he doesn't even dare to talk of it to the person by his side. What he daren't talk about is this – it is as if this person to whom he immediately refers all of his emotions were annulled. The other no longer exists. There is a sort of immediate external world, of manifestations perceived in what I will call a primitive real, a non-symbolised real, despite the symbolic form, in the usual sense of the term, that this phenomenon takes.

The subject is not at all psychotic. He just has a hallucination. He might be psychotic later on, but he isn't at the moment when he has this absolutely limited, nodal experience, quite foreign to his childhood, completely disintegrated. At this point in his childhood, nothing entitles one to classify him as a schizophrenic, but it really is a psychotic phenomenon we are dealing with.

Hence there is here, at the level of completely primitive experience, at the source-point in which the possibility of the symbol lays the subject open to a certain relation to the world, a correlation, a balancing that I would very much like you to understand – what is not recognised irrupts into consciousness in the form of the seen.

If you go deeply into this particular polarisation, you'll find it much easier to broach the ambiguous phenomenon known as déjà-vu, which lies between these two modes of relation, the recognised and the seen. In the déjà-vu, something in the external world is carried to the limit, and emerges with a special pre-signification. Retrospective illusion relates this perceived thing endowed with an original quality to the domain of the déjà-vu. Freud is talking of nothing other than this when he tells us that any experiencing[2] of the external world implicitly refers to something which has already been perceived in the past. This is true as far as you might want to take it – in a certain way, all varieties of the perceived necessarily include a reference to something previously perceived.

That is why we are here brought back to the level of the imaginary as such, to the level of the model image of the original form. What is at issue is not the recognised as symbolised and verbalised. Rather we rediscover the problems raised by Platonic theory, not of remembering but of reminiscence.

I promised you another example, which I am taking from the advocates of the so-called modern way of analysing. You'll see that these principles were already set out in 1925 in this text of Freud's.

A great deal is made of the fact that at first we analyse the surface, as they say. It would be the crowning glory to make it possible for the subject to progress by escaping this sort of chance represented by the intellectualised sterilisation of contents re-evoked by analysis.

Well, Kris, in one of his articles, gives an account of the case of a subject whom he took into analysis and who, it should be said, had already been analysed once. This subject is seriously hampered in his profession, an intellectual profession which appears to be, in the glimpses one catches of it, not far removed from what might be our preoccupations. This subject experiences all manner of difficulties producing, as they say. Indeed, his life is as it were fettered by the feeling he has of being, let's say for the sake of brevity, a plagiarist. He is continually discussing his ideas with someone who is very close to him, a brilliant scholar,[3] but he always feels tempted to take on the ideas his

---

[2] 'toute épreuve'. Cf. *Realitätsprufung, épreuve de la réalité*, reality-testing.
[3] English in the original.

interlocutor provides him with, and that is for him a perpetual impediment to everything that he wants to get out, to publish.

All the same, he manages to get one text into shape. But, one day, he turns up declaring almost triumphantly that the whole of his thesis is already to be found in the library, in a published article. So there he is, this time, a plagiarist despite himself.

What will the alleged interpretation of the surface that Kris offers us actually consist in? Probably in the following – Kris in actual fact gets interested in what happened and what the article contains. Looking into it more closely, he realises that none of the central theses brought forward by the subject are to be found there. Some issues are raised which address the same question, but there is nothing of the new views brought forward by his patient, whose thesis is thus clearly original. This is where you must start from, Kris says, it's what he calls – I don't know why – taking up things on the surface.

Now, Kris says, if the subject is bent on showing him that his entire behaviour is completely shackled, it is because his father never succeeded in producing anything, because he was crushed by a grandfather – in all the senses of the word – who himself had a highly constructive and fertile mind. He needs to find in his father a grandfather, a father who would be grand, who, in contrast, would be capable of doing something, and he satisfies this need by forging himself tutors, always grander than him, upon whom he becomes dependent by means of a plagiarism which he then reproaches himself for, and by means of which he destroys himself. He is thus doing nothing more than satisfying a need, the same need that tormented his childhood and in consequence dominated his history.

There's no question about it, the interpretation is valid. And it is important to see how the subject reacted to it. What does Kris consider as being the confirmation of the significance of what he put forward, which has such tremendous implications?

In what follows we see the whole history of the subject unfolding. We see that the symbolisation, properly speaking penile of this need for the real, creative and powerful, father, took the form of all sorts of games in childhood, fishing games – will the father catch a bigger or a smaller fish? etc. But the immediate reaction of the subject is the following. He remains silent, and at the next session he says – *The other day, on leaving, I went into such and such street* – it takes place in New York, it is the street where there are foreign restaurants where you can eat rather more spicy dishes – *and I sought out a place where I could find the dish I am particularly fond of, fresh brains.*

Here you can see what makes for a response elicited by an accurate interpretation, namely a level of speech which is both paradoxical and full in its meaning.

What makes this an accurate interpretation? Are we dealing with something which is at the surface? What does that mean? It means nothing, other than that Kris, via a detour that is doubtless diligent, but whose outcome he could easily have predicted, came to realise precisely the following – that the subject, in his manifestation in this special guise of the production of an organised discourse, in which he is always subject to this process which is called negation and in which the integration of his *ego* is accomplished, can only reflect his fundamental relation to his ideal ego in an inverted form.

In other words, the relation to the other, in so far as the primitive desire of the subject strives to manifest itself in it, always contains in itself this fundamental, original element of negation, which here takes the form of inversion.

This, as you see, only opens up new problems for us.

But to continue, it would be useful if one were to fix precisely the difference of level between the symbolic as such, the symbolic possibility, the opening up of man to symbols, and, on the other hand, its crystallisation in organised discourse in so far as it contains, fundamentally, contradiction. I think that M. Hyppolite's commentary has shown you that today in a magisterial fashion. I would like you to keep both the tool and the means to use it to hand, as milestones to which you will always be able to refer yourselves when you come to difficult crossroads in the rest of our discussion. That is why I thank M. Hyppolite for having given us the benefit of his extraordinary expertise.

10 February 1954

VI

Discourse analysis and ego analysis

ANNA FREUD OR MELANIE KLEIN

What I intend to do is to begin to draw you into the area marked out by the remarks I made last time. It is very precisely that area between the formation of the symbol and the discourse of the ego, and we have already been making our way into it from the start of this year. Today, I've entitled the seminar we'll be pursuing together 'Discourse analysis and ego analysis', but I cannot promise to live up to such an ambitious title in a single session. In opposing these terms, I mean them to take the place of the classical opposition between analysis of contents/analysis of resistances.

In the text on the *Verneinung* that he kindly commented on for us, M. Hyppolite brought out the importance of the complex meaning of *Aufhebung*. In German, this term signifies at once to deny, to suppress and also to preserve through suppression, to raise up. We have here an example of a concept which cannot be pondered over too much in order to reflect upon what we do in our dialogue, with the subject, as psychoanalysts have for some time noted.

1

Obviously we are dealing with the ego of the subject, with its limitations, its defences, its character. We have to get it moving. But what function does it have in this operation? The entire psychoanalytic literature is as it were at a loss over its exact definition.

All the recent discussions which take the ego of the analysand to be the ally of the analyst in the Great Analytic Work contain quite obvious contradictions. Indeed, apart from ending up with the notion, not only of the bipolarity or bi-functioning of the ego, but strictly speaking of its splitting,[1] the radical distinction between two egos, it is very difficult to define the ego as an autonomous function, while at the same time continuing to regard it as a master of errors, the seat of illusions, the locus of a passion proper to it, one

---

[1] English in the original.

which leads essentially to misunderstanding [*méconnaissance*]. In analysis, as moreover in one major philosophical tradition, misunderstanding is precisely its function.

There are paragraphs in Anna Freud's book, *The Ego and the Mechanisms of Defence*, where one has the feeling, if you overlook the sometimes disconcertingly reifying character of its language, that she is talking about the ego with the same kind of understanding as we are trying to sustain here. And at the same time one has the feeling that she is talking about *the-little-man-within-the-man*, who has an autonomous life within the subject and who is there to defend it – *Father, look out to the right, Father, look out to the left* – against whatever might assail him from without as from within. If we were to consider her book as the depiction of a moralist, then she incontestably is speaking of the ego as the seat of a certain number of passions, in a style not unworthy of the manner in which La Rochefoucauld points out the unflagging ruses of self-love.

The dynamic function of the ego in the analytic dialogue thus up to now remains fundamentally contradictory for lack of having its place rigorously specified and this fact comes to the surface each time we touch on the principles underlying technique.

I believe that many of you have read this book of Anna Freud's. It is extremely instructive and it is easy to pick out, on account of its being quite rigorous, those points where the weaker elements in its argument appear, still more apparent in the examples she gives.

Look at the passages where she tries to define the function of the ego. In analysis, she says, the ego is only made manifest through its defences, that is to say in so far as it is opposed to the work of analysis. Does that amount to saying that everything which is opposed to the work of analysis is a defence of the ego? Elsewhere she acknowledges that one cannot maintain this and that there are other elements of resistance than the defences of the ego. Isn't that the way I began broaching the problem with you? Many of the problems we've taken up here figure in this book, and one should read it pen in hand, because it has the status of a legacy, faithfully transmitted, of Freud's final detailed construction regarding the ego.

Someone close to us in the *Société*, seized at the 1950 Congress, I know not why, with a lyrical impulse – this dear friend – called Anna Freud *the plumb-line of psychoanalysis*. Well, the plumb-line doesn't make a building. A number of other instruments are needed, a water-level for instance. But in the end the plumb-line isn't that bad – it allows us to gauge the vertical of certain problems.

I am going to ask Mlle Gélinier to give you an account of an article of Melanie Klein's entitled 'The importance of symbol-formation in the development of the ego'. I don't think reading one of Anna Freud's texts dealing with the analysis of children, and especially the ego defences, can be a bad way of introducing it.

Here is a small example she gives us. It concerns one of her patients, who comes to be analysed on account of a state of acute anxiety which disrupts her life and her studies, all this, to obey her mother.

Her attitude toward me was friendly and frank, but I noticed that in all her communications she carefully avoided making any allusion to her symptom. She never mentioned anxiety attacks which took place between the analytic sessions. If I myself insisted on bringing her symptom into the analysis or gave interpretations of her anxiety which were based on unmistakable indications in her associations, her friendly attitude changed. On every such occasion the result was a volley of contemptuous and mocking remarks. The attempt to find a connection between the patient's attitude and her relation to her mother was completely unsuccessful. Both in consciousness and in the unconscious that relation was entirely different. In these repeated outbursts of contempt and ridicule the analyst found herself at a loss and the patient was, for the time being, inaccessible to further analysis. As the analysis went deeper, however, we found that these affects did not represent a transference reaction in the true sense of the term and were not connected with the analytic situation at all. They indicated the patient's customary attitude toward herself whenever emotions of tenderness, longing, or anxiety were about to emerge in her affective life. The more powerfully the affect forced itself upon her, the more vehemently and scathingly did she ridicule herself. The analyst became the recipient of these defensive reactions only secondarily, because she was encouraging the demands of the patient's anxiety to be worked over in consciousness. The interpretation of the content of the anxiety, even when this could be correctly inferred from other communications, could have no result so long as every approach to the affect only intensified her defensive reaction. It was impossible to make that content conscious until we had brought into consciousness and so rendered inoperative the patient's method of defending herself against her affects by contemptuous disparagement – a process which had become automatic in every department of her life. Historically this mode of defence by means of ridicule and scorn was explained by her identification of herself with her dead father, who used to try to train the little girl in self-control by making mocking remarks when she gave way to some emotional outburst. The method had become stereotyped through her memory of her father, whom she had loved dearly. The technique necessary in order to understand this case was to begin with the analysis of the patient's defence against her affects and to go on to the elucidation of her resistance in the transference. Then, and then only, was it possible to proceed to the analysis of her anxiety itself and of its antecedents. [2]

What is at stake in what is here presented as the necessity for analysing the ego defence? Nothing other than the correlate of an error. Indeed, Anna Freud immediately approached the material from the perspective of the dual relation between the patient and herself. She took the patient's defence to be what was its manifestation, namely an aggressive act toward her, Anna Freud. It is on the plane of her own ego, Anna Freud's, it is within the framework of the dual

[2] Anna Freud (1936) pp. 36–7.

relation with her, Anna Freud, that she perceived the manifestations of the ego defence. At the same time she wanted to see in it a manifestation of transference, according to the formula which makes of the transference the reproduction of a situation. Although it is often given, to the point where it is taken to be classical, this formula is incomplete, since it doesn't specify how the situation is structured. What I am now saying to you is related to what I pointed out in my lecture at the Collège Philosophique.

Anna Freud started by interpreting the analytic relation in accordance with the prototype of the dual relation, which is the relation of the subject to her mother. She immediately found herself in a position which not only marked time but was also perfectly sterile. What does she call *having analysed the defence against the affects?* Following this text, there seems no other alternative than her very own understanding. This path would not take her very far. She should have distinguished between the dual interpretation, in which the analyst enters into an ego to ego rivalry with the analysand, and the interpretation which moves forward in the direction of the symbolic structuration of the subject, which is to be located beyond the present structure of his ego.

Through this we come back to the question of knowing what *Bejahung*, what assumption by the ego, what *yes* is at issue in the progress of analysis. What *Bejahung* should be elicited, so as to constitute the unveiling essential to the progress of an analysis?

In a passage to be found in the *Outline of Psycho-analysis*, page 40 in the French edition,[3] but which is not outside of our purview since it is headed 'The technique of psycho-analysis', Freud tells us that it is the ratification of a pact that determines the point of entry into the analytic situation. *The sick ego promises us the most complete candour – promises, that is, to put at our disposal all the material which its self-perception yields it; we assure the patient of the strictest discretion and place at his service our experience in interpreting material that has been influenced by the unconscious. Our knowledge is to make up for his ignorance and to give his ego back its mastery over lost provinces of his mental life. This pact constitutes the analytic situation.*

Well – as my last lecture implied – if it is true that our knowledge comes to the rescue of the ignorance of the analysand, it is no less the case that we are also in ignorance, in as much as we are ignorant of the symbolic constellation dwelling in the subject's unconscious. What is more, this constellation should always be conceived of as structured, in accordance with a complex order.

The word *complex* surfaced in analytic theory through a kind of internal force since, as you know, it wasn't Freud who invented it, but Jung. When we get on the trail of the unconscious, what we encounter are structured, organised, complex situations. Freud gave us the first model of it, its standard, in the Oedipus complex. Those of you who have followed my seminar for some time

[3] (1940a) GW XVII 98; Stud Erg 412; SE XXIII 173.

have had the opportunity to see for themselves to what extent the Oedipus complex poses problems and to what extent it contains ambiguities, thanks to the commentary I made on those cases least subject to reservations on account of their having been so richly sketched in by Freud himself, namely three of the five great psychoanalyses. In short, the entire development of analysis has resulted from showing to advantage, one after another, each of the tensions implied within this triangular system. This fact alone requires us to see in it something quite different from this solid mass summed up in the classic formula – sexual attraction for the mother, rivalry with the father.

You are aware of the profoundly dissymmetrical character, right from the start, of each of the dual relations included within the Oedipal structure. The relation linking the subject to the mother is distinct from that linking him to the father, the narcissistic or imaginary relation to the father is distinct from the symbolic relation, and also from the relation that we really do have to call real – which is residual with respect to the edifice which commands our attention in analysis. All this demonstrates well enough the structure's complexity, and it is by no means inconceivable that another line of research will allow us to develop the Oedipal myth more clearly than has been done up to now.

Despite the wealth of material which has been included within the Oedipal relation, the schema laid down by Freud can hardly be said to have been departed from. This schema should be kept to in its essentials, because it is, and you'll see why, truly fundamental, not only for any understanding of the subject, but also for any symbolic realisation by the subject, of the id, of the unconscious – which is a self [*soi-même*] and not a set of unorganised drives, as a part of Freud's theoretical elaboration might lead one to think when one reads in it that within the psyche only the ego possesses an organisation.

Last time we saw that even the reduction of the negation bearing on what has been denied does not, for all that, render up to us, on behalf of the subject, his *Bejahung*. One should take a close look at the value of the criteria we demand – and on which we are, moreover, in agreement with the subject – in order to recognise a satisfactory *Bejahung*.

What is the source of the evidence? It is the analytic reconstruction that the subject must authenticate. The memory must be re-experienced with the help of empty spaces. And Freud quite rightly reminds us that we can never wholeheartedly trust memory. From then on, what, exactly, are we satisfied with when the subject tells us that things have got to that clicking-point where he has the feeling of truth?

This question brings us to the heart of the problem of the feeling of reality which I touched on the other day with respect to the genesis of the Wolfman's hallucination. I put forward the quasi-algebraic formula, which has the air of being almost too transparent, too concrete – the real, or what is perceived as such, is what resists symbolisation absolutely. In the end, doesn't the feeling of the real reach its high point in the pressing manifestation of an unreal, hallucinatory reality?

For the Wolfman, the symbolisation of the meaning of the genital plane was *verworfen*. So should we be surprised that a number of interpretations, which are called interpretations of contents, are not symbolised by the subject? They manifest themselves at a stage when they cannot in any way make available to him the revelation of his situation within this forbidden territory that is his unconscious, in so far as they are still located in the plane of negation or in that of the negation of the negation. Something has not yet been got over – which is precisely beyond discourse, and which necessitates a jump in discourse. Repression cannot purely and simply disappear, it can only be gone beyond, in the sense of *Aufhebung*.

What Anna Freud calls the analysis of the defences against affect is only one step in her own understanding and not in that of the subject. Once she realises that she is on the wrong track in believing that the subject's defence is a defence against herself, she can then analyse the resistance of the transference.

Where does this lead her? – to someone who isn't there, to a third party. She sifts out something that must greatly resemble Dora's position. The subject is identified with her father and this identification has structured her ego. This structuration of the ego is here referred to as a defence. It is the most superficial aspect of identification, but one is able, through this short cut, to make connection again with a deeper plane, and to recognise the subject's position in the symbolic order. Nothing other than this is at stake in analysis – recognising what function the subject takes on in the order of the symbolic relations which covers the entire field of human relations, and whose initial cell is the Oedipus complex, where the assumption of sex is decided.

Now I will let Mlle Gélinier speak – she will get you to grasp Melanie Klein's point of view. This point of view is opposed to that of Anna Freud – it is not for nothing that these two ladies confronted each other in Merovingian rivalries, a situation not without parallel.

Anna Freud's point of view is intellectualist, and leads her into putting forward the view that everything in analysis must be conducted from a median, moderate position, which would be that of the ego. For her everything starts with the education or the persuasion of the ego, and everything must come back to that. You are going to see the diametrically opposite starting point of Melanie Klein's approach to a particularly difficult subject, apropos of whom one may ask oneself how Anna Freud would have been able to make use of her categories of the strong ego and the weak ego, which presuppose a position of preliminary re-education. By the same token you will be able to judge which of the two is closer to the axis of the Freudian discovery.

Melanie Klein's article, 'The importance of symbol-formation in the development of the ego', published in 1930, is to be found in The Writings of Melanie Klein, *vol I, pp. 219–32.*

2

She slams the symbolism on him with complete brutality, does Melanie Klein, on little Dick! Straight away she starts off hitting him large-scale interpretations. She hits him a brutal verbalisation of the Oedipal myth, almost as revolting for us as for any reader – *You are the little train, you want to fuck your mother.*

Quite clearly, this way of doing things leads to theoretical discussions – which cannot be dissociated from a case-diagnostic. But it is clear that as a result of this interpretation something happens. Everything is there.

You will have noticed the lack of contact that Dick experiences. That's where the defect of his *ego* is. His *ego* isn't formed. Moreover Melanie Klein differentiates Dick from a neurotic, by his profound indifference, his apathy, his absence. In fact, it is clear that, for him, what isn't symbolised is reality. This young subject is completely in reality, in the pure state, unconstituted. He is entirely in the undifferentiated. Now, what constitutes a human world? – if not the interest brought to bear on objects as distinct entities or as equivalent ones. The human world is an infinite world as far as its objects are concerned. In this respect, Dick lives in a non-human world.

This text is a precious one because it comes from a therapist, a woman of experience. She feels things, she expresses them badly – one cannot blame her for that. The theory of the *ego* is incomplete here perhaps because she hadn't decided to provide one, but what she does show extremely well is the following – if, in the human world, objects become variegated, develop, with the luxuriance that makes for its originality, it is to the extent that they make their appearance within a process of expulsion linked to the instinct of primitive destruction.

What is at issue here is a primitive relation, at the very root, the instinctual root, of being. As these ejections out of the subject's primitive world each take place, a world which is not yet organised into the register of a properly human, communicable reality, so each time a new type of identification arises. That is what is insufferable, and anxiety arises simultaneously.

Anxiety is not a sort of energy that the subject has to apportion out in order to constitute objects, and Melanie Klein's text does not include any turn of phrase which might be read in this way. Anxiety is always defined as appearing suddenly, as arising.[4] To each of the objectal relations there corresponds a mode of identification of which anxiety is the signal. The identifications in

----

[4] English in the original.

question here precede the ego-identification. But even when this latter will have been achieved, every new re-identification of the subject will cause anxiety to arise – anxiety in the sense of its being a temptation, a giddiness, a loss of the subject as he finds himself at extremely primitive levels. Anxiety is a connotation, a signal, as Freud always very clearly formulated it, a quality, a subjective colouration.

Now this anxiety is exactly what is not generated in the subject in question. Dick cannot even engage in the first sort of identification, which would already be an essay in symbolism. He is, paradoxical as it may seem to say it, eyeball to eyeball with reality, he lives in reality. In Melanie Klein's office, there is neither other nor ego for him, just a reality pure and simple. The space between the two doors is the body of his mother. The trains and all that is doubtless something, but something which is neither nameable nor named.

It is at this point that Melanie Klein, with her animal instinct which has moreover allowed her to bore through a body of knowledge which was up to then impenetrable, dares to speak to him – to speak to a being who nonetheless allows himself to be apprehended as someone who, in the symbolic sense of the term, does not reply. He is there as if she didn't exist, as if she were a piece of furniture. And yet she is speaking to him. She literally gives names to what doubtless does indeed partake in the symbol, since it can be named immediately, but which was, up to that moment, for this subject, just reality pure and simple.

That is what gives signification to the term prematuration which she employs to say that Dick has already in some sense reached the genital stage.

Normally, the subject finds for those objects of his primitive identification a series of imaginary equivalents which diversify his world – he draws up identifications with certain objects, withdraws them, makes them up again with others, etc. Each time anxiety prevents a definitive identification, the fixation of reality. But these comings and goings will give its framework to that infinitely more complex real which is the human real. After this phase, in the course of which fantasies are symbolised, comes the so-called genital phase, in which reality is then fixed.

Now, for Dick, reality is clearly fixed, but that's because he cannot undertake these comings and goings. He is immediately in a reality which knows no development.

It is however not a completely dehumanised reality. It signifies, at its own level. It is already symbolised, since one can give it a meaning. But as it is above all a movement of coming and going, it only amounts to an anticipated, fixed symbolisation, with a single and unique primary identification, with the following names – the *void*, the *dark*. This gap is precisely what is human in the structure peculiar to the subject, and that is what replies within him. He only makes contact with this gap.

In this gap, he can count only a very limited number of objects, which he cannot even name, as you have already astutely noted. Certainly, he already has some sense of vocables, but to these vocables he hasn't given a *Bejahung* – he hasn't assumed them. At the same time, paradoxical as it may appear, a potentiality for empathy can be found in him, which is much greater than normal, because he is perfectly at ease in relation to reality, in a non-anxiogenic fashion. When he sees little pencil shavings on Melanie Klein's blouse, the result of a fragmentation, he says – *Poor Melanie Klein.*

Next time we will take up the problem of the relation between the symbolic and the real from the most difficult angle, at its point of origin. You will see the connection with what we singled out the other day in M. Hyppolite's commentary – the function of destructionism in the constitution of human reality.

17 February 1954

THE TOPIC OF THE IMAGINARY

VII

The topic of the imaginary

The small talk I will offer you today was announced under the title 'The topic of the imaginary'. Such a subject is quite enough to fill up several years of teaching, but since several questions concerning the place of the imaginary in the symbolic structure crop up while following the thread of our discourse, today's chat may justify its title.

It wasn't without some preconceived plan, the rigour of which will, I hope, become apparent as it is revealed in its entirety, that last time I brought your attention to a case whose particular significance resides in its showing in miniature the reciprocal interplay of those three grand terms we have already had occasion to make much of – the imaginary, the symbolic, and the real.

Without these three systems to guide ourselves by, it would be impossible to understand anything of the Freudian technique and experience. Many difficulties are vindicated and clarified when one brings these distinctions to bear on them. This is indeed the case with the incomprehensions Mlle Gélinier remarked upon the other day when dealing with Melanie Klein's text. What matters, when one tries to elaborate upon some experience, isn't so much what one understands, as what one doesn't understand. The value of Mlle Gélinier's report is precisely to have highlighted what, in this text, cannot be understood.

That is why the method of textual commentary proves itself fruitful. Commenting on a text is like doing an analysis. How many times have I said to those under my supervision, when they say to me – *I had the impression he meant this or that* – that one of the things we must guard most against is to understand too much, to understand more than what is in the discourse of the subject. To interpret and to imagine one understands are not at all the same things. It is precisely the opposite. I would go as far as to say that it is on the basis of a kind of refusal of understanding that we push open the door to analytic understanding.

It isn't enough for it to seem to hang together, a text. Obviously, it hangs together within the framework of pat phrases we've grown used to –

73

instinctual maturation, primitive aggressive instinct, oral, anal sadism, etc. And yet, in the register that Melanie Klein brings into play, there appear several contrasts, which I am going to return to in detail.

Everything turns on what Mlle Gélinier found to be peculiar, paradoxical, contradictory in the *ego*'s function – if too developed, it stops all development, but in developing, it reopens the door to reality. How is it that the gate to reality is reopened by a development of the *ego*? What is the specific function of the Kleinian interpretation, which appears to have an intrusive character, a superimposing upon the subject? These are the questions that we will have to touch upon again today.

You should have realised by now that, in the case of this young subject, real, imaginary and symbolic are here tangible, are flush with one another. I have taught you to identify the symbolic with language – now, isn't it in so far as, say, Melanie Klein speaks, that something happens? On the other hand, when Melanie Klein tells us that the objects are constituted by the interplay of projections, introjections, expulsions, reintrojections of bad objects, and that the subject, having projected his sadism, sees it coming back from these objects, and, by this very fact, finds himself jammed up by an anxious fear, don't you have the feeling that we are in the domain of the imaginary?

From then on the whole problem is that of the juncture of the symbolic and of the imaginary in the constitution of the real.

1

To clarify things a little for you, I've concocted a little model for you, a substitute for the mirror-stage.

As I have often underlined, the mirror-stage is not simply a moment in development. It also has an exemplary function, because it reveals some of the subject's relations to his image, in so far as it is the *Urbild* of the ego. Now, this mirror-stage, which no one can deny, has an optical presentation – nor can anyone deny that. Is it a coincidence?

The sciences, and above all those sciences in labour, as ours is, frequently borrow models from other sciences. My dear fellows, you wouldn't believe what you owe to geology. If it weren't for geology, how could one end up thinking that one could move, on the same level, from a recent to a much more ancient layer? It wouldn't be a bad thing, I'll note in passing, if every analyst went out and bought a small book on geology. There was once an analyst geologist, Leuba, who wrote one. I can't recommend you to read it too highly.

Optics could also have its say. At this point I find that I'm not in disagreement with the tradition established by the master – more than one of you must have noticed in the *Traumdeutung*, in the chapter 'The psychology of the dream-process', the famous schema into which Freud inserts the entire proceedings of the unconscious.

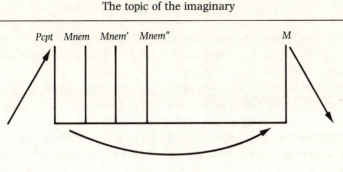

Freud's schema[1]

Inside, Freud places the different layers which can be distinguished from the level of perception, namely from the instantaneous impression – *Mnem'*, *Mnem"*, etc, both image and memory. These recorded traces are later repressed into the unconscious. It is a very pretty schema, which we will come back to since it will be useful to us. But I'd like to point out that it is accompanied by a commentary which doesn't appear to have ever attracted anyone's attention, even though it was used again in another form in Freud's quasi last work, the *Outline of Psycho-analysis*.

I will read it to you as it is to be found in the *Traumdeutung*. *What is presented to us in these words is the idea of psychical locality* – what is at issue here is precisely the field of psychical reality, that is to say of everything which takes place between perception and the motor consciousness of the ego. *I shall entirely disregard the fact that the mental apparatus with which we are here concerned is also known to us in the form of an anatomical preparation, and I shall carefully avoid the temptation to determine psychical locality in any anatomical fashion. I shall remain upon psychological ground, and I propose simply to follow the suggestion that we should picture the instrument which carries out our mental functions as resembling a compound microscope or a photographic apparatus, or something of the kind. On that basis, psychical locality will correspond to a point inside the apparatus at which one of the preliminary stages of an image comes into being. In the microscope and telescope, as we know, these occur in part at ideal points, regions in which no tangible component of the apparatus is situated. I see no necessity to apologise for the imperfections of this or of any similar imagery. Analogies of this kind are only intended to assist us in our attempt to make the complications of mental functioning intelligible by dissecting the function and assigning its different constituents to different component parts of the apparatus. So far as I know, the experiment has not hitherto been made of using this method of dissection in order to investigate the way in which the mental instrument is put together, and I can see no harm in it. We are justified, in my view, in giving free rein to our speculations so long as we retain the coolness of our judgement and do not mistake the scaffolding for the building. And*

[1] (1900a) SE V 538.

since at our first approach to something unknown all that we need is the assistance of provisional ideas, I shall give preference in the first instance to hypotheses of the crudest and most concrete description.[2]

I don't have to tell you that, seeing as advice is given so as not to be followed, since then we haven't missed an opportunity of taking the scaffolding for the building. On the other hand, the authorisation which Freud gives us to make use of supplementary relations so as to bring us closer to an unknown fact incited me into myself manifesting a certain lack of deference in constructing a schema.

Something almost infantile will do for us today, an optical apparatus much simpler than a compound microscope – not that it wouldn't be fun to follow up the comparison in question, but that would take us a bit far out of our way.

I cannot urge you too strongly to a meditation on optics. The odd thing is that an entire system of metaphysics has been founded on geometry and mechanics, by looking to them for models of understanding, but up to now it doesn't seem as though optics has been exploited as much as it could have been. Yet it should lend itself to a few dreams, this strange science which sets itself to produce, by means of apparatuses, that peculiar thing called *images*, in contrast to other sciences, which import into nature a cutting up, a dissection, an anatomy.

Don't think that, having said this, I am trying to make you believe that the moon is made of green cheese, or to make you take optical images for those images with which we are concerned. But, all the same, it is not for nothing that they share a name.

Optical images possess a peculiar diversity – some of them are purely subjective, these are the ones we call virtual, whereas others are real, namely in some respects, behave like objects and can be taken for such. More peculiar still – we can make virtual images of those objects which are real images. In such an instance, the object which is the real image quite rightly has the name of virtual object.

There is in truth something which is even more surprising, which is that optics is founded on a mathematical theory without which it is absolutely impossible to structure it. For there to be an optics, for each given point in real space, there must be one point and one corresponding point only in another space, which is the imaginary space. This is the fundamental structural hypothesis. It gives the impression of being overly simple, but without it one cannot write even one equation, nor symbolise anything – optics would be impossible. Even those who are not aware of this couldn't do a thing in optics if it didn't exist.

Here, too, the imaginary space and the real space fuse. Nonetheless they have to be conceived of as different. When it comes to optics, there are many

---

[2] (1900a) GW II/III 541; Stud II 512; SE V 536.

opportunities for employing certain distinctions which show you the extent to which the symbolic source counts in the emergence of a given phenomenon.

On the other hand, there is in optics a set of phenomena which can be said to be altogether real since we are also guided by experience in this matter, but in which, nonetheless, subjectivity is implicated at every moment. When you see a rainbow, you're seeing something completely subjective. You see it at a certain distance as if stitched on to the landscape. It isn't there. It is a subjective phenomenon. But nonetheless, thanks to a camera, you record it entirely objectively. So, what is it? We no longer have a clear idea, do we, which is the subjective, which is the objective. Or isn't it rather that we have acquired the habit of placing a too hastily drawn distinction between the objective and the subjective in our little thought-tank? Isn't the camera a subjective apparatus, entirely constructed with the help of an x and a y which take up residence in the domain which the subject inhabits, that is to say that of language?

I will leave these questions hanging, to move straight on to a small example that I will try to get into your heads before I put it on the blackboard, because there is nothing more dangerous than things on the blackboard – it's always a bit flat.

It is a classical experiment, which used to be performed in the days when physics was fun, in the days when physics was really physics. Likewise, as for us, we find ourselves at a moment in time when psychoanalysis is really psychoanalysis. The closer we get to psychoanalysis being funny the more it is real psychoanalysis. Later on, it will get run in, it will be done by cutting corners and by pulling tricks. No one will understand any longer what's being done, just as there is no longer any need to understand anything about optics to make a microscope. So let us rejoice, we are still doing psychoanalysis.

Put a vast cauldron in place of me – which perhaps could quite happily stand in for me on some days, as a sound-box – a cauldron as close as possible to being a half-sphere, nicely polished on the inside, in short a spherical mirror. If it is brought forward almost as far as the table, you won't see yourselves inside it – hence, even if I were turned into a cauldron, the mirage effect that occurs from time to time between me and my pupils would not come about here. A spherical mirror produces a real image. To each point of a light ray emanating from any point on an object placed at a certain distance, preferably in the plane of the sphere's centre, there corresponds, in the same plane, through the convergence of the rays reflected on the surface of the sphere, another luminous point – which yields a real image of the object.

I am sorry that I haven't been able to bring the cauldron today, nor the experimental apparatuses. You'll have to represent them to yourselves.

Suppose that this is a box, hollow on this side, and that it's placed on a stand, at the centre of the half-sphere. On the box, you will place a vase, a real one. Beneath it, there is a bouquet of flowers. So, what is happening?

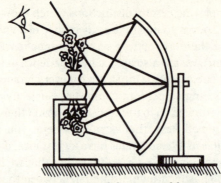

The experiment of the inverted bouquet

The bouquet is reflected in the spherical surface, meeting at the symmetrical point of luminosity. Consequently, a real image is formed. Note that the rays do not quite cross perfectly in my schema, but that is also true in reality, and for all optical instruments – one only ever gets an approximation. Beyond the eye, the rays continue their movement, and diverge once again. But for the eye, they are convergent, and give a real image, since the characteristic of rays which strike the eye in a convergent form is that they give a real image. Convergent in meeting the eye, they diverge in moving away from it. If the rays happen to meet the eye in the opposite sense, then a virtual image is formed. This is what happens when you look at an image in the mirror – you see it where it isn't. Here, on the contrary, you see it where it is – on the one condition that your eye be in the field of the rays which have already crossed each other at the corresponding point.

At that moment, while you do not see the real bouquet, which is hidden, if you are in the right field, you will see a very peculiar imaginary bouquet appear, taking shape exactly in the neck of the vase. Since your eyes have to move linearly in the same plane, you will have an impression of reality, all the while sensing that something is strange, blurred, because the rays don't quite cross over very well. The further away you are, the more parallax comes into play, and the more complete the illusion will be.

This is a fable we will put to a great deal of use. To be sure, this schema has no pretension to touch on anything which has a substantial relation to anything we deal with in analysis, the so-called real or objective relations, or the imaginary relations. But it allows us to illustrate in a particularly simple way what follows on from the strict intrication of the imaginary world and the real world in the psychic economy – now you are going to see how.

2

This little experiment pleased me. It is not me who invented it, it has been around for a long time, known as *the experiment of the inverted bouquet*. As it stands, in its innocence – these authors didn't make it up for us – it seduces us with its contingent details, the vase and the bouquet.

Indeed, the specific domain of the primitive ego, *Urich* or *Lustich*, is constituted by a splitting, by a differentiation from the external world – what is included inside is differentiated from what is rejected by the processes of exclusion, *Aufstossung*, and of projection. From then on, if there are any notions which are placed at the forefront of every psychoanalytic conception of the primitive stage of the ego's formation, it is clearly those of container and contained. This is how the relation of the vase to the flowers that it contains can serve us as a metaphor, a most precious one at that.

You know that the process of his physiological maturation allows the subject, at a given moment in his history, to integrate effectively his motor functions, and to gain access to a real mastery of his body. Except the subject becomes aware of his body as a totality prior to this particular moment, albeit in a correlative manner. That is what I insist upon in my theory of the mirror-stage – the sight alone of the whole form of the human body gives the subject an imaginary mastery over his body, one which is premature in relation to a real mastery. This formation is separated from the specific process of maturation and is not confused with it. The subject anticipates on the achievement of psychological mastery, and this anticipation will leave its mark on every subsequent exercise of effective motor mastery.

This is the original adventure through which man, for the first time, has the experience of seeing himself, of reflecting on himself and conceiving of himself as other than he is – an essential dimension of the human, which entirely structures his fantasy life.

In the beginning we assume there to be all the ids, objects, instincts, desires, tendencies, etc. That is reality pure and simple then, which is not delimited by anything, which cannot yet be the object of any definition, which is neither good, nor bad, but is all at the same time chaotic and absolute, primal. This is the level Freud is referring to in *Die Verneinung*, when he talks about judgements of existence – either it is, or it is not. And it is here that the image of the body gives the subject the first form which allows him to locate what pertains to the ego and what does not. Well then, let us say that the image of the body, if we locate it in our schema, is like the imaginary vase which contains the bouquet of real flowers. That's how we can portray for ourselves the subject of the time before the birth of the ego, and the appearance of the latter.

I'm schematising, as you're quite well aware, but developing a metaphor, a thinking apparatus, requires that from the start one give a sense of what its use is. You will see that this apparatus here possesses a versatility which allows for all sorts of movement. You can invert the experiment's conditions – the pot could just as well be underneath and the flowers on top. You could make what is real imaginary at your discretion, on condition that you retain the relation of the signs, $+ - +$ or $- + -$.

For there to be an illusion, for there to be a world constituted, in front of the eye looking, in which the imaginary can include the real and, by the same token, fashion it, in which the real also can include and, by the same token, locate the imaginary, one condition must be fulfilled – as I have said, the eye must be in a specific position, it must be inside the cone.

If it is outside this cone, it will no longer see what is imaginary, for the simple reason that nothing from the cone of emission will happen to strike it. It will see things in their real state, entirely naked, that is to say, inside the mechanism, a sad, empty pot, or some lonesome flowers, depending on the case.

You might say – *We aren't an eye, what is this eye which wanders around?*

The box represents your own body, the bouquet, instincts and desires, the objects of desire which rove about. And the cauldron, what's that? That could well be the cortex. Why not? It would be fun – we'll discuss that some other day.

In the middle of this, your eye doesn't rove about, it is fixed there, like a titillating little appendage of the cortex. So, why am I telling you that it roves around and that, according to its position, sometimes it works, sometimes it doesn't?

The eye is here, as so often, symbolic of the subject.

The whole of science is based on reducing the subject to an eye, and that is why it is projected in front of you, that is to say objectivated – I'll explain that to you another time. In relation to the theory of the instincts, some time back someone proposed a very beautiful construction, the most paradoxical that I have ever heard professed, which entified the instincts. At the end, not a single one was left standing, and it was, just on this account, useful to undertake this demonstration. In order to reduce us for a moment to being only an eye, we had to put ourselves in the shoes of the scientist who can decree that he is just an eye, and can put a notice on the door – *Do not disturb the experimenter*. In life, things are entirely different, because we aren't an eye. So, this eye, what does it mean?

It means that, in the relation of the imaginary and the real, and in the constitution of the world such as results from it, everything depends on the position of the subject. And the position of the subject – you should know, I've been repeating it for long enough – is essentially characterised by its place in the symbolic world, in other words in the world of speech. Whether he has the right to, or is prohibited from, calling himself *Pedro* hangs on this place. Depending on what is the case, he is within the field of the cone or he isn't.

That is what you have to get into your heads, even if it seems a bit much, to understand what follows.

3

We must accept Melanie Klein's text for what it is, namely the write-up of an experiment.

Here's a boy, who, we are told, is about four years old, whose general level of development is between fifteen and eighteen months. That is a question of definition, and you never know what is meant. What is the instrument of measurement? Specification is often omitted. An affective development of fifteen to eighteen months, this notion remains even more fuzzy than the image of a flower in the experiment I just set up for you.

The child possesses a very limited vocabulary, more than just limited in fact, incorrect. He deforms words and uses them inopportunely most of the time, whereas at other times it is clear that he knows their meaning. Melanie Klein insists on the most striking fact – this child has no desire to make himself understood, he doesn't try to communicate, his only activities, more or less playful, are emitting sounds and taking pleasure in meaningless sounds, in noises.

Even so, this child possesses something of language – otherwise Melanie Klein could not make herself understood by him. He has some of the elements of the symbolic apparatus at his disposal. On the other hand, Melanie Klein, from this first, so crucial, contact with the child on, characterises his attitude as one of apathy, indifference. He is nonetheless not lacking in direction. He does not give the impression of being an idiot, far from it. Melanie Klein distinguishes him from all the neurotic children she had previously seen by observing that he gave no sign of anxiety, even in the disguised forms which it assumes in neurotics, either explosion or else withdrawal, stiffness, timidity. It could not escape the notice of this therapist, with all her experience. There he is, this child, as if nothing was going on. He looks at Melanie Klein as he would look at a piece of furniture.

I am underlining these aspects because I want to highlight the uniform character of reality for him. Everything is equally real for him, equally indifferent.

This is where Mlle Gélinier's quandaries begin.

The child's world, Melanie Klein tells us, is manufactured out of a container – this would be the body of the mother – and out of the contents of the body of this mother.[3] In the course of the development of his instinctual relations with this privileged object, the mother, the child is led into instigating a series of relations of imaginary incorporations. He can bite, absorb the body of his mother. The style of this incorporation is one of destruction.

In this maternal body, the child expects to encounter a certain number of objects, themselves possessing a specific unity, though objects which may be dangerous for him are included amongst them. Why dangerous? For exactly the same reason whereby he is dangerous for them. Mirroring them, as one might well say, he clothes them with the same capacities for destruction as

---

[3] The term Lacan uses is '*contenu*', which covers both the English 'contents' (the term Klein uses, see *op. cit.* p. 232 and particularly p. 221) and 'contained', which is the English term most appropriate for some of the uses to which Lacan is putting the term in this seminar.

those of which he feels himself the bearer. It is in virtue of this that he will come to accentuate their exteriority in relation to the initial limitations of his ego, and reject them like bad, dangerous objects, poo-poo.

Certainly these objects will be externalised, isolated, from this primal universal container, from this primal large whole that is the fantasised image of the mother's body, the entire empire of the primal infantile reality. But they will nevertheless always be endowed with the same maleficent accent which marked his first relations with them. That is why he will reintroject them, and switch his attention to other, less dangerous objects. For example, he will construct what is called the equation *faeces-urine*. Different objects from the external world, more neutralised, will be set up as the equivalents of these first ones, will be linked up with them through the imaginary – I am underlining it – equation. Hence, the symbolic equation that we rediscover between these objects arises from an alternating mechanism of expulsion and introjection, of projection and absorption, that is to say from an imaginary interplay.

It is specifically this interplay that I am trying to symbolise for you in my schema through the imaginary inclusions of real objects, or inversely, through the capturing of imaginary objects within a real enclosure.

In Dick's case, we see clearly that there is the skeleton of imagination, if I may say, of the external world. It is there ready to surface, but only ready to.

Dick plays with the container and the contained. Already, he has quite naturally entified in several objects, the little train for example, a certain number of tendencies, of persons even – himself as little train, in comparison with his father who is the big train. Moreover, the number of objects of significance is, surprisingly, for him very limited, limited to the minimal signs capable of expressing the inside and the outside, the contained and the container. Hence the dark space is straightaway assimilated to the inside of the mother's body, in which he seeks refuge. What doesn't happen is the free play, the conjunction between the different forms, imaginary and real, of objects.

That is why, when he seeks refuge in the empty, dark inside of the maternal body, there are no objects there, to Mlle Gélinier's great surprise. For one simple reason – in his case, the bouquet and the vase cannot both be there at the same time. That is the key.

Mlle Gélinier's astonishment is based on the fact that, for Melanie Klein, everything takes place on a plane of equal reality – of unreal reality,[4] as she puts it, which, in fact, doesn't facilitate our conceiving the dissociation of different sets[5] of primitive objects. Melanie Klein has neither a theory of the imaginary nor a theory of the *ego*. It is up to us to introduce these notions, and to understand that, in so far as one part of reality is imagined, the other is real and inversely, in so far as one part is reality, the other becomes imaginary. One can

---

[4] English in the original.
[5] English in the original.

see why, in the beginning, the conjunction of different parts, of sets,[6] can never be accomplished.

Here, we are in the mirror relation.

We call this the plane of projection. But can one designate the correlate of projection? One has to find another word than *introjection*. As we use it in analysis, the word 'introjection' is not the opposite of projection. It is almost only ever used, you will notice, when it is a question of symbolic introjection. It is always accompanied by a symbolic denomination. Introjection is always the introjection of the speech of the other, which introduces an entirely different dimension from that of projection. Around this distinction you can discriminate between what is a function of the *ego* and what pertains to the order of the dual relation, and what is a function of the super-ego. It is not for nothing that they are distinguished within analytic theory, nor that it is accepted that the super-ego, the authentic super-ego, is a secondary introjection in relation to the function of the ideal *ego*.

These are asides. I'll return to the case described by Melanie Klein.

The child is there. He has a certain number of significant registers at his disposition. Melanie Klein – we can follow her at this point – underlines the extreme restrictedness of one of them – the imaginary domain. Normally it is through the possibilities of play in the imaginary transposition that the progressive valorisation of objects comes about, on the plane that we commonly designate as affective, through a diversification, a fanning-out of all the imaginary equations which allow the human being to be the only animal to have at his disposition an almost infinite number of objects – objects marked with the value of a *Gestalt* in his *Umwelt*, objects isolated as to their forms. Melanie Klein underlines the poverty of the imaginary world, and, by the same token, the impossibility of this child entering into an effective relation with objects *qua* structures. An important correlation to grasp.

If we now sum up everything that Melanie Klein describes of this child's attitude, the significant point is simply the following – he makes no call.

The call – this is a notion that I ask you to retain. You are going to say to yourselves – *Of course, being Doctor Lacan, he uses this to go on about language again*. But the child already has his own system of language, quite sufficient. The proof is that he plays with it. He even makes use of it to play a game of opposition against the adults' attempts to intrude. For example, he behaves in a way which is said in the text to be negativistic.[6] When his mother suggests a name to him, one he is capable of reproducing in a correct manner, he reproduces it in an unintelligible, deformed manner, which cannot be of any use whatever. Here we rediscover the distinction to be drawn between negativism and negation – as M. Hyppolite reminded us, thus demonstrating

---

[6] English in the original.

not only his culture, but also that he has seen patients with his own eyes. As to Dick, he uses language in a strictly negativistic manner.

In consequence, in introducing the call, it isn't language that I am covertly slipping in. I will even go further – not only isn't it language, but it isn't a higher level of language. It is in fact beneath language, if we're talking of levels. You have only to observe a pet to see that a being deprived of language is quite capable of making calls on you, calls to draw your attention to something which, in some sense or other, it lacks. To the human call a further, richer development is reserved, because it takes place precisely in a being who has already reached the level of language.

Let us be schematic.

A certain Karl Bühler put forward a theory of language, which is neither unique, nor the most complete, but in it you'll find something of interest – he differentiates three stages in language. Unfortunately he located them in registers which do not make them very comprehensible.

First of all, the level of the statement as such, which is almost a level of the natural datum. I am at the level of the statement when I say the simplest thing to someone, for example an imperative. It is at this level of the statement that everything concerning the nature of the subject must be placed. An officer, a professor, will not give an order in the same language as a worker or foreman. At the level of the statement, from its style to its very intonation, everything we learn bears on the nature of the subject.

In any imperative, there's another plane, that of the call. It is a question of the tone in which the imperative is uttered. The same text can have completely different imports depending on the tone. The simple statement *stop* can have, depending on the circumstances, completely different imports as a call.

The third level is communication properly speaking – what is at issue, and its reference to the totality of the situation.

With Dick we are at the level of the call. The call acquires its weight within the already acquired system of language. Now, what is crucial here is that this child does not voice any call. The system whereby the subject comes to locate himself in language is interrupted, at the level of speech. Language and speech are not the same thing – this child is, up to a certain point, a master of language, but he doesn't speak. There is a subject here who quite literally does not reply.

Speech has not come to him. Language didn't stick to his imaginary system, whose register is extremely limited – valorisation of trains, of door-handles, of the dark. His faculties, not of communication, but of expression, are limited to that. For him, the real and the imaginary are equivalent.

Hence Melanie Klein here has to give up on technique. She has the minimum of material. She doesn't even have games – this child does not play. When he picks up a little train for a while, he doesn't play, he does it in the same way he moves through the air – as if he were an invisible being, or rather as if everything were, in a specific manner, invisible to him.

Melanie Klein here doesn't, as she is vividly aware, offer an interpretation. She starts off, she says, from ideas she already has, which are well known, as to what happens at this stage. I won't beat about the bush, I just tell him – *Dick little train, big train daddy-train.*

Thereupon, the child starts to play with his little train, and he says the word, *station.*[7] Crucial moment, when the sticking of language to the subject's imaginary begins to sketch itself.

Melanie Klein plays this back to him – *The station is mummy. Dick is going into mummy.* From this point on, everything starts firing. She'll only feed him these kinds of lines, and no others. And very quickly the child makes progress. That's a fact.

So what did Melanie Klein actually do? – nothing other than to bring in verbalisation. She symbolised an effective relationship, that of one named being with another. She plastered on the symbolisation of the Oedipal myth, to give it its real name. It's from that point on that, after an initial ceremony, taking refuge in the dark in order to renew contact with the container, something new awakens in the child.

The child verbalises a first call – a spoken call. He asks for his nurse, with whom he came in and who he had allowed to leave as if it were nothing to him. For the first time, he reacts by calling, which is not simply an affective call, mimed by the whole being, but a verbalised call, which from then on includes a reply. This is his first communication in the strict, technical sense of the term.

Things then progress to the point where Melanie Klein brings into play all the other elements of a situation which is from then organised, right up to and including the father himself, who comes to take his own part. Outside of the sessions, Melanie Klein says, the child's relations unfold on the plane of the Oedipus complex. The child symbolises the reality around him starting from this nucleus, this little palpitating cell of symbolism which Melanie Klein gave him.

That is what she later calls – *gaining access to his unconscious.*[8]

What did Melanie Klein ever do, which would reveal the least comprehension of any kind of process, which might, in the subject, amount to his unconscious? She accepts it from the start, out of habit. Do all read the case again and you will see in it the spectacular demonstration of the formula that I am always giving you – *the unconscious is the discourse of the other.*

Here is a case where it is absolutely apparent. There is nothing remotely like an unconscious in the subject. It is Melanie Klein's discourse which brutally grafts the primary symbolisations of the Oedipal situation on to the initial ego-related [*moïque*] inertia of the child. Melanie Klein always does that with her subjects, more or less implicitly, more or less arbitrarily.

In the extreme case, in the case of the subject who hasn't acceded to human

---

[7] English in the original.

[8] *'avoir ouvert les portes de son inconscient'* – the phrase is taken from Klein's paper (p. 229).

reality, since no call can be heard from him, what are the effects of the symbolisations introduced by the therapist? They specify an initial position from which the subject can introduce an interplay between the imaginary and the real and master his development. He is swallowed up in a series of equivalences, in a system in which objects are substituted one for the other. He runs through an entire sequence of equations which drive him out of the space between the doors where he had gone to seek refuge in the absolute darkness of the total container, to those objects which he substitutes for it – the wash-basin, for example. In this way he unfolds and articulates his entire world. And then, from the wash-basin, he moves on to an electric radiator, on to objects which are more and more complex. He accedes to richer and richer contents [*contenus*], such as to the possibility of defining the contained [*contenu*] and the non-contained [*non-contenu*].

Why speak in this case of the development of the *ego*? That's to confuse, as always, the *ego* and the subject.

Development only takes place in so far as the subject integrates himself into the symbolic system, acts within it, asserts himself in it through the use of genuine speech. It isn't even essential, you should note, that this speech be his own. In the couple that is temporarily constituted in what is, however, its least affectivated form, between the therapist and the subject, genuine speech can be brought forth. To be sure, not any old speech – that's where we perceive the virtue of the symbolic situation of the Oedipus complex.

It really is the key – a very elementary key. I have already pointed out to you that there most probably was a whole bunch of keys. One day perhaps I will give you a lecture on what we gain in this respect from the myths of primitive peoples – I wouldn't say inferior, because they aren't inferior, they know much more than we do. When we study a mythology, for example one that might perhaps appear with respect to a Sudanese population, we discover that for them the Oedipus complex is just a rather thin joke. It is a very tiny detail within an immense myth. The myth allows the cataloguing of a set of relations between subjects of a wealth and complexity besides which the Oedipus complex seems only to be so abridged an edition that in the end it cannot always be used.

But no matter. Us analysts have been satisfied with it up to now. Certainly, one does try to elaborate it a bit, but it is all rather timid. One always feels terribly tangled up because one doesn't distinguish easily between the imaginary, symbolic and real.

Now I want to bring the following to your attention. When Melanie Klein offers him the Oedipal schema, the imaginary relation which the subject lives, though extremely impoverished, is already complex enough for us to say that he has a world of his own. But for us this primitive real is literally ineffable. As long as he doesn't tell us anything about it, we have no means of gaining access to it, except through symbolic extrapolations which constitute the ambiguity of all systems such as Melanie Klein's – she tells us, for instance, that within the empire of the maternal body, the subject is to be found with all his brothers, not to mention the father's penis, etc. Really?

It doesn't matter, since we can thus grasp in any case how this world is set in motion, how the imaginary and real begin to be structured, how the successive investments develop, investments which delineate the variety of human, that is nameable, objects. All of this process has its point of departure in this initial fresco constituted by a significative speech, formulating a fundamental structure which, in the law of speech, humanises man.

How can I put this in yet another way? Ask yourselves what the call represents in the field of speech. Well, it's the possibility of refusal. I say the *possibility*. The call doesn't imply refusal, it doesn't imply any dichotomy, any bipartition. But you can see for yourselves that it is when the call is made that dependency relations establish themselves in the subject. From then on he will welcome his nurse with open arms, and in deliberately hiding himself behind the door, he will all at once reveal in relation to Melanie Klein the need to have a companion in this cramped corner which he occupied for a while. Dependency will come in its train.

In this observation, then, you see, quite independently, the set of pre-verbal and post-verbal relations at play in the child. And you realise that the external world – what we call the real world, which is only a humanised, symbolised world, the work of transcendence introduced by the symbol into the primitive reality – can only be constituted when a series of encounters have occurred in the right place.

These positions belong to the same order as those which, in my schema, cause a given structuration of the situation to depend upon a given position of the eye. I will make further use of this schema. For today I only wanted to introduce a bouquet, but one can introduce the other.

Starting from Dick's case and by employing the categories of the real, the symbolic and the imaginary, I showed you how it can happen that a subject who has all the elements of language at his disposition, and who has the possibility of making several imaginary moves that allow him to structure his world, might not be in the real. Why isn't he in it? – simply because things didn't happen in a specific order. The figure is in its entirety upset. No way of giving this entirety any development whatsoever.

Are we dealing with the development of the *ego* here? Look at Melanie Klein's text again. She says that the *ego* had developed in too precocious a manner, in such a way that the child has too real a relation to reality, because the imaginary could find no place there – and then, in the second part of her sentence, she says that it is the *ego* which halts development. This simply means that the *ego* cannot be fruitfully employed as an apparatus in the structuring of this external world. For one simple reason – because of the poor position of the eye, the *ego* quite simply doesn't appear.

Let the vase be virtual. The vase doesn't appear, and the subject remains in a reduced reality, with a similarly reduced imaginary baggage.

The core of this observation, which is what you must understand – the virtue of speech, in so far as the act of speech is a mode of functioning coordinated to a symbolic system that is already established, typical and significant.

It would be worth your while to ponder the questions, to reread the text, also to get the feel of this little schema so that you could see for yourselves what use you could put it to.

What I've given you today is a theoretical discussion in complete contrast with the set of problems raised last time by Mlle Gélinier. The title of the next session, which will take place in two weeks time, will be – *The transference – the different levels on which it should be studied.*

24 February 1954

VIII

The wolf! The wolf!

THE CASE OF ROBERT
THEORY OF THE SUPER-EGO
THE CORE OF SPEECH

In the course of our dialogue, you have been able to get acquainted with the ambition which rules our commentary, namely that of reconsidering the fundamental texts of the analytic experience. The moving spirit of our excavation is the following idea – whatever in an experience is always best seen is at some remove. So it is not surprising that it should be here and now that we are led, in order to understand the analytic experience, to begin again with what is implied by its most immediate given, namely the symbolic function, or what in our vocabulary is exactly the same thing – the function of speech.

We rediscover this, the central domain of analytic experience, signalled throughout Freud's oeuvre, never named, but signalled at every step. I don't think I am pushing it when I say that that is what can be immediately translated, almost algebraically, from any Freudian text. And this translation yields the solution of a number of antinomies which become apparent in Freud with that honesty which ensures that any given one of his texts is never closed, as if the whole of the system were in it.

For the next session, I would very much like someone to undertake to give a commentary on a text which exemplifies what I've just been saying. This text is to be found between 'Remembering, repeating and working-through' and 'Observations on transference-love', which are two of the most important texts in the collection of Papers on Technique. I am referring to 'On narcissism: an introduction'.

It is a text that we cannot but bring into our course, as soon as we have touched on the situation of the analytic dialogue. You will agree with that, if you know the further implications of these terms, *situation* and *dialogue* – dialogue in inverted commas.

We tried to define resistance within its own field. Then, we formulated a definition of transference. Now, you will be well aware of the great distance which separates – resistance, which keeps the subject from this full speech which analysis awaits from him, and which is a function of that anxiogenic inflection constituted, in its most radical mode, at the level of symbolic exchange, by the transference – from this phenomenon which we handle in a technical manner in analysis and which seems to us to be the driving force,[1] as Freud put it, of the transference, namely love.

In 'Observations on transference-love', Freud did not hesitate to call the transference by the name, *love*. Freud is so little concerned to evade the phenomenon of love, of passionate love, in its most concrete sense, that he goes so far as to say that there is no really essential distinction between transference and what, in everyday life, we call love. The structure of this artificial phenomenon which is transference and that of the spontaneous phenomenon we call love, and more specifically passionate love, are, on the plane of the psychic, equivalent.

On Freud's part, there is no evading this phenomenon, no attempt to dissolve the scabrous into something symbolic, in the sense in which it is usually understood – the illusory, the unreal. Transference – is love.

Our inquiries are now going to centre on transference-love, to wind up our study of the Papers on Technique. This will take us to the heart of that other notion, which I am trying to bring in here, without which, what is more, it is not possible to arrive at a judicious apportioning of what we deal with in our experience – the function of the imaginary.

Don't get the idea that this function of the imaginary is absent from Freud's texts. It is no more so than the symbolic function. Freud quite simply didn't place it in the foreground, and didn't call attention to it everywhere it can be found. When we come to study 'On narcissism', you will see that Freud himself, in order to specify the difference between dementia praecox, schizophrenia, psychosis, on the one hand, and neurosis on the other, comes up with no other definition than the following, which may perhaps seem surprising to some of you. *A patient suffering from hysteria or obsessional neurosis has also, as far as his illness extends, given up his relation to reality. But analysis shows that he has by no means broken off his erotic relations to people and things. He still retains them in phantasy; i.e. he has, on the one hand, substituted for real objects imaginary ones from his memory, or has mixed the latter with the former; –* remember our schema from last time – *and on the other hand, he has renounced the initiation of motor activities for the attainment of his aims in connection with those objects. Only to this condition of the libido may we legitimately apply the term 'introversion' of the libido which is used by Jung indiscriminately. It is otherwise with the paraphrenic. He seems really to have withdrawn his libido from people and things in the external world, without replacing them by others in phantasy.* This simply means that he recreates this imaginative world . . . *When he does so replace them, the process seems to be a secondary one and to be part of an attempt at recovery, designed to lead the libido back to objects.*[2]

---

[1] (1915a) GW X 313; Stud Erg 224; SE XII 165 – *triebende Kräfte*.
[2] (1914c) GW X 139; Stud III 42; SE XIV 74.

Here we come to what is the essential distinction to be drawn between neurosis and psychosis, as to the functioning of the imaginary, a distinction which Schreber's analysis, which, I hope, we will be able to start before the end of the year, will enable us to consider in greater depth.

For today, I will yield the floor to Rosine Lefort, my student, here on my right, who, as I heard yesterday evening, presented her observations on a child, whom she had spoken of with me for a long time, to our sub-group dealing with the psychoanalysis of children. It is one of those serious cases which leave us with a great feeling of unease as to the diagnosis, and in a considerable quandary as to the nosology. But at all events, Rosine Lefort was able to penetrate deeply, as you will be able to see for yourselves.

Just as we started off, two lectures ago, with Melanie Klein's observation, today I yield the floor to Rosine Lefort. She will open up, in so far as time permits, questions to which I will provide answers which may well be included next time in my discussion entitled 'Transference in the imaginary'.

Dear Rosine, tell us about the case of Robert.

1

THE CASE OF ROBERT

MME LEFORT: *Robert was born on 4 March 1948. His past history has been reconstituted with some difficulty, and it is in large part owing to the material brought up in sessions that it has been possible to learn of the traumas he suffered.*

His father is not known. His mother is presently confined as a paranoiac. She kept him with her up to the age of five months, moving from house to house. She neglected his essential needs, to the point of forgetting to feed him. She had to be continually reminded to care for her child: washing, dressing, feeding. We have established that this child was so neglected as to suffer from hunger. He had to be hospitalised at the age of five months in an acute state of hypertrophy and wasting.

Scarcely had he been hospitalised when he suffered a bilateral otitis which necessitated a double mastoidectomy. He was then sent to Paul Parquet,[3] whose strict prophylactic practice is well known. There, he was isolated, and fed on a drip on account of his anorexia. He came out at nine months, and was returned almost by force to his mother. Nothing is known of the two months he then spent with her. We pick up his scent again after his hospitalisation at eleven months, when he was again in a state of acute wasting. He was definitively and legally abandoned five months later without having seen his mother again.

From that time up to the age of three years and nine months, this child underwent changes of residence twenty-five times, passing through institutions for children or hospitals, without ever being placed in a foster home, properly speaking. These

---

[3] Children's hospital in Paris.

hospitalisations were made necessary by childhood illnesses, by an adenoidectomy, by the neurological, ventriculographic, electro-encephalographic examinations he was given – result: normal. Health and medical evaluations were made indicating profound somatic disturbances, and then, the somatic ones having been improved upon, psychological deterioration. The last evaluation, at Denfert, when Robert was three and a half, suggested that he be confined, which could only have been definitive, on account of an unclearly defined para-psychotic state. Gesell's test gave an I.Q. of 43.

So he arrived, at the age of three and a half, at the institution, the unit at the Denfert repository, where I undertook his treatment. At that time, he was in the following condition.

From the point of view of height and weight, he was in very good shape, except for a chronic bilateral otorrhea. From the standpoint of motor activity, he had a swinging gait, extreme lack of coordination in his movements, a constant hyperagitation. From the point of view of language, complete absence of coordinated speech, frequent screams, guttural and discordant laughter. He yelled the only two words he knew – Miss! and wolf!, This word, wolf!, he repeated throughout the day, so I nicknamed him the wolf-child, *because that really was the image he had of himself.*

From the point of view of his behaviour, he was hyperactive, continually prey to jerky and disorderly movements, without aim. Unorganised prehensive activity – he would throw his arm out to take hold of an object and if he didn't reach it, he couldn't correct it, and had to start the movement all over again from the beginning. A variety of sleeping problems. With this permanent condition as a background, he experienced convulsive fits of agitation, without any true convulsions, with reddening of the face, piercing howls, during each of the routine moments of his daily life – the pot, and above all the emptying of the pot, undressing, feeding, open doors, which he couldn't stand, likewise darkness, other children's yelling, and as we will see, moving rooms.

Less often, he had crises of a diametrically opposed sort, in which he was completely prostrate, staring aimlessly, like a depressive.

With an adult, he was hyperagitated, undifferentiated, without any true contact. Children he appeared to ignore, but when one of them screamed or cried, he went into a convulsive fit. In these moments of crisis, he became dangerous, he became strong, he throttled other children, and he had to be kept isolated during the night and at meals. At those times he betrayed neither a hint of anxiety, nor any emotion.

We didn't really know what category to put him in. But we tried to treat him nonetheless, though we did ask ourselves if anything would come of it.

I am going to tell you about the first year of treatment, which was then discontinued for a year. There were several phases in the treatment.

During the preliminary phase, he retained his everyday behaviour. Guttural screams. He would arrive in the room running without stopping, howling, jumping in the air and crouching down, putting his head between his hands, opening and closing the door, switching the light on and off. With objects, he would either take them up or hurl them aside, or pile them on top of me. Very marked prognathism.

The only thing I could extract from these first few sessions was that he did not dare go near the feeding-bottle containing milk, or coming somewhat closer to it would blow on it. I also noted an interest in the wash-basin which, when full of water, seemed to spark off a real panic attack.

At the end of this preliminary phase, after one session, after having piled everything on top of me while in a very agitated state, he bolted and I heard him at the top of the staircase, which he didn't know how to go down by himself, saying in a pathetic voice, in a very low tone, for him unusual, Mummy, looking into the emptiness.

This preliminary phase came to an end outside the treatment. One evening, after going to bed, he tried to cut off his penis with a pair of plastic scissors, while standing on his bed in front of the other terrified children.

In the second part of the treatment, he started to reveal what Wolf! meant to him. He would scream it all the time.

He started, one day, by trying to strangle a little girl whom I had in treatment. They had to be separated and he was put in another room. He had a violent reaction, and was intensely disturbed. I had to come and bring him back into the room where he normally lived. As soon as he was there, he howled – Wolf!, and started to throw everything across the room – it was the dining-hall – food and plates. In the days that followed, each time that he passed by the room where he had been put, he howled – Wolf!

This also clarifies his behaviour towards doors, which he couldn't stand being left open, he spent the time of the session in opening them so as to make me close them again and howling – Wolf!

At this point we should recall his history – the shifting from place to place, the rooms, were for him a destruction, since he had never stopped changing places, nor adults. It had become a real principle of destruction for him, one which had intensely marked the primitive manifestations of his activity of ingestion and excretion. He expressed it mainly in two scenes, one with the feeding-bottle and the other with the pot.

He had at long last taken to the bottle. One day, he went to open the door, and held out the feeding-bottle to an imaginary person – whenever he was alone in a room with an adult, he carried on behaving as if there were other children around him. He held out the bottle. He came back tearing off the teat, he made me put it back on, held the bottle outside again, left the door open, turned his back on me, drank two gulps of milk, and, facing me, tore off the teat, threw back his head, covered himself in milk and spilt the rest over me. And, seized with panic he fled, unconscious and blind. I had to pick him up from the staircase which he'd started to roll down. At that moment I had the impression that he had swallowed the destruction and that the open door and the milk were linked.

The scene with the pot which followed was marked by the same destructive character. At the beginning of the treatment, he felt obliged to do his business in the session, thinking that if he gave me something, he would keep me. He could only do it pressed against me, sitting on the pot, holding my apron in one hand, and the bottle or a pencil in the other. He would eat before, and especially after. Not milk but sweets and cakes.

The emotional intensity betrayed great fear. The most recent of these scenes clarified the relation for him between defecation and destruction through changes.

In the course of this session, he had started to do his business, seated beside me. Then with his pooh beside him, he leafed through the pages of a book, turning the pages. Then he heard a noise from outside. Crazed with fear, he went out, took his pot, and set it down in front of the door of the person who had just gone into the room next door. Then he returned into the room where I was, and flattened himself against the door, howling – Wolf! Wolf!

I had the impression it was a propitiatory rite. He was incapable of giving this pooh to me. To some extent he knew that I didn't exact it from him. He went to put it outside, knowing full well that it would be thrown out, hence destroyed. So I interpreted his rite for him. Straightaway, he went to look for the pot, put it back in the room beside me, hid it with a piece of paper, saying, 'have no more, have no more',[4] so as not to be obliged to give it.

Then he started to be aggressive towards me, as if giving him permission to take possession of himself through this pooh which he had at his disposal, I had given him the possibility of being aggressive. Clearly, not being able to own, up until then, he didn't have a sense of aggressivity, but only of auto-destruction, specifically when he attacked the other children.

From that day on, he no longer felt obliged to do his business in the session. He used symbolic substitutes, sand. He was acutely confused as to his own self, the contents of his body, objects, children, and the adults who surrounded him. His state of anxiety, of agitation, became more and more acute. For the rest of the time he was becoming unbearable. I would actually witness truly hectic sessions in which I had considerable difficulty intervening.

That day, after having drunk a little milk, he spilt it on the floor, then threw sand into the wash-basin, filled the feeding-bottle with sand and water, peed in the pot, put sand in it. Then he shovelled up milk mixed with sand and water, added the lot to the pot, and placed the india-rubber baby and the bottle on top of it, and entrusted the whole of it to me.

Then, he went to open the door, and came back with fear written all over his face. He again took up the bottle which was in the pot and broke it, working feverishly on it until he had reduced it to little pieces. He then gathered them all carefully together, and buried them into the sand in the pot. He was in such a state that I had to take him down, feeling that I couldn't do anything for him any more. He brought the pot along.

---

[4] 'a pu, a pu'.

A bit of sand fell on the ground, unleashing unbelievable panic in him. He had to gather up every last bit of sand, as if it was a piece of himself, and he howled – Wolf! Wolf!

He couldn't stand being put in the group, he couldn't stand any child coming close to his pot. He had to be put to bed in a state of extreme tension, which, in a spectacular manner, was only relieved by a diarrhetic debacle, which he spread everywhere in his bed and on the walls, with his hands.

The whole of this scene was so pathetic, lived through with such anxiety, that I was very worried, and I started to get a sense of the idea he had of himself.

He gave it greater precision the next day, when I had to frustrate him – he ran to the window, opened it and cried out – Wolf! Wolf!, and, seeing his own image in the glass, he hit it, crying out – Wolf! Wolf!

That is the way Robert represented himself, he was the Wolf! It was his own image that he hit or that he evoked with such intensity. This pot into which he placed what comes into him and what comes out, the pee and the pooh, then a human image, the doll, then the pieces of the bottle, it really was an image of himself, akin to that of the wolf, as the panic generated when a bit of sand fell on the floor testified. In sequence and at the same time, he was all the elements that he put into the pot. He was just the series of objects through which he came into contact with daily life, symbols of the contents of his body. The sand is the symbol of faeces, the water that of urine, the milk that of what enters his body. But the scene with the pot shows that he differentiated very little between these things. For him, all of these contents are united in the same feeling of permanent destruction of his body, which, in opposition to these contents, represents the container, and which he symbolised with the broken bottle, whose pieces were buried under these destructive contents.

In the following phase, he exorcised the Wolf! I say exorcise because this child gave me the impression of being possessed. Thanks to my permanent presence, he was able to exorcise, with a little of the milk he had drunk, the scenes from daily life which did him such harm.

At that point, my interpretations above all tended to differentiate the contents of his body from the affective point of view. The milk is what one receives. Pooh is what one gives, and its value depends on the milk one has received. Pee is aggressive.

Many sessions went on in this way. Just when he was peeing in the pot, he would inform me – Not pooh, it's pee. He was sorry. I reassured him in telling him that he received too little to be able to give something without destroying him. That reassured him. He could then go and empty the pot in the toilet.

The emptying of the pot was surrounded with many protective rites. He started by emptying the urine into the sink in the toilet while letting the tap run so as to be able to replace the urine with water. He filled the pot, letting it amply overflow, as if a container only had an existence through its content and also had to overflow so as to contain it in its turn. There we have a syncretistic vision of being in time, as container and contained, exactly like an intra-uterine existence.

Here he rediscovered this confused image that he had of himself. He emptied the pee,

*while trying to catch it again, convinced that it was he who was leaving. He howled –
Wolf!, and the pot only had a reality for him when full. My whole concern was to show
him the reality of the pot, which was still there after having been emptied of his pee;
just as he, Robert, was still there after having peed, and the tap wasn't washed away
by the water which ran from it.*

*On account of these interpretations and my continued presence, Robert progres-
sively introduced a delay between emptying and filling, until the day when he was able
to return, triumphantly carrying an empty pot in his arms. He had quite clearly
acquired the idea of the permanence of his body. His clothes were for him his container,
and when he was stripped of them, it was certain death. The business of undressing
was for him the occasion for genuine crises, the most recent one having lasted three
hours, during which the staff described him as possessed. He howled –Wolf!, running
from one bedroom to the next, smearing the other children with faeces that he found in
the pots. It was only once he was tied up that he calmed down.*

*The next day, he came to the session, started to undress in an extreme state of
anxiety, and, completely naked, climbed into the bed. It took three sessions before he
was able to drink a little milk, completely naked in the bed. He pointed to the window
and the door, and hit his image while howling – Wolf!*

*In parallel, in daily life, undressing was easy, but was followed by a deep depression.
He started to sob without reason each evening, seeking comfort from the ward-sister
downstairs, going to sleep in her arms.*

*At the end of this phase, he had exorcised with me the emptying of the pot, as well as
the undressing scene, through my continuing presence, which had turned milk into a
constructive element. But, driven by the necessity of building up a minimum, he
hadn't touched on the past, he only counted on the present of everyday life, as if he
were deprived of memory.*

In the next phase, it was I who became the Wolf!

*He made use of the little bit of construction he had succeeded in accomplishing to
project on to me all the badness he had drunk, and, in some way, to rediscover his
memory. He was thus progressively able to become aggressive. This was to turn
tragic. Driven by the past, he had to be aggressive towards me, and yet, at the same
time, in the present I was the one he needed. I had to reassure him by my
interpretations, speak to him about the past which was forcing him to be aggressive,
and assure him that it wouldn't cause me to disappear, nor shift him from where he
was, something he always took as a punishment.*

*When he had been aggressive towards me, he would try to destroy himself. He
would represent himself by the bottle, and would try to break it. I would take it out of
his hands, because he wasn't in a fit state to cope with breaking it. He would then take
up the thread of the session, and his aggressivity towards me continued.*

*At that point, he made me play the role of his starving mother. He forced me to sit on
a chair on which a mug of milk was sat, so that I would knock it over, thus depriving*

him of his good food. Then he started howling – Wolf!, took the cot and wash-tub and threw them out of the window. He turned against me, and, with great violence made me swallow dirty water while howling – Wolf! Wolf! Here this feeding-bottle stood for bad food, and was a throwback to his separation from his mother, who had deprived him of food, and to all the changes which he was made to suffer.

In parallel, he conferred another aspect of the bad mother on me, the role of the one who leaves. One evening, he saw me leaving the institution. The next day, he reacted, even though he had seen me leave on other occasions without being capable of expressing the emotion that he must have felt. That day, he peed on me whilst in a highly aggressive, and also anxious, state.

This scene was only the prologue to a final scene, which resulted in my being definitively burdened with all the bad things that had happened to him, and in projecting on to me the Wolf!

So, because I used to leave, I was made to swallow the bottle of dirty water and was on the receiving end of the aggressive pee. So I was the Wolf! Robert separated himself from it during one session, by shutting me in the toilets, then returned to the room where we had the sessions, all alone, climbed into the empty bed, and started to moan. He could not call me, yet I did have to come back, since I was the permanent person. I came back. Robert was stretched out, pathetic, his thumb now within an inch of his mouth. And, for the first time in a session, he held out his arms to me and let himself be consoled.

From this session on, the institution witnessed a total change in his behaviour.

I had the impression that he had exorcised the Wolf!

From this point on, he no longer talked about it, and could move on to the next phase – intra-uterine regression, that is to say the construction of his body, of the body-ego,[5] which he hadn't been able to do up till then.

To use the dialectic that he himself had always used, that of the contained-container, Robert was obliged, in order to construct himself, to be my content, but had to make sure of his possession of me, that is to say of his future container.

He started this period by using a bucket full of water, the handle of which was made of rope. He absolutely could not stand this rope being attached to the two ends. It had to hang on one side. I had been struck by the fact that when I had had to tie the rope up again for carrying the bucket, he had experienced pain that seemed almost physical. One day, he put the bucket full of water between his legs, took the rope and brought its end up to his navel. I then had the impression that the bucket was me, and he was attaching himself to me with an umbilical cord. Then, he overturned the contents of the bucket of water, took all his clothes off, and then lay down in the water, in a foetal position, curled up, stretching himself out from time to time, and going so far as opening and closing his mouth on the liquid, just as a foetus drinks the amniotic fluid,

---

[5] English in the original.

as the most recent American experiments have shown. I had the impression that this was how he was constructing himself.

Exceedingly agitated at the beginning, he became aware of a certain reality of pleasure, and everything came to a climax in two key scenes, enacted in an extraordinarily collected manner, and with an astonishing completeness, given his age and his general condition.

In the first of these scenes, Robert, completely naked and facing me, collected up the water in his cupped hands, raised it to the level of his shoulders and let it run the length of his body. He started afresh like this several times, and then he said to me, softly – Robert, Robert.

This baptism in water – because it was a baptism, given the collected manner in which he accomplished it – was followed by a baptism in milk.

He started by playing in the water with more pleasure than contemplativeness. Then, he took his glass of milk and drank it. Then he put the teat back on and started running the milk from the feeding-bottle the length of his body. As it didn't flow fast enough, he took the teat off, and started afresh, making milk run over his chest, his stomach and along his penis with an intense feeling of pleasure. Then he turned towards me, showed me this penis, taking it in his hand, with an air of complete rapture. Then he drank some milk, thus putting some both inside and outside him, in such a way that the content was both contained and container at once, rediscovering the same scene that he had enacted with the water.

In the subsequent phases, he moved on to the stage of oral construction.

This stage is extremely difficult, very complex. First of all, he was four years old and he was living through the most primitive of the stages. What is more, the other children that I then had in treatment in this institution were girls, which created a problem for him. Finally Robert's patterns[6] of behaviour had not entirely disappeared and had a tendency to return whenever he encountered frustration.

After his baptism by water and milk, Robert started to experience the symbiosis which characterises the primitive mother-child relationship. But when the child actually lives through it, there is normally no problem of sexuality, at least in the direction, new-born to the mother. Whereas here, there was one.

Robert had to set up a symbiosis with a feminine mother, which thus presented him with the problem of castration. The problem was to get him to accept food without this entailing his castration.

At first he experienced this symbiosis in a simple form. Seated on my knees, he ate. Then, he took my ring and my watch and put them on, or he took a pencil from my smock and broke it with his teeth. Then I interpreted it for him. This identification with a castrating phallic mother remained from then on within the plane of the past, and was accompanied by a reactional aggressivity whose motivations changed over time. He now only broke the lead of his pencil to punish himself for this aggressivity.

[6] English in the original.

After that, he could drink milk from the bottle, resting in my arms, but it was he who held the bottle. It was only later that he could cope with my holding the bottle, as if the whole of the past forbade him from taking into him, from me, the contents of so essential an object.

His desire for symbiosis was still in conflict with his past. That's why he opted for the expedient of giving himself the bottle. But as he acquired the experience, by means of other foods, such as pap and cakes, that the food he received from me in the course of this symbiosis didn't make him into a girl, he could then accept it from me.

He first tried to differentiate himself from me by sharing with me. He gave me everything to eat, saying, while touching himself – Robert, then touching me – Not Robert. I made great use of this in my interpretations to help him differentiate himself. The situation then ceased being only between him and me, and he brought in the little girls who I had in treatment.

It was a castration problem, since he knew that a little girl came up for sessions with me before him and after him. So the logic of emotions required that he turn himself into a girl, since it was a girl who broke the symbiosis he needed with me. The situation was one of conflict. He played it out in different ways, peeing seated on the pot, or else doing it standing up, while showing himself to be aggressive.

Robert was now capable of receiving, and capable of giving. He gave me his pooh without fear of being castrated by this gift.

So we had got to a stage in the treatment that can be summarised as follows – the contents of his body are no longer destructive, bad, Robert is capable of expressing his aggressivity in peeing standing up, without the existence and integrity of the container, that is to say his body, being put into question.

The Gesell IQ had changed from 43 to 80, and on the Terman-Merill, he had an IQ of 75. The clinical picture had changed, his motor difficulties had disappeared, as well as the prognathism. With the other children, he had become friendly and often protective of the smaller ones. One could start to integrate him into the group activities. Only his language remained rudimentary, Robert never put together sentences, he only used key words.

Then I left on holiday. I was away for two months.

On my return, he made a scene which showed the coexistence in him both of patterns[7] from the past and of the present construction.

While I was away, his behaviour had remained as it had been – what the separation meant to him, his fear of losing me, was expressed in the old way, but in a very rich fashion, on account of what he had since acquired.

When I returned, he emptied out, as if to destroy them, the milk, his pee, his pooh, then took off his smock and threw it in the water. He thus destroyed his old contents and his old container, rediscovered through the trauma of my absence.

The next day, overwhelmed by his psychological reaction, Robert expressed himself

---

[7] English in the original.

on the somatic plane – profuse diarrhoea, vomiting, fainting. He emptied himself completely of his past image. Only my continuous presence could make the connection with a new image of himself – like a new birth.

At that moment, he acquired a new image of himself. We saw him re-enacting in the session ancient traumas we knew nothing of. Robert drank from the bottle, put the teat in his ear, and then broke the bottle, in a condition of acute violence.

Now, he could do it without the integrity of his own body suffering from it. He separated himself from the symbol of the bottle, and could express himself through the bottle qua object. This session was so striking – he repeated it twice – that I made inquiries about what happened when he had had the antrotomy at the age of five months. We then learned that in the E.N.T. ward where he had been operated upon, he had not been given an anaesthetic, and that throughout the painful operation a bottle of sweetened water had been kept forced in his mouth.

This traumatic episode clarified the image that Robert had constructed of a starving, paranoiac, dangerous mother, who certainly attacked him. Then the separation, a bottle held by force, making him swallow his cries. The force-feedings with the tube, twenty-five moves in succession. I had the impression it was Robert's tragedy that all his oral-sadistic fantasies had been realised in the actual events of his life. His fantasies had become reality.

Lately, I have had to confront him with something real. I was away for a year, and I returned eight months pregnant. He saw me pregnant. He started playing with fantasies of the destruction of this child.

I disappeared for the birth. While I was away, my husband took him into treatment, and he acted out the destruction of this child. When I returned, he saw me thin, and childless. So he was convinced that his fantasies had become reality, that he had killed the child, and hence that I was going to kill him.

He has been extremely disturbed in the last fortnight, up until the day when he was able to tell me about it. Then and there, I confronted him with reality. I brought him my daughter, in such a way that he would now be able to make the break. His level of agitation subsided instantly, and the next day, when I had him for a session, he started at last to demonstrate some jealousy. He was becoming attached to something living and not to death.

This child had always remained at the stage in which fantasies are realities. That is what explains why his fantasies of intra-uterine form had been reality in the treatment, so that he could perform an astonishing construction. If he had gone past this stage, I wouldn't have been able to have secured this construction of himself.

As I was saying yesterday, I had the impression that this child had sunk under the real, that at the beginning of the treatment there was no symbolic function in him, still less an imaginary function.

But he did have two words.

2

M. HYPPOLITE: *I want to ask a question about the word* Wolf! *Where did* Wolf! *come from?*

MME LEFORT: *In children's homes, you often see nurses scaring them with the wolf. In the home where I had him in treatment, one day when the children were impossible to deal with, they were shut in the children's garden, and a nurse went outside to howl like a wolf so as to make them be good.*

M. HYPPOLITE: *It still has to be explained why fearing the wolf took hold in him, just as with so many other children.*

MME LEFORT: *The wolf was quite clearly the devouring mother, in part.*

M. HYPPOLITE: *Do you think that the wolf is always the devouring mother?*

MME LEFORT: *In children's stories, the wolf is always about to eat. At the oral-sadistic stage, the child wishes to eat its mother, and thinks that its mother is going to eat it. Its mother becomes the wolf. I think that that is probably its genesis but I'm not sure. In this child's history there are many things of which I am ignorant, which I wasn't able to find out about. When he wanted to be aggressive towards me, he didn't go on all fours, nor did he bark. At the moment he does. Now he knows that he is human, but he needs, from time to time, to identify himself with an animal, just like a child of eighteen months. And when he wants to be aggressive, he gets on all fours, and goes* wouh, wouh, *without the least anxiety. Then he stands up and carries on with the rest of the session. He can still only express his aggressivity at this stage.*

M. HYPPOLITE: *Yes, it's between* zwingen *and* bezwingen.[8] *There's a world of difference between the word implying constraint, and the one which doesn't. Constraint,* Zwang, *is the wolf who creates anxiety in him, and once the anxiety is overcome,* Bezwingung, *that's when he plays the wolf.*

MME LEFORT: *Yes, I quite agree.*

Naturally the wolf raises all the problems of symbolism: it isn't a function with a limit, since we are forced to search out its origin in a general symbolisation.

Why the wolf? We are not particularly familiar, in this part of the world, with this character. The fact that it is the wolf who is chosen to produce these effects ties us straightaway to a broader function on the mythical, folkloric, religious, primitive plane. The wolf is part of a complete filation, which connects up with secret societies, with everything that implies in the way of initiation, either in the adoption of a totem, or in the identification with a character.

---

[8] *Zwingen* and *bezwingen* are both often roughly translated as 'to overcome, to vanquish'. *Zwang* is the term most often rendered in English by 'compulsion' (cf. '*Zwangsneurose*', '*Zwangsvorstellung*' – 'obsessional neurosis', 'obsessional idea').

It is difficult to draw these distinctions in relation to such an elementary phenomenon, but I would like to draw your attention to the difference between the super-ego and the ego-ideal, in the determination of repression.

I don't know if you have realised the following – here we have two conceptions which seem to lead in exactly opposite directions, as soon as one brings them into play, in any kind of dialectic, in order to explain the behaviour of a patient. The super-ego is constraining and the ego-ideal exalting.

These are things that one tends to gloss over, because we move from one term to the other as if the two were synonymous. It is a question which is worth pursuing in relation to the transference relationship. When one looks for the basis of therapeutic action, one says that the subject identifies the analyst with his ego-ideal or on the contrary with his super-ego, and, in the same text one substitutes one for the other in accordance with the unfolding of the demonstration, without really explaining what the difference is.

Certainly I will be led to examine the question of the super-ego. I should say from the start that, if we don't limit ourselves to a blind, mythical usage of this term, this key-word, this idol, the super-ego is essentially located within the symbolic plane of speech, in contrast to the ego-ideal.

The super-ego is an imperative. As is indicated by common sense and by the uses to which it is put, it is consonant with the register and the idea of the law, that is to say with the totality of the system of language, in so far it defines the situation of man as such, that is to say in so far as he is not just a biological individual. On the other hand, one should also emphasise, as a counter to this, its senseless, blind character, of pure imperativeness and simple tyranny. What path will allow us to bring these notions into a synthesis?

The super-ego has a relation to the law, and is at the same time a senseless law, going so far as to become a failure to recognise [méconnaissance] the law. That is always the way we see the super-ego acting in the neurotic. Isn't it because the morality of the neurotic is a senseless, destructive, purely oppressive, almost always anti-legal morality, that it became necessary to elaborate on the function of the super-ego in analysis?

The super-ego is at one and the same time the law and its destruction. As such, it is speech itself, the commandment of law, in so far as nothing more than its root remains. The law is entirely reduced to something, which cannot even be expressed, like the *You must*, which is speech deprived of all its meaning. It is in this sense that the super-ego ends up by being identified with only what is most devastating, most fascinating, in the primitive experiences of the subject. It ends up being identified with what I call *the ferocious figure*, with the figures which we can link to primitive traumas the child has suffered, whatever these are.

In this very special case, we see, embodied there, this function of language, we touch on it in its most reduced form, reduced down to a word whose meaning and significance for the child we are not even able to define, but which nonetheless ties him to the community of mankind. As you have quite aptly remarked, this isn't a wolf-child who might have lived in a savage state, but a speaking child, and it is through this *Wolf!* that you had the possibility, right from the beginning, of establishing a dialogue.

What is remarkable in this case is the moment when, after a scene which you described, the use of the word *Wolf!* disappeared. It is around this pivot of language, of the relationship to this word, which for Robert is the summary of a law, that the turning-point from the first to the second phase occurs. There then follows this extraordinary elaboration, brought to a close by this touching self-baptism, when he utters his own Christian name. At that point we come close to the fundamental relation, in its most reduced form, of man to language. It is extraordinarily moving.

What questions do you still want to raise?

MME LEFORT: *What is the diagnosis?*

Well, there are some people who have already taken a stand on this. Lang, I've been told that you had said something on this subject yesterday evening, something which appeared to me to be interesting. I think the diagnosis you made is only analogical. By making a reference to the categories that exist in nosography, you uttered the word. . . .

DR LANG: *Hallucinatory delirium.*[9] *One can always try to look for an analogy between relatively deep disturbances in the behaviour of children and what we are familiar with in adults. And most often we talk about infantile schizophrenia when we don't quite know what is happening. An essential element is lacking here, needed in order to talk of schizophrenia, namely dissociation. There is no dissociation, because there is scarcely any construction. It seemed to me reminiscent of certain forms of organisation of hallucinatory delirium. I had great reservations yesterday evening, because there is a margin between direct observation of the child at this age and what we know from our usual nosography. In this particular case many things would have to be clarified.*

Yes. That is how I understood what you had said when it was passed on to me. A hallucinatory delirium, by which you mean a chronic hallucinatory psychosis, has only one thing in common with what is happening in this subject, and that is this dimension, which Mme Lefort subtly highlighted, which is that this child lives only the real. If the word *hallucination* means something, it is this feeling of reality. In hallucination there is something which the patient truly takes to be real.

[9] The French term is '*délire*', notoriously difficult to translate, since it has a wider range than 'delirium'; it has occupied an important place in French psychiatric terminology for well over a century.

You know how much this remains a problem, even in a hallucinatory psychosis. In an adult chronic hallucinatory psychosis, there is a synthesis of the imaginary and the real, which is the entire problem of psychosis. Here we find a secondary imaginary elaboration which Mme Lefort has highlighted, which is literally non-inexistence in the nascent state.

It's a long time since I have re-examined the case. And yet, the last time we met, I had put before you the grand schema of the vase and the flowers, in which the flowers are imaginary, virtual, illusory, and the vase real, or inversely, because one can set up the apparatus the other way round.

At this juncture, all I can do is point out to you the pertinence of this model, constructed around the relation between the contained-flowers and the container-vase. The container-contained system, which I already placed in the foreground with the significance that I give to the mirror-stage, is here seen being played out to the full, and quite nakedly. We see the child behaving in accordance with the more or less mythical function of the container, and, as Mme Lefort has noted, only being able to endure it being empty at the end. To be capable of enduring its emptiness is, in the end, to identify it as a truly human object, that is to say, an instrument, capable of being detached from its function. And it is essential in so far as in the human world, there is not only utility, but also the tool,[10] that is to say instruments, which exist as things in their own right.

M. HYPPOLITE: *Universal.*

DR LANG: *The way in which the wolf changes from being vertical to horizontal is rather delightful. It does seem to me precisely that the wolf of the beginning is lived through.*

It is neither him nor anyone else, at the beginning.

DR LANG: *It's reality.*

No, I think that it is essentially speech reduced down to its core. It is neither him nor anyone else. He is clearly the *wolf!* in so far as he says this very word. But the *wolf!* is anything in so far as it can be named. Here you see the nodal state of speech. Here the ego is completely chaotic, speech has come to a halt. But, starting with the *wolf!* he will be able to take his place and construct himself.

DR BARGUES: *I noticed the fact that there was a change at a particular moment, when the child played with his excrement. He gave, transformed and took sand and water. I think that it is the imaginary which he started to construct and reveal. He could already take a greater distance from the object, his excrement, and then he distanced himself further and further. I don't think that one can talk of the*

---

[10] '*l'utile*' and '*l'outil*'.

symbol in the sense in which you understand it. However, yesterday, I had the impression that Mme Lefort talked about them as symbols.

It's a difficult question. It is the one we are addressing here, in as much as it may be the key to what we designate as the ego. What is the ego? These aren't homogeneous agencies. Some are realities, others are images, imaginary functions. The ego itself is one of them.

This is what I would like to turn to before we leave. What musn't be left out is what you described to us in such an absorbing way at the beginning – the motor activity of this child. This child seems to have suffered no lesion of the organic systems. What sort of motor behaviour has he now? How are his grasping gestures?

MME LEFORT: *To be sure, he no longer is as he was at the beginning.*

At the beginning, as you have described him, when he wanted to reach an object, he could only grasp it in one complete gesture. If this gesture failed him, he had to start again from the beginning. So he is in control of visual adaptation, but he suffers from disturbances of his sense of distance. This wild child can always, like a well organised animal, catch what he wishes. But if there is something wrong or lacking in the act, he can only correct it in doing the whole thing over again. Consequently, we can say that there doesn't seem to have been any deficiency or backwardness bearing on the pyramidal system in this child, but we are confronted with signs of failures in the functions of ego-synthesis, in the sense in which we understand the ego in analytic theory.

The lack of attention, the unarticulated agitation that you also observed, at the beginning, must also be linked to failures of the ego's functions. Besides, one should take note that, in certain respects, analytic theory goes so far as to make sleep a function of the ego.

MME LEFORT: *From the memorable day when he locked me up, his motor disturbances diminished, and this child, who neither slept nor dreamt, began to dream in the night, and to call his mother in his dreams.*

That is what I was trying to get at. I am not overlooking the direct relation between the atypicality of his sleep and the anomalous character of his development, whose backwardness is to be placed precisely on the plane of the imaginary, on the plane of the ego in so far as it is an imaginary function. This observation shows us that, from the backwardness of a given point in imaginary development, there ensues disturbances of certain functions which are apparently of a lower level than what we may call the superstructural level.

What gives this case its special interest is the relation between the strictly sensorimotor maturation and the function of imaginary mastery by the subject. That is the question. The point is to know to what extent it is this particular articulation which is involved in schizophrenia.

According to our inclination and the idea each of us has of schizophrenia, of its mechanism and of its fundamental source, we can include or exclude this case from the category of schizophrenic illness.

It is clear that it isn't schizophrenia in the sense of a state, in as much as you have showed us its significance and its movement. But there is here a schizophrenic structure of the relation to the world and an entire set of phenomena that we could, if need be, bring into line with the catatonic set of phenomena. To be sure, strictly speaking there is no symptom of it, so that we can place the case, as Lang did, in any one given category, only in order to give it an approximate location. But some deficiencies, some failures in adaptation to the human, point towards something which later, analogically speaking, would present itself as a schizophrenia.

I think that one can't say any more about it, except that it is what one calls an exemplary case. After all, we have no reason to think that the nosological categories have been there all along, awaiting us from eternity. As Péguy said, the little pegs always fit into the little holes, but there comes a time when the little pegs no longer correspond to the little holes. That it is a question of phenomena of a psychotic nature, more exactly of phenomena which may terminate in psychosis, seems indisputable to me. Which doesn't mean that all psychoses have analogous beginnings.

Leclaire, I'm asking you specifically to work out something for next time from 'On narcissism: an introduction', which is to be found in volume IV of the *Collected Papers*, or in volume X of the complete works. You'll see that what is at issue are the questions raised by the register of the imaginary, which we are in the course of studying here.

10 March 1954

IX

On narcissism

For those who weren't here last time, I am going to appraise the utility as I see it of bringing Freud's article *'Zur Einführung des Narzissmus'* in at this point.

1

How can we take stock of our findings to date? This week, I realised, not without satisfaction, that some of you have started to be seriously concerned about the systematic usage that I recommend to you here, and have done for some time, of the categories of the symbolic and the real. You know that I insist on the notion of the symbolic by telling you that it is always advisable to start with that notion in order to understand what we are doing when we intervene in analysis, and especially when we intervene in a positive fashion, namely through interpretation.

We have been led to emphasise that aspect of resistance which is to be located at the very level of the utterance of speech. Speech can express the being of the subject, but, up to a certain point, it never succeeds in so doing. So we have now reached the point where we ask ourselves the question – in relation to speech how should one locate all these affects, all these imaginary references which are ordinarily invoked when one wants to define the action of the transference in the analytic experience? You have clearly perceived that it is not a matter of course.

Full speech is speech which aims at, which forms, the truth such as it becomes established in the recognition of one person by another. Full speech is speech which performs.[2] One of the subjects finds himself, afterwards, other than he was before. That is why this dimension cannot be evaded in the analytic experience.

[1] *'De ce qui fait acte'* – *faire acte* means 'to act as, to give proof of'. The term 'performative' is taken from J. L. Austin, *How To Do Things With Words*, Oxford: Oxford University Press, 1962.
[2] *'qui fait acte'*.

We cannot think of the analytic experience as a game, a lure, an intrigue based on an illusion, a suggestion. Its stake is full speech. Once this point has been made, as you might have already noticed, lots of things sort themselves out and are clarified, but lots of paradoxes and contradictions appear. The value of this conception is precisely to bring out these paradoxes and contradictions, which doesn't make them opacities and obscurities. On the contrary, it is often what appears to be harmonious and comprehensible which harbours some opacity. And inversely it is in the antinomy, in the gap, in the difficulty, that we happen upon opportunities for transparency. This is the point of view on which our method is founded, and so, I hope, is our progress.

The first of the contradictions to appear is the remarkable fact that the analytic method, if it aims at attaining full speech, starts off on a path leading in the diametrically opposed direction, in so far as it instructs the subject to delineate a speech as devoid as possible of any assumption of responsibility and that it even frees him from any expectation of authenticity. It calls on him to say everything that comes into his head. It is through these very means that it facilitates, that is the least one can say, his return on to the path which, in speech, is below the level of recognition and concerns the third party, the object.

Two planes have always been distinguished within which the exchange of human speech is played out – the plane of recognition in so far as speech links the subjects together into this pact which transforms them, and sets them up as human subjects communicating – the plane of the *communiqué*, in which one can distinguish all sorts of levels, the call, discussion, knowledge, information, but which, in the final analysis, involves a tendency to reach an agreement on the object. The term 'agreement' is still there, but here the emphasis is placed on the object considered as external to the action of speech, which speech expresses.

To be sure, the object is not devoid of reference to speech. From the start, it is already partially given in the system of objects, or objective system,[3] in which one should include the accumulated prejudices which make up a cultural community, up to and including the hypotheses, the psychological prejudices even, from the most sophisticated generated by scientific work to the most naive and spontaneous, which most certainly do not fail considerably to influence scientific references, to the point of impregnating them.

So here is the subject invited to abandon himself entirely to this system – it is just as much the scientific knowledge he possesses or what he can imagine on

---

[3] '*système objectal, ou objectiv*' – '*objectal*' is a word coined within the technical vocabulary of psychoanalysis (Robert gives 1951 as its date of introduction) to describe whatever relates to the objects independent of the subject's ego. '*Objectif*' has a venerable history, in philosophy, linguistics and ordinary usage – it corresponds roughly to 'objective', including therein the often neglected philosophical senses in English (and such uses as in 'the objective of a telescope').

the basis of the facts he possesses as to his condition, his problem, his situation, as the most naive of his prejudices, upon which his illusions are founded, including his neurotic illusions, in so far as what is at stake there is an important part of the constitution of the neurosis.

It would seem – and this is where the problem lies – that this speech act can only progress along the path of intellectual conviction which emerges from educational intervention, that is to say a higher intervention, which comes from the analyst. Analysis progresses through indoctrination.

It is this indoctrination one has in mind when one talks about the first phase of analysis as having been intellectualist. Of course it never existed. Perhaps some intellectualist conceptions of analysis were around then, but that doesn't mean that intellectualist analyses actually took place – the forces authentically at work were there from the beginning. If they hadn't been, analysis would never have had the opportunity to show its mettle, and assert itself as an obvious method of psychotherapeutic intervention.

What is called intellectualism in this context is something completely different from what is connoted were we to speak of something intellectual. The better we analyse the various levels of what is at stake, the better we will be able to distinguish what has to be distinguished and unify what has to be unified, and the more effective our technique will be. That is what we will try to do.

So, there really must be something other than indoctrination to explain the effectiveness of the analyst's interventions. That is what experience has shown to be efficacious in the action of transference.

That's where the opacity begins – what, after all, is transference?

In its essence, the efficacious transference which we're considering is quite simply the speech act. Each time a man speaks to another in an authentic and full manner, there is, in the true sense, transference, symbolic transference – something takes place which changes the nature of the two beings present.

But there what is at issue is a transference other than the one which is initially encountered in analysis not only as a problem, but as an obstacle. Indeed, this function should be located on the imaginary plane. So it is to specify it, that the notions you are familiar with, the repetition of prehistoric situations, unconscious repetition, the putting into effect of a reintegration of history – history in the opposite sense to the one I once put forward, since it is a question of an imaginary reintegration, the past situation only being experienced in the present, without the knowledge of the subject, in so far as its historical dimension is misrecognised [*méconnue*] by him – you'll note that I didn't say *unconscious*. All these ideas have been put forward so as to define what we observe, and their reward is a guaranteed empirical finding. They don't uncover, however, the reason, the function, the signification of what we observe in the real.

To expect an explanation for whatever is observed is, you'll perhaps tell me, to expect too much, to manifest too great a thirst for theory. Several hard-headed characters would perhaps like to impose a damper on us at this point.

However it seems to me that the analytic tradition doesn't distinguish itself by its lack of ambition in this respect – there must be reasons for that. Besides, whether justified or not, whether carried away or not by Freud's example, few are the psychoanalysts who have not succumbed to the theory of mental evolution. This particular metapsychological business is in truth completely impossible, for reasons which will become apparent later. But one cannot practice psychoanalysis, not even for one second, without thinking in metapsychological terms, just as M. Jourdain[4] was pretty well obliged to speak prose, whether he wanted to or not, as soon as he started speaking. This fact is truly structural to our activity.

Last time I alluded to Freud's article on transference-love. You are well aware of the strict economy of Freud's works, and to what extent it can be said that he never truly addressed himself to a subject which was not urgent, indispensable for him to deal with – in the course of a career which had almost the span of a human life, especially if one thinks at what point in his actual life, his biological life, he began his teaching.

We cannot but see that one of the most important questions in analytic theory is to know what is the connection between the bonds of transference and the characteristics, both positive and negative, of the love relation. Clinical experience vouchsafes it, as does, by the same token, the theoretical history of the discussions arising around what is called the source of therapeutic efficaciousness. In short, this subject has been on the agenda roughly since the 1920s – the Berlin Congress first of all, the Salzburg Congress, the Marienbad Congress. Since that time, the usefulness of the function of transference in the manipulation we undertake of the patient's subjectivity has never stopped being questioned. We have even separated out something which some go so far as to call, not just transference neurosis – a nosological label designating what the subject is affected with – but a secondary neurosis, an artificial neurosis, an actualisation of the neurosis in the transference, a neurosis which knots the imaginary persona of the analyst in its threads.

We know all that. But the question as to what constitutes the mainspring of what takes effect in analysis remains obscure. I am not talking about the courses of action we sometimes undertake, but about the very source of therapeutic efficacity.

The least one can say is that there is an enormous diversity of opinion in the analytic literature on this subject. To go back to the venerable discussions, all you have to do is take a look at the last chapter of Fenichel's little book. I'm not often one to recommend reading Fenichel, but as far as the historical data are

---

[4] See p. 3 n1 above.

concerned, he is a very instructive witness. You will see the diversity of opinion – Sachs, Rado, Alexander – when the question was broached at the Salzburg Congress.[5] You will also see the said Rado announce in what direction he intends to push the theorisation of the source of analytic efficacity. Strangely enough, having promised to spell out in black and white the solution to these problems, he never did so.

It seems that there's some mysterious resistance at work, acting so as to keep the question in comparative darkness, not only on account of its own obscurity, since little glimmers of light sometimes appear in this or that researcher's work, the more reflective subjects. One really has the feeling that the question is often caught sight of, that someone gets as close as is possible to it, but that it exerts some sort of repulsion which forbids it being rendered into concepts. Perhaps here more than elsewhere, it is possible that the completion of the theory, and even its progress, are experienced as a threat. That isn't to be excluded. It is no doubt the most propitious hypothesis.

The opinions expressed in the course of discussions on the nature of the imaginary link established in the transference bear a very close relation to the notion of the object relation.

This latter idea has now come to the foreground in analytic theoretical work. But you are aware of the extent to which the theory wavers on this issue.

Take for example the fundamental article of James Strachey, which appeared in the *International Journal of Psycho-analysis*, dealing with the source of therapeutic efficacity. It is one of the best argued of texts, whose entire emphasis falls on the super-ego. You can see the difficulties that this conception gets one in, and the number of supplementary hypotheses that the above-mentioned Strachey is required to introduce in order to sustain it. He suggests that the analyst takes on, in relation to the subject, the function of the super-ego. But the theory according to which the analyst is purely and simply the mainstay of the super-ego's function cannot stand up, since this function is precisely one of the most important sources of the neurosis. So the argument is circular. To get out of it, the author finds himself forced to introduce the idea of a parasitical super-ego – a supplementary hypothesis which is completely unjustified, but which the contradictions in his argument necessitate. Besides, he is obliged to go too far. So as to argue for the existence of this parasitical super-ego in analysis, he is obliged to posit that a set of exchanges, of introjections and projections, take place between the analysand subject and the analyst subject, which bring us to the level of the mechanisms by which good and bad objects – introduced by Melanie Klein into the practice of the English school – are constituted. This brings with it the risk of re-creating them *ad nauseam*.

One can locate the question of the relations between the analysand and the

[5] See p. 164 n1 below.

analyst on a completely different plane – on the plane of the ego and the non-ego, that is to say, on the plane of the narcissistic economy of the subject.

Moreover, the question of transference-love has from the start been too closely linked with the analytic study of the notion of love. We are not dealing with love in the guise of Eros – the universal presence of a power binding subjects together, underlying the whole of the reality in which analysis is played out – but of passionate love, as it is concretely lived by the subject, as a sort of psychological catastrophe. It raises the question, as you know, of knowing how this passionate love is, in its very essence, linked to the analytic relation.

Having said something nice about Fenichel's book, let me tell you something nasty about it. It is as delightful as it is striking to note the sort of revolt, of insurrection even, that the extremely pertinent remarks of two authors on the relations between love and transference seem to elicit in Mr Fenichel. They emphasise the narcissistic character of the relationship of imaginary love, and show how and to what extent the loved object is confounded, by means of one whole facet of its qualities, of its attributes, and also of its impact on the psychic economy, with the subject's ego-ideal. One thus sees the general syncretism of Mr Fenichel's thought linked up in a curious fashion with this middle way which is his and which leads him to experience such repugnance, a real phobia when faced with the paradox generated by this imaginary love. Imaginary love in its essence partakes of illusion, and Mr Fenichel experiences a kind of horror in thus seeing the very function of love devalued.

That is precisely what is at issue – what is this love, which enters in as an imaginary mainspring in analysis? Fenichel's horror tells us something about the subjective structure of the character in question.

Well, for us, what we have to locate is the structure which articulates the narcissistic relation, the function of love in its widest sense and the transference in its practical efficacy.

There is more than one way to help you find your sense of direction in the midst of all the ambiguities which, as I think you have become aware, make their appearance again and again at every twist and turn in the analytic literature. I hope to teach you new categories, which introduce essential distinctions. These are not external distinctions, scholastic or ever-expanding ones – juxtaposing this or that field, proliferating bipartitions off to infinity, a mode of procedure which consists in always introducing supplementary hypotheses. No doubt this method is open to those who want it; but for my part I am aiming at progress in understanding.

It is a matter of bringing into focus what is implied by simple ideas, which already exist. There is no point in taking apart indefinitely, as one could – as has been done in a remarkable work on the idea of transference. I am rather inclined to leave intact the empirical totality of the notion of transference, all the while remarking that it is plurivalent and that it acts in several registers at a time, in the symbolic, the imaginary and the real.

These are not three fields. Even in the animal kingdom, you have been able to see that it is in relation to the same actions, the same behaviour, that we can distinguish precisely the functions of the imaginary, the symbolic and the real, for the simple reason that they do not belong in the same order of relations.

There are a number of ways of introducing these ideas. Mine has its limits, like any dogmatic account. But its usefulness is in being critical, that is to say in arising just where the empirical efforts of researchers meet with a difficulty in handling a pre-existing theory. That is what makes for the value of the path of textual commentary.

2

Doctor Leclaire starts the reading and commentary on the initial pages of 'On narcissism: an introduction'.   Interruption.

What Leclaire is saying here is quite right. For Freud there is a relation between a thing x which has moved on to the plane of the libido, and the disinvestment of the external world characteristic of the forms of dementia praecox – take this in as extended a sense as you can. Now, to set up the problem in these terms creates great difficulties in analytic theory, as it was constituted at that time.

In order to understand it one must look at the *Three Essays on the Theory of Sexuality*, where the notion of a primitive auto-erotism comes from.[6] What is this primitive auto-erotism, whose existence Freud postulates? It is a libido which constitutes the objects of interest, and which is allocated, through a sort of evasion, of extension, of pseudopodia. Beginning with this emission by the subject of libidinal investments, its instinctual development unfolds, its world is built up, in accordance with an instinctual structure peculiar to it. This conception does not give rise to any difficulties so long as Freud leaves out of the libido's mechanism everything pertaining to a register other than that of desire as such. The register of desire is, for him, an extension of the concrete manifestations of sexuality, an essential relation maintained by the animal being with the *Umwelt*, its world. So you see that this is a bipolar conception – on one side the libidinal subject, on the other the world.

Now this conception breaks down, as Freud knew very well, if one generalises excessively the notion of libido, because, in so doing, one neutralises it. Isn't it quite clear, moreover, that it adds essentially nothing to an understanding of the facts of neurosis if the libido functions roughly in the same way as M. Janet called the function of the real? On the contrary, the libido takes on its meaning by being distinguished from the real, or realisable, relations,

[6] (1905d) GW V 82–3; Stud V 88–9; SE VII 181–2; *et seq.*

from all the functions which have nothing to do with the function of desire, from everything touching on the relations of the ego and of the external world. It has nothing to do with instinctual registers other than the sexual, with, for example, whatever has to do with the domain of nutrition, of assimilation, of hunger in so far as it is conducive to the preservation of the individual. If the libido is not isolated from the entire range of functions for the preservation of the individual, it loses all meaning.

Now, in schizophrenia, something happens which completely disturbs the relations of the subject to the real, swamping the foundation with form. This fact, all of a sudden, raises the question of knowing whether the libido doesn't go much further than the definition given it by taking the sexual register as its organising, central core. That's the point at which the libido theory begins to create problems.

It creates such problems that it has been effectively put in question. I'll show you that when we analyse Freud's commentary on the text written by Senatspräsident Schreber. It is in the course of this commentary that Freud becomes aware of the difficulties created by the problem of libidinal investment in the psychoses. And he then makes use of notions that are ambiguous enough for Jung to say that he had given up defining the nature of the libido as being uniquely sexual. Jung does take this step decisively, and introduces the notion of introversion, which is for him – that is the criticism which Freud made of him – a notion *ohne Unterscheidung*,[7] lacking in capacity to discriminate. And he ends up with the vague notion of psychic interest, which collapses into one single register what belongs to the order of the preservation of the individual and what belongs to the order of sexual polarisation of the individual in its objects. All that remains is a kind of relation of the subject to himself which Jung says pertains to the libidinal order. What the subject must do is realise himself as an individual in possession of genital functions.

Since then, psychoanalytic theory has been vulnerable to a neutralisation of the libido, which consists, on the one hand, in firmly asserting that the libido is what is involved, and on the other, in saying that it is simply a property of the soul, the creator of its world. Such a conception is extremely difficult to distinguish from analytic theory, in so far as the Freudian idea of a primordial auto-erotism forming the basis upon which objects are progressively constituted is almost equivalent, in terms of its structure, to Jung's theory.

That is why, in his article on narcissism, Freud harks back to the necessity of distinguishing egoistical libido and sexual libido. Now you understand one of the reasons why he wrote this article.

The problem is an extremely knotty one for him to resolve. All the while

---

[7]   (1914c) GW X 139; Stud III 42; SE XIV 74, quoted on p. 90 above, where it is translated as 'indiscriminately'.

maintaining the distinction between the two libidos, throughout the entire article he continually skirts around the notion of their equivalence. How can these terms be clearly distinguished if one maintains the idea that they are equivalent in energetic terms, which is what allows one to say that it is in so far as the libido is disinvested from the object that it returns back on to the *ego*? There's the problem raised. As a result, Freud is led to conceive of narcissism as a secondary process. A unity comparable to the ego does not exist at the beginning, *nicht von Anfang*, is not to be found in the individual from the start, and the *Ich* has to develop, *entwickelt werden*.[8] The auto-erotic instincts, in contrast, are there right from the start.

Those of you who are somewhat familiar with what I am putting before you will see that this idea confirms the usefulness of my conception of the mirror-stage. The *Urbild*, which is a unity comparable to the ego, is constituted at a specific moment in the history of the subject, at which point the ego begins to take on its functions. This means that the human ego is founded on the basis of the imaginary relation. The function of the ego, Freud writes, must have *eine neue psychische Aktion, . . . zu gestalten*.[9] In the development of the psyche, something new appears whose function it is to give form to narcissism. Doesn't that indicate the imaginary origin of the ego's function?

In the next two or three lectures, I will specify what use, simultaneously limited and various, should be made of the mirror-stage. For the first time, I will teach you, in the light of Freud's text, that there are two registers implied in this stage. Finally, if last time I showed you that the imaginary function contains the plurality of experience of the individual, I am going to show you that one cannot limit it to that – because of the need to distinguish the psychoses from the neuroses.

3

What is now important to bear in mind from the article's opening is the difficulty Freud experiences in defending the originality of the psychoanalytic dynamic against the Jungian dissolution of the problem.

According to the Jungian schema, psychic interest comes and goes, goes out, comes back, colours, etc. It drowns the libido in the universal magma which will be the basis of the world's constitution. Here we come upon a very traditional mode of thought clearly distinct from orthodox analytic thought. Psychic interest is here nothing other than an alternating spotlight, which can come and go, be projected, be withdrawn from reality, at the whim of the pulsation of the psyche of the subject. It's a pretty metaphor, but it throws no light on practice, as Freud underlines. It does not allow one to grasp the

---

[8] GW X 142; Stud III 144; SE XIV 77.   [9] *Ibid.*

differences that there might be between a directed, sublimated retreat of interest in the world which the anchorite may achieve, and that of the schizophrenic, whose result is however structurally quite distinct, since the subject discovers that he is completely stuck. No doubt a considerable number of clinical points have been brought out by the Jungian investigation, which intrigues by its quaintness, its style, the parallels it establishes between what some mental or religious ascesis produces and what a schizophrenic produces. That, perhaps, is a way of working which has the advantage of adding some colour and life for the benefit of the researchers, but which quite clearly has illuminated nothing in the way of mechanisms – Freud doesn't miss the opportunity of quite mercilessly underlining that in passing.

What is crucial for Freud is grasping the difference in structure which exists between the withdrawal from reality which we observe in the neuroses and that which we observe in the psychoses. One of the crucial distinctions is established in a surprising manner – surprising at least for those who haven't come to grips with these problems.

In the refusal to recognise [*méconnaissance*], in the refusal, in the barrier opposed to reality by the neurotic, we note a recourse to fancy. Here we have *function*, which in Freud's vocabulary can only refer to the imaginary register. We know the extent to which people and objects in the neurotic's milieu change significance entirely, in relation to a function there is no problem in naming – without going further than ordinary linguistic usage – as imaginary. *Imaginary* here refers – in the first instance, to the subject's relation to its formative identifications, which is the true meaning of the term 'image' in analysis – secondly, to the relation of the subject to the real whose characteristic is that of being illusory, which is the facet of the imaginary most often highlighted.

Now, whether rightly or wrongly, it doesn't matter at this stage, Freud emphasises that nothing comparable is to be found in psychosis. When it comes to the psychotic subject, if he loses the realisation of the real, he doesn't find any imaginary substitute. That is what distinguishes him from the neurotic.

This conception may appear extraordinary at first glance. You are well aware that one has to make some headway in conceptualisation at this point in order to follow Freud's thinking. One of the most widespread of conceptions is that the deluded [*délirant*] subject is dreaming, that he is bang in the middle of the imaginary. So, in Freud's conception, the function of the imaginary cannot be the function of the unreal. Otherwise there'd be no point in his denying the psychotic access to the imaginary. And since in general Freud knows what he is saying, we will have to find a means of filling in what he meant on this topic.

This will lead us into a coherent exposition of the relations between the imaginary and the symbolic, since that is one of the points on which Freud brings this difference of structure to bear with great energy. When the psychotic reconstructs his world, what is invested to start off with? You will see along what path, for many of you unexpected, this will take us – the answer is words. There, you cannot but recognise the category of the symbolic.

We will push what this critique opens up further. We will see that it may be the case that the specific structure of the psychotic should be located in a symbolic unreal, or in a symbolic unmarked by the unreal. The function of the imaginary is to be located somewhere entirely different.

You're beginning to see, I hope, the difference between Freud's and Jung's appreciation of the place of the psychoses. For Jung, the two domains of the symbolic and the imaginary are there completely confused, whereas one of the preliminary articulations that Freud's article allows us to pinpoint is the clear distinction between the two.

Today is only a curtain-raiser. But when it comes to matters as important as these, you can't raise the curtain too slowly. I have only managed to introduce – as moreover the very title of the article puts it – a limited number of questions, which have never been raised. It will give you the time to turn things over in your minds, and to do a little work from now to the next time.

Next time I would like to see, in commenting on this text, as close a collaboration as possible from our friend Leclaire. I would rather like to see Granoff engage in this work – he seems to have a particular inclination and interest in Freud's article on transference-love – this may well be an opportunity for him to contribute by introducing this article. There's a third article that I would like to entrust to someone for next time. It's a text which comes from the metapsychology of the same period, and which pertains directly to our object – '*Compléments métapsychologiques à la doctrine des rêves*',[10] which is translated into French as '*La théorie des rêves*'. I'll give it to whoever doesn't mind taking it on himself – for example our dear Perrier, for whom this will be the chance to comment on the subject of schizophrenics.

17 March 1954

[10] 'Metapsychological supplement to the theory of dreams' (1917d) GW X 412–26; Stud III 179–91; SE XIV 222–35.

X

The two narcissisms

THE NOTION OF DRIVE

THE IMAGINARY IN ANIMALS AND IN MAN

SEXUAL BEHAVIOUR IS PARTICULARLY PRONE TO THE LURE

THE *URICH*

'On narcissism: an introduction' dates from the beginning of the 1914 war, and it is quite moving to think that it was at that time that Freud was developing such a construction. Everything which we include under the meta-psychological rubric emerges between 1914 and 1918, following the publication in 1912 of Jung's work translated into French under the title *Métamorphoses et Symboles de la Libido*.[1]

1

Jung's approach to the mental illnesses had an entirely different perspective from Freud's, since his experience was with the gamut of schizophrenias, whereas Freud's was with the neuroses. His 1912 work puts forward a grandiose unitary conception of psychic energy, fundamentally different in its inspiration, and even in its definition, from the notion developed by Freud under the name of libido.

Nevertheless, the theoretical difference is still recalcitrant enough to state for Freud to be struggling with difficulties which one can sense throughout the article.

The point, for him, is to maintain a clearly demarcated usage – these days we would say *operational* – of the notion of libido, which is essential to sustaining his discovery. On what, in short, is the Freudian discovery based – if not on this fundamental realisation that the symptoms of the neurosis reveal an indirect form of sexual satisfaction. Freud had very concretely demonstrated the sexual function of symptoms with respect to neurotics, by means of a series of equivalents, the last of which is a therapeutic sanction. With this as a foundation, he always maintained that it wasn't a new, totalising conception of

---

[1] The original work, *Wandlungen und Symbole der Libido* (1911–12) was translated as *The Psychology of the Unconscious* (New York, 1916). The revised, better known version is that to be found in *The Collected Works of C. G. Jung*, vol 5, Princeton: Bollingen, 1953–1979, under the title *Symbols of Transformation*.

the world that he was offering, but a well defined theory, based on a clearly, yet entirely new, demarcated field, comprising several human realities, particularly psychopathological ones – subnormal phenomena, that is to say those which normal psychology does not study, dreams, slips, mishaps, which disturb some of the so-called higher functions.

The problem which Freud faced at this point in time was that of the structure of the psychoses. How to map out the structure of the psychoses within the framework of the general theory of the libido?

Jung gives the following solution – the profound transformation of reality apparent in the psychoses is due to a metamorphosis of the libido, analogous to that which Freud had caught a glimpse of with respect to the neuroses. Except that, in the psychotic, Jung says, the libido is introverted into the internal world of the subject – a notion left hanging in the greatest ontological uncertainty. It is on account of this introversion that for him reality fades into a twilight. The mechanism of the psychoses is thus perfectly continuous with that of the neuroses.

Being intent on the working out, starting off from experience, of extremely well defined mechanisms, always concerned with its empirical reference, Freud sees analytic theory transformed by Jung into a vast psychic pantheism, a series of imaginary spheres each enveloping the other, which leads to a general classification of contents, of events, of the *Erlebnis* of the individual's life, and finally to what Jung calls the archetypes. This is not the path down which a clinical, psychiatric working out of the objects of research can be undertaken. And that is why he now attempts to ascertain the relation which the sexual drives are capable of maintaining amongst themselves, those sexual drives to which he had given such prominence owing to their having been hidden and to their having been revealed by his analysis, and the ego drives, which up to that point he had not brought to the fore. Can one say, yes or no, whether the one is the shadow of the other? Is reality constituted by this universal libidinal projection which is at the heart of the Jungian theory? Or is there on the contrary a relation of opposition, a relation of conflict, between the ego drives and the libidinal drives?

With his usual honesty, Freud makes it clear that his determination to maintain this distinction is based on his experience of the neuroses, and, after all, that is only a limited experience. That is why he says no less clearly that one may postulate, at a primitive stage, prior to that which psychoanalytic investigation permits one to penetrate, a condition of narcissism, in which it is impossible to distinguish the two fundamental propensities, the *Sexuallibido* and the *Ichtriebe*.[2] They are inextricably mixed together, *beisammen*,[3] confused, and are not distinguishable - *ununterscheidbar* – by our coarse analysis. Nonetheless he explains why he strives to maintain the distinction.

[2] GW X 142; Stud III 44; SE XIV 76.
[3] '*beisammen*' usually means 'together (in the same place)'.

First of all there is the experience of the neuroses. Next, he says, the fact that the distinction between the ego-drives and the sexual drives lacks clarity at the moment should perhaps be attributed simply to the fact that the drives constitute, for our theory, the final point of reference. The theory of drives is not at the base of the construction, but right up at the top. It is eminently abstract, and Freud later was to call it our mythology. That is why, with the concrete always within his sights, always putting his own speculative projects in their place, he underlines their limited value. He compares the notion of drive to the highest-level notions from physics, matter, force, attraction, which have only been developed in the course of the historical evolution of the science, and whose initial form was uncertain, in truth confused before they were purified and then applied.

We are not following Freud, we are accompanying him. The fact that an idea occurs somewhere in Freud's work doesn't, for all that, guarantee that it is being handled in the spirit of the Freudian researches. As for us, we are trying to conform to the spirit, to the watchword, to the style of this research.

Freud backed up his theory of the libido with what the biology of his time made available to him. The theory of instincts cannot but take into account a fundamental bipartition between the final ends of the preservation of the individual and those of the continuity of the species. What we find in the background is nothing other than Weissmann's theory, of which you must remember something from your time spent in philosophy classes. This theory, which hasn't been definitely proved, posits the existence of an immortal substance made up of sexual cells. These would make up a unique sexual line of descent through continuous reproduction. The germ-plasm would, still according to this theory, be what preserves the existence of the species, and what is perpetuated from one individual to the next. In contrast, the somatic plasm would be like an individual parasite which, from the point of view of the reproduction of the species, would have carried on growing in a lateral fashion, with the sole aim of being the vehicle for the eternal germ-plasm. Freud immediately makes it clear that his own construction does not pretend to be a biological theory. Whatever value he attaches to this reference, on which he decided to rely until further notice and with reservations, he would not hesitate to abandon it, if an examination of the facts within the domain specific to analytic investigation were to render it useless and detrimental.

Similarly there is no reason, he says, to swamp the *Sexualenergie* in the as yet unexplored field of psychic facts. The point is not to seek for the libido a universal kinship with every single psychic manifestation. That would be as if, he says, in a question of inheritance, someone were to invoke, as a proof to the lawyer of his rights, the universal kinship which, according to the monogenetic hypothesis, links all men together.[4]

[4] GW X 144; Stud III 46; SE XIV 79.

I'd like to make a remark here, which may perhaps seem to you to contrast sharply with those we usually make. But you will see that it will help us with our task, which is to clarify Freud's ongoing discussion, whose obscurities and impasses he in no way keeps from us, as you have already seen, if only through our commentary on the first few pages of this article. He doesn't offer a solution, but opens up a series of questions, into which we must try to penetrate.

At the time Freud was writing, there was, as he himself says somewhere, no ready-made,[5] ready-to-wear theory of instincts. Even today, it hasn't been brought to completion, but some progress has been made since the work of Lorenz and Tinbergen – which justifies these perhaps over-speculative remarks that I'm now going to make.

What follows from endorsing the Weissmannian notion of the immortality of the germ-plasm? If the individual which develops is quite distinct from the fundamental living substance which the germ-plasm constitutes, and which does not perish, if the individual is parasitic, what function does it have in the propagation of life? None. From the point of view of the species, individuals are, if one can put it this way, already dead. An individual is worth nothing alongside the immortal substance hidden deep inside it, which is the only thing to be perpetuated and which authentically and substantially represents such life as there is.

Let me clarify this. From the psychological point of view, what exactly is this individual led to propagate, by the infamous sexual instinct? – the immortal substance enclosed in the germ-plasm in the genital organs, represented in vertebrates by spermatozoa and ova. Is that all? – obviously not, since what is propagated is, after all, an individual. Only, it doesn't reproduce as an individual, but as a type. It only manages to reproduce the type already brought into being by the line of its ancestors. In this respect, not only is it mortal, but it is already dead, since properly speaking it has no future. It isn't this or that horse, but the prop, the embodiment of something which is *The* Horse. If the concept of species is valid, if natural history exists, it is because there are not only horses, but also *The* Horse.

This really is where the theory of instincts ends us up. In fact, what serves as support for the sexual instinct on the psychological plane?

What is the basic mainspring determining the setting into motion of the gigantic sexual mechanism? What is its releasing mechanism, as Tinbergen puts it, following Lorenz?[6] It isn't the existence of the sexual partner, the particularity of one individual, but something which has an extremely intimate relation with what I have been calling the type, namely an image.

[5] English in the original.

[6] The French term here translated 'releasing mechanism' is '*déclencheur*', which means 'trigger, starter (as in starter for a car)'. It was thought best to make this term consistent with English language works in ethology, despite the connotations, which Lacan exploits, borrowed from other semantic fields.

In the functioning of pairing mechanisms, ethologists have proved the dominance of the image, which appears in the guise of a transitory phenotype through modification of the external appearance and whose manifestation serves as a signal, of a constructed signal, that is to say a *Gestalt*, which sets the reproductive behaviour in motion. The mechanical throwing into gear of the sexual instinct is thus essentially crystallised in a relation of images, in – I now come to the term you're expecting – an imaginary relation.

This is the framework within which we must articulate the *Libidotriebe* and the *Ichtriebe*.

The libidinal drive is centred on the function of the imaginary.

Try as an idealist and moralising transposition of analytic doctrine might to make us believe, this does not mean that the subject makes his way in the imaginary towards an ideal state of genitality which would be the ultimate sanction and final source for the installation of the real. So we now have to define more precisely the relations of the libido with the imaginary and the real, and to resolve the problem as to the real function that the *ego* has in the psychic economy.

O. MANNONI: *Can I put in a word? For some time I've been perplexed by a problem that seems to me simultaneously to complicate and simplify matters. It is that the investment of objects by the libido is at bottom a realist metaphor since it only invests the image of objects. Whereas the investment of the ego can be an intra-psychic phenomenon, whereby the ontological reality of the ego is invested. If the libido has become object-libido, it can then only invest something symmetrical to the ego's image. Such that we will have two narcissisms, according to whether it is a libido which intra-physically invests the ontological ego, or an object-libido which invests something which may perhaps be the ego-ideal, and is in any case an image of the ego. We would then have a well-founded distinction between primary narcissism and secondary narcissism.*

You do know, don't you, that, step by step, I want to take you somewhere. We are not proceeding entirely aimlessly, although I am open to welcome discoveries that we make along the way. I am happy to see our friend Mannoni taking an elegant jump[7] into the subject – one needs to make one every now and then – but let us first go back to where we left off.

What am I trying to get at? – to get to grips with this fundamental experience made available to us by the contemporary development of the theory of instincts in relation to the cycle of sexual behaviour, which reveals that the subject is there essentially prone to the lure.

For example, the male stickleback has to have beautiful colours on its belly and back, before the copulation dance with the female can get going. But we

---

[7] English in the original.

can quite easily make a cut-out which, even when poorly put together, will have exactly the same effect on the female, provided that it possesses certain markings – *Merkzeichen*. Sexual behaviour is quite especially prone to the lure. This teaches us something which is important in working out the structure of the perversions and the neuroses.

2

Since we've got to this point, I am going to introduce a complement to the schema that I gave you during that little course on the topic of the imaginary.

I pointed out to you that this model faithfully follows Freud's very wishes. He spelled out in several places, particularly in the *Traumdeutung* and the *Abriss*, that the fundamental psychic agencies should be primarily conceived of as representing what takes place in a camera, namely as images, which are either virtual or real, produced through its functioning. The organic apparatus represents the mechanism of the camera, and what we apprehend are the images. Their functions are not homogeneous, because a real image and a virtual image are not the same thing. The agencies that Freud constructs should not be taken to be substantial, nor epiphenomenal in relation to the modification of the apparatus itself. Hence the agencies should be interpreted by means of an optical schema. A conception that Freud drew attention to on many occasions, but which, in his hands, never materialised.

On the left you see the concave mirror, thanks to which the phenomenon of the inverted bouquet is produced, which I have here transformed since it is more convenient, into that of the inverted vase. The vase is in the box, and the bouquet is on top.

Through the play of reflection of light rays, the vase will be reproduced in the form of a real, and not virtual, image, to which the eye can accommodate. If the eye becomes accommodated to the level of the flowers that we have placed there, it will see the real image of the vase encompassing the bouquet, and will give a style and unity to it – a reflection of the unity of the body.

For the image to have some consistency, it must be a genuine image. What is the definition of an image in optics? – to every point on the object there must correspond a point on the image, and all the rays issuing from a point must intersect again somewhere in a unique point. An optical apparatus is uniquely defined by a univocal or bi-univocal convergence of rays – as one says in axiomatics.

If the concave apparatus is placed here where I am, and the conjurer's little set-up in front of the desk, the image cannot be seen with clarity sufficient to produce an illusion of reality, a real illusion. You have to be positioned at a certain angle. Obviously, depending on the various positions of the eye doing the looking, we might distinguish a given set of circumstances which could perhaps allow us to understand the different positions of the subject in relation to reality.

To be sure, a subject is not an eye, I've told you that. But this model can be applied because we are in the imaginary, where the eye has a great importance.

Someone raised the question of the two narcissisms. You are well aware that this is what is at issue - the relation between the constitution of reality and the relation with the form of the body, which Mannoni, more or less felicitously, called *ontological*.

First let us go back to the concave mirror, on to which, as I've pointed out to you, we could probably project all manner of things whose meaning is organic, in particular the cortex. But let's not turn it into a substance too quickly, because the point here isn't, as you will see more clearly from what follows, the pure and simple exposition of the theory of the little-man-inside-the-man. If I wanted to use it to redo the-little-man-inside-the-man, there would be no point in my criticising it all the time. And if I am giving in on that, it's because there is a reason why I'm giving in.

The eye now, this hypothetical eye I've been telling you about, let us put it somewhere between the concave mirror and the object.

For this eye to have precisely the illusion of the inverted vase, that is to say for this eye to see it under optimal conditions, as clearly as if it were at the end of the

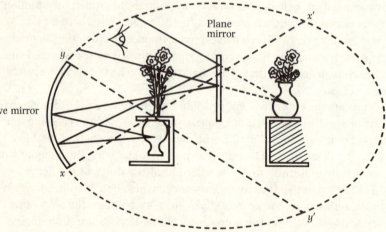

Schema with two mirrors

room, one thing only is both necessary and sufficient – that there be a plane mirror in the middle of the room.

To put it another way, if one put a mirror in the middle of the room, while I turn my back on the concave mirror, I would see the image of the vase as clearly as if I were at the end of the room, even though I wouldn't see it in a direct manner. What am I going to see in the mirror? Firstly, my own face, there where it isn't. Secondly, at a point symmetrical to the point where the real image is, I am going to see this real image appear as a virtual image. Are you with me? It isn't difficult to understand – when you get home, set yourself in front of a mirror, put your hand in front of you . . .

This little schema is only a very simple elaboration of what I've been trying to explain to you for years with the mirror stage.

Just now, Mannoni mentioned the two narcissisms. First of all, there is, in fact, a narcissism connected with the corporeal image. This image is identical for the entirety of the subject's mechanisms and gives his *Umwelt* its form, in as much as he is man and not horse. It makes up the unity of the subject, and we see it projecting itself in a thousand different ways, up to and including what we can call the imaginary source of symbolism, which is what links symbolism to feeling, to the *Selbstgefühl*, which the human being, the *Mensch*, has of his own body.

This initial narcissism is to be found, if you wish, on the level of the real image in my schema, in so far as it makes possible the organisation of the totality of reality into a limited number of preformed frameworks.

To be sure, this way of functioning is completely different in man and in animals, which are adapted to a uniform *Umwelt*. For the animal there is a limited number of pre-established correspondences between its imaginary structure and whatever interests it in its *Umwelt*, namely whatever is important for the perpetuation of individuals, themselves a function of the perpetuation of the type of the species. In man, by contrast, the reflection in the mirror indicates an original noetic possibility, and introduces a second narcissism. Its fundamental pattern[8] is immediately the relation to the other.

For man the other has a captivating value, on account of the anticipation that is represented by the unitary image as it is perceived either in the mirror or in the entire reality of the fellow being.

The other, the alter ego, is more or less confused, according to the stage in life, with the *Ichideal*, this ego-ideal invoked throughout Freud's article. Narcissistic identification – the word identification, without differentiation, is unusable – that of the second narcissism, is identification with the other which, under normal circumstances, enables man to locate precisely his imaginary and libidinal relation to the world in general. That is what enables him to *see* in its place and to structure, as a function of this place and of his world, his being. Mannoni said *ontological* just now, I'm quite happy with that. What I would

---

[8] English in the original.

precisely say is – his *libidinal being*. The subject sees his being in a reflection in relation to the other, that is to say in relation to the *Ichideal*.

Hence you see that one has to distinguish between the functions of the ego – on the one hand, they play for man, as they do for every other living creature, a fundamental role in the structuration of reality – what is more, in man they have to undergo this fundamental alienation constituted by the reflected image of himself, which is the *Urich*, the original form of the *Ichideal* as well as that of the relation to the other.

Is this sufficiently clear for you? I had already given you an initial element of this schema, I'm giving you another one today – the reflexive relation to the other. Later on you'll see what use it may serve, this schema. You're right in thinking that it is not for the fun of it that I've made up these delightful constructions. It will be extremely useful, since it will allow you to locate almost all the clinical, concrete questions raised by the function of the imaginary, and in particular in relation to those libidinal investments whose meanings one eventually ceases to understand when handling them.

Reply to Doctor Granoff's intervention concerning the application of the optical schema to the theory of the state of being in love.

The exact equivalence of the object and the ego-ideal in the love relation is one of the most fundamental notions in Freud's work, and one comes across it again and again. The loved object, when invested in love, is, through its captative effect on the subject, strictly equivalent to the ego-ideal. It is for this reason that, in suggestion, in hypnosis, we encounter the state of dependency, such an important economic function, in which there is a genuine perversion of reality through the fascination with the loved object and its overestimation. You're acquainted with the psychology of love which Freud so subtly expounded. We are offered such a large, important slice, that, as you see, we have scarcely come to terms with it today. But you'll find all manner of things on the topic of what he calls the choice of the object.

So, you cannot but see the contradiction that exists between this notion of love and certain mythical conceptions of the libidinal ascesis of psychoanalysis. I know not what vague fusion, or communion between genitality and the constitution of the real is recommended to us as the culmination of affective maturation. I am not saying that there isn't something essential to the constitution of reality in all this, but one must understand what. Because, it is either one or the other – either love is what Freud is describing, an imaginary function in its very foundation, or it is the foundation and the base of the world. Just as there are two narcissisms, so there must be two loves, Eros and Agapè.

Reply to Doctor Leclaire's question about the ambiguities concerning the Ichideal *and the* Idealich *in Freud's text.*

We are in a seminar here, we are not professing an ex cathedra teaching. We are trying to find our bearings, and to draw the greatest profit from a text and above all from someone's thinking as it develops.

God knows how others, amongst them the best, Abraham and Ferenczi included, have tried to get the development of the *ego* and its relations to the development of the libido sorted out. This question is the subject of the latest article brought out by the New York school, but for now let's stay with Ferenczi and Abraham.

Freud relied on the article published in 1913 by Ferenczi on the sense of reality. It is very poor. Ferenczi is the one who started to put the famous stages into everyone's heads. Freud refers to it. At that point in time, we are still at the stage of the very first theoretical attempts to articulate the constitution of the real, and the mere fact of receiving a reply was in itself a great help to Freud. Ferenczi brought him something, and he made use of it.

The article in question had a decisive influence. It's like repressed things, which have all the more importance for being unknown. Similarly, when some chap writes something truly stupid, it's not because no one reads it that it doesn't have consequences. Because, without having read it, everyone repeats it. Some inanities circulate like that, playing on a mixing up of planes which people don't watch out for. Hence, the first analytic theory of the constitution of the real is impregnated with ideas in the air at the time, expressed in more or less mythical terms, concerning the stages of the evolution of the human mind. The idea is to be found everywhere, in Jung also, that the human mind has made decisive progress in very recent times, and that before that we were still at a stage of prelogical confusion – as if it weren't clear that there is no structural difference between the thought of Mr Aristotle and that of some of the others. These ideas bring with them their power of confusion and disseminate their poison. You can see it clearly in the embarrassment which Freud himself experiences when he refers to Ferenczi's article.

When one talks of primitives, of so-called primitives, and of mental patients, it works fine. But where the evolutionary point of view finds complications is with children. There, Freud is forced to say that development is far from being that transparent.

Perhaps it would be better, in fact, not to refer here to falsely evolutionary notions. This probably isn't the place for the fertile idea of evolution. It is a question, rather, of elucidating structural mechanisms, which are at work in our analytic experience, which is centred on adults. Retroactively, one may clarify what happens in children, in a hypothetical and more or less verifiable manner.

In taking up this structural point of view, we are directly following Freud, because that is where he ended up. The final development of his theory distanced itself from analogical evolutionary adventures, embarked on through a superficial use of several shibboleths. Actually, what Freud always insisted upon was exactly the opposite, namely the preservation, at every level, of what may be considered as different stages.

We'll try to go one step further next time. Think of all this as a starter. You will come to see its strict relation with the phenomenon of the imaginary transference.

24 March 1954

XI

Ego-ideal and ideal ego

FREUD LINE BY LINE

THE LURES OF SEXUALITY

THE SYMBOLIC RELATION DEFINES THE POSITION OF

THE SUBJECT IN THE IMAGINARY

Leclaire, who has worked for us on the difficult text, 'On narcissism: an introduction', is going to continue today to share his reflections and questions with us. Take up the second section again and try to quote a lot.

1

DR LECLAIRE: *It's an impossible text to summarise. One would have to quote almost the whole of it. The first part postulates the fundamental distinction in the libido, with those arguments to which you have paid some attention concerning the germ-plasm. In the second part, Freud tells us that it is unquestionably the study of the dementia praecoxes, which he calls the group of paraphrenias, which continues to provide the surest access to a study of the psychology of the ego. But that is not what he will go on to consider. He mentions several other paths which might lead to reflections concerning the psychology of the ego. He starts off with the influence of organic illness on the distribution of libido, which may be considered an excellent introduction to psycho-somatic medicine. He makes a reference to a discussion that he had had with Ferenczi on this subject, and starts with the observation that, in the course of an illness, of a painful episode, the patient withdraws his libidinal investment in to his ego in order to free it once more when he is cured. He concludes that this is a banal consideration, but nevertheless one which merits examination. During the phase in which he withdraws his libidinal investment from objects, the libido and the ego's interest are once again confused, once again share the same destiny, and become impossible to tell apart.*

Do you know Wilhelm Busch? He's a humourist you should drink deep from. There's an unforgettable creation of his called *Balduin Bählamm*, the poet in shackles. His toothache puts a stop to all his idealist and platonising daydreams, as well as to the promptings of love. He forgets the prices on the stock exchange, taxes, the multiplication table, etc. All the habitual forms of being are suddenly

129

found to be without interest, turned to nothing. And now, in the little hole, lives the molar. The symbolic world of the prices on the stock exchange and the multiplication table is entirely invested in pain.

DR LECLAIRE: *Freud then turns to another point, the state of sleep in which there is a similar narcissistic withdrawal of libidinal investments. He then returns to hypochondria, to its differences and points of similarity with organic illness. He thus arrives at the notion that the difference between the two, which is perhaps of no importance, is the existence of an organic lesion. The study of hypochondria and organic illnesses allows him above all to make it clear that, in the hypochondriac, there are doubtless also organic changes of the order of vaso-motor difficulties, of circulatory difficulties, and he expounds on the similarity between the excitation of any bodily zone and sexual excitation. He introduces the notion of erotogenicity,[1] of erogenous zones which can, he says, replace the genitals and behave like them, that is to say, they can be the seat of activity and relaxation. And he tells us that there may be a variation in the libidinal investment of the ego in parallel with each variation of this type in the erotogenicity of an organ. And this raises the psycho-somatic problem again. In any case, following on from the study of erotogenicity, and the possibilities of erotogenization[2] of any part of the body, he is led to suppose that hypochondria may be classified with the neuroses which depend on the libido of the ego, whereas the other actual neuroses depend on object-libido. I had the impression that this passage, which, when the second part is considered as a whole, forms a kind of paragraph, is less important than the second paragraph of the second part, in which he defines the two types of object choice.*

Freud's essential point is that it is almost of no importance whether a working over of the libido – you know how difficult it is to translate *Verarbeitung* and *élaboration* isn't quite it[3] – is produced with real objects or with imaginary objects. The distinction only appears later, when the libido becomes oriented towards unreal objects. This leads to a *Stauung*, to a damming of the libido, which brings us to the imaginary character of the *ego*, since it is its libido which is in question.

O. MANNONI: *This German word must mean the construction of a dike. It appears to have a dynamic meaning, and at the same time means a raising of the level, and consequently a greater and greater energy of libido, which is well rendered in English by damming.[4]*

---

[1] '*érogénéité*'. Freud's term is '*Erogeneität*' (GW X 151; Stud III 51), translated as 'erotogenicity' (SE XIV 84).
[2] A neologism in French (*érogénéisation*). At the corresponding point in his text, Freud uses the same term as in note 1 above, as does SE.
[3] *Verarbeitung* is translated in SE as 'working over' (GW X 152; Stud III 52; SE XIV 86).
[4] English in the original.

Damming up,[4] even. In passing, Freud quotes four verses of Heinrich Heine's from the *Schöpfungslieder*, usually found in collection with the *Lieder*. It is a very strange little group of seven poems, whose irony and humour reveal many things which touch on the psychology of *Bildung*. Freud asks himself the question why does man get out of narcissism. Why is man dissatisfied? At this truly crucial moment in his scientific argument, Freud quotes Heine's verses to us. God is speaking, and says, *Illness is no doubt the final cause of the whole urge to create. By creating, I could recover. By creating, I became healthy.*[5]

DR LECLAIRE: *That is to say that this internal work, in which real objects and imaginary objects are equivalent . . .*

Freud doesn't say that they are equivalent. He says that at the point we have reached in the formation of the external world, it is a matter of indifference whether one considers them as real or imaginary. The difference only makes its appearance later, when the damming up has had its effects.

DR LECLAIRE: *So I come to the second sub-chapter of the second part, in which Freud tells us that another important point in the study of narcissism is to be found in the analysis of the difference in modalities of the love life of man and woman. He thereby comes to the distinction between two types of choice which one may translate by anaclitic and narcissistic, and he studies their genesis. He is led to putting it as follows – A human being has originally two sexual objects – himself and the women who takes care of him.*[6] *We might start from there.*

Himself, that's to say his image. It's absolutely clear.

DR LECLAIRE: *He goes into greater detail prior to the genesis, to the form, even, of this choice. He notes that the initial auto-erotic sexual satisfactions serve a function in the preservation of the self. Then, he notes that the sexual drives are at first employed in the satisfaction of the ego-drives, only becoming autonomous later. Thus the child at first loves the object which satisfies the ego-drives, that is to say the person who takes care of him. Finally, he is led to define the narcissistic type of object choice, clearly seen, above all, he says, in those whose libidinal development has been disturbed.*

That is to say in neurotics.

DR LECLAIRE: *These two basic types correspond - as he had mentioned earlier – to the two basic types, masculine and feminine.*

The two types – narcissistic and *Anlehnung*.

---

[4] English in the original.
[5] A modification of Strachey's translation (SE XIV 85 n3), following Lacan's more exact and literal French rendering of the German (GW X 151; Stud III 51).
[6] GW X 155; Stud III 55; SE XIV 88.

DR LECLAIRE: Anlehnung *has the meaning of support.*

The notion of *Anlehnung* does have some connection with the notion of dependency developed since. But it is a much larger and richer idea. Freud draws up a list of the different types of fixation in love, which has no reference whatsoever to what one might call a mature relationship – that myth of psychoanalysis. First of all, within the field of fixation in love, there is *Verliebtheit*, the narcissistic type. It is characterised as follows, that one loves – firstly, what one is oneself, that is to say, as Freud specifies in brackets, oneself – secondly, what one was – thirdly, what one would like to be – fourthly, the person who was a part of one's own self. That's the *Narzissmustypus*.

The *Anlehnungstypus* is no less imaginary, since it is also based on a reversal of identification. The subject thus takes his bearings on a primitive situation. One loves the woman who feeds and the man who protects.

DR LECLAIRE: *Here, Freud puts forward a number of considerations which count as indirect proofs for the conception of the primary narcissism of the child, which he locates essentially – strange as it may seem – in the manner in which parents see their child.*

That's the seduction exercised by narcissism. Freud points out what every human being finds fascinating and satisfying in the apprehension of a being whose perceived characteristics are those of this enclosed world, shut in on itself, satisfied, full, which the narcissistic type represents. He compares it to the supreme seduction a beautiful animal exerts.

DR LECLAIRE: *He says* – His Majesty the Baby. *The child is what the parents make of it, in so far as they project the ideal on to it. Freud makes it clear that he will leave to one side the disturbances of the child's primary narcissism, even though that is a subject of great importance, since the question of the castration complex is linked to it. He takes the opportunity to give a more precise sense of where Adler's notion of the masculine protest belongs, by putting it back in its proper place . . .*

. . . which is by no means negligible.

DR LECLAIRE: . . . *yes, it is of great importance, but he links it up with disturbances of the original primary narcissism. We thus come to the following important question – what happens to the ego libido in the normal adult? Are we forced to admit that it is completely subsumed in the object investments? Freud rejects this hypothesis, and reminds us of the existence of repression, which has, in the end, a normalising function. Repression, he says, and this is the essential point in the argument,* proceeds from the ego, from its ethical and cultural requirements. The same impressions, experiences, impulses and desires that one man indulges or at least works over consciously will be rejected with the utmost indignation by another, or even stifled before they enter consciousness.[7] *We have here a difference in behaviour, depending on the individual, depending on the person. Freud attempts to formulate this difference as follows* - We can say that the one man has set up an ideal in himself by which he measures his actual[8] ego, while the other has formed no such ideal. For the ego the formation of an ideal would be the conditioning factor of repression. This ideal is now the target of the self-love which was enjoyed in childhood by the true[9] ego. *And he goes on . . .*

It isn't the true ego, it's the real ego – *das wirkliche Ich.*

DR LECLAIRE: *The text goes on* – Narcissism seems to make its appearance displaced on to this new ideal ego, which finds itself in possession of all the ego's precious perfections, in the same way as the infantile ego was. As always where the libido is concerned, man has here again shown himself incapable of giving up a satisfaction he had once enjoyed. *For the first time Freud uses the term 'ideal ego' in this sentence* – this ideal ego is now the target of the self-love which was enjoyed in childhood by the true[10] ego. *But he then says* – He is not willing to forgo the narcissistic perfection of his childhood and [. . .] he seeks to recover it in the new form of an ego-ideal.[11] *Here we find the two terms 'ideal ego' and 'ego-ideal'.*

Given the rigour of Freud's writing, one of the puzzles of this text, very well brought out by Leclaire, is the coexistence in the same paragraph of the two terms.

DR LECLAIRE: *It is amusing to observe how the word 'form' is substituted for the word 'ego'.*

Exactly. And Freud makes use there of the *Ichideal*, which is precisely symmetrical and opposed to the *Idealich*. It's the sign that Freud is here designating two different functions. What does that mean? We are going to try and clarify it in a moment.

DR LECLAIRE: *What caught my attention is that just when he substitutes the term* ideal ego *for* ego-ideal, *the* ego-ideal *is preceded by* new form.

Of course.

DR LECLAIRE: *The new form of his ego-ideal is what he projects before him as his ideal.*

---

[7] GW X 160; Stud III 60; SE XIV 93. The first sentence of this passage is a loose paraphrase of the original German: 'Repression, we have said, proceeds from the ego; we might say with greater precision that it proceeds from the self-respect of the ego.'

[8] *'aktuelles'* in German; 'actual' in SE; *'actuel'* in French.

[9] SE gives 'actual'; French has *'véritable'*; as Lacan points out the German is *'wirkliche'*.

[10] *'wirkliche Ich'.*   [11] GW X 161; Stud III 61; SE XIV 94.

The next paragraph clears up this difficulty. For once, quite exceptionally in his work, Freud spells out the difference between sublimation and idealisation. Go on.

DR LECLAIRE: *So Freud has postulated the existence of the ideal ego, which he then calls the ego-ideal, or form of the ideal ego. He says, from there, there is only one step to the searching out of the relations of the formation of the ideal to sublimation. Sublimation is a process involving object libido. In contrast, idealisation deals with the object which has been ennobled, elevated, and it does so without any modification in its nature. Idealisation is no less possible in the domain of ego libido than in that of object libido.*

Once again, that amounts to saying that Freud places the two libidos on the same plane.

DR LECLAIRE: *The idealisation of the ego may coexist with a failed sublimation. The formation of the ego-ideal heightens the demands of the ego and encourages repression to the full.*

One is on the plane of the imaginary, and the other is on the plane of the symbolic – since the demand of the *Ichideal* takes up its place within the totality of demands of the law.

DR LECLAIRE: *Hence sublimation opens up the expedient of satisfying this demand without involving repression.*

That is successful sublimation.

DR LECLAIRE: *That's how he rounds off this short paragraph dealing with the relations of the ego-ideal to sublimation.* It would not surprise us, *he goes on to say,* if we were to find a special psychical agency which performs this task of seeing that narcissistic satisfaction from the ego-ideal is ensured and which, with this end in view, constantly watches the actual [*aktuelle*] ego and measures it by that ideal.[12] *This hypothesis of a special psychical agency, which would thus have vigilance and security as its function, will eventually lead us to the super-ego. And Freud supports his argument with an example drawn from the psychoses in which, he says, this agency is clearly visible in delusions of being watched.*[13] *Before he discusses the syndrome of being watched, he makes it clear that, if such an agency exists, we are not in a position to discover it, but can only presuppose[14] it as such. To me, it seems singularly important that, in this, his first way of introducing the super-ego, he says that this agency does not exist, that one will not discover it, but can only presuppose it.*

---

[12] GW X 162; Stud III 62; SE XIV 95.

[13] *Ibid.* '*Beachtungs- oder richtiger Beobachtungswahnes*', rendered by Leclaire as '*syndrome d'influence*', a nosological conception found primarily in French psychiatry following Séglas.

[14] Freud's verb, '*agnoszieren*', is rendered by Strachey as 'recognise'. The French verb Leclaire employs is '*supposer*' (assume, presuppose, suppose). See p. 152 n8 below.

He adds that what we call our conscience fulfils this function, has this characteristic. The recognition of this agency throws light on paranoid symptomatology. A patient of this type complains of being watched, of hearing voices, of having his thoughts known, of being observed. They are right, *Freud says,* this complaint is justified. A power of this kind, watching, discovering and criticising all our intentions, does really exist. Indeed, it exists in every one of us in normal life. *Then we find . . .*

That is not quite the intended meaning. Freud says that, if such an agency exists, it is not possible that it is the sort of thing that we would not yet have discovered. That's because he identifies it with the censorship, as the examples he chooses reveal. He comes upon this agency again in delusions of being watched,[15] in which it becomes confused with the person who commands the subject's actions. He then recognises it in what is defined by Silberer as the functional phenomenon. According to Silberer, the subject's internal perception of his own mental states, of his mental mechanisms in so far as they are functions, just when he is sliding into a dream, plays a formative role. The dream symbolically transposes this perception, in the sense in which *symbolic* simply means imagistic. Here we have a spontaneous form of splitting of the subject. Freud always had an ambiguous attitude towards this conception of Silberer's, saying both that this phenomenon is extremely important, and that it is nonetheless secondary in relation to the manifestation of desire in the dream. Perhaps that is due to the fact, he remarks somewhere,[16] that he himself has a make-up such that this phenomenon does not possess the importance in his own dreams that it may have in other people's. This vigilance of the ego which Freud highlights, ever present in the dream, is the guardian of sleep, placed on the margins, as it were, of the dream's activity, and very often ready to comment on it in its own right. This residual participation of the ego is, like all the agencies which Freud takes account of under the rubric of the censorship, an agency which speaks, that is to say a symbolic agency.

DR LECLAIRE: *A sort of synthesis then follows, in which he opens up a discussion of the sense of self,[17] in the normal individual and the neurotic. The sense of self has three origins, which are – primary narcissistic satisfaction, the measure of success, that is to say the satisfaction of the desire for omnipotence, and the gratification received from love objects. These are the three roots of the sense of self which Freud seems to retain. It's not necessary, I think, to go into the detail of the discussion here. I would prefer to return to the first of the complementary remarks. What seems to me to be extremely important is this –* The development of the ego consists in an

---

[15] *'le délire d'influence'.* See p. 134 n13 above.

[16] (1900a) GW II/III 508–9; Stud II 484–5; SE V 504–5.

[17] *'sentiment de soi'.* Freud's term, *Selbstgefühl,* is translated in SE as 'self-regard' (SE XIV 98 *et passim*). The broader term 'sense of self' has been employed, despite its clumsiness, because it reflects French and German more faithfully.

estrangement from primary narcissism and gives rise to a vigorous attempt to recover that state. This departure is brought about by means of the displacement of libido on to an ego-ideal imposed from without, and satisfaction is brought about from fulfilling this ideal.[18] *So the ego experiences a kind of estrangement, passing via a middle term, which is the ideal, and returns later to its primitive position. This movement seems to me to be the very image of development.*

O. MANNONI: *Its structuration.*

Yes, structuration, that's quite right.

DR LECLAIRE: *This displacement of the libido on to an ideal needs to be made more precise because it may be one of two things – either this displacement of the libido is carried out once again on to an image, on to an image of the ego, that is to say on to a form of the ego, which we call an ideal, since it is not similar to the one that is already there, or that was there – or else we will apply the term ego-ideal to something going beyond a form of the ego, to something which is quite properly an ideal, and which comes closer to the idea, to the form.*

Agreed.

DR LECLAIRE: *It's in this sense that we come to perceive, it seems to me, all of the richness of the sentence. But also its degree of ambiguity in as much as, if one talks of structuration, one then takes the ego-ideal to be the form of the ego-ideal. But that isn't made clear in this text.*

M. HYPPOLITE: *Could you read Freud's sentence again?*

DR LECLAIRE: The development of the ego consists in an estrangement from primary narcissism and gives rise to a vigorous attempt to recover that state.

M. HYPPOLITE: *But does one have take that to be the begetting of the ego-ideal?*

DR LECLAIRE: *No. Freud talks about the ego-ideal before. The estrangement is brought about by means of a displacement of the libido on to an ego-ideal imposed from without. And satisfaction is brought about by fulfilling this ideal. Obviously, to the extent that this ideal is fulfilled . . .*

M. HYPPOLITE: *. . . incapable of being fulfilled, because when all is said and done that is the origin of transcendence, destructive and fascinating.*

DR LECLAIRE: *It isn't made explicit, however. The first time that he talks of the ideal ego, it's in order to say that self-love now moves towards this ideal ego.*

O. MANNONI: *In my opinion, one often gets the impression that we are speaking several different languages. I think that one should perhaps distinguish between a*

---

[18] GW X 168; Stud III 67; SE XIV 100.

development of the person and a structuration of the ego. Something of this sort will
allow us to understand one another, because it is truly an ego which structures, but
within a being which is developing.

Yes, we are deep in structuration. Precisely at the point where the entire
analytic experience unfolds, at the joint of the imaginary and the symbolic. Just
now, Leclaire raised the question about the function of the image and the
function of what he called the idea. We know very well that the idea never lives
all by itself. It lives with all the other ideas, Plato has already taught us that.

In order to bring a little light to bear, let's get the little apparatus going, the
one I have been showing you these last few sessions.

2

Let's start with the animal, an animal which is also an ideal, that is to say
successful – the unsuccessful one is the animal we managed to capture. This
ideal animal gives us a vision of completeness, of fulfilment, because it
presupposes the perfect fit, indeed the identity of the *Innenwelt* and the *Umwelt*.
That's what makes this living form seductive, as its appearance harmoniously
unfolds.

What does the development of instinctual functioning teach us in this
respect? The extraordinary importance of the image. What comes into play in
releasing the complementary behaviour of the male and female sticklebacks?
Gestalten.

Let us simplify matters, and consider this functioning solely at one given
moment. The male or female animal subject is captivated, as it were, by a
Gestalt. The subject literally identifies itself with the releasing stimulus. The
male is caught up in the zigzag dance on the basis of the relation that is set up
between himself and the image which governs the releasing of the cycle of his
sexual behaviour. The female is caught up in the same way in this mutual
dance. This is not just the external manifestation of something which always
has the aspect of a dance, of two-body gravitation. Up to now that has been one
of the most difficult problems for physics to solve, but it comes about quite
harmoniously in the natural world in the pairing relation. At that moment, the
subject is found to be completely identical to the image which governs the
complete releasing of a specific motor behaviour, which itself produces and
echoes back to the partner, in a certain style, the command which makes it
engage in the other part of the dance.

The natural appearance of this closed world of two gives us the image of the
conjunction of the object libido and the narcissistic libido. In effect, each
object's attachment to the other is produced by the narcissistic fixation on this
image, because it is this image, and it alone, that it was expecting. That explains

why, in the world of living things, only a partner of the same species – we never pay sufficient attention to this – is able to release this special form which we call sexual behaviour. With very few exceptions, which must be placed within the margin of error which natural events display.

Let us say that, in the animal world, the entire cycle of sexual behaviour is dominated by the imaginary. On the other hand, it is in sexual behaviour that we find the greatest possibilities of displacement occurring, even in animals. We already make use of it for experimental purposes when we present the animal with a lure, a false image, a male partner which is only a shadow bearing the dominant characteristics of the said animal. At the time of the manifestations of the phenotype that, in many species, occur at this biological moment which calls for sexual behaviour, the offering of this lure is sufficient to release the sexual behaviour. The possibility of displacement, the illusory, imaginary dimension, is essential to everything pertaining to the order of sexual behaviour.

Is this true for man, yes or no? This image could be it, this *Idealich* we've just been talking about. Why not? Still, it wouldn't occur to us to call this lure the *Idealich*. So where are we going to put it? Here my little apparatus reveals its virtues.

What are its implications? I've already explained to you the physical phenomenon of the real image, which can be produced by the spherical mirror, be seen in its place, be inserted into the world of real objects, be accommodated in it at the same time as real objects, even bringing to these real objects an imaginary disposition, namely by including, excluding, locating and completing them.

This is nothing other than the imaginary phenomenon which I just spelt out in detail for you in the animal. The animal makes a real object coincide with the image within him. And, what is more, as is indicated in Freud's texts, I would add that the coincidence of the image with a real object strengthens it, gives it substance, embodiment. At this moment, behaviour is released, such that the subject will be guided towards its object, with the image as go-between.

Does this happen in man?

In man, as we know, an eminent disorder characterises the manifestations of the sexual function. Nothing in it adapts. This image, around which we, we psychoanalysts, revolve, presents, whether in the neuroses or in the perversions, a sort of fragmentation, of rupture, of breaking up, of lack of adaptation, of inadequation. Here we come upon a game of hide and seek between the image and its normal object – if indeed we adopt the ideal of a norm at all in the functioning of sexuality. From then on how can we find a way of representing the mechanism whereby this disordered imagination finally succeeds, in spite of everything, in fulfilling its function?

I am trying to use simple terms so as to guide your thinking. We could make use of more complicated ones. But you see that this really is the question which analysts distractedly ask themselves, as they vigorously – and publicly – scratch their heads.

Take up any article, it doesn't matter which, for example the last one, which I read for your sake, by our dear friend Michael Balint – whose forthcoming visit to our Society I'll announce shortly. He asks the question – what is the end of the treatment? For the last session of our course this term, I would like – perhaps I won't do it, I don't know, it will depend whether I'm feeling inspired – I would like to talk to you about the termination of analysis. It's a jump, but doesn't our scrutiny of the mechanisms of resistance and of the transference allow it?

Well, what is the end of the treatment? Is it analogous to the end of a natural process? Genital love – this Eldorado promised to analysts, which we quite imprudently promise to our patients – is it a natural process? Isn't it, on the contrary, simply a series of cultural approximations which are only capable of being realised in certain cases? Is analysis, its termination, thus dependent on all sorts of contingencies?

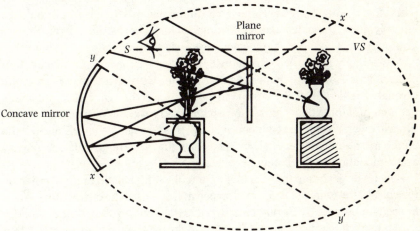

Simplified schema of the two mirrors

What is the point? – if not to see what the function of the other, of the human other, is, in the adequation of the imaginary and the real.

Here we'll take up the little schema again. The finishing touch I added to it in our last session constitutes an essential element of what I am trying to demonstrate. The real image can only be seen in a consistent fashion within a limited field of the real space of the apparatus, the field in front of the apparatus, as constituted by the spherical mirror and the inverted bouquet.

We have placed the subject at the edge of the spherical mirror. But we know that the seeing of an image in the plane mirror is strictly equivalent for the subject to an image of the real object, which would be seen by a spectator beyond this mirror, at the very spot where the subject sees his image. We can therefore replace the subject by a virtual subject, *VS*, placed inside the cone which limits the possibility of the illusion – that's the field $x'y'$. The apparatus that I've invented shows, then, how, in being placed at a point very close to the real image, one is nevertheless capable of seeing it, in a mirror, as a virtual image. That is what happens in man.

What follows from this? A very special symmetry. In fact, the virtual subject, reflection of the mythical eye, that is to say the other which we are, is there where we first saw our *ego* – outside us, in the human form. This form is outside of us, not in so far as it is so constructed as to captate[19] sexual behaviour, but in so far as it is fundamentally linked to the primitive impotence of the human being. The human being only sees his form materialised, whole, the mirage of himself, outside of himself. This notion doesn't figure as yet in the article we are studying, it only emerges later in Freud's work.

What the subject, the one who exists, sees in the mirror is an image, whether sharp or broken up, lacking in consistency, incomplete. This depends on its position in relation to the real image. Too much towards the edge, and you'll see it poorly. Everything depends on the angle of incidence at the mirror. It's only from within the cone that one can have a clear image.

So whether you see the image more or less clearly depends on the inclination of the mirror. As for the virtual spectator, the one who becomes your substitute through the fiction of the mirror in order to see the real image, all that's necessary is for the plane mirror to be inclined in a specific way for him to be in the field in which one sees very poorly. From this fact alone, you will also see the image in the mirror very poorly. Let's say that this represents the uneasy accommodation of the imaginary in man.

Now let us postulate that the inclination of the plane mirror is governed by the voice of the other. This doesn't happen at the level of the mirror-stage, but it happens subsequently through our overall relation with others – the symbolic relation. From that point on, you can grasp the extent to which the regulation of the imaginary depends on something which is located in a transcendent fashion, as M. Hyppolite would put it – the transcendent on this occasion being nothing other than the symbolic connection between human beings.

What is the symbolic connection? Dotting our i's and crossing our t's, it is the fact that socially we define ourselves with the law as go-between. It is through the exchange of symbols that we locate our different selves [*mois*] in relation to one another – you, you are Mannoni, and me Jacques Lacan, and we have a certain symbolic relation, which is complex, according to the different planes on which we are placed, according to whether we're together in the police station, or together in this hall, or together travelling.

---

[19] See p. 146 n2 below.

In other words, it's the symbolic relation which defines the position of the subject as seeing. It is speech, the symbolic relation, which determines the greater or lesser degree of perfection, of completeness, of approximation, of the imaginary. This representation allows us to draw the distinction between the *Idealich* and the *Ichideal*, between the ideal ego and the ego-ideal. The ego-ideal governs the interplay of relations on which all relations with others depend. And on this relation to others depends the more or less satisfying character of the imaginary structuration.

A schema like this one shows you that the imaginary and the real act on the same level. To understand this, all we have to do is to make another little improvement in the apparatus. Think of the mirror as a pane of glass. You'll see yourself in the glass and you'll see the objects beyond it. That's exactly how it is – it's a coincidence between certain images and the real. What else are we talking about when we refer to an oral, anal, genital reality, that is to say a specific relation between our images and images? This is nothing other than the images of the human body, and the hominisation of the world, its perception in terms of images linked to the structuration of the body. The real objects, which pass via the mirror, and through it, are in the same place as the imaginary object. The essence of the image is to be invested by the libido. What we call libidinal investment is what makes an object become desirable, that is to say how it becomes confused with this more or less structured image which, in diverse ways, we carry with us.

So this schema allows you to represent to yourself the difference which Freud always carefully drew, and which often remains puzzling to readers, between topographical regression and genetic, archaic regression, regression in history as we are also taught to designate it.

Depending on the inclination of the mirror, the image in the spherical mirror is more or less successfully set up at the centre or on the edges. One might even conceive of it being modified. How does the primitive mouth get transformed, in the end, into a phallus? – it would perhaps be easy to knock up a little model of entertaining physics for this problem. This shows you that, in man, no truly effective and complete imaginary regulation can be set up without the intervention of another dimension. Which is what analysis, mythically at least, aims at.

What is my desire? What is my position in the imaginary structuration? This position is only conceivable in so far as one finds a guide beyond the imaginary, on the level of the symbolic plane, of the legal exchange which can only be embodied in the verbal exchange between human beings. This guide governing the subject is the ego-ideal.

This distinction is absolutely essential, and it allows us to make sense of what happens in analysis on the imaginary plane, which we call transference.

To get hold of it – this is the value of Freud's text – one has to understand what *Verliebtheit* is, what love is. Love is a phenomenon which takes place on the imaginary level, and which provokes a veritable subduction of the symbolic, a sort of annihilation, of perturbation of the function of the ego-ideal. Love reopens the door – as Freud put it, not mincing his words – to perfection.

The *Ichideal*, the ego-ideal, is the other as speaking, the other in so far as he has a symbolic relation to me [*moi*], which, within the terms of our dynamic manipulation, is both similar to and different from the imaginary libido. Symbolic exchange is what links human beings to each other, that is, it is speech, and it makes it possible to identify the subject. That isn't a metaphor – the symbol begets intelligent beings, as Hegel says.

The *Ichideal*, considered as speaking, can come to be placed in the world of objects on the level of the *Idealich*, that is, on the level where this narcissistic captation which Freud talks about over and over again throughout this text can take place. You can rest assured that when this confusion occurs, the apparatus can't be regulated any longer. In other words, when you're in love, you are mad, as ordinary language puts it.

I would like at this point to give an illustration of love at first sight. Remember the first time Werther sees Lotte, as she is cuddling a child. It's an entirely satisfying image for the *Anlehnungstypus* on the anaclitic plane. It is the way the object coincides with Goethe's hero's fundamental image that triggers off[20] his fatal attachment – next time we must clarify why this attachment is fundamentally fatal. That's what love is. It's one's own ego that one loves in love, one's own ego made real on the imaginary level.

People go crazy thinking about this problem – how can a transference be so easily generated in neurotics, when they are so fettered when it comes to love? The production of transference has an absolutely universal character, truly automatic, whereas the demands of love are, on the contrary, as everyone knows, so specific . . . It's not every day that you come upon something which is constructed so as to give you the very image of your desire. How is it, then, that within the analytic relation, the transference, which has the same nature as love – Freud says it in the text which I gave Granoff to go through – arises, one can say *even before* the analysis has started? To be sure, it isn't perhaps quite the same thing before and during analysis.

I see that the clock ticks on, and I don't want to keep you after quarter to two. I will start off with these questions next time – how does the function of transference, triggered off[20] almost automatically in the analysand/analyst relation – before it has even begun, on account of the presence and function of analysis – how does it allow us to bring into play the imaginary function of the *Idealich*?

31 March 1954

---

[20] '*déclenche*'. See p. 121 n6 above.

XII

Zeitlich-Entwicklungsgeschichte

It was Alain who pointed out that no one counts the number of columns on his mental image of the Pantheon. To which I would have liked to have answered him – except the architect of the Pantheon. So here we are, ushered through this little gateway, into the relations between the real, the imaginary and the symbolic.

1

M. HYPPOLITE: *Can one ask a question about the structure of the optical image? I want to ask for some material specifications. If I've correctly understood the material structure, there is a spherical mirror, and the real image of the object is inverted in the middle of the mirror. This image would be on a screen. Instead of being formed on a screen, we can look at it with the eye.*

Exactly. Because it's a real image, in as much as the eye accommodates itself within a specific plane, designated by the real object. In the amusing experiment which I drew inspiration from, there was an inverted bouquet which was placed in the neck of a real vase. In so far as the eye accommodates itself to the real image, it sees it. It is clearly delineated in as much as the light rays all converge on the same point in virtual space, that is to say in as much as, for every point on the object, there corresponds a point on the image.

M. HYPPOLITE: *If the eye is placed within the luminous cone, it sees the image. If not, it doesn't see it.*

The experiment proves that, for it to be perceived, the observer must be not very far removed from the axis of the spherical mirror, within a sort of continuation of the outward curvature of this mirror.

M. HYPPOLITE: *In that case, if we introduce a plane mirror, the plane mirror gives a virtual image of the real image we are considering as the object.*

Everything which can be directly seen can also be seen in a mirror. It is exactly the same as if it were seen as making up a set composed of symmetrical parts, one real, the other virtual, corresponding to one another. The virtual part corresponds to the opposed real part, and inversely, in such a manner that the virtual image in the mirror is seen in the same way as the real image would be by an imaginary, virtual observer, who occupies the symmetrical position in the mirror, the real image functioning on this occasion as the object.

M. HYPPOLITE: *I've gone back to construction sets again, just as in the days of exams or prelims.*[1] *But here, there's also an eye which looks in the mirror in order to see the virtual image of the real image.*

As long as I can see the real image, I will see it just as well, placing the mirror at a half-way point, either appearing from where I am, that is at a place which may vary between the real image and spherical mirror, or even behind it. What I'll see appearing in the mirror, if it is appropriately positioned, that is to say if it is perpendicular to the axis of a moment ago, is the self-same real image outlined against the confused background given by the concavity of a spherical mirror in a plane one.

M. HYPPOLITE: *When I look in the mirror, I simultaneously perceive the virtual bouquet of flowers and my virtual eye.*

Yes, as long as my real eye exists, and isn't itself an abstract point. For I've emphasised that we aren't eyes. And, in saying this, I'm beginning to slip into abstraction.

M. HYPPOLITE: *So, I've properly understood the image. There remains the symbolic correspondence.*

That is what I am going to try to explain a bit to you.

M. HYPPOLITE: *What play of correspondences is there between the real object, the flowers, the real image, the virtual image, the real eye and the virtual eye? Let's start with the real object – what do the real flowers represent for you?*

The point of this schema is, of course, that it can be put to a variety of uses. Freud had already constructed something similar, and quite specifically pointed out to us in the *Traumdeutung* and the *Abriss* that the psychic agencies should be conceived of on the basis of imaginary phenomena. In the *Traumdeutung* he made use of the schema of layers, in which perceptions and memories are inscribed, the former forming the conscious, the latter the unconscious, which comes to be projected on to consciousness, eventually closing the stimulus-response circuit, with which one tried to explain the

[1] 'bachot ou du PCB', colloquial terms for 'baccalauréat' (final secondary school examinations) and 'Certificat d'études de physique, chimie et biologie', a preliminary medical examination.

organism's circuit at that time. We can see in it something like the superposition of photographic films. But it is quite clear that his schema is imperfect. Because . . .

M. HYPPOLITE: *I've already got the hang of your schema. I am looking for the initial correspondences.*

The original correspondences? To clarify matters, we can give the real image, which has the function of containing and, at the same time, of excluding several real objects, the signification of the limits of the ego. However, if you give such a function to one element of the model, other elements necessarily take on other functions. All that counts here is the way the relations are put to use.

M. HYPPOLITE: *Could one, for example, say that the real object signifies the* Gegenbild, *the sexual replica of the ego? In the animal schema, the male finds the* Gegenbild, *that is to say his complementary counterpart in the structure.*

Since you need a *Gegenbild* . . .

M. HYPPOLITE: *The word is Hegel's.*

The very term *Gegenbild* implies correspondence with an *Innenbild*, which boils down to the correspondence of the *Innenwelt* with the *Umwelt*.

M. HYPPOLITE: *Which prompts me to say that if the real object, the flowers, represents the real object correlative to the perceiving animal subject, then the real image of the flower pot represents the reflected imaginary structure of this real structure.*

You couldn't have put it better. That's exactly what happens when one is dealing with an animal. And that is what happens in my first construction, where there is only the spherical mirror, when the experiment is limited to showing how the real image is mixed in with real things. That, in fact, is one way of representing the *Innenbild* which allows the animal to seek out its specific partner, in the manner in which the key seeks out a keyhole, or the keyhole seeks out the key, directing its libido where it has to be for the propagation of the species. I've pointed out to you that, from this point of view, we can already grasp in an impressionistic way the essentially transitory character of the individual in relation to the type.

M. HYPPOLITE: *The cycle of the species.*

Not only the cycle of the species, but the fact that the individual is so much a captive of the type that, in relation to this type, it is annihilated. It is, as Hegel would say – I don't know if he said it – already dead in relation to the eternal life of the species.

M. HYPPOLITE: *I made Hegel say this sentence, in commenting on your image –
that in fact, knowledge, that is to say humanity, is the failure of sexuality.*

That's going a bit too far.

M. HYPPOLITE: *For me what is important is that the real object can be understood
as the real counterpart, which pertains to the order of the species, of the real
individual. But then a development in the imaginary takes place, which allows this
counterpart in the single spherical mirror also to become a real image, an image which
fascinates, as such, in the very absence of the real object which is projected into the
imaginary, an image which fascinates the individual and captates[2] him right up to the
plane mirror.*

You know what a delicate matter it is to measure what is and what isn't
perceived by an animal, because, for it just as for man, perception seems to
extend much further than one is able to bring out in experimental, that is to say
artificial behaviour. Sometimes we realise that it is capable of making choices
with the help of things the existence of which we did not suspect. Nonetheless,
we know that, when it is engaged in a cycle of behaviour of the instinctual type,
there takes place in it a thickening, a condensation, a dulling, of its perception of
the external world. The animal is then so stuck within a number of imaginary
conditions that we can lure it most easily, just when it would be of the greatest
use for it not to be fooled. Libidinal fixation on certain terms here appears as a
kind of funnel.

That is our starting point. But, if it is necessary to construct an apparatus
which is a little more complex and tricky for man, it is because, for him, it
doesn't happen like that.

Since you have been kind enough to get me started again today, I don't see why
I shouldn't begin by reminding you of the fundamental Hegelian theme – man's
desire is the desire of the other.

That is exactly what is made plain in the model by the plane mirror. That is
also where we again come upon Jacques Lacan's classical mirror phase, this
turning point [*moment de virage*] in development, in which the individual makes
a triumphant exercise of his own image in the mirror, of himself. Through
certain correlations in his behaviour, we can understand that what occurs here
for the first time, is the anticipated seizure of mastery.

Here we are also touching on something else, which I've called the *Urbild*,
using *Bild* in a different sense from the way you used it just now – the first model
in which man's delay, the unsticking of man in relation to his own libido, is

---

[2] *'capter'*. The verb 'to captate', obsolete according to the O.E.D., is here revived in a quasi-
technical sense – Lacan and Hyppolite use it to refer exclusively to the imaginary effects of the image
in the other, a relation of seduction and fascination.

noticeable. This gap means that there's a radical difference between the satisfaction of a desire and the pursuit of the fulfilment of desire – desire is essentially a negativity, introduced at a point in time which is not especially primary, but which is crucial, a turning-point [*tournant*]. Desire is first grasped in the other, and in the most confused form. The relativity of human desire in relation to the desire of the other is what we recognise in every reaction of rivalry, of competition, and even in the entire development of civilization, including this sympathetic and fundamental exploitation of man by man whose end is by no means yet in sight, for the reason that it is absolutely structural to, and constitutes, as Hegel acknowledged once and for all, the very structure of the idea of labour. To be sure, it is no longer a question of desire here, but of the total mediation of activity in so far as it is specifically human, in so far as it has taken the path of human desires.

The subject originally locates and recognises desire through the intermediary, not only of his own image, but of the body of his fellow being. It's exactly at that moment that the human being's consciousness, in the form of consciousness of self, distinguishes itself. It is in so far as he recognises his desire in the body of the other that the exchange takes place. It is in so far as his desire has gone over to the other side that he assimilates himself to the body of the other and recognises himself as body.

Nothing allows us to assert that the animal has a consciousness separated from its body as such, that its corporeality is an objectifiable entity for it . . .

M. HYPPOLITE: *Statutory, in both senses.*

Exactly. Whereas it is certain that, if there is for us a fundamental given even before the register of the unhappy consciousness has emerged at all, it's precisely the distinction between our consciousness and our body. This distinction makes our body into something factitious, from which our consciousness is entirely incapable of detaching itself, but on the basis of which it conceives itself – these are not perhaps the most adequate terms – as distinct.

The distinction between consciousness and body is set up in this abrupt interchange of roles which takes place in the experience of the mirror when the other is involved.

Mannoni yesterday evening remarked that, in interpersonal relations, something factitious is always brought in, namely the projection of others on to ourselves. This is no doubt because we recognise ourselves as body in so far as these others, who are indispensable for the recognition of our desire, also have bodies, or more exactly, in so far as we have one like them.

M. HYPPOLITE: *What I fail to understand, is not so much the distinction between oneself and the body, as the distinction between two bodies.*

Of course.

M. HYPPOLITE: *Since the self represents itself as the ideal body, and since there is also the body I feel, there are two . . .?*

No, certainly not. That's where the Freudian discovery acquires its full importance – man, in his initial stages, does not from the first in any way accede to a surmounted desire. What he recognises and fixes in this image of the other is a fragmented desire. And the apparent mastery of the mirror image is given to him, at least virtually, as complete. It is an ideal mastery.

M. HYPPOLITE: *That is what I call the ideal body.*

It is the *Idealich*. As for his desire, that, in contrast, is not constituted. What the subject finds in the other is first of all a series of ambivalent planes, of alienations of his desire – of a desire still in pieces. Everything we know about the evolution of instincts yields us its schema, since Freud's libido theory is built upon the preservation, upon the progressive compounding of a number of partial drives, which may or may not succeed in leading to a mature desire.

M. HYPPOLITE: *I think that we are in complete agreement. Yes? But, you were saying no just now. We are in complete agreement. If I say two bodies, that simply means that what I see as being constituted either in the other, or in my own image in the mirror, is what I am not, and in fact is what is beyond me. That is what I call the ideal, statutory body, or statue. As Valéry says in* La Jeune Parque *– But my statue quivers at the same time,[3] that is to say disintegrates. Its disintegration is what I call the other body.*

The body as fragmented desire seeking itself out, and the body as ideal self, are projected on the side of the subject as fragmented body, while it sees the other as perfect body. For the subject, a fragmented body is an image essentially dismemberable from its body.

M. HYPPOLITE: *The two project themselves on to each other in the sense that, all at once, it sees itself as statue and dismembers itself at the same time, projecting the dismembering on to the statue, within a dialectic which cannot be brought to an end. I apologise for repeating what you have said, just to be sure that I've really understood.*

In a moment, if you want, we'll go one step further.

After all, the real is obviously right here, on this side of the mirror. But what is beyond it? First of all, there is, as we have already seen, the primitive imaginary of the specular dialectic with the other.

This fundamental dialectic already introduces the fatal dimension of the death instinct, in two senses. Firstly, the libidinal captation has an irremediably fatal significance for the individual, in so far as it is subjected to the x of eternal

[3] '*Mais ma statue en même temps frissonne.*'

life. Secondly – and this is the point emphasised by Freud's thought, but isn't fully made out in *Beyond the Pleasure Principle* – the death instinct in man takes on another signification in that his libido is originally constrained to pass through an imaginary stage.

In addition, this image of an image is what disrupts the maturity of the libido in man, disrupts the smooth fitting together of reality and the imaginary which should in principle exist, according to our hypothesis – since, after all, what do we know about it? – in animals. In animals, the securing of the guide-rails is so much more in evidence that it is precisely what has given rise to the great fantasy of *natura mater*, the very idea of nature, in relation to which man portrays his original inadequacy to himself, which he expresses in a thousand different ways. You can spot it, in a perfectly objectifiable manner, in his quite special impotence at the beginning of life. This prematurity of birth hasn't been invented by the psychoanalysts. Histologically, the apparatus which in the organism plays the role of nervous system, still a matter for debate, is not complete at birth. Man's libido attains its finished state before encountering its object. That is how this special fault is introduced, perpetuated in man in the relation to the other who is infinitely more fatal for him than for any other animal. This image of the master, which is what he sees in the form of the specular image, becomes confused in him with the image of death. Man can be in the presence of the absolute master. He is in his presence from the beginning, whether he has been taught this or not, in so far as he is subjected to this image.

M. HYPPOLITE: *The animal is bound by death when he makes love, but he doesn't know anything about it.*

Whereas man knows it. He knows it and feels it.

M. HYPPOLITE: *That amounts to saying that he himself takes his own life. Through the other he wants his own death.*

We are all completely agreed that love is a form of suicide.

DR LANG: *There's one point you have insisted on, and I haven't fully grasped the significance of your insistence. It is the fact that one has to be within a certain field in relation to the apparatus we're studying.*

I see that I haven't shown you enough petticoat, since you've seen the frills but not how they're tied on.

What's at issue here can once again come into play on several planes. We can interpret things at the level of structuration, or of description, or of the management of the cure. It is particularly useful to have a schema such that the apparition of the image at a given moment be dependent upon the activation of a plane of reflection – the subject remaining always in the same place. Only from a specific virtual point of observation can one see the image with sufficient completeness. You can shift this virtual point around as you wish. Now, when the mirror veers round, what changes?

It will not only be the backdrop, that is, what the subject can see at the back, for example himself – or an echo of himself, as M. Hyppolite has observed. In fact, when you move a plane mirror, there comes a point when a certain number of objects leave the field. Clearly the closest ones are the last to leave, which may already be useful in explaining some of the ways in which the *Idealich* is placed in relation to something else which for the moment I leave in an enigmatic form, and which I have called the observer. Quite obviously it's not just an observer. In the end what is involved is the symbolic relation, namely the point from which one speaks, it is spoken.

But it is not only this which changes. If you put the mirror at an angle, the image itself changes. Without the real image moving, simply because the mirror changes, the image that the subject, placed on the side of the spherical mirror, will see in this mirror, will pass from having the form of a mouth to that of a phallus, or from a more or less complete desire to that type of desire which a moment ago I called fragmented. In other words, this mode of functioning allows us to see what was always Freud's idea, namely the possible correlations between the notion of topographical [*topique*] regression and the regression he called *zeitlich-Entwicklungsgeschichte* – which clearly shows how embarrassed by the temporal relation he himself was. He says *zeitlich*, that's to say *temporal*, then a hyphen, and – *history of development*, whereas you're well aware what an internal contradiction there is between the term *Entwicklung* and the term *Geschichte*.[4] He joins these three terms together, then, sort that one out for yourselves!

But if we didn't have to sort it out, we wouldn't need to be here. And that would be a great pity.

Go on, Perrier, with the 'Metapsychological supplements to the theory of dreams'.

2

DR PERRIER: *Yes, this text . . .*

Did this text seem a bit of a problem to you?

DR PERRIER: *As a matter of fact, yes. I think the best thing to do would without doubt be to make a schema of it. It's an article that Freud opens by telling us that it is instructive to set out a parallel between certain morbid symptoms and the normal*

---

[4] The passage Lacan is referring to, (1917d) GW X 418; Stud III 184; SE XIV 227, reads 'zeitlichen *oder entwicklungsgeschichtlichen*' ('*zeitlichen*' emphasised in the original).

prototypes which allow us to study them, for example, mourning and melancholia, the dream, sleep and certain narcissistic states.

By the way, he uses the term *Vorbild*, which has much the same meaning as the term *Bildung*, to designate the normal prototype.

DR PERRIER: *Freud comes to the study of the dream with an aim which comes clear at the end of the article, of going more deeply into the study of those phenomena which one comes across in the narcissistic disorders, in schizophrenia for example.*

The normal prefigurations in a morbid disorder, *Normalvorbilder krankhafter Affektionen.*[5]

DR PERRIER: *So, he says that sleep is a state of psychic undressing, which restores the sleeper to a state analogous to the primitive foetal state, and which in the same way brings him to divest himself of an entire part of his psychic organisation, just as one takes off a wig, false teeth, clothes, before going to sleep.*

With regard to this image of the subject's narcissism which he gives us, and which he takes to be the fundamental essence of sleep, it's rather funny to see Freud add the remark, which doesn't quite seem to fit within a straight-forwardly physiological perspective, that it is not true for all human beings. Sure, you usually do take off your clothes, but you put on others. Look at the picture that he paints all of a sudden, of taking off one's glasses – some of us are endowed with infirmities which make them necessary – but also one's false teeth, one's false hair. A hideous picture of a disintegrating being. We thus come upon this partially decomposable, collapsible character of the human ego, whose limits are so imprecisely defined. Surely false teeth are not a part of my ego, but to what extent are my real teeth? – if they are so easily replaced. The idea of the ambiguous, uncertain character of the limits of the ego is put to the fore here, in the portico of the introduction to the metapsychological study of the dream. The preparation for sleep reveals its importance.

DR PERRIER: *In the next paragraph, Freud takes up something which appears to be the short cut to everything he is going to study from then on. He recalls that when one studies the psychoses, in every case one finds oneself in the presence of temporal regressions, that is to say of those points in the stages of its own evolution to which every case returns.*[6] *He then says that one comes across similar regressions, one in the evolution of the ego, and the other in the evolution of the libido. The regression of the evolution of the libido in the dream*[7] *which corresponds to all of this will, he says, lead to the re-establishing of primitive narcissism. The regression of the evolution of the*

---

[5] GW X 412; Stud III 179; SE XIV 222.

[6] See (1900a) GW II/III 554; Stud II 524; SE V 548: 'what is in question [in *zeitliche* regression] is a harking back [*Rückgreifen*] to older psychical structures'.

[7] GW X 412–3; Stud III 179–80; SE XIV 222–3).

ego in the dream will in the same way lead to the hallucinatory satisfaction of desire. This, a priori, *doesn't seem to be particularly clear, at least not to me.*

It might be a bit clearer with our schema.

DR PERRIER: *You can already get an inkling of it, in seeing how Freud starts with temporal regressions, of regressions in the subject's history. Consequently, regression in the evolution of the ego leads to this completely elementary, primordial, unelaborated state, which is the hallucinatory satisfaction of desire. He will, first of all, enjoin us to go over with him once again the study of the dream-processes, and in particular, the study of the narcissism of sleep, in terms of what takes place in it, that is to say the dream. First of all he talks about the dream's egoism, which is a term which shocks a bit when comparing it with narcissism.*

How does he justify the egoism of the dream?

DR PERRIER: *He says that in the dream, the principal protagonist is always the sleeper.*

Who also plays the leading role. Who can tell me exactly what *agnoszieren* means? It's a German term which I haven't been able to find. But its meaning is not in doubt – it's a question of this person who must always be recognised as the person himself, *als die eigener [Person] zu agnoszieren.*[8] Can someone give me some idea of the use of this word? Freud doesn't use *anerkennen*, which would imply the dimension of recognition in the sense in which we always understand it in our dialectic. The person of the sleeper is to be recognised, at which level, that of our interpretation or that of our mantic? It is not quite the same thing. Between *anerkennen* and *agnoszieren*, there's all the difference between what we understand and what we know, a difference which nonetheless bears the mark of a fundamental ambiguity. See how Freud himself analyses for us the celebrated dream of the botanical monograph in the *Traumdeutung*. The further we get the more we see how inspired these initial approaches towards the meaning of the dream and its scenario actually were.

Mme X, can you give us a hint about this *agnoszieren?*

MME X: *Sometimes Freud uses Viennese words. This word is no longer used in German, but the meaning you have given is correct.*

Indeed, it's interesting, the significance of the Viennese milieu.

In this connection, Freud gives us a very deep sense of his relation with the fraternal character, with this friend-enemy, who he says is a character absolutely fundamental to his existence – there must always be someone

---

[8] GW X 413; Stud III 180; SE XIV 223. *Agnoszieren* is used in the passage which Lacan and Leclaire commented upon (pp. 134 n14 above) – there, it is rendered into French as 'supposer' (assume, suppose), the sense that Leclaire highlights, opposing it to 'discover'. Lacan emphasises the fact that it is impossible that we haven't *yet* discovered it. On both occasions, SE translates '*agnoszieren*' as 'recognise'.

masked by this sort of *Gegenbild*. But, at the same time, it is with this character as go-between, embodied by his colleague from the laboratory – I've mentioned this character in earlier seminars, right at the beginning, when we talked a bit about the first stages of Freud's scientific life – it is in relation to and through the intermediary of this colleague, of his acts, of his feelings, that Freud projects, brings to life in this dream what is its latent desire, namely the claims of his own aggression, of his own ambition. Such that this *eigene Person* is entirely ambiguous. It is right at the heart of the dream's consciousness, more exactly at the heart of the mirage of the dream that we have to search, in the person who plays the leading role, for the sleeper's own person. But the point is that, it is not the sleeper, it is the other.

DR PERRIER: *He then asks if narcissism and egoism are not in fact one and the same thing. And he tells us that the word narcissism serves only to underline the libidinal character of egoism. In other words, narcissism may be considered as the libidinal complement of egoism. In a parenthetical clause, he talks about the diagnostic capacity of the dream, by reminding us that one often perceives in dreams, in a way that is completely unapparent in the waking state, organic modifications which allow one to offer a diagnosis of something still unapparent in the waking state. At this point, the problem of hypochondria makes its appearance.*

Here, then, is something a bit crafty, a bit more clever. Think hard about what it means. I talked to you about the exchange that takes place between the subject's image and the image of the other in so far as it is libidinalised, narcissised, in the imaginary situation. By the same token, in the same way as in animals, certain parts of the world are rendered opaque and become fascinating, it too is rendered thus. We have the capacity to *agnoszieren* in the dream the sleeper's own person in a pure state. The power of understanding of the subject is expanded in proportion. On the contrary, in the waking state, at least if he hasn't read the *Traumdeutung*, he won't be able to perceive in its sufficiency those bodily sensations capable of telling him, while he is sleeping, about something internal, something coenaesthetic. It is precisely in so far as the libidinal obscuring in the dream is on the other side of the mirror, that his body is, not felt any the less, but perceived better, understood by the subject.

Do you grasp the mechanism here?

In the waking state, the body of the other is reflected back to the subject, he thus fails to recognise lots of things about himself. That the *ego* is a capacity to fail to recognise [*méconnaissance*] is the very foundation of the technique of analysis.

This goes a very long way. As far as structuration, organisation and by the same token scotomisation – here, I am happy enough to use the term – and all manner of things, which are so many pieces of information which can be passed from ourselves to ourselves – a special game which reflects back to us our corporeality, that corporeality which also has an alien origin. Even as far as

– They have eyes in order not to see. You must always take the phrases of the Evangelist literally, if you don't it's obvious you won't understand anything – people think that it is ironic.

DR PERRIER: *The dream is also a projection, an externalisation of an internal process. Freud reminds us that the externalisation of an internal process is a means of defence against waking. In hysterical phobias, there is the same projection, which is itself a means of defence, and which replaces an internal function. Except, he says, why does the intention to sleep find itself thwarted? It can be either through a stimulus coming from outside, or through an excitation coming from within. The case of the internal obstacle is the more interesting, that is the one we are going to study.*

One must go over this passage carefully, because it allows one to introduce a bit of rigour into the usage, in analysis, of the term projection. It is continually employed in the most confused way. In particular, we slide all the time into the classical usage of the term, in speaking of the projection of our feelings on to our fellow beings. That is not quite what is involved when we are obliged, by force of circumstance, that is to say by the law of the system's coherence, to make use of the term in analysis. If we manage to get to the Schreber case and the question of the psychoses next term, we will have to spell out in its fine detail the meaning to be given to projection.

   If you followed what I said just now, you must see that what is here called the internal process always comes from the outside. It is first recognised through the intermediary of the outside.

DR PERRIER: *This is a problem that I encountered with Father Beirnaert and Andrée Lehmann, who helped me yesterday evening – the preconscious desire of the dream, what is it?*

What Freud calls the desire of the dream is the unconscious element.

DR PERRIER: *Exactly. Freud says that first the preconscious desire of the dream is formed, in the waking state I presume, which allows the unconscious drive to express itself, thanks to the material, that is to say, in the preconscious residues of the previous day. That's the point at which my perplexing question arose. Having used the term preconscious desire of the dream, Freud says that there was no need of its presence in the waking state, and it may already possess the irrational character peculiar to everything which is unconscious. One translates it in terms of the conscious.*

Which is important.

DR PERRIER: *One must be careful, he says, not to confuse the dream's desire with everything that pertains to the order of the preconscious.*

That's it!

   See how one usually understands this after having read it. One says – here's the manifest and there's the latent. Then one gets caught up in a number of complications. What is manifest is the composition. The work on the dream makes it possible – through a very pretty turnaround of its initial aspect, as memory – for the subject to evoke for you what is manifest. But what makes up the dream is something which we must look for, and which truly belongs to the unconscious. This desire, we find it or we don't find it, but we only ever see it silhouetted at the back. The unconscious desire is like the directing force which has forced all the *Tagesresten*, these vaguely lucid investments, to become organised in a certain way. This composition results in the manifest contents, that is to say in a mirage which in no way corresponds to what we are obliged to reconstruct, which is the unconscious desire.

<h2 style="text-align:center">3</h2>

How can we represent this with my little schema? M. Hyppolite, in a timely manner, made me pull out all the stops at the beginning of this session. We won't be able to settle this question today. But we must at least make some headway.

At this point, it is indispensable to bring in what one might call the controls of the apparatus.

So, the subject becomes aware of his desire in the other, through the intermediary of the image of the other which offers him the semblance of his own mastery. Just as we quite frequently reduce the subject to an eye in our scientific reasoning, we could just as well reduce him to an actor momentarily caught up in the anticipated image of himself, quite independently of his development. But there's no escaping the fact that he's a human being, born in a state of impotence, and, very early on, words, language were what he used to call with, and a most miserable call it was, when his food depended on his screams. This primitive mothering has already been related to his states of dependency. But really that is no reason to hide the fact that, no less early, this relation to the other is named, and is so by the subject.

That a name, however confused it may be, designates a specific person, is exactly what makes up the transition to the human state. If one has to define the moment at which man becomes human, we can say that it is the moment when, however little it be, he enters into the symbolic relation.

As I've already emphasised, the symbolic relation is eternal. And not simply because effectively there must always be three people – it is eternal because the symbol introduces a third party, an element of mediation, which brings the two actors into each other's presence, leads them on to another plane, and changes them.

I want to take up this point again, and at length, even if that means breaking off in the middle today.

M. Keller, who is a gestalt philosopher, and who, by virtue of this, believes himself to be very much superior to the mechanicist philosophers, is very ironical about the theme of the stimulus-response. Somewhere he says the following – it really is odd to receive from Mr So-and-so, a publisher in New York, an order for a book, because if we were in the register of stimulus-response, one would believe that I had been stimulated by this order and that my book is the response. Oh, dear me, says Keller, appealing to our so well founded everyday intuitions, things aren't so simple. I am not just satisfied to reply to this request, I also find myself in a state of terrible tension. My equilibrium – a gestalt notion – will only be restored when this tension has taken on the form of a realisation of the text. This call I have received produces a dynamic state of disequilibrium in me. It will only be satisfied when it has been assumed, that is to say, when the circle has been closed, that circle which here and now is anticipated by the very existence of this call for a full response.[9]

This is by no means a sufficient description. Keller assumes that a preformed model of the right response exists in the subject, and introduces an element of the already-there. At the limit, it's having a response to everything through a dormative power. He is satisfied with postulating that the register of relations which generate any action means that the subject hasn't actualised the model which is already entirely inscribed within him. That is only the transcription, at a slightly more developed level, of the mechanistic theory.

No, you must not misconceive [méconnaître] the symbolic register here, through which the human being as such is constituted. In fact, from the moment that M. Keller receives the order, has replied *yes*, has signed a contract, M. Keller is not the same M. Keller. There's another Keller, a contracted Keller, and also another publishing house, a publishing house which has one more contract, one more symbol.

I am using this crude, obvious example because it brings us to the heart of the dialectic of labour. Simply as a result of having defined myself in relation to some man as his son, and of my having defined him as my father, something happens which, however intangible it may appear to be, weighs just as heavily as the carnal procreation which unites us. And, practically speaking, within the human order, it weighs even more heavily. Because, even before I am capable of pronouncing the words father and son, and even if he is gaga and can no longer pronounce these words, the entire human system around us already defines us, with all the impending consequences that that brings with it, as father and son.

So, the dialectic of the ego and the other is transcended, is placed on a higher plane, in relation to the other, solely through the function of language, in so far as it is more or less identical, and at all events is fundamentally linked up with

[9] The French word '*réponse*' covers both the English 'response' (as in 'stimulus-response') and the term 'reply' (as in 'reply' to a call from the other).

what we should call the rule, or better still, the law. At each instant of its intervention, this law creates something new. Every situation is transformed by its intervention, whatever it is, except when we talk to no purpose.

But even this, as I've explained elsewhere, has its meaning. This realisation of language, now only serving *as an effaced coin passed from hand to hand in silence* – a phrase I quoted in my Rome report, which comes from Mallarmé – indicates the pure function of language, which is to assure us that we are, and nothing more.[10] That one is capable of speaking to no purpose is just as significant as the fact that, when one speaks, in general it is for a purpose. What is striking is that there are many instances when one speaks although one might just as well remain silent. Ah, but to keep silent just then is precisely what is most cunning.

Here we are, introduced to this elementary level where language immediately adheres to our first experiences. Because it is a vital necessity which makes of man's environment a symbolic one.

In my little model, in order to conceive of the incidence of the symbolic relation, all you have to do is assume that it is the introduction of linguistic relations which produces the swings of the mirror, which will offer the subject, in the other, in the absolute other, the various aspects of his desire. There is a connection between the imaginary dimension and the symbolic system, so long as the history of the subject is inscribed in it – not the *Entwicklung*, the development, but the *Geschichte*, that is, that within which the subject recognises himself, correlatively in the past and in the future.

I know that I am saying these words quickly, but I will go over them again more slowly.

The past and the future correspond precisely to one another. And not any old how – not in the sense that you might believe that analysis indicates, namely from the past to the future. On the contrary, precisely in analysis, because its technique works, it happens in the right order – from the future to the past. You may think that you are engaged in looking for the patient's past in a dustbin, whereas on the contrary, it is as a function of the fact that the patient has a future that you can move in the regressive sense.

I cannot tell you why just now.

All human beings share in the universe of symbols. They are included in it and submit to it, much more than they constitute it. They are much more its supports than its agents. It is as a function of the symbols, of the symbolic constitution of his history, that those variations are produced in which the

---

[10] Lacan is referring to a phrase of Stéphane Mallarmé's: 'To relate, to teach, even to describe is all right and although perhaps enough for each one to exchange human thought, by taking or putting a coin silently in someone else's hand, the elementary use of talk serves the universal *reportage* of which, with the exception of literature, everything among the different kinds of contemporary partakes.' (Mallarmé, *The Poems*, trans. and introduction by Keith Bosley, Harmondsworth: Penguin, pp. 44–7)

subject is open to taking on the variable, broken, fragmented, sometimes even unconstituted and regressive, images of himself. That is what we see in the normal *Vorbilden* in the subject's everyday life, just as we see it, in a more controlled manner, in analysis.

What are the unconscious and the preconscious in all this?

I can't satisfy you today. But even so you should recognise that the first approximation we can give of it, from today's point of view, is that what is at issue are certain differences or more exactly certain impossibilities linked to the subject's history, in as much as his development is in fact inscribed in it.

We will now reappraise Freud's ambiguous formula, *zeitlich-Entwicklungs-geschichte*. But let's limit ourselves to history, and let's say that it's on account of certain peculiarities in the subject's history that some parts of the real image or some abrupt phases exist. We thus are dealing with a mobile relation.

In the intra-analytic game, certain phases or faces – let us not baulk at plays on words – of the real image can never be given as the virtual image. On the contrary, whatever is accessible through the simple mobility of the mirror in the virtual image, whatever you are able to see of the real image in the virtual image, should be located rather in the preconscious. Whereas the parts of the real image which can never be seen, those places where the apparatus seizes up, where it blocks up – having pushed the metaphor this far, we needn't shy away from pushing further – that is the unconscious.

If you think you have understood, you are bound to be wrong. You will see the difficulties that this notion of the unconscious gives rise to, and my only ambition is to show you them. On the one hand, the unconscious is, as I have just defined it, something negative, something ideally inaccessible. On the other hand, it is something quasi real. Finally, it is something which will be realised in the symbolic, or, more precisely, something which, thanks to the symbolic progress which takes place in analysis, *will have been*. I'll show you, following Freud's texts, that the notion of the unconscious must satisfy these three conditions.

But just now I am going to illustrate the third of them, whose irruption may seem surprising to you.

Don't forget this – Freud initially explains repression as a fixation. But at the moment of the fixation, there is nothing which could be called repression – that of the Wolf-man happens a long time after the fixation. The *Verdrängung* is always a *Nachdrängung*. How then should one explain the return of the repressed? As paradoxical as it may seem, there is only one way to do it – it doesn't come from the past, but from the future.

To give you a fair idea of what the return of the repressed is in a symptom, one must take up the metaphor that I've gleaned from the cyberneticists – this spares me from having to invent it myself, because one shouldn't invent too many things.

Wiener posits two beings each of whose temporal dimension moves in the opposite direction from the other. To be sure, that means nothing, and that is how things which mean nothing all of a sudden signify something, but in a quite different domain. If one of them sends a message to the other, for example a square, the being going in the opposite direction will first of all see the square vanishing, before seeing the square. That is what we see as well. The symptom initially appears to us as a trace, which will only ever be a trace, one which will continue not to be understood until the analysis has got quite a long way, and until we have discovered its meaning. In addition, one can say that, just as the *Verdrängung* is only ever a *Nachdrängung*, what we see in the return of the repressed is the effaced signal of something which only takes on its value in the future, through its symbolic realisation, its integration into the history of the subject. Literally, it will only ever be a thing which, at the given moment of its occurrence, *will have been.*

You'll see it better with the help of my little apparatus. I'm going to let you in on a secret – I add a little bit to it every day. I don't bring it here all finished, like Minerva emerging from the head of a Jupiter which I am not. We'll stay with it right to the day when it begins to seem a bit tiresome to us, then we'll drop it. Until then, it will help us reveal the construction of these three necessary facets of the notion of the unconscious so that we understand it, by eliminating all these contradictions which Perrier is encountering in the text he's presenting.

Let's leave it there for today. I still haven't shown you why the analyst is to be found where the virtual image is. The day you will have understood why the analyst is to be found there, you will have understood almost everything that happens in analysis.

7 April 1954

BEYOND PSYCHOLOGY

XIII

The see-saw of desire

CONFUSION OF TONGUES IN ANALYSIS
BIRTH OF THE *I*
MISRECOGNITION [*MÉCONNAISSANCE*] IS NOT IGNORANCE
THE MYSTIQUE OF INTROJECTION
ON PRIMARY MASOCHISM

We are beginning a third term which, thank God, is going to be short.

I had thought to start on the Schreber case before we went our separate ways this year. I would really have liked that, especially since I am getting the original work of President Schreber translated, for whatever purpose it may serve. It is a book Freud worked on and he advised us to consult it. A recommendation made in vain up to now, since it is impossible to find this work – I know of only two copies in Europe. I managed to get hold of one of them from which I have had two microfilms made up, one for my own use, the other I've given to the library of the Société Française de Psychanalyse.

Reading Schreber is entrancing. In it one finds everything one needs in order to write a complete treatise on paranoia and to supply a rich commentary on the mechanism of the psychoses. M. Hyppolite said that my knowledge started off from paranoiac knowledge – if it started there, I hope that it hasn't stayed there.

There's a gap here. But we are not going to fall into it straightaway, because we might easily remain imprisoned there.

Up to now, we have been making our way through Freud's Papers on Technique. I believe that it is now impossible not to push a bit further the comparison that I have implicitly always been making with present-day analytic technique, with what one can call, in inverted commas, *its most recent advances*. I've been referring implicitly to the teaching that is given you in supervisions, according to which analysis is analysis of resistances, analysis of the systems of the ego's defences. This conception remains poorly centred, and we can only refer to specific, but unsystematised, and sometimes even unformulated teachings.

Despite the paucity, which everyone remarks upon, of analytic literature dealing with technique, a few authors have addressed the topic. When they have not written a book, strictly speaking, they have written articles – some of them, strangely enough, remain working papers, and these are among the most interesting. There is here, in fact, a considerable corpus to work through. I hope that at this point I'll be able to count on the collaboration of some of you, to whom I'll lend several of these texts.

First of all, there are the three articles of Sachs, Alexander and Rado, taken from the Salzburg symposium.[1] You must know them if you have looked through Fenichel's book.

Then at the Marienbad Congress, you'll find the symposium on the results – as they call them – of analysis. In reality, it's less a question of the result than of the procedure which leads to these results. You can already see there the beginnings, and even the blossoming forth, of what I call the confusion of tongues in analysis, namely the extreme diversity of conceptions, whichever one holds, concerning active methods in the analytic process.

The third stage is what is happening now. There are good grounds for emphasising the recent development of the theory of the ego by the American troika, Hartmann, Loewenstein and Kris. These writings are sometimes quite disconcerting in the way they disengage concepts. They are always referring to the *desexualised* libido – they almost get to the point of saying *delibidinised* – or of deaggressivated aggression. The function of the ego more and more plays there the problematical role it already has in the writings of Freud's third period – which I have left outside our field of investigation, which I've limited to the median period 1910–1920 during which what was to be the final theory of the ego begins, with the notion of narcissism, to be developed. Read the volume which in its French edition is called *Essais de Psychanalyse*, which brings together *Beyond the Pleasure Principle, Group Psychology and the Analysis of the Ego*, and *The Ego and the Id*. We cannot analyse it this year, but it is indispensable for anyone who wants to understand the developments that the authors I have been talking about have brought to the theory of the cure. The theories of treatment which have been brought forward since 1920 have always centred around the final formulations of Freud. With great clumsiness most of the time, which stems from the very great difficulty of understanding what Freud is saying in these truly monumental articles, if one hasn't got to the bottom of the very genesis of the notion of narcissism. That is what I've tried to draw your attention to regarding the analysis of resistances and transference in the Papers on Technique.

1

Essentially, mine is a discursive path. Starting from the Freudian texts, I try to put before you here a problematic. But, from time to time, we have to focus on a

[1] The symposium on technique Lacan is referring to took place on 21 April 1924, at the International Congress at Salzburg. See *Int. J. Psa.* 6 1925.

didactic formula and bring into line the diverse formulations of these problems to be found in the history of analysis.

I'm adopting a middle way in placing before you a model, which doesn't pretend to be a system, but only a pictorial reference. That's why I've led you step by step to the optical schema we've started to construct here.

This apparatus is now beginning to become familiar to you. I've showed you how we may imagine that the real image formed thanks to the concave mirror is produced inside the subject, at a point which we call O. The subject sees this real image as a virtual image in the plane mirror, at O', in so far as he finds himself placed in the virtual symmetrical position in relation to the plane mirror.

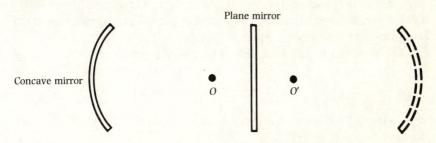

Simplified schema of the two mirrors

Here we have two points O and O'. Why O and O'? Because a little girl – a virtual woman, hence a being much more engaged in the real than males – one day came up with this pretty phrase – *Oh, you musn't think my whole life will unfold in O and in O'*.[2] Poor little thing! Your life will unfold in O and in O', the same as for everyone else. But still, by this she is telling us what she aspires to. In her honour I will call these points O and O'.

With that, one can already manage to do something.

You have to start, against all odds, from O and from O'. You already know that what is at issue relates to the constitution of the *Idealich*, and not the *Ichideal* – in other words, to the fundamentally imaginary, specular origin of the ego. That's what I am trying to make you understand using several texts, the principal one being '*Zur Einführung des Narzissmus*'.

I hope you have grasped the strict relation that exists, in this text, between the formation of the object and that of the ego. It is because they are strictly correlative and because their appearance is truly contemporaneous that the problem of narcissism arises. At this point in Freud's thinking, the libido seems to be subject to a dialectic other than its own – that, I would say, of the object.

Narcissism is not the biological individual's relation to his natural object,

[2] '*Ah! il ne faut pas croire que toute ma vie se passera en O et en O'*.'

which is then made richer and more variously complicated. There is a special narcissistic investment. It is a libidinal investment in something which should be conceived of as different from an image of the *ego*.

I'm putting things very crudely at this stage. I could put them in more sophisticated, philosophical language, but I want to make you see them clearly. What is absolutely certain is that from a certain point on in the development of the Freudian experience, attention becomes centred around the imaginary function of the ego. After Freud, the entire history of psychoanalysis becomes confused with a return to the academic, and not the traditional, conception of the ego as the psychological function of synthesis. Now if the ego has a contribution to make in the psychology of human beings, it can only be conceived of in a trans-psychological plane, or, as Freud says it explicitly – because Freud, despite the difficulties that he had with the conception of the ego, never lost the thread – *metapsychological*.

What does that mean, if not that it is beyond psychology?

2

What is it to say *I*? Is it the same thing as the *ego*, the analytic concept? One must start here.

When you use it, you cannot fail to recognise that the *I* has above all a psychological reference, in the sense in which one starts doing psychology when it is a question of observing what goes on in a human being. How does he learn to say it, this *I*?

I is a verbal term, whose use is learned through a specific reference to the other, which is a spoken reference. The *I* is born through the reference to the *you*. Everyone knows that the psychologists have used this to erect a scaffolding of remarkable things, the relation of reciprocity for example, which is either consolidated or isn't, and which determines I know not what stage in the intimate development of the child. As if one could, just like that, be sure of it, and deduce it from the initial clumsiness of the child in sorting out the personal pronouns. The child repeats the sentence one says to him using *you* instead of inverting it with the *I*. There is a hesitation in the learning of language. We don't have the right to go beyond that. But it is enough to warn us that the *I* is constituted at first in a linguistic experience, in reference to the *you*, and that this takes place within a relation in which the other shows him, what? – orders, desires, which he must recognise, his father's, mother's, educators', or his peers' and mates'.

It is clear that at the beginning, the chances are extremely slight that he will achieve recognition for his own, for his desires, except in the most immediate manner. We don't know anything, at least when we begin, about the precise point of resonance where, in the little subject's way of thinking, the individual is to be found. It is precisely that which makes him so unhappy.

Besides, how would he achieve recognition for his desires? He hasn't got a clue about them.[3] Let's say that we have every reason for believing that he hasn't got a clue about them. That is what our experience of adults shows us, us analysts. The adult, in fact, has to search out his desires. Otherwise he wouldn't need analysis. Which is enough to show us that he is cut off from what's related to his ego, namely from what of himself he is capable of securing recognition for.

I say – *he hasn't got a clue about them*. A vague formula, but analysis teaches us things in stages – which incidentally is the point of following the development of Freud's work. Let us now clarify this formula.

What is ignorance? Certainly it is a dialectical notion, since it is only within the perspective of truth that it is constituted as such. If the subject does not refer himself to the truth, there is no ignorance. If the subject doesn't begin to ask himself the question what is and what is not, there is no reason for there to be a true and a false, nor even, beyond that, reality and appearance.

Careful. We are beginning to get deep into philosophy. Let us say that ignorance is constituted in a polar fashion in relation to the virtual position of a truth to be attained. So it is a state of the subject in so far as he speaks.

In analysis, starting from the point when we implicitly engage the subject in a search for the truth, we are beginning to constitute his ignorance. It is we who create this situation, and hence this ignorance. When we say that the ego hasn't a clue about the subject's desires, it is because the examination of the experience in Freud's work teaches us that. So this particular ignorance is not ignorance pure and simple. It is what is concretely expressed in the process of *Verneinung*, and which, in the subject's static totality, is called misrecognition [*méconnaissance*].

Misrecognition is not ignorance. Misrecognition represents a certain organisation of affirmations and negations, to which the subject is attached. Hence it cannot not be conceived without correlative knowledge. If the subject is capable of misrecognising something, he surely must know what this function has operated upon. There must surely be, behind his misrecognition, a kind of knowledge of what there is to misrecognise.

Take someone who is deluded, who lives in a state of misrecognition of the death of someone close to him. One would be wrong to believe that he confuses him with a living being. He misrecognises, or refuses to recognise, that he is dead. But everything in the way he behaves indicates that he knows that there is something that he doesn't want to recognise.

So what is this misrecognition implied behind the function of the ego, which is essentially that of knowledge? That will be our point of entry into the question of the ego. That is, perhaps, the effective, concrete origin of our experience – we are led into devoting ourselves, in the presence of what is analysable, to an operation employing a mantic, in other words a translation, whose aim is to

[3] *'Il n'en sait rien.'*

loosen up, beyond the subject's language, ambiguous as it is on the plane of knowledge, a truth. To make progress in this register, one must ask oneself what is the knowledge which guides and directs the misrecognition.

In animals, knowledge is a coaptation, an imaginary coaptation. The structuration of the world in the form of the *Umwelt* is accomplished through the projection of a certain number of relations, of *Gestalten*, which organise it, and specify it for each animal.

In fact, the psychologists of animal behaviour, the ethologists, define certain mechanisms of structuration, certain paths of discharge as innate in the animal. Its world is the environment in which it evolves, which weaves and separates out from the indistinctness of reality these paths which are preferred from the outset, to which its behavioural activities are committed.

In man, there is nothing of the kind. The anarchy of his elementary drives is demonstrated by analytic experience. His partial behaviour-patterns, his relation to the object – to the libidinal object – is subject to all sorts of risks. Synthesis miscarries.

So what corresponds in man to this innate knowledge which in the animal is quite simply its guide in life?

Here one should separate out the function which the image of his own body possesses in man – all the while noting that in animals it also assumes enormous importance.

Here I jump on a bit because I presume that we have already gone over these steps together.

You know that the attitude of the infant between six and eighteen months in front of a mirror informs us about the fundamental relation to the image of the human individual. Last year, I was able to show you the infant's jubilation in front of the mirror throughout the whole of this period in a film made by M. Gesell, who, however, had never so much as heard of my mirror stage, and has never asked himself any question of an analytical nature, believe you me. This makes the fact that he has so well isolated the significant moment even more impressive. Certainly, *he* does not himself underline its fundamental feature, which is its exalting character. Because it isn't the appearance of this behaviour at six months which is the most important thing, but rather its dissolution at eighteen months. All of a sudden, the behaviour changes completely, as I showed last year, so as to be nothing more than an appearance, *Erscheinung*, one experience amongst others upon which is exerted the action of control and of instrumental play. All the signs so clearly accentuated in the previous period disappear.

To explain what happens, I will make use of a term which some of your reading must at least have made familiar to you, one of those terms which we use in a confused manner, but which all the same corresponds in us to a mental schema. You know that at the moment of the dissolution of the Oedipus complex, something happens which we call *introjection*.

I beg you not to be hasty in giving this term too definite a meaning. Let us say that it is used when something like a reversal takes place – what was the outside becomes the inside, what was the father becomes the super-ego. Something takes place at the level of this invisible, unthinkable subject, which is never named as such. Is it at the level of the ego, of the id? Somewhere between the two. That's why we call it the super-ego.

So one then embarks on this quasi-mythology for specialists, with which our minds usually busy themselves. After all, these schemata are acceptable, we perpetually inhabit a world whose schemata are acceptable. But if one asked a psychoanalyst – *Do you really believe, then, that the child devours his father, that it gets into his stomach, and that that becomes the super-ego?*

We operate as if all that goes without saying. There are innocuous ways of using the term introjection, which go a long way. Suppose there's an ethnologist who had never heard anyone speak of this godforsaken analysis, and suddenly turns up here to listen to what's going on. He would say – *Very peculiar primitives, these analysands, who bit by bit devour their analysts.*

So look at the treatise of Balthasar Gracián, whom I consider to be a fundamental author – Messrs Nietzsche and La Rochefoucauld are rather insignificant alongside *The Oracle* and *Criticón*. As long as one believes in the communion, there is no reason for not thinking that one eats Christ, and hence his dainty ear-lobe as well. Why not make the communion a communion *à la carte?* Well, that would be fine for those who believe in transubstantiation. But what about the rest of us, the reasonable analysts, the analysts concerned with science? What we discover above Stekel's signature, and that of other authors, is only, when all is said and done, a measured introjection of the analyst and an outside observer could but transpose it on to the mystical plane of communion.

All the same it is a long way from what we really think – in so far as we think. Thank God, we don't, which is our excuse. That is the great mistake that is always made – to imagine that people think what they say.

We do not think, but that is not a reason for not trying to understand why such manifestly senseless words have been uttered.

Let us pick up the thread again. The point at which the mirror stage vanishes is analogous to the moment of see-sawing which occurs at certain points in psychic development. We can observe it in these phenomena of transitivism in which one finds the infant taking as equivalent his own action and that of the other. He says – *François hit me*, whereas it was him who hit François. There's an unstable mirror between the child and his fellow being. How are we to explain these phenomena?

There's a moment when the infant in jubilation assumes a mastery which he has not yet attained, through the mediation of the image of the other. Now, the subject shows himself entirely capable of assuming this mastery within himself. See-saw.

To be sure, he can only do it in a state of empty form. This form, this envelope of mastery, is something so certain that Freud, who came to it along paths quite different from mine, along the paths of the dynamic of libidinal investment, could find no other way of putting it – read *The Ego and the Id*. When Freud speaks of the *ego*, it is not at all a question of something so incisive, so determining, so imperative, that it gets confused with what in academic psychology are called the *higher agencies*. Freud underlines that it must have an intimate connection with the surface of the body. Not the sensitive, sensory, impressionistic surface, but this surface in so far as it is reflected in a form.[4] There is no form which lacks a surface, a form is defined by the surface – by difference in the identical, that is to say the surface.

The image of the other's form is assumed by the subject. Thanks to this surface, situated within the subject, what is introduced into human psychology is this relation between the outside and the inside whereby the subject knows himself, gets acquainted with himself as body.

Besides, it is the sole truly fundamental difference between human and animal psychology. Man knows himself as body, whereas there is, after all, no reason why he should know himself, since he is inside it. The animal is also inside it, but we have no reason for thinking that he represents it to himself.

It is within the see-saw movement, the movement of exchange with the other, that man becomes aware of himself as body, as the empty form of the body. In the same way, everything which is then within him in a pure state of desire, original desire, unconstituted and confused, which finds expression in the wailing of the child – he will learn to recognise it through its inversion in the other. He will learn, because he has not yet learned, in as much as we have not brought communication into play.

This anteriority is not chronological, but logical, and here we are only performing a deduction. It is no less fundamental for all that, since it allows us to distinguish the planes of the symbolic, of the imaginary and of the real, without which one can only make progress in the analytic experience by using expressions bordering on the mystical.

Before desire learns to recognise itself – let us now say the word – through the symbol, it is seen solely in the other.

At first, before language, desire exists solely in the single plane of the imaginary relation of the specular stage, projected, alienated in the other. The tension it provokes is then deprived of an outcome. That is to say that it has no other outcome – Hegel teaches us this – than the destruction of the other.

The subject's desire can only be confirmed in this relation through a competition, through an absolute rivalry with the other, in view of the object towards which it is directed. And each time we get close, in a given subject, to this primitive alienation, the most radical aggression arises – the desire for the disappearance of the other in so far as he supports the subject's desire.

[4] See (1923b) GW XIII 253; Stud III 294; SE XIX 26.

Here we meet up again with what the simple psychologist can observe in the behaviour of subjects. Saint Augustine, for example, notes, in a phrase I've often repeated, this all-consuming, uncontrollable jealousy which the small child feels for his fellow being, usually when the latter is clinging to his mother's breast, that is to say to the object of desire which is for him essential.

This is a key function. The relation of the subject to his *Urbild*, his *Idealich*, through which he enters into the imaginary function and learns to recognise himself as a form, can always see-saw. Each time the subject apprehends himself as form and as ego, each time that he constitutes himself in his status, in his stature, in his static, his desire is projected outside. From whence arises the impossibility of all human coexistence.

But, thank God, the subject inhabits the world of the symbol, that is to say a world of others who speak. That is why his desire is susceptible to the mediation of recognition. Without which every human function would simply exhaust itself in the unspecified wish for the destruction of the other as such.

Inversely, each time that, in the phenomenon of the other, something appears which once again allows the subject to reproject, to recomplete, to *feed*, as Freud says somewhere, the image of the *Idealich*, each time that the jubilant assumption of the mirror stage is retrieved along similar lines, each time that the subject is captivated by one of his fellow beings, well, then the desire revives in the subject. But it is revived verbally.

In other words, each time that the object identifications of the *Idealich* come about, so this phenomenon of *Verliebtheit* occurs, to which I've drawn your attention from the beginning. The difference between *Verliebtheit* and transference is that *Verliebtheit* does not happen automatically – there have to be certain conditions for it, as determined by the subject's development.

In the article on *The Ego and the Id* – which is read so sloppily, because attention is paid solely to the famous, idiotic schema,[5] with the stages, the little bob, the irrelevancies, the gadget he brings in which he calls the super-ego, what got into him, to come up with that, when he must have had other schemata – Freud writes that the ego is constructed out of its successive identifications with the loved objects which allowed it to acquire its form. The ego is constructed like an onion, one could peel it, and discover the successive identifications which have constituted it.[6] He writes in a similar vein in the articles I mentioned to you just now.

The perpetual reversion of desire to form and of form to desire, in other words of consciousness and body, of desire in so far as it is a part of the loved object, in which the subject literally loses himself, and with which he is identified, is the fundamental mechanism around which everything relating to the *ego* turns.

We really must understand that this game is, in its essence, an all-consuming one, and leads to immediate extermination, as soon as the subject is capable of

[5] *'fameux schéma à la con'*.   [6] See (1923b) GW XIII 257; Stud III 297; SE XIX 29.

doing something. And, believe me, he is capable of it very quickly.

The little girl I mentioned earlier, who wasn't particularly awful, found refuge in a country garden, where she became very peaceably absorbed, at an age when she was scarcely walking on her feet, in the application of a good-sized stone to the skull of a little playmate from next door, who was the person around whom she constructed her first identifications. The deed of Cain does not require very great motor sophistication to come to pass in the most spontaneous, I must even say in the most triumphant, of fashions. She had no sense of guilt – *Me break Francis head*. She spoke that with assurance and peace of mind. Nonetheless, I still don't predict a criminal future for her. She simply displayed the most fundamental structure of the human being on the imaginary plane – to destroy the person who is the site of alienation.

What were you trying to say, Granoff?

3

DR GRANOFF: *How then should one understand the masochistic outcome of the mirror stage?*

Give me time. That's what I'm here for, to explain it to you. As soon as you start to call it the masochistic outcome, you won't be able to see the wood for the trees.

The masochistic outcome – I never fold when raised, even if it holds up my argument for a bit – we cannot understand it without the dimension of the symbolic. It is located at the juncture between the imaginary and the symbolic. What, in its structurating form, is generally called primary masochism is located at this juncture. That is also where one must locate what is usually called the death instinct, which is constitutive of the fundamental position of the human subject.

Don't forget that, when Freud described primary masochism, he found its most precise embodiment in the play of a child. He was exactly eighteen months old, that child. For the painful tension engendered by the inevitable fact of the presence and absence of the loved object, he substituted, Freud tells us, a game, in which he himself manipulated the absence and presence in themselves and took pleasure in controlling them. He achieved it by means of a little reel at the end of a thread, which he threw away and pulled back.

Since at this point I am not myself engaged in a dialectic, but am trying to respond to Freud, to clarify the basic elements of his thought, I will emphasise what Freud does not underline, but which is implicit in it – as always, his observations enable one to complete the theorisation. This game with the cotton-reel is accompanied by a vocalisation which from the linguist's point of view is characteristic of the very foundation of language [*langage*], and which is the only way one may grasp the problem of a language [*langue*], namely a simple opposition.

What is important is not that the child said the words *Fort/Da*, which, in his mother tongue, amounts to *far/here* – besides, he pronounced them in an approximate fashion. It is rather that here, right from the beginning, we have a first manifestation of language. In this phonematic opposition, the child transcends, brings on to the symbolic plane, the phenomenon of presence and absence. He renders himself master of the thing, precisely in so far as he destroys it.

Since from time to time we read a bit of Freud's text, for the first time we are going to turn to one of Jacques Lacan's texts. I read it again recently, and I found that it was comprehensible. But it is true that I was in a privileged position.

I wrote⁷ – *These are the games of occultation which Freud, in a flash of genius, revealed to us so that we might recognise in them that the moment when desire becomes human is also the moment when the child is born into language. We can now thereby grasp that that subject does not just in this master his privation in assuming it* – that's what Freud says – *but he also raises his desire to a second power. For his action destroys the object that it causes to appear and disappear in the provocation* – in the true sense of the word, through the voice – *in the anticipating provocation of its absence and its presence. It thus renders negative the field of forces of desire, in order to become its own object for itself. And this object, by quickly taking shape in the symbolic couple of the two elementary exclamations, announces in the subject the diachronic integration of the dichotomy of the phonemes* – that simply means that it is the gate of entry into what already exists, the phonemes making up a language – *whose synchronic structure the existing language offers to his assimilation; for that matter he is already engaged in the system of the concrete discourse of his surroundings, in reproducing more or less approximately in his* Fort *and his* Da *the vocables that he has received from these surroundings* – so, it is from outside that he receives it, the *Fort/Da* – *it is in fact already in his solitude that the desire of the little man has become the desire of an other, of an* alter ego, *who dominates him and whose object of desire is henceforth his own affliction.*

Whether the child now turns to an imaginary or a real partner, he will see him obeying equally the negativity of his discourse and his call – because don't forget that, when he says *Fort*, it is because the object is here, and when he says *Da* the object is absent – *and since his call has the effect of making him slip away, he will search in a banishing affirmation* – very early on he will learn the force of refusal – *the provocation of the return which brings his object back to this desire.*

So you see here that – already before the introduction of the no, of the refusal of the other, when the subject learns to constitute what M. Hyppolite showed us

⁷ E 318–19/103–4.

the other day – the negativation of the simple call, the appearance of a simple pair of symbols when confronted with the contrasted phenomenon of presence and absence, that is to say the introduction of the symbol, reverses the positions. Absence is evoked in presence, and presence in absence.

This seems foolish, and to go without saying. But you still have to say it and reflect on it. Because it is in so far as the symbol allows this inversion, that is to say cancels the existing thing, that it opens up the world of negativity, which constitutes both the discourse of the human subject and the reality of his world in so far as it is human.

Primal masochism should be located around this initial negativation, around this original murder of the thing.

4

Just a word by way of conclusion.

We haven't got as far as I had hoped. Nonetheless, I have been able to get you to grasp the fact that desire, alienated, is perpetually reintegrated anew, reprojecting the *Idealich* outside. It is in this way that desire is verbalised. Here there is a game of see-saw between two inverted relations. The specular relation of the *ego*, which the subject assumes and realises, and projection, which is always ready to be renewed, in the *Idealich*.

The primary imaginary relation provides the fundamental framework for all possible erotism. It is a condition to which the object of Eros as such must be submitted. The object relation must always submit to the narcissistic framework and be inscribed in it. Certainly it transcends it, but in a manner which it is impossible to realise on the imaginary plane. That is what introduces for the subject the necessity of what I would call love.

A creature needs some reference to the beyond of language, to a pact, to a commitment which constitutes him, strictly speaking, as an other, a reference included in the general or, to be more exact, universal system of interhuman symbols. No love can be functionally realisable in the human community, save by means of a specific pact, which, whatever the form it takes, always tends to become isolated off into a specific function, at one and the same time within language and outside of it. That is what we call the function of the sacred, which is beyond the imaginary relation. We will come back to it.

Perhaps I am going a bit too quickly. Bear this in mind, that desire is only ever reintegrated in a verbal form, through symbolic nomination – that is what Freud called the *verbal nucleus* of the *ego*.

Through that, we come to understand analytic technique. In analysis one lets go of all the moorings of the speaking relationship, one eschews courtesy, respect, and dutifulness towards the other. *Free association*, this term is a very poor one for defining what is involved – we try to cut off the moorings of the conversation with the other. From then on, the subject finds himself relatively mobile in relation to this universe of language in which we engage him. While he adjusts his desire in the other's presence, this oscillation of the mirror occurs on the imaginary plane, allowing those imaginary and real things, which are not in the habit of co-existing for the subject, to encounter one another in a relative simultaneity, or in specific contrasts.

Here we find an essentially ambiguous relationship. What do we try to show to the subject in analysis? Where do we try to guide him to in authentic speech? All our attempts and instructions have as their aim, at the moment when we free the subject's discourse, to deprive him of every possible genuine function of speech – so through what paradox do we manage to rediscover it? This paradoxical path consists in extracting speech from language. Given this, what will the full significance of the phenomena which take place in the interval be? Such is the horizon of the question which I am trying to spread out in front of you.

Next time I will show you the results of this experiment in unanchored discourse, the oscillation of the mirror which allows the play of the see-saw between O and O', at the end of properly conducted analyses. Balint gives us a terrific definition of what we usually obtain *at the end of those rare analyses which may be considered to be terminated* – it is he who puts it like that. Balint is one of the rare souls who know what they are saying, and what he depicts as happening is quite alarming, as you will see. Now, what we're talking about here is a properly conducted analysis . . .

Besides this, there is analysis as it is usually practised, which I have shown you to be improper. *Analysis of resistances* – that is a legitimate rubric, but it isn't a practice, as I will show you, implied by the premises of analysis.

5 May 1954

XIV

The fluctuations of the libido

AGGRESSIVITY ≠ AGGRESSION

THE WORD *ELEPHANT*

THE MOORINGS OF SPEECH

TRANSFERENCE AND SUGGESTION

FREUD AND DORA

Let's go back to where we left off. Can someone start off with a question?

DR PUJOL: *You say the desire of the other. Is it the desire which is in the other? Or the desire that I have for the other? For me, they are not the same thing. In what you said last time at the end, it was desire in the other, and which the ego can recapture by destroying the other. But at the same time it is a desire which it has for the other.*

1

Isn't it the original, specular foundation of the relation to the other, in so far as it is rooted in the imaginary?

The first alienation of desire is linked to this concrete phenomenon. If play is of value to the child, it is because it constitutes the plane of reflection in which he sees appearing in the other an activity which anticipates his own, in that it is that little bit more perfected, better mastered, than his own, his ideal form. From that point on the first object has value.

The pre-development of the child already shows that the human object differs fundamentally from the object of the animal. The human object is originally mediated through rivalry, through the exacerbation of the relation to the rival, through the relationship of prestige and physical presence. It is already a relation belonging to the order of alienation since it is initially in the rival that the subject grasps himself as ego [*comme moi*]. The original notion of the totality of the body as ineffable, as lived, the initial outburst of appetite and desire comes about in the human subject via the mediation of a form which he at first sees projected, external to himself, and at first, in his own reflection.

Second point. Man knows that he is a body – although he never perceives it in a complete fashion, since he is inside it, but he knows it. This image is the ring, the bottle-neck, through which the confused bundle of desires and needs must pass in order to be him, that is to say in order to accede to his imaginary structure.

The formula *man's desire is the desire of the other* has to be, like all formulae, used in the right context. It is not valid in only one sense. It is valid on the plane on which we started, that of imaginary captation. But, as I said to you at the end of the last session, it doesn't stop there. Were that not the case, as I pointed out in a mythical way, the only inter-human relation that would be possible would be this mutual and radical intolerance of the coexistence of consciousnesses, as Mr Hegel puts it – every *other* remaining essentially what frustrates the human being, not only of his object, but of the very form of his desire.

Here we have a destructive and fatal relation between human beings. Moreover, it is always there, subjacent. Lots of things have been made to fit within the political myth of the 'struggle for life'.[1] If it was Darwin who wrought it, that was because he came of a nation of privateers, for whom racism was the basic industry.

In fact, everything tells against this thesis of the survival of the fittest species. It is a myth which goes against the facts. Everything goes to prove that there are points of invariability and of equilibria proper to each species, and that species live in a sort of coordinated way, even amongst eaters and eaten. It never gets to the point of radical destruction, which would quite simply lead to the annihilation of the eating species, who would no longer have anything to eat. The strict inter-adjustment which exists in the living world is not brought about by the struggle to the death.

We must gain a deeper appreciation of the notion of aggressivity, which we use in such a brutal fashion. People believe that aggressivity is aggression. It has got absolutely nothing to do with it. At the limit, virtually, aggressivity turns into aggression. But aggression has got nothing to do with the vital reality, it is an existential act linked to an imaginary relation. That is a key which enables one to think through a great many problems anew, and not just our own, in an entirely different register.

I asked you to bring up a question. You did well to raise it. Are you satisfied, however? It seems to me that we got further last time.

In the human subject, desire is realised in the other, by the other – *in* the other,[2] as you put it. That is the second moment, the specular moment, the moment when the subject has integrated the form of the ego. But he is only capable of integrating it after a first swing of the see-saw when he has precisely exchanged his ego for this desire which he sees in the other. From then on, the desire of the other, which is man's desire, enters into the mediation of language. It is in the other, by [*par*] the other, that desire is named. It enters into the symbolic relation of *I* and *you*, in a relation of mutual recognition and transcendence, into the order of a law which is already quite ready to encompass the history of each individual.

---

[1] English in the original.   [2] *'chez l'autre'*, which could be rendered as 'that the other has'.

I talked about the *Fort* and *Da* with you. It is an example of the way in which the child enters naturally into this game. He starts to play with the object, to be more exact, with the simple fact of its presence and its absence. So it is a transformed object, an object with a symbolic function, a devitalised object, already a sign. When the object is there he chases it away, when it isn't there he calls it. Through these first games, the object passes, as if naturally, on to the plane of language. The symbol comes into being and becomes more important than the object.

I've repeated this time and again. If you can't get it into your heads . . .

For the human being the word or the concept is nothing other than the word in its materiality. It is the thing itself.[3] It is not just a shadow, a breath, a virtual illusion of the thing, it is the thing itself.[3]

Think for a moment in the real. It is owing to the fact that the word *elephant* exists in their language, and hence that the elephant enters into their deliberations, that men have been capable of taking, in relation to elephants, even before touching them, decisions which are more far-reaching for these pachyderms than anything else that has happened to them throughout their history – the crossing of a river or the natural decimation of a forest. With nothing more than the word *elephant* and the way in which men use it, propitious or unpropitious things, auspicious or inauspicious things, in any event catastrophic things have happened to elephants long before anyone raised a bow or a gun to them.

Besides, it is clear, all I need do is talk about it, there is no need for them to be here, for them really to be here, thanks to the word *elephant*, and to be more real than the contingent elephant-individuals.

M. HYPPOLITE: *That is Hegelian logic.*

Is it liable to attack on that account?

M. HYPPOLITE: *No, it is not liable to attack. Just now Mannoni said that it was politics.*

O. MANNONI: *That is how human politics comes about. In the broad sense. If men don't act like animals, it is because they exchange their knowledge by means of language. As a consequence, it is politics. The politics of elephants is possible thanks to the word.*

M. HYPPOLITE: *But not only that. The elephant himself is affected. That's the Hegelian logic.*

All this is pre-political. I simply want to help you be clear about the importance of the name.

---

[3] *'la chose même'.*

Here we are simply entering on to the plane of the name. There isn't even any syntax yet. But really, it is quite clear that this syntax originates at the same time. The child, as I have already hinted, articulates taxic[4] elements before phonemes. The *if sometimes* appears all by itself on occasion. To be sure, this does not allow us to decide upon a logical anteriority, because we are only dealing with the emergence, properly speaking, of a phenomenon.

Let me sum up. The projection of the image is invariably succeeded by that of desire. Correlatively, there is a reintrojection of the image and a reintrojection of desire. Swing of the see-saw, a play of mirrors.[5] To be sure, this articulation doesn't happen only once. It is repeated. And, in the course of the cycle, the child reintegrates, and reassumes his desires.

I will now place the accent on the manner in which the symbolic plane connects up with the imaginary plane. In fact, as you see, the desires of the child initially pass via the specular other. That is where they are approved or reproved, accepted or refused. And that is how the child serves his apprenticeship in the symbolic order and accedes to its foundation, which is the law.

This also has its experimental sureties. Susan Isaacs mentions in one of her texts – and the Koehler school also highlights it – that very early on, at an *infans* age still, between eight and twelve months, the child simply does not react in the same way to an accidental knock, to a fall, a brutal mechanical act related to a piece of clumsiness, and, on the other hand, to a slap with a punitive intention. In this instance we can distinguish two entirely different reactions of the child, well before the exteriorised appearance of language. That is because the child already has an initial appreciation of the symbolism of language. Of the symbolism of language and of its function as a pact.

Now we are going to try to grasp what the function of speech is in analysis.

2

Speech is the mill-wheel whereby human desire is ceaselessly mediated by re-entering the system of language.

I emphasise the register of the symbolic order because we must never lose sight of it, although it is most frequently forgotten, although we turn away from it in analysis. Because, in the end, what do we usually talk about? What we go on and on about, often in a confused, scarcely articulate fashion, are the subject's imaginary relations to the construction of his ego. We talk all the time about the dangers, the commotions, the crises that the subject undergoes at the level of his ego's construction. That is why I started by explaining the relation O-O', the imaginary relation to the other.

On its first emergence, the genital object is no less premature than everything

---

[4] '*taxième*' – not to be found in dictionaries, but clearly relating to the 'ordering', the syn*tax*. See p. 54 above.   [5] '*Jeu de bascule, jeu en miroir*'.

else that one observes in the development of the child, and it founders. Except that the libido which is related to the genital object is not on the same level as the primitive libido, whose object is the subject's own image. That is a crucial phenomenon.

It is in so far as the child comes into the world in a structurally premature state, from top to bottom and from end to end, that he has a primitive libidinal relation to his image. The libido here at issue is the one whose resonances you know, which belongs to the order of *Liebe*, of love. It is the grand X of the entire theory of analysis.

You think it's a bit much to call it the grand X? I would have no difficulty showing you the texts, and from the best analysts – because you don't demonstrate something by searching out references in the writings of people who don't know what they are talking about. I will ask someone to read Balint. What is it, this supposedly accomplished genital love? It remains entirely problematical. The question of knowing whether it is a natural process or a cultural achievement has not yet been, so Balint tells us in the text, decided upon by analysts. That is a quite extraordinary ambiguity, which remains at the very heart of everything which is apparently most openly accepted in our circles.

However that may be, if the primitive libido is relative to prematuration, the nature of the second libido is different. It goes beyond, it responds to an initial maturation of desire, if not of organic development. That at least is what we have to assume if the theory is to hold up and if an explanation of our experience is to be given. Here there is a complete change of level in the relation of the human being to the image, to the other. It is the pivotal point of what is called maturation, upon which the entire Oedipal drama turns. It is the instinctual correlative of what, in Oedipus, takes place on the situational plane.

So what happens? In so far as the primitive libido comes to maturity, the relation to the narcissistic image, to use the final edition of the Freudian vocabulary, passes on to the plane of *Verliebtheit*. The captivating narcissistic image, which is alienating on the imaginary plane, finds itself invested with *Verliebtheit*, which phenomenologically speaking pertains to the register of love.

To explain things in this way means that the filling up, even the overflowing, of the primitive gap of the immature subject's libido depends on an internal maturation linked to the organic development of the subject. The pre-genital libido is the sensitive spot, the moment of mirage between Eros and Thanatos, between love and hate. That is the simplest way to render comprehensible the crucial role played by the so-called desexualised libido of the ego in the possibility of reversion, of instantaneous swerving of hate into love, of love into hate. That is the problem whose solution apparently gave Freud the greatest of difficulties – go and take a look in his work, *The Ego and the Id*.[6] In the text I'm discussing, he even seems to turn it into an objection to the theory which postulates as distinct the death instincts and life instincts. I think, on the contrary, that this fits in perfectly – on condition that we have an adequate theory of the imaginary function of the ego.

If you found this too difficult, I can give you an illustration of it right away.

The aggressive reaction to Oedipal rivalry is related to one of these changes of level. At first, the father constitutes one of the most conspicuous of the imaginary figures of the *Idealich*, and as such is invested with a *Verliebtheit* which is clearly isolated, named and described by Freud. It is in so far as a regression of the libidinal position takes place that the subject reaches the Oedipal phase, between three and five years of age. Then the aggressive feeling of rivalry and hate towards the father makes its appearance. A very slight change of libidinal level in relation to a specific threshold transforms love into hate – moreover, it oscillates for a while.

Now let us take up the thread where I left it last time.

I pointed out to you that the imaginary relation definitively provides the frameworks within which the libido will fluctuate. And I left open the question of the symbolic functions in the cure. What use do we make of language and of speech in the cure? In the analytic relation there are two subjects linked by a pact. This pact is set up on levels which are very diverse, even very confused, at the beginning. It isn't, in essence, any the less a pact. And we do everything, via the preliminary rules, to establish this aspect quite firmly at the beginning.

Within this relation, the initial task is to untie the moorings of speech. In his way of speaking, in his style, in his manner of addressing himself to his allocutor,[7] the subject is freed of the obligation, not only to be polite, to be courteous, but even to be coherent. One lets go of a certain number of the moorings of speech. If we think that there is a direct, permanent link between the way in which a subject expresses himself, achieves recognition, and the genuine, experiential dynamic of his relations of desire, we are forced to see that this alone introduces a certain uncoupling, a floating, a possibility of oscillation in the mirror relation to the other.

That is the why and the wherefore of my model.

For the subject, the uncoupling of his relation to the other causes the image of his ego to fluctuate, to shimmer, to oscillate, renders it complete and incomplete. So that he can recognise all the stages of his desire, all the objects which have given consistency, nourishment and body to this image, he has to perceive it in its completeness, to which he has never had access. Through the

---

[6] '*Le Moi et le Soi*'.

[7] '*allocutaire*' – according to *Robert*, a recent neologism in lingustics, meaning the person who receives the message of the speaker.

successive identifications and revivals, the subject must constitute the history of his ego.

The floating, spoken relation with the analyst tends to produce, in the self-image, sufficiently repeated and wide-ranging variations, albeit infinitesimal and limited, for the subject to perceive the captating images which lie at the base of the constitution of his ego.

I have talked about small oscillations. I don't need to enlarge on what makes up their smallness right now. Clearly there is some braking, several occasions when things grind to a halt, which technique teaches us to surmount, to fill in, even, sometimes, to reconstruct.

Such a technique produces in the subject an imaginary mirage relation with himself above and beyond anything everyday experience may procure him. It tends to create artificially, as a mirage, the fundamental condition for any *Verliebtheit*.

It is the breaking of the moorings of speech which allows the subject to see, at least as a sequence, the diverse parts of his image, and to procure what we can call a maximal narcissistic projection. In this respect analysis is still rather rudimentary, since at the beginning it consists, we must admit, in letting everything go, to see what will happen. Things could have been, could be handled differently – it is not inconceivable. The fact remains that it can only tend to produce, at best, narcissistic revelation on the imaginary plane. And that is precisely the fundamental condition of *Verliebtheit*.

Being in love, when it happens, happens in an entirely different way. There has to be a surprising coincidence there, because it doesn't happen with just any partner or with just any image. I have already alluded to the maximal conditions for Werther's love at first sight.

In analysis, the point around which the subject's identification at the level of the narcissistic image focuses is what we call the transference. The transference, not in the dialectical sense which I explained to you in the Dora case for example, but the transference such as it is commonly understood as an imaginary phenomenon.

I am going to show you the moot point to which the handling of the imaginary transference leads. It leads to a point where, in terms of technique, there's a parting of the ways.

Balint is one of the most self-aware of analysts. His description of what he does is extremely lucid. At the same time, it offers one of the best examples of the tendency to which the entire technique of analysis has little by little become committed. He simply says in a more coherent and more open manner what in others is entangled in scholasticism where one cannot see the wood for the trees. So, this is exactly what Balint says – the entire development of analysis consists in the tendency of the subject to rediscover what he calls 'primary love'.[8]

---

[8] English in the original.

The subject feels the need to be the object of love, of care, of affection, of the interest of another object without his having any regard for the needs or even the existence of this object. That is what Balint quite clearly spells out, and I am grateful to him for spelling it out – which doesn't mean that I approve of it.

Locating the entire activity of analysis on such a plane, with no qualification, with no other element, is startling in itself. However this conception is right in the mainstream of that development of analysis which places the accent more and more on relations of dependency, on instinctual satisfactions, even on frustration – which is the same thing.

Given that, how does Balint describe what we observe at the end of analysis, at the end of a completed analysis, one that is truly terminated – by his own admission, that amounts to no more than a quarter. A state of narcissism is induced in the subject, he says quite explicitly, which reaches the point of an unrestrained exaltation of his desires. The subject becomes intoxicated with a quite illusory sensation of absolute mastery over reality, but which he has a need of in the post-termination period. He must free himself of it by progressively putting the nature of things back into place. As for the final session, it never fails to elicit, in both partners, the strongest desire to cry. That is what Balint writes, and this is valuable as extremely precious testimony as to the high point of a whole segment of the analytic movement.

Don't you have the feeling that that is an extremely unsatisfactory game, a Utopian ideal? – which something in us is bound to be disappointed by.

One way of understanding analysis, or to be more precise, of not understanding some of its essential mainsprings, quite certainly must lead to a conception like this one and to results like these.

I will leave this question hanging for the moment. We'll comment on Balint's texts later on.

3

Now I am going to make use of an example which you are already familiar with, since I have gone over it dozens of times – the case of Dora.

What is overlooked in analysis is quite obviously speech as a function of recognition. Speech is that dimension through which the desire of the subject is authentically integrated on to the symbolic plane. It is only once it is formulated, named in the presence of the other, that desire, whatever it is, is recognised in the full sense of the term. It is not a question of the satisfaction of desire, nor of I know not what primary love,[9] but, quite precisely, of the recognition of desire.

Remember what Freud does with Dora. Dora is a hysteric. At that point in time, Freud is not sufficiently aware – he wrote it, re-wrote it, repeated it

---

[9] English in the original.

everywhere in notes, and even in the text – of what he calls the *homosexual component* – which means nothing, but still, it is a label. It comes down to this – he didn't perceive what Dora's position was, that is to say who Dora's object was. He didn't perceive, in a word, that for her O' is occupied by Frau K.

How does Freud conduct his intervention? He tackles Dora on the plane of what he himself calls resistance. What does that mean? I have already explained it to you. It is absolutely obvious that Freud brings into play his *ego*, the conception he himself has of what girls are made for – a girl is made to love boys. If something isn't right, if something torments her, something repressed, in Freud's eyes it can only be this – she loves Herr K. And perhaps, by the same token, she loves Freud a little. Once you look at things this way, it is entirely self-evident.

For reasons which are likewise linked to his erroneous starting point, Freud doesn't even interpret for Dora the signs of her so-called transference to him – which at least spares him from erring here. Quite simply, he talks to her about Herr K. What does that mean? – save that he is speaking to her at the level of the experience of others. It is at this level that the subject has to recognise her desires and get them recognised. And if they are not recognised, they are forbidden as such, and that is indeed where repression begins. So, when Dora is still at the stage at which, if I can put it this way, she has learnt to understand nothing, Freud intervenes at the level of the recognition of desire, at a level which corresponds point by point with the experience of chaotic, even aborted, recognition, which had already made up her life.

Here's Freud, saying to Dora – *You love Herr K.* It so happens, what is more, that he says it clumsily enough for Dora to break off immediately. If he had at that time been initiated into what we call the analysis of resistances, he would have spoon-fed her slowly, he would have started by teaching her which things in her were defences, and, by dint of this, he would in fact have removed an entire set of minor defences. He would thus, strictly speaking, have employed an act of suggestion, that is to say he would have introduced into her *ego* a supplementary element, a supplementary motivation.

Somewhere Freud writes that the transference is just that. And to a certain extent, he is right, it *is* just that. Except you have to know at which level. Because he might have been able to modify Dora's *ego* sufficiently for her to have married Herr K. – a marriage as unhappy as any other marriage.

If, on the contrary, the analysis had been handled properly, what should have happened? What would have happened if, instead of making his speech intervene in O', that is to say putting his own *ego* into play with the aim of remoulding, of modelling that of Dora, Freud had pointed out to her that it was Frau K. whom she loved?

In fact, Freud intervened just when, in the swing of the see-saw, Dora's desire is in O', when she desires Frau K. The whole of Dora's story is to be found in this oscillation whereby she does not know if she loves only herself, her image as magnified in Frau K., or if she desires Frau K. It is precisely because this oscillation occurs again and again, because there is a perpetual see-sawing, that Dora can't get out of it.

It is when the desire is in O' that Freud had to name it, because, at that particular moment, it can be realised. If the intervention is repeated often enough, in a complete enough manner, the *Verliebtheit*, which is misrecognised [*méconnue*], broken, continually refracted, like an image on water which one can never quite keep a hold of, can be realised. At that moment, Dora could have recognised her desire, the object of her love, as being in fact Frau K.

That is an illustration of what I was saying to you just now – if Freud had revealed to Dora that she was in love with Frau K., she would then have actually have been so. Is that the aim of analysis? No, that is only the first stage. And, if you have bungled it, either you wreck the analysis, like Freud did, or you are engaged in something different, an orthopaedics of the *ego*. But you are not doing an analysis.

There is no reason why analysis, conceived of as a process of fleecing, of peeling away the systems of defence, should not work. That is what analysts call *finding an ally in the healthy part of the* ego. In effect they manage to pull over on to their side a half of the subject's *ego*, then a half of a half, etc. And why doesn't it happen like that with the analyst, since that is how the *ego* is constituted in real life? Except, the point is to know whether that is what Freud has taught us.

Freud has shown us that speech must be embodied in the very history of the subject. If the subject has not embodied it, if this speech is muzzled and is to be found latent in the subject's symptoms, do we, or do we not, have to release it, like Sleeping Beauty?

If we don't have to release it, let us then engage in a resistances type of analysis. But that is not what Freud meant when he first started talking about the analysis of resistances. We will see what the legitimate meaning of this expression is.

If Freud had intervened by allowing the subject to name her desire – because he didn't have to name it for her himself – the state of *Verliebtheit* would have been produced in O'. But one should not overlook the fact that the subject would have been very well aware that it was Freud who had given her this object of *Verliebtheit*. The process doesn't come to an end there.

Once this see-saw is accomplished, whereby the subject, at the same time as his speech, reintegrates the analyst's speech, recognition of his desire becomes possible for him. This doesn't happen in one go. Because the subject sees this so precious completeness approaching, he forges ahead into the storm-clouds, as towards a mirage. And it is in as much as he makes a fresh conquest of his *Idealich* that Freud can then take his seat at the level of the *Ichideal*.

We will leave it there for today.

The relationship of the analyst and the *Ichideal* raises the question of the super-ego. Besides, you know that *Ichideal* is sometimes taken to be a synonym for the super-ego.

I chose to climb the mountain. I could have taken the slope that leads down and straightaway asked the question – what is the super-ego? Only now are we coming to it. Because the reply seems to be self-evident, but it is not. Up to now, all the analogies which have been proposed for it, the references to the categorical imperative, to the moral conscience, are extremely confused. But let us leave matters there.

The first phase of analysis is accomplished in the passage from O to O' – from what, in the ego, is unknown to the subject to this image in which he recognises his imaginary investments. Each time, this projected image awakens in the subject the feeling of an exaltation without limit, of a mastery of every outcome, which is already laid down at the beginning of the experience of the mirror. But now, he can name it, because he has since learnt to speak. If he hadn't, he wouldn't be here, in analysis.

That is the first stage. It appears to be strictly analogous to the point where Balint breaks off. What is this narcissism without restraint, this exaltation of desires? – if not the point Dora could have reached. Are we going to leave her there, in this contemplation? At some point in the case-history, we see her lost deep in contemplation of this painting – the image of the Madonna, before which a man and a woman stand in adoration.

How should we conceive of the rest of the process? To take the next step, we will have to get to the bottom of the function of the *Idealich*, whose place you see the analyst occupy for a while, in so far as he intervenes in the right position, at the right time, at the right place.

So the next chapter will bear on the handling of the transference. I am leaving it open.

12 May 1954

XV

The nucleus of repression

To the extent that we are making any progress this year, which is beginning to take on the form of a year as it wanes, I find it satisfying to have received confirmation, through the questions which have been put to me, that some of you are beginning to understand that what I am in the process of teaching you involves the whole of psychoanalysis, involves the very meaning of your action. I am thinking of those of you who have understood that one can only propose a technical rule given the meaning of analysis.

Everything isn't as clear as it could be as yet, in what I am spelling out to you little by little. But have no doubt that nothing less is at stake here than taking a fundamental stand on the nature of psychoanalysis, which will later animate your activity, since it transforms your understanding of the existential position of the analytic experience and its ends.

1

Last time, I tried to give you a picture of that process which we are always bringing, in an enigmatic manner, into analysis, which in English is called working-through. In French, it is translated, not without some difficulty, by *élaboration*, or *travail*. It is this dimension, at first glance mysterious, which requires us to go over our work with our patient hundreds of times,[1] so that some progress, some subjective breakthroughs, come about.

What is embodied in the mill-wheel's turning, as expressed by these two arrows, from O to O', and from O' to O, in this game of coming and going, is the shimmering of the before and the beyond of the mirror, which the subject's image goes through. The point is to bring it, in the course of the analysis, to its completion. At the same time, the subject reintegrates his desire. And each time

---

[1] '*qu'il nous faut avec le patient cent fois sur le métier remettre notre ouvrage*' – a quotation from Boileau, *L'Art Poetique*, Chant I.

the completion of this image is brought a step nearer, the subject sees his desire suddenly emerging within him in the form of a particularly heightened tension. The completion of a single cycle does not bring this movement to a halt. There are as many cycles as it takes for the different phases of imaginary, narcissistic, specular identification – the three adjectives are equivalent when it comes to representing these matters in theory – to give an image in focus.

That does not exhaust the phenomenon, since in any case, nothing can be conceived of without the intervention of this third element, which I introduced last time – the speech of the subject.

That is when desire is sensed by the subject – which cannot happen without the conjunction of speech. And it is a moment of pure anxiety, and nothing but. Desire emerges in a confrontation with the image. Once this image which had been rendered incomplete is completed, once the imaginary facet which was non-integrated, suppressed, repressed, looms up, anxiety then makes its appearance. That is the fertile moment.

Some authors have wanted to specify it. Strachey tried to delimit what he calls the transference-interpretation, more precisely the mutative interpretation. See volume XV of the *International Journal of Psycho-analysis*, for 1934, numbers 2 and 3. In fact, he emphasises that interpretation is only capable of having positive effect at a precise point in time in the analysis. Such moments are not frequent, and cannot be grasped in just an approximate manner. It is neither around, nor roundabout, neither before, nor after, but at the exact moment when what is close to bursting open in the imaginary is then also present in the verbal relation with the analyst, that the interpretation must be given so that its decisive value, its mutative function, can have an effect.

What does that mean? – save that that is the moment when the imaginary and the real of the analytic situation are confused. That is what I am trying to explain to you. The subject's desire is there, in the situation, both present and inexpressible. To name it, so Strachey says, is what the analyst's intervention must confine itself to. It is the only occasion when his word should be added to that which the patient foments in the course of his long monologue, a mill-wheel of speech the movement of whose arrows on the schema would be a good enough justification for the metaphor.

To illustrate it, last time I reminded you of the function of Freud's interpretations in the Dora case, the sense in which they were inadequate and the blockage which resulted from them, the mental wall. That was only a first stage in the Freudian discovery. One must follow it as it moves on. Did some of you come, two years ago, to my commentary on the *Wolfman?* . . . not many. I would like one of them – Father Beirnaert? – to treat himself to another reading of this text of Freud's. You will see how helpful the schema I've given you is.

The Wolfman comes across as having what we would today call a character neurosis, or maybe a narcissistic neurosis. As such, this neurosis offers considerable resistance to treatment. Freud chose, quite deliberately, to give us an exposition of a part of it. In fact, the infantile neurosis – that is the title of the *Wolfman* in the German edition – was then of great use to him for raising certain theoretical questions concerning the function of trauma.

So we are in 1913, hence in the middle of the years 1910 to 1920, which are the object of our commentary this year.

The *Wolfman* is indispensable for understanding what Freud is working out at that particular point in time, namely the theory of trauma, unsettled then by Jung's persistent comments. There are a great many things in this study, not to be found anywhere else in Freud, certainly not in his purely theoretical writings – here we find essential complements to his theory of repression.

Firstly, I will remind you that repression is, in the Wolfman's case, bound up with a traumatic experience, that of the spectacle of his parents copulating in an *a tergo* position. The patient was never able to evoke, to remember, this scene directly, and it is reconstructed by Freud. The copulatory position could only be restored on the basis of the traumatic consequence it had on the actual behaviour of the subject.

To be sure, we have here patient historical reconstructions, which are remarkably surprising. Freud here proceeds as if with monuments, with archival documents, employing textual criticism and exegesis. If, at a certain point, an element comes to light in complex guise, it is certain that the point at which it appears in a less elaborated form is prior to it. In this way Freud manages to determine the date of the copulation in question. He fixes it unhesitatingly, with an absolute rigour, at a date defined by $n + \frac{1}{2}$ years. Now n cannot be higher than 1, because it could not have happened at two and a half for reasons which must be conceded on account of the consequences for the young subject of this spectacular revelation. It is not impossible that it happened at six months, but Freud sets this date aside because it appeared to him, given his thinking at that time, a trifle violent. I would just like to remark in passing that he does not exclude the possibility of it having occurred at six months. And, in truth neither do I. I must say that I'm rather inclined to think that it's the correct date, rather than at one and a half. I might tell you why later on.

Let us get back to the essentials. The traumatic force of the imaginary break-in produced by this spectacle is under no circumstances to be located immediately after the event. The scene acquires traumatic significance for the subject between the ages of three years three months and four years. We know the exact date because the subject was born on Christmas Day, a coincidence which is, furthermore, decisive for his history. It is in anticipation of the events of Christmas, for him as for all children invariably accompanied by the arrival of presents coming to him from a descending being, that for the first time he has the anxiety-dream, the pivot of this case-history. This anxiety-dream is the first manifestation of the traumatic significance of what a moment ago I called the imaginary break-in. To borrow a term from the theory of instincts such as it has been developed in recent times, in a manner that is certainly more meticulous than in Freud's day, especially for birds, it is the *Prägung* – this term possesses resonances of *striking*, striking a coin – the *Prägung* of the originating traumatic event.[2]

This *Prägung* – Freud explains in the most clearcut fashion – is at first located in a non-repressed unconscious – we will render this approximate expression more precise later. Let us say that the *Prägung* has not been integrated into the verbalised system of the subject, that it has not even reached verbalisation, and not even, one might say, attained signification. This *Prägung*, strictly limited to the domain of the imaginary, re-emerges in the course of the subject's progress into a symbolic world which is more and more organised. That is what Freud is explaining in telling us the subject's entire history, as it then unfolds out of his statements, between *x* the original moment and the age of four, where he locates the repression.

Repression only occurs to the extent that the events of the early years of the subject are historically sufficiently turbulent. I cannot tell you the whole story - his seduction by his older sister, who is more virile than he is, the object both of rivalry and of identification – his drawing back and his refusal in the face of this seduction, for which, at that early age, he had neither the resources nor the elements – then his attempt to approach and actively seduce the governess,[3] the famous Nania, a seduction that is normatively directed along the line of a primary genital Oedipal development, but whose opening move is warped because of the sister's initial captivating seduction. From the terrain on which he was engaged, the subject is thus forced back towards the sado-masochistic positions, whose register and ensemble of elements Freud supplies us with.

Now I will show you two signposts.

Firstly, all the outcomes, the most favourable outcomes which can be hoped for, stem from the subject's introduction to the symbolic dialectic. Furthermore, the symbolic world will not cease to exert a determining attraction throughout the entire development of this subject since, as you know, later on there will be occasions when the solution found is a happy one, in so far as the elements that are educative in the strict sense of the word enter into his life. The whole of the dialectic of rivalry with the father, which renders him passive, will become, at a given point in time, quite relaxed, through the intervention of prestigious individuals, this or that teacher, or, earlier on, through the introduction of the religious register. What Freud shows us then is the following – it is in as much

---

[2] Translated in ethological works in English as 'imprinting'. Lorenz and others also employ the term '*Objektbindung*' (translated as 'object-fixation').

[3] '*gouvernante*', usually the term for 'governess'. See (1918b) GW XII 42–5; Stud VIII 139–41; SE XVII 19–21 and GW XII 48; Stud VIII 144; SE XVII 24.

as the subjective drama is integrated into a myth which has an extended, almost universal human value, that the subject brings himself into being.

On the other hand, what happens in this period between three years one month and four years? – save that the subject learns how to integrate the events of his life into a law, into a field of symbolic significations, into a human field which universalises significations. That is why, at least at this point in time, this *infantile neurosis* is exactly the same thing as a psychoanalysis. It plays the same role as a psychoanalysis, namely it accomplishes the reintegration of the past, and it brings into the play of symbols the *Prägung* itself, which here is only attained through an effect that is retroactive, *nachträglich*, as Freud puts it.

To the extent that, in the course of events, it becomes integrated in the form of a symbol, in history, the stamp comes very close to emerging. Then, when it does in fact emerge exactly two and a half years after having entered into the life of the subject – and perhaps, given what I've said, three and a half years later – on the imaginary plane it takes on its status as trauma, as a result of the form of the first symbolic integration, a form that was especially shocking for the subject.

The trauma, in so far as it has a repressing action, intervenes *after the fact* [*après coup*], *nachträglich*. At this specific moment, something of the subject's becomes detached in the very symbolic world that he is engaged in integrating. From then on, it will no longer be something belonging to the subject. The subject will no longer speak it, will no longer integrate it. Nevertheless, it will remain there, somewhere, spoken, if one can put it this way, by something the subject does not control.

In other words, there is no essential difference between this moment in the analysis which I have described to you, and the intermediary moment, between the stamp and the symbolic repression.

There is just one difference, which is that at that particular moment, there is no one there to give him his cue. Repression begins, having constituted its original nucleus. Now there is a central point around which symptoms, successive repressions, and by the same token – since repression and the return of the repressed are the same thing – the return of the repressed will later be organised.

2

Aren't you amazed that the return of the repressed and repression are the same thing?

DR X: *Oh, nothing amazes me any longer.*

It amazes some people. Though X tells us that, as far as he's concerned, nothing amazes him any more.

O. MANNONI: *That gets rid of the notion one sometimes comes across of successful repression.*

No, it doesn't get rid of it. To show you this, we would have to go into the entire dialectic of forgetting. Every successful symbolic integration involves a sort of normal forgetting. But that would take us a very long way into the Freudian dialectic.

O. MANNONI: *A forgetting without the return of the repressed, then?*

Yes, without the return of the repressed. Integration into history evidently brings with it the forgetting of an entire world of shadows which are not transposed into symbolic existence. And if this symbolic existence is successful and is fully taken on by the subject, it leaves no weight behind it. One would then have to bring in Heideggerian notions. In every entry of being into its habitation in words, there's a margin of forgetting, a λήθη[4] complementary to every ἀλήθεια.[5]

M. HYPPOLITE: *It is the word* successful *in Mannoni's formula that I don't understand.*

It is a therapist's expression. Successful repression is essential.

M. HYPPOLITE: Successful *could mean the most profound forgetting.*

That is what I am talking about.

M. HYPPOLITE: *So this* successful *means, in certain respects, total failure. To arrive at the integration of being, man must forget the essential. This* successful *is a failure. Heidegger would not accept the word* successful. *You can only say* successful *from the therapist's point of view.*

It is a therapist's point of view. Nonetheless, the margin of error there is to be found in every realisation of being is always, it seems, reserved by Heidegger to a sort of fundamental λήθη, or shadow of the truth.

M. HYPPOLITE: *The therapist's success – nothing could be worse for Heidegger. It is the forgetting of the forgetting. Heideggerian authenticity consists in not being engulfed by the forgetting of the forgetting.*

Yes, because Heidegger made a sort of philosophical law out of this return to the sources of being.

Let us take up the question again. To what extent can a forgetting of the forgetting be successful? To what extent must every analysis open out on to a resurgence into being? Or on to a certain recoil into being, opted for by the subject with regard to his own destiny? Since I always jump at any opportunity

---

[4] Forgetting, forgetfulness.   [5] Truth.

that comes my way, I am going to forestall somewhat those questions which might be raised. If the subject starts off from point O, the point of confusion and innocence, where is the dialectic of the symbolic reintegration of desire going to lead? Is it enough simply for the subject to name his desires, for him to have permission to name them, for the analysis to be terminated? That is the question that I may perhaps raise at the end of this session. You will also see that I will not leave it there.

At the end, right at the end of analysis, after having gone through a specific number of circuits and brought about the complete integration of his history, will the subject still be at O? or else, a bit further over there, towards A?[6] In other words, will a part of the subject still remain on the level of this sticking-point which we call his *ego*? Does the analysis only deal with what we consider to be a given, namely the subject's *ego*, the internal structure which could be improved by exercise?

That is how someone like Balint and one whole trend of analysis have come to think that, either the *ego* is strong, or else it is weak. And if it is weak, they are obliged, by the internal logic of their position, to think it has to be strengthened. As soon as one holds the *ego* to be the straightforward exercising of self-mastery by the subject, the high point of the hierarchy of the nervous functions, one is completely committed to the task of teaching it to be strong. From whence the notion of education through practice, through learning,[7] even, as a mind as clear-headed as Balint's has written, through performance.

With respect to the strengthening of the *ego* in the course of the analysis, Balint goes so far as to comment on the extent to which the ego is perfectible. Only a few years ago, he says, what was considered in any given exercise or sport to be the world record is now just about good enough to qualify an athlete as average. So the human ego, when it is made to compete with itself, accomplishes more and more extraordinary feats. Considering which, one is led to deduce – we have no proof of it, and for good reasons – that an exercise such as analysis could structure the ego, could introduce into its functions a training which will strengthen it and will render it capable of tolerating a greater amount of excitation.

But what could render analysis – a verbal game – fit for whatever goes on in this type of training?

The fundamental fact which analysis reveals to us and which I am in the process of teaching you, is that the *ego* is an imaginary function. If you blind yourself to this fact, you'll find yourself in step with the line that the whole, or nearly the whole of analysis, has taken.

If the *ego* is an imaginary function, it is not to be confused with the subject.

[6] The diagram in the French edition, reproduced here on p. 139, does not have A; the very similar diagram on E 674 names the plane mirror A.   [7] English in the original.

What do we call a subject? Quite precisely, what, in the development of objectivation, is outside of the object.

One might say that the ideal of science is to reduce the object to what can be closed and fastened within a system of interacting forces. In the end, the object is only ever like that for science. and there is only ever one subject – the scientist who considers the whole, and hopes one day to reduce everything to a determinate play of symbols encompassing all the interactions between objects. Except, when it comes to organised beings, the scientist finds himself obliged after all always to imply that action exists. Certainly one can always consider an organised being as an object, but as long as one grants it the status of organism, one retains, if only implicitly, the idea that it is a subject.

During analysis, for example of a piece of instinctual behaviour, one can ignore the subjective position for a while. But this position can under no circumstances be ignored when it comes to the speaking subject. We are necessarily obliged to admit the speaking subject as subject. But why? For one simple reason – because he can lie. That is, he is distinct from what he says.

Well, the dimension of the speaking subject, of the speaking subject *qua* deceiver, is what Freud uncovered for us in the unconscious.

In science, the subject is only sustained, in the end, on the plane of consciousness, since the subject *x* in science is in fact the scientist. It is whoever possesses the system of the science that sustains the dimension of the subject. He is the subject, in so far as he is the reflection, the mirror, the support of the objectal world. In contrast, Freud shows us that in the human subject there is something which speaks, which speaks in the full sense of the word, that is to say something which knowingly lies, and without the contribution of consciousness. That restores – in the obvious, strict, experimental sense of the term – the dimension of the subject.

By the same token, this dimension is no longer confused with the *ego*. The ego is deprived of its absolute position in the subject. The ego acquires the status of a mirage, as the residue, it is only one element in the objectal relations of the subject.

Are you with me?

That is why I took up on the way what Mannoni was putting forward. The question is indeed whether, in analysis, it is solely a matter of enlarging the correlative objectivations of the *ego*, when considered as a centre that is completely given, but which is more or less restricted – that is how Miss Anna Freud puts it. When Freud writes – *Where id was, there ego must be* – must we take it to mean that the task is to enlarge the field of consciousness? Or is it a matter of displacement? *Where id was, there . . .* – don't think that it is there.[8] It

---

[8] The word '*là*', here translated as 'there', is to be found in the standard French translation of Freud's dictum, '*Wo Es war, soll Ich werden*' – '*Là où le ça était, l'ego doit être.*' See Freud (1933a) SE XXII 80, which gives 'Where id was, there ego shall be.' The 'shall' [*soll*] has been corrected to 'must', but 'there' (which is not to be found in the German) has been retained to correspond to the French '*là*'. See the more extensive discussion in E 128–9, 299–300.

is in a great many places. For example, in my schema, the subject is looking at the mirror game in A. For a moment, let us identify the id with the subject. Are we to understand that there where the id was, in A, the *ego* must be? That the *ego* must move to A and, at the end of the most refined of ideal analyses, no longer be there at all?

That is quite conceivable, since everything pertaining to the *ego* must be realised in what the subject recognises as himself. That, in any case, is the question I am putting to you. I hope that this is sufficient indication of the direction I am taking. I haven't exhausted it.

However that may be, given the point I've reached with my remarks about the *Wolfman*, I think that you see the usefulness of the schema. In conformity with the best analytic traditions, it unifies the original formation of the symptom, the signification of repression itself, with what takes place in the analytic process, considered, at least in its beginnings, as a dialectical process.

With this simple beginning, I will leave it up to Reverend Father Beirnaert to take his time in once again reading the case-history of the *Wolfman*, to give us someday a résumé, indeed to highlight some questions when he has drawn together the elements that I have brought out for you in this text.

3

Since we will leave the subject of the *Wolfman* there, I want to make a little further progress towards understanding what is the therapeutic procedure, the source of therapeutic action, in analysis. What, precisely, does the naming, the recognition of desire signify, at the point where it is arrived at, in O? Does everything have to stop there? Or is it necessary to go a step further?

I am going to try and get you to understand the meaning of this question.

There is an absolutely essential function in the process of the symbolic integration of his history by the subject, a function in relation to which, as everyone has long noticed, the analyst occupies a significant position. This function is called the super-ego. It is impossible to understand anything about it if you don't relate it to its origins. The super-ego at first appeared in the history of Freudian theory in the form of the censorship. I could just as well a moment ago have directly illustrated the remark I made you by saying that, from the beginning, we are placed, with the symptom and just as much with all of the unconscious functions of daily life, in the dimension of speech. The task of censorship is to deceive through lying, and it is not for nothing that Freud chose the term of censorship. Here we are dealing with an agency which splits the subject's symbolic world, cuts it in two, into one accessible part, which is recognised, and one inaccessible, forbidden part. It is this idea that we rediscover, hardly transformed, with almost the same emphasis, in the register of the super-ego.

Straightaway I am going to emphasise what brings the idea of the super-ego, one of whose facets I am reminding you of, into opposition with the idea we commonly make use of.

In general, the super-ego is always thought of within the register of a tension, and this tension is within a hair of being reduced down to purely instinctual principles, like primary masochism for example. Such a conception is not alien to Freud. Freud goes even further. In the article *Das Ich und das Es*, he maintains that the more the subject suppresses his instincts, that is to say, if you wish, the more moral his conduct is, and the more the super-ego exacerbates its pressure, the more severe, demanding and imperious it becomes.[9] That clinical observation is not universally true. But Freud here lets himself get carried away by his object, which is neurosis. He goes so far as to consider the super-ego to be one of these toxic products which, through their organic activity, would release other toxic substances which, under given conditions, would bring their reproductive cycle to an end. That is pushing things very far. But you will rediscover this idea implicit within a whole conception of the super-ego prevalent in analysis.

As a counter to this conception, the following may be apt. In a general fashion, the unconscious is, in the subject, a schism of the symbolic system, a limitation, an alienation induced by the symbolic system. The super-ego is an analogous schism, which is produced in the symbolic system integrated by the subject. This symbolic world is not limited to the subject, because it is realised in a language which is the common language, the universal symbolic system, in so far as it establishes its empire over a specific community to which the subject belongs. The super-ego is this schism as it occurs for the subject – but not only for him – in his relations with what we will call the law.

I am going to illustrate this with an example, because what you are taught in analysis familiarises you so little with this register, that you are going to think that I am overstepping its limits. Nothing of the kind.

It concerns one of my patients. He had already been in analysis with someone else before coming to me. He had quite peculiar symptoms connected with the use of the hand, an organ of some significance for those entertaining activities on which analysis has shed so much light. An analysis conducted along classical lines did its utmost, without success, to organise, at any cost, his various symptoms around, obviously, infantile masturbation, and the prohibitions and the repressions that it would have brought with it in his environment. These prohibitions did exist, since they still exist. Unfortunately, it explained nothing, nor did it resolve anything.

This subject was – I can't dissimulate this element of his history, although it is always a delicate matter to bring particular cases into teaching – of the Islamic religion. But one of the most striking elements of the story of his subjective

[9] Freud (1923b) GW XIII 284; Stud III 320; SE XIX 54.

development was his estrangement from, his aversion to the Koranic law. Now, this law is something infinitely more complete than we can imagine, in our cultural sphere, defined as it is by *Render unto Caesar the things which be Caesar's, and unto God the things which be God's*. In the Islamic sphere, on the contrary, the law has a totalitarian character which will on no account permit the isolation of the juridical from the religious plane.

So this subject manifested a failure to recognise [*méconnaissance*] the Koranic law. In a subject who belonged, through his ancestry, his functions, his future, to this cultural sphere, this was something which struck me in passing, in line with the idea, which I believe to be sound enough, that one should not fail to recognise the symbolic appertinances of a subject. This put us hot on the trail of what was at issue here.

In fact, the Koranic law decrees the following, with respect to the person who is found guilty of theft – *The hand will be cut off*.

Now, the subject had, in his childhood, been caught up in a whirlwind both private and public, which amounted to the following, that he had heard it said – and it was quite a scene, his father being a civil servant and having lost his position – that his father was a thief and must therefore have his hand cut off.

To be sure, for a long time now the prescription has not been put into effect – no more than that belonging to the laws of Manu,[10] *whosoever has committed incest with his mother must tear off his genitals and, carrying them in his hand, will go towards the West*. But it does not remain any the less inscribed in the symbolic order which founds interhuman relations, and which is called the law.

This proposition was for this subject thus isolated off from the rest of the law in a privileged manner. And it became lodged in his symptoms. All the other symbolic references of my patient, all these primitive arcana around which such a subject finds his most fundamental relations to the universe of the symbol organised, were forfeited on account of the particular emphasis that this prescription had acquired for him. For him it lies at the centre of an entire series of inadmissible, conflictual, symptomatic unconscious expressions, linked to this primal childhood experience.

In the course of analysis, as I have pointed out to you, it is when the traumatic elements – grounded in an image which has never been integrated – draw near that holes, points of fracture appear in the unification, the synthesis, of the subject's history. I have pointed out how it is in starting from these holes that the subject can realign himself within the different symbolic determinations which make him a subject with a history. Well, in the same way, for every human being, everything personal which can happen to him is located in the relation to the law to which he is bound. His history is unified by the law, by his symbolic universe, which is not the same for everyone.

---

[10] Manu is the first man and giver of laws in Hindu mythology.

Tradition and language diversify the reference to the subject. A discordant statement, unknown in law, a statement pushed into the foreground by a traumatic event, which reduces the law down to a point with an inadmissible, unintegrable character – this blind, repetitive agency is what we usually define in the term super-ego.

I hope that this little case will have been striking enough to give you an idea of a dimension analysts are not often to be found reflecting upon, but which they cannot manage to ignore entirely. Every analyst, in fact, is a witness to the fact that no resolution of an analysis is possible, whatever the diversity, the iridescence of the archaic events that it brings into play, if it does not end by knotting itself around this legal, legalising coordinate, which is called the Oedipus complex.

The Oedipus complex is so essential to the very dimension of the analytic experience that its pre-eminence is revealed right from the start of Freud's work and is sustained right up to its end. That is because the Oedipus complex occupies a privileged position, in the present state of Western civilization.

Just now I alluded to the division into several planes of the register of the law in our cultural sphere. God knows that the multiplicity of planes does not make life very easy for the individual, because conflicts ceaselessly are bringing them into opposition. In as much as the different languages of a civilisation gain in complexity, its tie to the most primitive forms of the law comes down to this essential point – this is Freudian theory at its purest – which is the Oedipus complex. That is what, in the life of the individual, resonates with the register of the law, as one discovers in the neuroses. It is the most uniform point of intersection, the minimum requirement.

That is not to say that it is the only one, nor that it would amount to straying outside of the field of psychoanalysis to refer to the totality of the symbolic world of the subject, which can be extraordinarily complex, even antinomic, and to his own personal position, which is a function of his place in society, of his future, of his projects, in the existential sense of the term, of the education and tradition which is his.

We are in no way relieved of the problems raised by the relations of the subject's desire – which emerges there, at point O – to the totality of the symbolic system in which the subject is called, in the full sense of the term, to take up his place. The fact that the structure of the Oedipus complex is an ubiquitous requirement does not exempt us, for all that, from perceiving that other structures belonging to the same level, to the plane of the law, can, in a given case, play just as decisive a role. That is what we just now encountered in this last clinical case.

Once the number of cycles necessary for the subject's objects to appear have been accomplished, and his imaginary history is completed, once the successive tensed-up, suspended, anxiety-provoking desires of the subject are named and reintegrated, all is not, for all that, brought to term. What was initially there, in O, then here, in O', then again in O, has to be referred to the completed system of symbols. The very outcome of the analysis requires it.

Where should this adjournment come to a stop? Do we have to extend analytic intervention to the point of becoming one of those fundamental dialogues on justice and courage, in the great dialectical tradition?

That is a question. It is not easy to answer, because in truth, modern man has become singularly unused to broaching these grand themes. He prefers to resolve things in terms of conduct, of adaptation, of group morale and other twaddle. From whence the gravity of the problem posed by the analyst's education in humanity.

That is where I will leave you today.

19 May 1954

MICHAEL BALINT'S
BLIND ALLEYS

XVI

Preliminary interventions on Balint

THEORY OF LOVE

DEFINITION OF CHARACTER

OBJECTIVATION

It's all very fine saying that theory and technique are the same thing. Do let us get something out of it. Let us try and understand each individual's technique, when his theoretical ideas are sufficiently articulated to allow us to make some assumptions about it.

Except, the theoretical ideas pushed to the fore by some minds, even fine minds, are not on that account usable. Those people who work with concepts are not always clearly aware of what they are saying. In contrast, in certain cases, one has a strong feeling that the concepts truly express something of the experience. and that is the case with our friend Michael Balint.

I wanted to seek the support of someone who is, in lots of ways, close, even congenial to us, and who without question has an orientation which converges with some of the demands we are here making explicit as to what the intersubjective relation in analysis must be. At the same time, the way in which he expresses himself gives us the feeling that he has come under the sway of the dominant mode of thought.

In order to render palpable what I will call a certain contemporary deviationism in relation to the fundamental analytic experience which is my constant point of reference, it would be all too easy to pick out crude, even obviously crazy people. It is when they are subtle, and when they attest less to a clearcut aberration than to a specific way of missing the point, that one should take them up.

This is how I wanted to put to the test what has to be the point of any teaching, namely that one follows it. I have entrusted this to Granoff, who, as he has made crystal-clear, is unquestionably to be numbered as one of those most interested in the path along which I am trying to lead you, so that he may communicate to us today what he has been able to gather from his reading of Balint's book, *Primary Love and Psycho-analytic Technique*.

According to what he himself says, Balint started his career around about 1920. This book is a collection of articles written between 1930 and 1950. It is a very interesting book, extremely pleasurable to read, clear, lucid, often bold, full of humour. It will be in all your interests to get to grips with it – when you have the time, because it is holiday reading, like a prize at the end of term. Treat yourselves to a copy, because our *Société* is not rich enough this year to give you all one.

1

Interventions in the course of Dr Granoff's presentation.

Two modalities of love are being opposed. First of all there is the pregenital mode. An entire article, entitled 'On love and hate', has as its axis the notion that what is involved is a love in which the object possesses absolutely no interests of its own. Absolute unselfishness[1] – the subject does not recognise any of its demands, any of its own needs. Everything which is good for me is right for you – that is the implicit formula which the subject's behaviour expresses. Primary love,[2] the later stage, is always characterised as the rejection of any kind of reality, the refusal to recognise the partner's requirements. That is what contrasts it to genital love.[2] As you'll see, I have massive objections to this conception; my objections will show how it literally dissipates everything which analysis has contributed.

You are entirely right, Granoff, to point out that Balint's conception is centred on a theory of love which is more than just normative, or moralising. Quite rightly, you highlight that it leads to this question – is what we consider to be normal a natural state or is it a cultural end-product, something artificial, indeed something which he calls a happy chance?[3] And, further on, he asks – what should we call health, when analysis is terminated? Is the analytic cure a natural or an artificial process? Are there processes in the mind which, if they are not halted, disturbed, will lead development towards equilibrium? Or, on the contrary, is health a happy chance, an improbable event? About that, Balint remarks, the ambiguity of the analytic chorus is complete. Which may lead one to think that the question has not been put very clearly.
. . . .
You are not bringing out clearly enough the Balintian definition of character, which is, however, extremely interesting.

Character controls man's relations to his objects. Character always signifies a more or less extensive limitation of the possibilities of love and of hatred. So character signifies limitation of the capacity for love and enjoyment.[4] The dimension of enjoyment [*joie*], which is extremely extensive, goes well beyond

---

[1] English in the original. See Alice Balint, 'Love for the mother and mother love', pp. 110–11.
[2] English in the original.   [3] English in the original.
[4] Last four words in English in the original.

the category of *jouissance* in a way that one should spell out. Enjoyment [*joie*] implies a subjective plenitude which well deserves being expanded on.[5]

If the article didn't date from 1932, I would say that it is responsible for the promulgation of a certain puritanical moral ideal. In Hungary there are Protestant historical traditions, which have precise historical parallels with the history of Protestantism in England. Hence, we see a peculiar convergence of the thought of this student of Ferenczi's, guided by his master along trails which I am going to make you follow today, with his destiny, which has eventually integrated him so well into the English community.

Character is for him preferable in its strong form, the one which brings with it all its limitations. The weak character[6] is someone who lets himself be overrun. There's no need to add that this results in complete ambiguity between what he calls character analysis, and, something he feels no qualms in venturing out in the same context, logical character. He does not seem to see that these are completely different characters – on the one hand, character is the reaction to the libidinal development of the subject, the web within which this development is caught, and limited, on the other, there are innate elements which, for the characterologists, divide individuals into classes, which are constitutional.

Balint thinks that analytic experience will tell us more about this. I myself have pretty well been brought round to think so too, but on condition that one realises that analysis can profoundly modify character.

. . . .

Quite rightly you highlight Balint's remark to the effect that, beginning in 1938–40, an entire vocabulary disappeared from analytical articles, while the orientation which centres psychoanalysis upon object relations was being consolidated. This vocabulary is the one whose connotation, Balint says, is *too libidinal* – the term *sadistic*, for example, disappears.

This confession is very revealing. That really is what's going on, the growing puritanism of the analytic atmosphere.

. . . .

Balint fully realises that there must be something that exists between two subjects. Since he is completely lacking in the conceptual apparatus necessary for introducing the intersubjective relation, he is led to speak of a two-body psychology.[7] He thinks that is the way out of one-body psychology.[7] But it is clear that two-body psychology is still a relation of object to object.

Theoretically, this would not be serious, if it did not have technical consequences in the concrete, therapeutic exchange with the subject. The point is that in actual fact it is not a relation of object to object. Balint is, as you put it so well just now, *entangled in a dual relation, and denying it.* We won't be

---

[5] Lacan here counterposes the notoriously untranslateable *jouissance* (bliss, pleasure, enjoyment, orgasm) and 'joy'.   [6] English in the original.   [7] English in the original.

able to find a more felicitous formula, and I congratulate you on it, for saying how the explanation of the analytic situation is usually expressed.

To make any advances, all knowledge [*connaissance*] must objectify the parts which are objectifiable. How does an analysis make progress? – if not through the interventions which impel the subject to objectify himself, to take himself as object.

Balint objectifies the subject, but in a different sense. He proposes what I would call a recourse to a call on the real, which is only an effacement, through a failure to recognise, as you put it just now, the symbolic register. In fact, this register disappears completely in the object relation, and by the same token the imaginary register as well. That is why the objects take on an absolute value.

Balint tells us how to act – *create an atmosphere, your own atmosphere, a comfortable atmosphere*. That is all he has to say. It is extremely uncertain, hesitating on the edge of the unsayable, and he then brings in reality, what he calls the event. Clearly, analysis is not set up so that we fall into our patient's arms, and he into ours. The limitation of the analyst's means raises the question as to what plane his action occurs on. Balint is induced to call to attention all the registers of the real.

It is not for nothing that the real is always in the background, and that I never refer to it directly in our commentaries here. It is, quite precisely, and quite properly speaking, excluded. And Balint, no more than anyone else, will not make it come back. But that is the implication of his recourse to the call. A failure of the theory which corresponds to this deviation in technique.

2

It is late now. I don't want to go beyond a quarter to two.

I think we can give Granoff full marks. He has achieved everything I hoped of him, and has given you a full presentation of all the problems raised by this book of Balint's, his one and only book, which is the fruit of his reflections as well as of his professional practice.

Some questions may have emerged from it for you. I will come back to them next time. What I want to highlight now is the article which you didn't talk about, 'Transference of emotions', from 1933. Is it emotions which are transferred? Nobody seems scandalised by a title like that.

It isn't an article specifically addressed to analysts, it is also addressed in part to those who aren't, so that they grasp the phenomenon of tranference which, he says, gives rise to many misconceptions, and of which the scientific world in general had a less adequate conception at that time than of the phenomenon of resistance. He gives several examples. You'll see, it is quite delightful.

I will start off with this hole which Granoff left at the heart of his presentation so as to throw light once again on the rest. Because Balint lacks a correct definition of the symbol, the latter is necessarily everywhere.

In this same article, he tells us that the interpretation of their own experience by analysts is naturally a psychology, or a characterology of the psychoanalyst himself. So it is not me who says it, it is him who makes the remark. The author himself offers us the belief that one should undertake the psychoanalysis of the theoretician analyst so as to locate some of the modern tendencies of theory and of practice.

Till next Wednesday.

26 May 1954

XVII

The object relation and the intersubjective relation

BALINT AND FERENCZI

THE SATISFACTION OF NEED

THE MAP OF TENDERNESS

INTERSUBJECTIVITY IN THE PERVERSIONS

SARTRIAN ANALYSIS

So let us look at this conception which we call Balint's, which is, in fact, linked to a very specific tradition, which may be said to be Hungarian in so far as it has been, quite incidentally, dominated by the personality of Ferenczi. Certainly we will have to broach, in many little anecdotal ways, the relations between Freud and Ferenczi. It is all rather diverting.

Ferenczi was to some extent considered, up to 1930, to be the *enfant terrible* of psychoanalysis. In relation to the analytic group in general, he remained a free-wheeler. His way of raising questions showed no concern for couching itself in a manner which was, at that time, already *orthodox*. Hence, on a number of occasions, he raised questions which can be classified under the rubric *active psychoanalysis* – and, having said this, which seems so crucial, we think we have understood something.

Ferenczi started by asking himself what role, at any given moment of the analysis, the analyst's initiative, in the first instance, and later on, the analyst's being, should play. One has to see under what terms any intervention is made, before qualifying it as active. For example, yesterday evening you heard the question regarding prohibitions raised, apropos of the case which Dr Morgan reported to us. As I reminded you yesterday evening, that is a question which is already sounded out in Freud's Papers on Technique. Freud always took it to be absolutely self-evident that, in certain cases, one must know how to intervene in an active way by imposing prohibitions – *Your analysis cannot continue if you indulge in that activity which, through in some way saturating the situation, sterilises, in the full sense of the term, what might happen in the analysis.*

Starting from where we are, and going back in history from Balint on, we will try to see what the notion of active psychoanalysis means for Ferenczi, who is credited with its introduction.

I'll point out to you in passing that, in the course of his life, Ferenczi changed his position several times. He reconsidered some of his attempts, concluding that experience had shown them to be excessive, almost unfruitful, even injurious.

Balint thus belongs to this Hungarian tradition which blossomed around the questions raised by the relation of the analysand and analyst, conceived of as an interhuman situation involving persons and, as a consequence, implying a certain reciprocity. Today these questions are spoken of in terms of transference and counter-transference.

Around about 1930, the personal influence of Ferenczi came to an end. From then on, it is that of his pupils which makes itself felt.

Balint is to be located in this period extending from 1930 to today, which is marked by the growing influence, within analysis, of the notion of the object relation. I believe that that is the central point in the conception of Balint, of his wife, and of their collaborators who took an interest in animal psychology. That is what comes across in a book which, even though it is only a collection of rather variable, disparate articles, spread over a period of twenty years, is nevertheless characterised by a remarkable unity, which one can extract.

1

I presume that the terrain has been reconnoitred, because Granoff's presentation has enabled you to locate, in their gross outlines, the problems that Balint raises. So let us start off with the object relation. It lies at the heart of all the problems, as you will see.

Let us go straight to the knot. Balint's main focus in the elaboration of the notion of the object relation comes down to this – the object relation is one which conjoins to a need an object which satisfies it.

In his conception, an object is first and foremost an object of satisfaction. This is not about to surprise us, since analytic experience moves within the order of libidinal relations, within the order of desire. Does that mean that defining the object, in human experience, as what saturates a need is a valid point of departure, from which one will be able to develop, to group together and to explain what experience teaches us is encountered in analysis?

For Balint, the fundamental object relation satisfies what one can call the full form, the typical form. It assumes its most characteristic form in what he calls primary love,[1] namely the relations between mother and infant. The key article on this point is 'Mother's love and love for the mother', by Alice Balint. According to the latter, what is specific to the infant's relation to the mother is that the mother as such satisfies all the needs of the infant. This doesn't mean, obviously, that that's how things always turn out. But it is a structural feature of the human infant's situation.

Here the entire animal backdrop is implicit. The little human being, like the little animal for a limited period, is stitched into the maternal companionship which saturates a certain primitive need he has, while he takes his very first

---

[1] English in the original.

steps in life. But he is much more so than any other, on account of the backwardness of his development. You are aware that one can say that the human being is born with foetalised traits, that is to say deriving from premature birth. Balint scarcely touches on this point, and only in an aside. But he notes it, and he has good reason to.

However that may be, the mother-child relation is so fundamental for him that he goes so far as to say that, if it comes to pass in a happy manner, problems can only arise by accident. This accident may be the rule – that doesn't change anything, it is an accident with respect to the essentials of the relation. If there is satisfaction, which is the desire of this primary relation, this primary love[2] doesn't even have to come to light. Nothing does. So everything pertaining to it which becomes manifest is simply a hitch in the fundamental set-up, the enclosed, two-sided relation.

I cannot linger over this, but I must just say that Alice Balint's paper develops this conception to the point of heroism. Let us follow its reasoning.

For the infant, everything which is good for it, coming from the mother, goes without saying. There is nothing to imply that this partner is autonomous, nothing to imply that it is another subject. The need is imperious. And everything in the object relation tends, all by itself, towards the satisfaction of need. If there thus exists a pre-established harmony, an enclosing of the first object relation of the human being, a tendency towards perfect satisfaction, in all strictness exactly the same has to hold for the other side, for the mother's side. Her love for her offspring has exactly the same characteristic of pre-established harmony on the primitive plane of need. For her as well, the care, the contact, the breast-feeding, everything which links her in an animal fashion to her offspring satisfies a need, complementary to the first one's.

Hence Alice Balint is obliged to prove – and this is the extreme heroism of her demonstration – that maternal need displays exactly the same limits as every vital need, namely that *when one no longer has anything to give, well one takes*. One of the most clinching points she puts forward is that, in any given so-called primitive society – this term is less an allusion to the social or communitarian structure of these societies than it is to the fact that they are much more exposed to terrible crises in the realm of need, whether it is a question of eskimos or tribes wandering in an abject state across the Australian deserts – when there is nothing left to eat, you eat your child. This forms part of the same system, the register of the satisfaction of vital needs, there is no gap between feeding and eating – you are all his and, by the same token, he is all yours. Consequently, when there is no longer any other way of getting by, it is easy enough to gulp him down. Absorption is a part of inter-animal relations, of object relations. In the normal run of events, the infant feeds on his mother, absorbing her to the

---

[2] English in the original.

extent that he can. The inverse is true. When the mother can no longer do otherwise she tucks into him.

Balint goes to great lengths in supplying extraordinarily suggestive ethnographic detail. I do not know if they are accurate – one should always be wary of reports from afar. Nevertheless, ethnographers recount that, in times of hardship, during the atrocious famines which form a part of the rhythms of isolated populations, which have remained at a very primitive stage, in certain Australian tribes for example, the pregnant women are capable, with that remarkable dexterity which is a characteristic of some primitive behaviour, of inducing abortion so as to feed on the object of the pregnancy, born prematurely in this fashion.

In short, the infant-mother relation is here presented as the starting-point of a complementarity of desire. There is a direct stitching together of desires, which dovetail together, bind together. Any discordances, gaps are only accidental.

This definition, the starting-point and pivot of the Balint conception, is in contradiction with the analytic tradition on one essential point, concerning the development of instincts. In fact, the definition of the infant-mother relation runs counter to the positing of a primitive stage of so-called auto-erotism, which is however vouchsafed, to a great extent, by Freud's texts, although not without considerable qualifications – very important qualifications which always leave matters subject to a certain ambiguity.

In the classical, Viennese conception of libidinal development, there is a stage in which the infantile subject knows only its need, in the sense in which it has no relation with the object which satisfies it. It knows only its sensations, and it reacts on the plane of stimulus-response. It does not have a pre-determined primary relation, only the feeling of its pleasure or its unpleasure. The world is the world of sensations. And these sensations direct, dominate, govern its development. One doesn't have to take account of its relation to an object, since no object yet exists for it.

It is this classic thesis – that Wälder sets out in his article 'Earliest stages', which appeared in the *International Journal* for 1937, page 416 – which made the Viennese circle particularly impermeable to what was beginning to emerge in the English circle. It was highlighting what emerged later on in Kleinian theory, namely the idea of original traumatic elements, linked to the notion of the good and the bad object, to primitive projections and introjections.

What are the consequences of the Balint conception of the object relation? To begin with, let us postulate the following – it is clear that Balint and those who follow him are on the track of a truth. Who can seriously deny, if he has observed a baby of fifteen to twenty days at the breast, that it takes an interest in specific objects? So, the traditional idea that the original vicissitude of the libido is auto-erotism has to be interpreted. It is certain that it has some value, but it is false if we locate it on the behaviourist plane of the relation of the living organism with its *Umwelt*, since observation shows us that there really is an object relation. Such theoretical developments, which are spliced on to the theory of analysis, figure as a deviation in relation to the fundamental inspiration of the conception of the libido. For the moment, a large section, the largest section, of the analytic movement is pursuing it.

So Balint defines the object relation through the satisfaction of a need to which the object corresponds in a closed, completed fashion, in the form of a primary love, the original model of which is found in the mother-infant relation. I could have introduced you to Balint's thought via another path. But, because it is a coherent body of thought, whichever entrance gains you access to it, you will always find the same blind alleys and the same problems in it. If one starts off with an object relation like this, there is no getting away from it. The libidinal relation, whatever its progressive steps, its stages, its breakings of limits, its phases, its metamorphoses, will always be defined in the same way.

2

Once such a definition of the object has been given, however varied the qualities of desire are in passing from the oral to the anal, and then to the genital, there will just have to be an object to satisfy and saturate it.

So, the genital relation, in its completed aspects, in its fulfilment on the instinctual plane, is theorised in the same manner as the infant-mother relationship. In the achievement of genital satisfaction, the satisfaction of the one, I won't say is concerned for the satisfaction of the other, but is saturated in this satisfaction. And it goes without saying that the other is satisfied in this essential relation. That is the axis of the Balints' conception of genital love.[3] It is the same as that for primary love.[3]

Balint cannot conceive of matters in any other way, once the object is defined as an object of satisfaction. As it is clear that this becomes much more complicated when the adult human subject has actually to put into effect his capacities for genital possession, what he needs here is an extension. But it is never anything more than an extension, that is, one does not understand where the subject's initiative could arise from, his perception of the existence or the *reality*, as one says, of the partner.

What makes genital love[4] different from primary love[4] is acceding to the reality of the other as a subject. The subject takes into account the existence of the other subject as such. He concerns himself, not only with the enjoyment [*jouissance*] of his partner, but with many other requirements which are

---

[3] English in the original.   [4] English in the original.

associated with it. All of this isn't a matter of course. For Balint, this is part of the given. That's the way it is because an adult, well, is far more complicated than a child. Fundamentally, the register of satisfaction is the same. There is a closed satisfaction, for two, in which the ideal is that each finds in the other the object which satisfies his desire.

But these faculties for appreciating the needs and requirements of the other, which are necessary at the genital stage, where are you going to get them from? What can introduce the recognition of others into the closed system of the object relation? Nothing can, and that is what is striking.

Yet they do have to come from somewhere, these elements which he calls tenderness, idealisation, which are these mirages of love with which the genital act is draped – the map of Tenderness.[5] Balint cannot deny this dimension, since clinical work demonstrates it. So, he says – and this is where his theory comes apart, from top to bottom – the origin of all this is pregenital.

That is incredible. It means that he is forced to build on to primary love[6] an original dimension of the genital stage, which brings with it this extremely complex relation to others through which copulation becomes love. Now, up to that point he has devoted himself to defining primary love[6] as an object relation which is closed in on itself, without intersubjectivity. The genital once reached, he wants the stuff on which the intersubjective relation is made to emerge out of this same primary love.[6] That is the contradiction of his doctrine.

Balint thinks of the pregenital as formed in an object relation, let us say an animal one, in which the object is not selfish,[6] is not subject. The term is never used, but the very formulae he does use show clearly what is at issue. In the pregenital, there is no self[7] at all, besides the one which organically exists. The object is there so as to saturate its needs. When we arrive at the level of the genital relation, one cannot escape from such a definition of the object relation, there is no way of making it develop any further, since, change as desire might, the object will still always have to be complementary to it. Yet Balint does find himself obliged to say – without being able to fill in the gap which results from doing so – that intersubjectivity, that is to say the experience of the selfishness of the other, stems from this pregenital stage from which he had previously excluded it. It is true. One can see this perfectly palpable fact revealing itself in the analytic experience. But this contradicts the entire theory of primary love.[6] And it is here, on the very plane of the theoretical statement, that one can see the blind alley one is led into when one takes the object relation to belong to the register of satisfaction.

[5] 'la carte du Tendre'. A reference to Madeleine de Scudéry's Clélie (1654–60) vol. I, in which she recounts a salon conversation in which an allegorical map of the country of the tender sentiments was drawn up.

[6] English in the original.

[7] The term 'self' became accepted into the French language in the mid-twentieth century, first in medicine and then in psychology and psychoanalysis.

DR LANG: *It seems to me that there is another contradiction, which also emerges from the presentation you've given. For in the closed world of primary love,* [8] *need and desire are completely confused. Besides, you yourself have sometimes used the one, sometimes the other term. Perhaps it is in paying attention to this point that we will see where the weakness lies.*

Balint uses the two alternately. The basis of his thought is need,[8] and it is accidentally, in lacking, that need makes itself manifest as wish.[8] And that really is what is at issue – is the human wish[8] simply the lack inflicted on need?[8] Does desire emerge only out of frustration? Analysts have gone a long way down this path, in a manner which is far less coherent than Balint, to the point of making frustration the pivot of analytic theory – the primary frustration, secondary, primitive, complex frustrations, etc. You must extricate yourself from this fascination to fall on your feet again. That is what I am going to try to remind you of now.

3

If analysis has made any positive discovery about libidinal development, it is that the child is a pervert, even a polymorphous pervert.

Before the stage of genital normalisation, first sketched around the Oedipus complex, the child is given over to an entire series of phases connoted by the term component drives. These are its first libidinal relations to the world. On the basis of this sketch, analysis today is engaged in applying the notion of the object relation, which is caught – Lang's idea is extremely fruitful at this point – within that of frustration.

What is this primary perversion? One has to recall that analytic experience started off with a select number of clinical phenomena, amongst which are the perversions. If one introduces the perversions into the pregenital, you must bear in mind what they are when they are seen in a clearcut and delineated fashion.

Is the Balint notion of object relation applicable both in the phenomenology of the perversions, in which the pregenital phase is involved, and in the phenomenology of love?

Quite the opposite! There is not one form of the perverse phenomena whose very structure is not, in every moment of its being lived through, sustained by the intersubjective relation.

Let us leave to one side the voyeuristic and exhibitionistic relations – that's too easy to prove. Let us take as our example the sadistic relation, whether in an imaginary form or in a paradoxical clinical form.

One thing is certain – the sadistic relation can only be sustained in so far as

---

[8] English in the original.

the other is on the verge of still remaining a subject. If he is no longer anything more than reacting flesh, a kind of mollusc whose edges one titillates and which palpitates, the sadistic relation no longer exists. The sadistic subject will stop there, suddenly encountering a void, a gap, a hollow. The sadistic relation implies, in fact, that the partner's consent has been secured – his freedom, his confession, his humiliation. The proof of this is manifest in the forms which one may call benign. Is it not true that most sadistic manifestations, far from being taken to extremes, remain rather on the threshold of execution – playing the waiting-game, playing on the fear of the other, with pressure, with threat, keeping to the forms, more or less secret, of the participation of the partner.

You know the extent to which by far the largest part of our clinical experience of the perversions is restricted to the plane of an exclusively playful execution. We are not dealing here with subjects prey to a need. In the mirage of play, each identifies himself with the other. Intersubjectivity is the essential dimension.

I cannot refrain at this point from referring to the author who has described this play in the most magisterial manner – I am referring to Jean-Paul Sartre, and the phenomenology of the apprehension of others in the third part of *Being and Nothingness*. It is a work which one can demolish, from a philosophical point of view, can be made to crumple under the weight of numerous criticisms, but which surely, in this description, becomes, if only through its talent and its verve, something which is quite especially convincing.

The author's entire demonstration turns around the fundamental phenomenon which he calls the gaze. The human object is originally distinguished, *ab initio*, in the field of my experience, and cannot be assimilated to any other perceptible object, by virtue of being an object which is looking at me. Sartre makes, on this point, some very subtle distinctions. The gaze in question must on no account be confused with the fact, for example, of seeing his eyes. I can feel myself under the gaze of someone whose eyes I do not even see, not even discern. All that is necessary is for something to signify to me that there may be others there. This window, if it gets a bit dark, and if I have reasons for thinking that there is someone behind it, is straightaway a gaze. From the moment this gaze exists, I am already something other, in that I feel myself becoming an object for the gaze of others. But in this position, which is a reciprocal one, others also know that I am an object who knows himself to be seen.

The entire phenomenology of shame, of modesty, of prestige, of the specific fear engendered by the gaze, is quite admirably described there, and I recommend you to look it up in Sartre's book. It is essential reading for an analyst, above all given the pass that analysis has come to, forgetting intersubjectivity even in the perverse experience, where it is so firmly woven into a register in which you have to recognise the plane of the imaginary.

We do indeed observe, in those phenomena which one calls perverted, nuances which cannot possibly be confused with what I am teaching you to place as the axis of the symbolic relation, that is to say recognition. These forms are extremely ambiguous – it is not for nothing that I mentioned shame. Were we to analyse prestige in a more subtle manner, we would also come upon its derisory forms, upon for example the way it appears in children, for whom it is a form of excitation, etc.

A friend told me an anecdote about this joke[9] that precedes bull fights, in which, in Spain, boobies are obliged to take part. He described an extraordinarily beautiful scene of collective sadism. You'll see how far the ambiguity extends.

So, one of these semi-idiots is made to file past, dressed up in a most beautiful matador costume. He files past into the arena before the little animals who partake in these games. As you know, they are not entirely innocuous. And the crowd is shouting out – *But that one, there, isn't he beautiful!* The character in question, whose semi-idiocy is firmly in the tradition of the grand games of the court of old Spain, gets into a sort of panic and starts to feel incompetent. His comrades say to him – *Go on, you see, everybody wants you.* Everybody joins in the game. The man's panic increases. He baulks, wants to get out of it. He is pushed beyond the barriers, and, finally, the see-saw takes place. All of a sudden, he breaks away from the people pushing him, and, carried away by the crushing insistence of the crowd, he becomes transformed into a sort of comic hero. Caught up in the structure of the situation, he walks up to the beast, taking on all the characteristics of the sacrificial attitude, with this difference, that it does after all remain on the level of a farce. He is immediately flattened to the ground. And he is carted off.

This sensational scene appears to me to illustrate perfectly the ambiguous zone in which intersubjectivity is essential. You could say that the symbolic element – the pressure of the clamour – plays an essential role in it, but it is almost cancelled out because of the mass phenomenon character which it assumes on this occasion. The whole phenomenon is thus reduced to that level of intersubjectivity whose manifestations we connote, provisionally, as perverse.

One can go further. And Sartre does go much further, in giving a structuration to the phenomenology of the love relation which to me appears irrefutable. I cannot go over the whole of it for you, because I would be obliged to go through all the phases of the dialectic of the for-itself and the in-itself. You will have to take the trouble of turning to the book yourselves.

Very astutely, Sartre makes the remark that, in the experience of love, it is not an entirely free commitment which we require from the object by whom we desire to be loved. The initial pact, the *you are my wife* or *you are my husband* to

---

[9] English in the original.

which I often allude when I talk to you about the symbolic register, contains nothing, in its Corneille-like abstraction, to saturate our basic requirements. The nature of the desire is expressed in a sort of bodily agglutinating of freedom. We want to become for the other an object that has the same limiting value for him as does, in relation to his freedom, his own body. We not only want to become for the other that in which his freedom is alienated – without a shadow of a doubt, freedom has to enter into it, since commitment is an essential element of our requirement to be loved – but it must also be much more than a free commitment. We require that a freedom accept its own renunciation so as to be, from that moment on, limited to everything capricious, imperfect, in truth inferior, the paths along which it is swept by its captation by that object which we ourselves are.

In this way, to become, through our contingence, through our specific existence in its most carnal aspect, in its most limiting aspect for our own selves, for our own freedom, to become the limit to which the other consents, to become the form of abdication of the other's freedom, that is the requirement which phenomenologically locates love in its concrete form – genital love,[10] as our good friend Balint said just now. That is what sets it down in this intermediate, ambiguous zone, between the symbolic and the imaginary.

If love is entirely caught up and glued within this imaginary inter-subjectivity, upon which I would like to focus your attention, it requires, in its completed form, participation in the register of the symbolic, the freedom-pact exchange, which is embodied in giving one's word [*parole donneé*]. There, a tiered zone is established in which you will be able to distinguish the planes of identification, as we put it in this so often imprecise language of ours, and a whole range of nuances, an entire fanning out of forms at play between the imaginary and the symbolic.

By the same token, you see that, contrary to Balint's perspective, and much more in conformity with our experience, we must start off with a radical intersubjectivity, with the subject's total acceptance by the other subject. It is by starting with the experience of the adult that we must grapple retrospectively, *nachträglich*, with the supposedly original experiences, in ranging the various degradations in tiers, without ever leaving the domain of intersubjectivity. In so far as we remain within the register of analysis, we will be obliged to admit an original intersubjectivity.

There is no transition possible between the two registers, between that of animal desire, in which the relation is object, and that of the recognition of desire. There has to be intersubjectivity at the beginning, since it is there at the end. And if analytic theory has qualified as polymorphously perverse this or that mode or symptom in the child's behaviour, it is in so far as perversion

---

[10] English in the original.

implies the dimension of imaginary intersubjectivity. Just now, I tried to get you to grasp it, in this double gaze whereby I see that the other sees me, and that any intervening third party sees me being seen. There is never a simple duplicity of terms. It is not only that I see the other, I see him seeing me, which implicates the third term, namely that he knows that I see him. The circle is closed. There are always three terms in the structure, even if these three terms are not explicitly present.

In adults, we are aware of the palpable richness of perversion. Perversion, in sum, is the privileged exploration of an existential possibility of human nature – its internal tearing apart, its gap, through which the supra-natural world of the symbolic was able to make its entry. But, if the child is a polymorphous pervert, does this mean that one has to project on to him the qualitative value of the perversion as it is experienced in the adult? In the child, are we obliged to search out an intersubjectivity of the same type as that which we see to be constitutive of perversion in the adult?

Well, no. What do the Balints base themselves on when they tell us about this primary love which takes no account of the other's selfishness?[11] On words like those of the child who, loving his mother the best, can say, quite coldly, to her – *When you are dead, Mummy, I'll have your hats.* Or – *When grandad dies*, etc. Words which elicit the adult's adulation of the child, because the latter then appears to be a scarcely conceivable divine being, whose feelings are quite beyond him. When one comes across phenomena as paradoxical as those, when one no longer understands and when one has to resolve the question of the transcendental, one thinks one is confronted either with a god or an animal. We take children far too much for gods to admit it, so we tell ourselves that we take them for animals. And that is what Balint does in thinking that the child does not recognise the other, except in relation to his own need. A complete error.

This simple example of *when you are dead* tells us where the basic intersubjectivity really shows itself in the child – it shows in the fact that he can make use of language.

Granoff was right to say the other day that Balint's work presages the role of what, following Freud, I have emphasised, in the first games of the child, which consists in evoking – I am not saying in calling – presence in absence, and in rejecting the object from presence. But Balint fails to recognise that this is a linguistic phenomenon. He only sees one thing, which is that the child does not take the object into account. Whereas what is important is that this little human being is able to make use of the symbolic function, thanks to which, as I have explained to you, it is possible for the elephants to make their entry here, however strait be the gate.

---

[11] English in the original.

To start with, intersubjectivity is given in the manipulation of the symbol, and this is the case right from the beginning. Everything begins with the possibility of naming, which is both destructive of the thing and allows the passage of the thing onto the symbolic plane, thanks to which the truly human register comes into its own. It is from that point on that, in a more and more complicated manner, the embodiment of the symbolic within imaginary experience takes place. The symbolic will shape all those inflections which, in the life of the adult, the imaginary commitment, the original captation, can take on.

In neglecting the intersubjective dimension, one slips into the register of that object relation from which there is no means of escape, and which leads us to theoretical no less than to technical blind alleys.

Have I wrapped things up enough this morning to be able to leave you at this point? That doesn't mean that there won't be a sequel.

For the child, to start with there is the symbolic and the real, contrary to what one might think. Everything which we see taking on consistency, becoming enriched and being diversified in the register of the imaginary begins with these two poles. If you think that the child is more a captive of the imaginary than of the rest, you are right in a certain sense. The imaginary is there. But it is completely inaccessible to us. It is only accessible to us when we start from its realisations in the adult.

The past history, the lived history, of the subject, which we try to get at in our practice, is not what the person you heard yesterday evening present to you as the snoozing, the fiddling about of the subject while in analysis. We can only get at it – and that is what we do, whether we know it or not – through the adult's childish language. I will prove it to you next time.

In magisterial fashion, Ferenczi saw the importance of this question – what is it in an analysis which makes the child within the adult participate? There is no doubt about the answer – whatever is verbalised in an irruptive fashion.

2 June 1954

XVIII

The symbolic order

PERVERSE DESIRE

MASTER AND SLAVE

NUMERICAL STRUCTURATION OF THE INTERSUBJECTIVE FIELD

THE HOLOPHRASE

SPEECH IN THE TRANSFERENCE

ANGELUS SILESIUS

Last time I left you on the dyadic relation in primary love. You were able to see that this leads Balint to end up conceptualising the analytic relation itself on this model – what he calls, quite rigorously, the two body psychology.[1] I think you have understood what blind alleys this leads one into, if one takes as a central idea the supposedly harmonious imaginary relation, which saturates natural desire.

I tried to show you this in the phenomenology of the perverse relation. I put the accent on sadism and scopophilia, leaving to one side the homosexual relation, which would require an infinitely more subtle study of imaginary intersubjectivity, of its uncertainty, of its unstable equilibrium, of its critical character. I thus centred the study of the imaginary intersubjective relation around the phenomenon, in the true sense, of the gaze.

The gaze is not located just at the level of the eyes. The eyes may very well not appear, they may be masked. The gaze is not necessarily the face of our fellow being, it could just as easily be the window behind which we assume he is lying in wait for us. It is an x, the object when faced with which the subject becomes object.

I gave you an introduction to the experience of sadism, which I took to be elective in revealing this dimension to you. I pointed out that, in the gaze of the being whom I torment, I have to sustain my desire with an act of defiance, a challenge[2] at every instant. If it does not rise above the situation, if it is not glorious, desire sinks into shame. This is equally true of the scopophilic relation. According to Jean-Paul Sartre's analysis, for anyone surprised in the middle of looking, the entire colour of the situation changes, in one swerving moment, and I become a pure thing, a maniac.

---

[1] English in the original.   [2] English in the original.

1

What is perversion? It is not simply an aberration in relation to social criteria, an anomaly contrary to good morals, although this register is not absent, nor is it an atypicality according to natural criteria, namely that it more or less derogates from the reproductive finality of sexual union. It is something else in its very structure.

A certain number of perverse inclinations have not without reason been said to arise out of a desire which dare not speak its name. Perversion in fact is to be placed at the limit of the register of recognition, and that is what fixes it, stigmatises it as such. Structurally, perversion such as I have delineated it for you on the imaginary plane, can only be sustained with a precarious status which, at every moment is contested, from within, for the subject. It is always fragile, at the mercy of an inversion, a subversion, which makes one think of the change of sign which occurs in certain mathematical functions – at the point when one passes from one value of a variable to the value immediately following, the correlative changes from plus to minus infinity.

The fundamental uncertainty of the perverse relation, the fact that it can find no way of becoming grounded in any satisfying action, makes up one aspect of the drama of homosexuality. But it is also this structure which gives perversion its value.

Perversion is an experience which allows one to enter more deeply into what one can call, in the full sense, the human passion, to use the Spinozistic term, that is to say what there is in man which is open to this division from himself which structures the imaginary, namely, between O and O', the specular relation. It becomes a profound experience, on account of the fact that within this gap of human desire, all manner of nuances are called forth, rising up in tiers from shame to prestige, from buffoonery to heroism, whereby human desire in its entirety is exposed, in the deepest sense of the term, to the desire of the other.

Remember the quite stupendous analysis of homosexuality which unfolds in Proust in the myth of Albertine. It hardly matters that this character is feminine – the structure of the relation is eminently homosexual. The requirement of this style of desire can only be satisfied in an inexhaustible captation of the desire of the other, pursued even in his dreams by the dreams of the subject, implying at each moment a complete abdication of the true desire of the other. An incessant see-saw of the lark-mirror which, at each moment, makes a complete turn on itself – the subject exhausts himself in pursuing the desire of the other, which he will never be able to grasp as his own desire, because his own desire is the desire of the other. It is himself whom he pursues. Therein lies the drama of this jealous passion, which is also a form of the imaginary intersubjective relation.

The intersubjective relation which subtends perverse desire is only sustained by the annihilation either of the desire of the other, or of the desire of the subject. It can only be grasped at the limit, in its inversions, whose meaning is made clear in a flash. This means – do think hard – that in the one as in the other, this relation dissolves the being of the subject. The other subject is reduced to being only the instrument of the first, who thus remains the only subject as such, but the latter is reduced to being only an idol offered to the desire of the other.

Perverse desire finds its support in the ideal of an inanimate object. But it cannot rest content with the realisation of this ideal. As soon as it realises it, at the very moment when it catches up with it, it loses its object. Its satiation is hence by its very structure condemned to be realised prior to the embrace through the extinction of desire or else the disappearance of the object.

I underline *disappearance*, because you find in analyses like this one the secret key to this *aphanisis* which Jones talked of when he tried to grasp, beyond the castration complex, what he touched on in the experience of certain infantile traumas. But here we are getting lost in a kind of mystery, because we do not rediscover the plane of the imaginary in it.

When all is said and done, an entire segment of the analytic experience is nothing other than – the exploration of blind alleys of imaginary experience, of their continuations, which are not innumerable, since they rest on the very structure of the body in so far as as such it defines a concrete topography. In the subject's history, or rather in his development, certain fertile, temporalised moments come to light, in which the different styles of frustration are revealed. These hollows, these cracks, these chasms that come to light in development are what define these fertile moments.

Something always goes limp when people talk to you about frustration. Owing to something like a naturalistic inclination of language, when the observer draws up the natural history of his fellow being, he omits to inform you that the subject *experiences* the frustration. Frustration is not a phenomenon that one can objectivate in the subject in the form of a deviation of the act which unites it to this object. It is not animal aversion. However premature it may be, the subject himself experiences the bad object as a frustration. And, by the same token, the frustration is experienced in the other.

Here we find a reciprocal relation of annihilation, a fatal relation structured by the following two abysses – either desire is extinguished, or the object disappears. That is why, at every turn, I take my bearings from the master-slave dialectic, and I re-explain it.

2

The master-slave relation is a limit-example, because, to be sure, the imaginary register in which it is deployed appears only at the limit of our experience. The analytic experience is not a total one. It is defined on another plane than that of the imaginary – the symbolic plane.

Hegel gives an account of the interhuman bond. He has to account not only for society, but for history. He cannot neglect any of its aspects. Now, one of these essential aspects, which is neither collaboration between men, nor the pact, nor the bond of love, is struggle and labour. And he focusses on this aspect, in order to structure the fundamental relation within an original myth, on the plane which he himself defines as negative, as marked by negativity.

What differentiates human society from animal society – the term doesn't frighten me – is that the former cannot be grounded upon any objectifiable bond. The intersubjective dimension as such must come into it. The master-slave relation does not therefore involve the domestication of man by man. That cannot be enough. So, what grounds this relation? It is not that the one who declares himself vanquished pleas for mercy, it is rather that the master enters into this struggle for reasons of pure prestige, and has risked his life. This risk establishes his superiority, and it is in the name of that, not of his strength, that he is recognised as master by the slave.

This situation begins with an impasse, because his recognition by the slave is worth nothing to the master, since only a slave has recognised him, that is to say someone that he does not recognise as a man. The initial structure of this Hegelian dialectic seems thus to lead to a dead end. You can see therefore that it is not without its affinities with the impasse of the imaginary situation.

However, this situation does unfold further. Its point of departure, being imaginary, is hence mythical. But its extensions lead us on to the symbolic plane. You know the extensions – that is what makes us speak of the master and the slave. Indeed, beginning with the mythical situation, an action is undertaken, and establishes the relation between pleasure [*jouissance*] and labour. A law is imposed upon the slave, that he should satisfy the desire and the pleasure [*jouissance*] of the other. It is not sufficient for him to plea for mercy, he has to go to work. And when you go to work, there are rules, hours – we enter into the domain of the symbolic.

If you look at it closely, this domain of the symbolic does not have a simple relation of succession to the imaginary domain whose pivot is the fatal intersubjective relation. We do not pass from one to the other in one jump from the anterior to the posterior, once the pact and the symbol are established. In fact, the myth itself can only be conceived of as already bounded by the register of the symbolic, for the reason that I underlined just now – the situation cannot be grounded in goodness knows what biological panic at the approach of death. Death is never experienced as such, is it – it is never real. Man is only ever afraid of an imaginary fear. But that is not all. In the Hegelian myth, death is not even structured like a fear, it is structured like a risk, and, in a word, like a stake. From the beginning, between the master and the slave, there's a rule of the game.

I won't push this today. I am only saying it for those of you who are most open – the intersubjective relation, which unfolds in the imaginary, is at the same time, in so far as it structures a human action, implicitly implicated in a rule of the game.

Let us once again take up, under another aspect, the relation to the gaze.

We are at war. I am moving forward over a plain, and I assume myself to be under a gaze lying in wait for me. If I am assuming that, it is not so much that I am afraid of some sign of my enemy, some attack, because as soon as that happens the situation becomes more relaxed and I know who I am dealing with. What matters the most to me is knowing what the other imagines, what the other detects of these intentions of mine, I who am moving forward, because I must screen my movements from him. It is a matter of ruse.

The dialectic of the gaze is maintained on this plane. What counts is not that the other sees where I am, but that he sees where I am going, that is to say, quite precisely, that he sees where I am not. In every analysis of the intersubjective relation, what is essential is not what is there, what is seen. What structures it is what is not there.

The theory of games, as it is called, is a fundamental method for the study of this relation. Simply because it is a mathematical theory, we are already on the symbolic plane. However simply you define the field of an intersubjectivity, its analysis always requires a certain number of numerical givens, which, as such, are symbolic.

If you read the book of Sartre's I was referring to the other day, you will see that he allows something extremely disturbing to emerge. Having defined the intersubjective relation so clearly, he seems to imply that, if there is a plurality in this world of imaginary inter-relations, this plurality is not enumerable, in so far as each of the subjects is by definition the unique centre of reference. This holds if one remains on the phenomenological plane of the analysis of the in-itself and the for-itself. But its consequence is that Sartre does not perceive that the intersubjective field cannot but open on to a numerical structuration, on to the three, the four, which are our bench-marks in the analytic experience.

Primitive as it is, this symbolism brings us immediately on to the plane of language, in so far as, outside of that, there is no numeration conceivable.

Another small parenthesis. I was reading, not much longer than three days ago, an old book from the beginning of the century, *The History of the New World of America*. The topic was the origin of language, a problem which attracted the attention of quite a number of linguists, even provoking their consternation.

Every discussion of the origin of language is vitiated by an irremediable puerility, even with indisputable cretinism. On every occasion, someone tries to make language emerge out of some or other advance in thought. Quite evidently, it is a circle. Thought, on this account, would pinpoint the detail in a situation, delimit the particularity, the combinatory element. It would by itself go beyond the stage of the detour, which is the mark of animal intelligence, to accede to that of the symbol. But how, if the symbol, which is the very structure of human thought, is not there in the first place?

To think is to substitute the word *elephant* for elephants, and a ring for the sun. You realise of course that there is an abyss between this thing which is phenomenologically the sun – the centre of which runs through the world of appearances, the unity of light – and a ring. And even if one spans it, what progress is there over animal intelligence? None. Because the sun in so far as it is designated by a ring is valueless. It only has a value in so far as this ring is placed in relation with other formalisations, which constitute with it this symbolic whole within which it has its place, at the centre of the world for example, or at the periphery, it doesn't matter which. The symbol only has value if it is organised in a world of symbols.

Those who speculate about the origin of language, and try to engineer the transitions between an appreciation of the whole situation and symbolic fragmentation have always been struck by what have been called holophrases. In the usages of certain peoples, and you won't need to go far to find common usages, there are phrases, expressions which cannot be broken down, and which have to be related to a situation taken in its entirety – these are holophrases. Here, it is thought, one has got hold of a juncture between the animal, who gets about without structuring situations, and man, who inhabits a symbolic world.

In the work I cited just now, I read that the Fijians, in certain specific situations, use the following phrase, which is not a phrase belonging to their language [*langage*] and cannot be reduced down to anything else – *Ma mi la pa ni pa ta pa*. The phonetisation is not indicated in the text, and I can only say it to you like that.

In what situation is the holophrase in question spoken? Entirely innocently, our ethnographer writes – *State of events of two persons looking at the other hoping that the other will offer to do something which both parties desire but are unwilling to do*.[3]

Here we find defined with an exemplary precision a state of inter-gaze where each expects the other to decide on something which has to be done by the two, which is between the two, but which neither of them wishes to enter into. And, by the same token, you see clearly that the holophrase is not an intermediary step between a primitive assumption of the situation as a whole, which would be the register of animal action, and symbolisation. It is not some vague sort of

[3] English in the original.

original gluing together of the situation into a verbal mode. On the contrary, what is involved is something in which what pertains to the register of the symbolic composition is defined at the limit, at the periphery.

I will leave you the task of bringing me some holophrases taken from our everyday usage. Listen carefully to the conversation of your contemporaries and you will see to what extent it is imbued with them. You will also see that every holophrase is connected with limit situations, in which the subject is suspended in a specular relation to the other.

3

This analysis had as its aim to get you to overturn that psychological perspective in which the intersubjective relation is reduced to an inter-objectal relation, grounded on a natural, complementary satisfaction. We have now got to Balint's article, 'On transference of emotions', whose title gives notice as to what I could call the delirious plane on which it unfolds – in the original, technical sense of the term delirious [délirant].

What is at issue is transference. The first paragraph invokes the two fundamental phenomena of analysis – resistance and transference. Resistance is defined, extremely well in fact, relating it to the phenomenon of language – everything which brakes, alters, slows up the blarney, or else completely interrupts it. You cannot go further than that. No conclusion is drawn from this, and we pass on to the phenomenon of transference.

How can an author as subtle as Balint, as refined, as delicate a practitioner, as admirable a writer, I would go so far as to say, undertake a study of some fifteen pages starting off with so psychological a definition of transference? It amounts to saying the following – what must come into it is something which exists inside the patient, so it is quite clearly something or other, feelings, emotions – the word *emotion* gives a better image. The problem is then to show how these emotions are embodied, projected, disciplined, symbolised. Now, the symbols of these supposed emotions evidently have no relation to them. So, he tells us about the national flag, the lion and the unicorn of Britain, the epaulets of officers, and everything else you fancy, about the two houses with their two roses of contrasting colours, judges who wear wigs.

I would be the last person to deny that one is capable of finding something to meditate upon in these examples skimmed from the surface of everyday British life. But, for Balint, it is a pretext for considering the symbol solely from the perspective of displacement. And with good reason – since he takes as the starting-point so-called emotion, a phenomenon of psychological surging forward, which would in this case be the real, the symbol in which it has to find its expression and come into being can only be displaced in relation to it.

There can be no doubt that the symbol has a role to play in every displacement. But the question is rather of knowing whether, as such, it is defined within the vertical register, by virtue of being displacement. That is the wrong road. Balint's remarks contain nothing erroneous in themselves, it is simply that the path that has been taken cuts across the right one – instead of going in the forwards direction, it goes in the direction in which everything comes to a halt.

Balint then reminds us what a metaphor is – the face of a mountain, the foot of a table, etc. Are we finally going to investigate the nature of language? No. We are told that the mode of operation of the transference is the following – you are angry, so you give the table a punch. As if it was really the table I was punching! There's a fundamental error in this.

Nonetheless, this really is the issue – how does the aim of the act come to be displaced? How does the emotion come to be displaced in its object? The real structure and the symbolic structure enter into an ambiguous relation which is constructed in the vertical direction, each of these two universes corresponding to the other, but for the fact that since the notion of a universe is not to be found here, there is no way of introducing that of correspondence.

According to Balint, transference is transference of emotions. And what is emotion transferred on to? In all of his examples, on to an inanimate object – note in passing that this word, *inanimate*, has already made its appearance just now as the limit of the imaginary dialectical relation. This amuses Balint, this transference on to the inanimate – I am not asking you, he says, what the object makes of all this. To be sure, he adds, if one thinks that the transference is made on to a subject, one ends up with a complication you will never see the end of.

That's right! That really is what happens, and for some time now – there is no way of doing analysis. Such a song and dance is made out of the notion of counter-transference, so much swaggering, boasting, promising the earth – yet somehow or other something gets in the way, it is just that this means that in the end – you will never see the end of it. With a two body psychology,[4] we come upon the famous problem, which is unresolved in physics, of two bodies.

In fact, if you restrict yourselves to the level of two bodies, there is no satisfactory symbolisation available. So is it by taking this path, and by maintaining that the transference is essentially a phenomenon of displacement, that one grasps the nature of transference?

Balint then tells us a pretty story. A gentleman comes to see him. He is on the brink of analysis – we know this situation very well – and he can't decide. He has been to see several analysts, and in the end he came to see Balint. He tells him a long story, very rich, very complicated, with details about his feelings, and his sufferings. And it is at this point that our Balint – whose theoretical positions by the way I am in the process of slandering, and God knows I'm sorry to do it – shows himself to be the wonderful character he is.

Balint does not fall into the counter-transference – that is to say, in plain

----

4 English in the original.

language, he is not an idiot – in the coded language we wallow in, we call the fact of hating someone ambivalence, and the fact of being an idiot counter-transference. Balint is not an idiot, he listens to this bloke, as a man who has already heard a great many things, a great many people, a man of experience. And he doesn't understand. That happens. There are stories like that, you don't understand them. When you don't understand a story, don't blame yourself immediately, say to yourself – the fact that I don't understand must mean something. Not only does Balint not understand, but he considers that he has the right not to understand. He says nothing to this bloke, and asks him to come back.

The bloke comes back. He carries on telling his story. And lays it on a bit thick. And Balint still doesn't understand. What the other tells him, are things which are as likely as anything else, the thing is that they just don't fit together. Experiences like that happen, they are clinical experiences to which you must always accord considerable weight, and sometimes they incline us towards the diagnosis of something organic. But that's not what this is about. So, Balint says to his client. *What's strange is that you are telling me lots of really interesting things, but I must confess that I can't make head or tail of your story.* Then the bloke brightens up, with a big smile on his face. *You're the first honest man I have met, because I've told all those things to some of your colleagues, who straightaway saw in them an intimation of an interesting, sophisticated structure. I told you all this as a test, to see if you were like all the others, a charlatan and a liar.*

You must have a sense of the gulf there is between Balint's two registers, when he expounds on the blackboard that it is the emotions of the English citizens which are displaced on to the British lion[5] and the two unicorns, and when he is on the job, talking intelligently about what he is trying out. One may say – *No doubt this bloke is within his rights, but isn't it rather uneconomic*[5]? *Isn't it rather a long detour?* Well, there, you start to go astray. Because the issue is not one of knowing whether it is economic or not. The bloke's way of going about things is nobly sustained, within his register, in so far as at the start of the analytic experience, one encounters the register of mendacious[6] speech.

The instauration of the lie in reality is brought about by speech. And it is precisely because it introduces what isn't, that it can also introduce what is. Before speech, nothing either is or isn't [*rien n'est, ni n'est pas*]. Everything is already there, no doubt, but it is only with speech that there are things which are – which are true or false, that is to say which are – and things which are not. Truth hollows out its way into the real thanks to the dimension of speech. There is neither true nor false prior to speech. Truth is introduced along with it, and so is the lie, and other registers as well. Before we go our various ways today, let us put them in a sort of triangle with three apexes. There, the lie. Here, the

---

[5] English in the original.   [6] *'menteresse'* – an Old French form for 'lying'.

mistake – not error, to which I will come back. And then, what else? – ambiguity, to which, by its very nature, speech is doomed. Because, the very act of speech, which founds the dimension of truth, always remains, by this fact, behind, beyond. Speech is in its essence ambiguous.

Symmetrically, the hole, the gap of being as such is hollowed out in the real. The notion of being, as soon as we try to grasp it, proves itself to be as ungraspable as that of speech. Because being, the very verb itself, only exists in the register of speech. Speech introduces the hollow of being into the texture of the real, the one and the other holding on to and balancing each other, exactly correlative.

Let us move on to another example, which Balint offers us, no less significant than the first one. How can he integrate them into this register of displacement within which he expounded on the transference? That is another story.

This time we have a charming lady patient, who belongs to the type, well illustrated in some English films, who chatter,[7] *talk-talk-talk-talk-to-say-nothing*. That is how the sessions go by. She has already done long stretches of analysis with someone else before coming into the hands of Balint, who understands very clearly – and even the patient confesses to it – that when something is troubling her, she covers it over by saying anything.

Where is the decisive turning-point? One day, after a painful hour of chatter,[7] Balint ends up putting his finger on what it is she didn't want to say. She didn't want to say that she had received a letter of recommendation for a job from a doctor friend of hers, which said that she was a completely trustworthy[7] person. A pivotal moment, from then on she makes an about turn, and will be able to commit herself to the analysis. In fact Balint gets the patient to acknowledge that, right from the start, that was exactly what mattered to her – she must not be considered trustworthy, that is to say someone bound by her word. Because if her word binds her, she will have to get to work, like the slave just now, she will have to enter the world of labour, that is to say of the homogeneous adult relationship, of the symbol, of the law.

It's clear. From the beginning, she understood very well the difference between the way one treats the words of a child and the way one treats the words of an adult. So as not to be committed, located in the world of adults, where one is always more or less reduced to slavery, she chatters away so as to say nothing and fill the sessions with hot air.

We can stop for a moment, and ponder on the fact that the child also has speech. It is not empty. It is as full of meaning as the speech of the adult. It is so full of meaning that adults spend their time marvelling at it – *See how clever he is, the sweet little thing! Did you hear what he said the other day?* In fact, that's the whole point.

---

[7] English in the original.

Indeed, here we have, just as a moment ago, this element of idolification which comes into the imaginary relation. The wonderful speech of the child may perhaps be transcendental speech, the revelation of heaven, the oracle of the little god, but it is clear that it doesn't commit him to anything.

And we make strenuous efforts, when things aren't going well, to extract some words from him which will tie him down. Lord knows how the adult's dialectic skids! The point is to link the subject to his contradictions, to make him sign what he says, and to pledge his speech in a dialectic.

In the transference situation – it is not me who says this, but Balint, and he is right, though this is something completely different from a displacement – what is at issue is the value of speech, no longer this time in so far as it creates the fundamental ambiguity, but in so far as it is a function of the symbolic, of the pact which links the subjects together in one action. The human action *par excellence* is originally founded on the existence of the world of the symbol, namely on laws and contracts. And it is truly around this register that Balint, when he is working at the level of the concrete, in his capacity as analyst, makes the situation between him and the subject revolve.

From this day on, he can make remarks to her about all manner of things – for example the way she behaves in her various jobs, that is to say, as soon as she begins to be trusted by everyone, she makes sure that some trivial matter gets her the sack. Even the kind of jobs she finds is significant – she is on the telephone, she receives things or she sends [*envoie*] others off to do various things, in short she shunts things around so that she can feel herself outside the situation, and in the end, she always makes sure to get the sack [*renvoyer*].

So this is the plane on which the transference relation comes to be played out – it is played out around the symbolic relation, whether it be a question of its institution, of its extension, or of its maintenance. The transference includes incidents, projections of imaginary articulations, but it is to be located entirely within the symbolic relation. What does that imply?

Speech is not deployed on one plane alone. By definition, speech always has its ambiguous backdrops, which attain the moment of the ineffable, in which it can no longer be spoken, can no longer provide its own foundations as speech. But this beyond is not the one that psychology searches for in the subject, finding it in God knows what mimicry, cramps, agitations, and all the emotional correlates of speech. The so-called psychological beyond is in fact on the other side, it is a be-fore [*en-deçà*]. The be-yond involved is to be found in the very dimension of speech.

By *being of the subject*, we do not mean its psychological properties, but what is hollowed out in the experience of speech, which constitutes the analytic situation.

This experience is constituted in analysis by extremely paradoxical rules, since what is involved is a dialogue, but a dialogue which is as much of a monologue as possible. It unfolds according to a rule of the game, and entirely within the symbolic order. Do you follow? What I wanted to exemplify today is the symbolic register in analysis, in bringing out the contrast that exists between the concrete examples that Balint gives, and his theorisation.

What for him is brought out by these examples is the mainspring of the situation, that is, the use that each of these two people, the bloke and the lady, made of speech. Now, that is an illicit extrapolation. Speech in analysis is not at all the same as that speech, which is both triumphant and innocent, which the child can make use of before he enters into the world of work. To speak in analysis is not equivalent to sustaining on purpose an insignificant discourse in the world of work. It is only by analogy that one can link the two together. Their basis is entirely different.

The analytic situation is not just an ectopia of the infantile situation. It is obviously an atypical situation, and Balint tries to take account of this by seeing it as an attempt at maintaining the register of primary love.[8] That's true, from certain points of view, but not all. In limiting oneself to this point of view, one embarks upon interventions which will lead the subject astray.

The facts prove it. In saying to the lady patient that she was reproducing some situation or other from her childhood, the analyst who preceded Balint didn't succeed in turning the situation around. That only started to happen given the concrete fact that the lady had with her that morning a letter which allowed her to find a position. Without theorising it, without knowing it, Balint intervened there in the symbolic register, put into play by the assured guarantee, by the simple fact of answering for someone. And it was precisely because he was on this plane that he had an effect.

His theory is out of joint, and botched as well. And yet, when one reads his text, one finds, as you have just seen, gloriously enlightening examples. The excellent practitioner Balint cannot, despite his theory, fail to recognise the dimension within which he manoeuvres.

4

Amongst Balint's references, there is one I want to take up here. It is a couplet by someone that he calls one of our colleagues – and why not? – Johannes Scheffler.

Having, at the beginning of the sixteenth century, undertaken very advanced medical studies – that probably had more meaning at that time than in our day – the latter wrote some very striking couplets, under the name of Angelus Silesius. Mystical? That is not quite the right way to describe them. The question of the deity is to be found in them, and of his relations with creativity

---

[8] English in the original.

which in its essence depends on human speech, and which goes as far as speech, to the point, even, where it ends up falling silent. The rather unorthodox perspective which Angelus Silesius always maintained is, in fact, a puzzle for historians of religious thought.

That he finds a place in Balint's text is certainly not just a matter of chance. The two verses he quotes are very beautiful. Their subject is nothing less than being in so far as it is tied, in the realisation of the subject, to the contingent or the accidental, and for Balint this has resonances with how he conceives the final moment of analysis, namely this state of narcissistic eruption, which I have already talked about in one of our meetings.

This rings a bell for us as well. Except, I don't think of the analytic termination in this manner. Freud's formula – *Where id was, ego must be* – is usually understood in line with crass spatialisation, and the analytic reconquest of the id is in the end reduced to the action of a mirage. The *ego* sees itself in a self which is simply a final alienation of itself, just better finished than all those it has known up to then.

No, it is the act of speech which is constitutive. The progress of an analysis does not consist in the enlarging of the field of the *ego*, it is not the reconquest by the *ego* of its margin of the unknown, rather it is a genuine inversion, a displacement, like a minuet executed by the *ego* and the *id*.

It is time to give you the couplet of Angelus Silesius – the thirtieth from the second book of *The Cherubinic Wanderer*.

> *Zufall und Wesen*
> *Mensch werde wesentlich: denn wann die Welt vergeht*
> *So fällt der Zufall weg, das Wesen das besteht.*

This couplet translates as follows –

> Contingence and essence
> Man, become essential: for when the world fails at last,
> The contingent falls away, but Essence, that stands fast.[9]

That really is what is at issue, at the end of analysis, a twilight, an imaginary decline of the world, and even an experience at the limit of depersonalisation. *That is when the contingent falls away* – the accidental, the trauma, the hitches of history – *And it is being which then comes to be constituted*.

Clearly Angelus wrote this at the time when he was studying medicine. The end of his life was troubled by the dogmatic wars of the Reformation and the Counter-Reformation, with respect to which he took up an extremely impassioned position. But the books of the *Cherubinic Wanderer* strike a transparent, crystalline note. It is one of the most significant moments in human meditation on being, a moment richer in resonances for me than the

---

[9] Translation adapted from *Selections from The Cherubinic Wanderer*, translated with an introduction by J. E. C. Flitch, London, 1932, p. 166.

Dark Night of St John of the Cross, which everyone reads and no one understands.

I cannot recommend anyone who is in analysis too highly to go out and acquire the works of Angelus Silesius. They are not that long, and they are translated in French, published by Aubier. You will find in them lots of other things to meditate on, for example the pun on *Wort*, speech, and *Ort*, place, and aphorisms which are spot on concerning temporality. Perhaps I will have an occasion next time to touch on some of these admirable formulae, which are extremely closed and yet open up, and lend themselves to meditation.

9 June 1954

SPEECH IN
THE TRANSFERENCE

XIX

The creative function of speech

Our friend Granoff has something to tell us, which seems to fit in with what I discussed last time. I am exceedingly happy when people take such initiatives, as they are completely in conformity with the spirit of dialogue which I desire in what is – let us not forget it – first and foremost a seminar. I do not know what he is going to tell us this morning.

Granoff's presentation concerned two articles from the April 1954 number of the Psycho-analytic Review: *'Emotion, instinct and pain-pleasure', by A. Chapman Isham, and 'A study of the dream in depth, its corollary and consequences' by C. Bennitt.*

1

These two extensive articles, pitched at a high theoretical level, converge with what I am doing here. But each of them draws attention to different points.

The first puts the emphasis on the information of emotion, which is said to be the ultimate reality with which we have to deal, and, strictly speaking, is the object of our experience. This conception answers to the desire to find an object somewhere which is similar, in so far as it is possible, to objects belonging to other registers.

Alexander wrote an important article, which we may perhaps discuss some day, called 'Logic of emotions', which no doubt places him at the heart of analytic theory.

Just as in this recent article of Chapman Isham, the question is how to introduce a dialectic into what we usually consider to be the affective register. Alexander starts with the well known logico-symbolic schema in which Freud deduces the various forms of delusion in accordance with the various ways of denying *I love him – It is not me who loves him – It is not him that I love – I do not love him – He hates me – It is him who loves me* – which accounts for the genesis of various delusions – the jealous, the impassioned, the persecutive, the erotomaniacal, etc. Hence we grasp the transformations, the very metabolism, which occur in the preconscious order, in a symbolic structuration, at a high level, since it includes very elaborate grammatical variations.

The first article that Granoff commented upon is thus interesting on account of its being at odds with the theoretical current dominant in analysis today. The second seems even more interesting to me, in so far as it seeks the beyond, the reality, the *fact*, as the article puts it, to which signification refers. It is a crucial problem.

So, you will get caught up in paths which are always dead ends, as is clearly seen in view of the impasses in which analytic theory finds itself today, if you fail to take account of the fact that signification only ever refers back to itself, that is to say to another signification.

Each time that we are obliged, in the analysis of language, to look for the signification of a word, the only correct method is to enumerate all of its usages. If you want to know the signification of the word *main* in the French language, you must draw up the catalogue of its usages, and not only when it represents the organ of the hand, but also when it figures in *main d'oeuvre* [manpower], *mainmise* [manumission], *mainmorte* [mortmain], etc. The signification is given by the sum of these usages.

This is what we are concerned with in analysis. We don't have to try very hard to find additional references. What need is there to talk of a reality which would sustain the so-called metaphorical usages? Every kind of usage, in a certain sense, is always metaphorical. Metaphor is not to be distinguished, as Jones thought, at the beginning of his article on 'The theory of symbolism', from the symbol itself and from its usage. Were I to address another being, whether created or not, in calling him *sun of my heart*, it would be an error to believe, as Jones does, that it is a question of a comparison, between what you are in my heart and what the sun is, etc. Comparison is only a secondary development of the original emergence of the metaphorical relation to being, one that is infinitely richer than anything I could now illuminate.

This emergence implies everything which will come to be linked with it in the future, and which I do not believe to have said. Simply from my having formulated this relation, it is me, my being, my avowal, my invocation, which enters into the domain of the symbol. Implied in this formula is the fact that the sun heats me up, the fact that it allows me to live, and also that it is the centre of my gravitation, and for that matter that it gives rise to Valéry's *morne moitié d'ombre*,[1] that it also blinds, lending false clarity and a deceptive glitter to everything. Because, the greatest light is also, is it not, the source of all obscurity. All that is already implied in the symbolic invocation. The

[1] Paul Valéry, 'Le cimitière marin: '. . . rendre la lumière/Suppose d'ombre une morne moitié.'

emergence of the symbol *creates*, literally, a new order of being in the relations between men.

But you'll say, there are, all the same, irreducible expressions. And you will object, furthermore, that we can always reduce the creative utterance of this symbolic call down to the level of fact, and that one could find simpler, more organic, more animal formulae for the metaphor that I gave you as an example. Try it out for yourselves – you will see that you will never leave the world of the symbol behind.

Let us suppose that you have recourse to the organic index, to the *Mets ta main sur mon coeur*,[2] said to Léonor by the infanta at the beginning of *Le Cid*, to express her feelings of love for the young knight. Well, if the organic index is invoked, it is still there at the centre of the confession, like a testimony, a testimony which only gains its edge in so far as – *Je m'en souviens si bien que j'épandrais mon sang Avant que je m'abbaisse à démentir mon rang*.[3] It is, in fact, only in as much as she forbids herself this feeling that she invokes a factual element. The fact of her heart beating only acquires its meaning within the symbolic world traced out in the dialectic of the feeling which is refused, or which is implicitly refused recognition by the person who experiences it.

We have, as you can see, come back to the point our discourse had reached last time.

2

Each time that we find ourselves within the order of speech, everything which founds another reality in reality, at the limit, only acquires its meaning and its edge in relation to this same order. If the emotion can be displaced, inverted, inhibited, if it is engaged in a dialectic, it is due to its being taken up into the symbolic order, in accordance with which the other orders, the imaginary and the real, find their place and their disposition.

Once more, I will try to make you see it. Here is a little fable.

One day, Odysseus's companions – as you know, a thousand misadventures befell them, and I think almost none completed the excursion – were turned, because of their unfortunate tendencies, into swine. The theme of the metamorphosis is well calculated to interest us, since it raises the question of the limit between the human and the animal.

So, they are turned into swine, and the story goes on.

One is still obliged to think they nonetheless retain some links with the human world, since in the middle of the pigsty – but the pigsty is a society – they

---

    [2] Pierre Corneille, *Le Cid*, Act I, Scene 2: 'Put your hand on my heart.'
    [3] *Ibid*. 'I remember it so well that I would spill my own blood/Before I would abase myself in denying my rank.'

communicate, through their grunts, their different needs, hunger, thirst, their sensuality, indeed their group feeling. But that is not all.

What can one say about these grunts? Aren't they also messages addressed to the other world? Well, here, at any rate, is what I hear. Odysseus's companions grunt the following – *We miss Odysseus, we miss his being with us, we miss his teaching, what he was for us in life.*

How do we recognise that a grunt which comes to us out of this silky mass filling the enclosed space of the pigsty is speech? Is it because some ambivalent feeling is expressed in it?

On this occasion there really does exist what we call, in the order of emotions and feelings, ambivalence. Because, for his companions, Odysseus is somewhat of a liability as a guide. However, once changed into swine, they no doubt have grounds for missing his presence. From whence the doubt about what they are communicating.

This dimension is not to be overlooked. But is it enough to turn a grunt into speech? No, because the emotional ambivalence of the grunt is a reality, in its essence unconstituted.

The pig's grunt only becomes speech when someone raises the question as to what it is that they want to make you believe. Speech is precisely only speech in as much as someone believes in it.

And what, through grunting, do these companions of Odysseus turned into swine want to have us believe? – that they are still somewhat human. To give expression to their nostalgia for Odysseus is, on this occasion, to lay claim to recognition for themselves, the swine, as being the companions of Odysseus.

It is within this dimension that speech is to be located, before all else. Speech is essentially the means of gaining recognition. It is there before anything lying behind. And, on account of that, it is ambivalent, and absolutely unfathomable. What it says – is it true? Is it not true? It is a mirage. It is this initial mirage which guarantees that you are in the domain of speech.

Without this dimension, a communication is just something which transmits, roughly of the same order as a mechanical movement. A moment ago I alluded to the silky rustling, the rustling communication within the pigsty. That is it – the grunt is entirely analysable in terms of mechanics. But, as soon as it wants to have something believed and demands recognition, speech exists. That is why, in a sense, one can speak of the language of animals. Animals have a language [*langage*] to the degree that there is someone there to understand it.

3

Let us take another example which I will borrow from Nunberg's article, 'Transference and reality', from 1951, which raises the question as to what the transference is. It is the same problem.

It is extremely gratifying to see both how far the author goes and the extent to which he is nonplussed. According to him, everything happens at the level of the imaginary. The foundation of the transference is, he thinks, the projection into reality of something which is not there. The subject requires that his partner be a form, a model, of his father for example.

To start with, he refers to the case of a patient who spent her time vehemently scolding the analyst, bawling him out even, reproaching him for never being good enough, for never making the correct interventions, for making mistakes, for being in bad taste. Is this an instance of transference, Nunberg asks himself?

Interestingly enough, but not without some justification, he replies – no, here it is rather more like an aptitude – readiness[4] – for transference. For the moment, in her recriminations, the subject makes her requirement heard, her primitive requirement for a real person, and what motivates her dissatisfaction is the discordance which the real world manifests in comparison with this prerequisite. That is not the transference, but its condition.

When does transference really start? When the image which the subject requires becomes confused for the subject with the reality in which he is placed. The whole progress of the analysis is to show him the distinction between these two planes, to unstick the imaginary and the real. Classical theory – the subject displays so-called delusive behaviour, which one brings him to see is rather ill adapted to the actual situation.

Except, we spend our time realising that the transference is in no way a delusive phenomenon. You are not analysing the subject if you say to him – *But my dear chap, the feeling you have for me is only transference.* That has never settled anything. Luckily, when the authors are clear-headed in their practice, they give examples which give the lie to their theory and which prove that they have some feeling for the truth. That is true of Nunberg. The example that he gives as being typical of the experience of transference is particularly instructive.

He had a patient who brought him masses of material, and expressed himself with an authenticity, a care for detail, a regard for being complete, with a surrender . . . And yet nothing budged. Nothing budged until Nunberg realised that the analytic situation happened to reproduce, for the patient, a situation from his childhood, in which he indulged in making as complete confessions as possible, based upon the total confidence that he had in his interlocutor, who was none other than his mother, who came every evening to sit at the foot of his bed. The patient, like Scheherezade, took pleasure in giving her an exhaustive account not only of day-to-day events, but also of his acts, of his desires, of his inclinations, of his scruples, of his self-reproaches, never hiding anything. The warm presence of his mother, clad in her night-gown, was for him the source of a continuous pleasure in and of itself, consisting in making out the outline of her breasts and body under her gown. So he conducted his first sexual investigations on his beloved partner.

[4] English in the original.

How do you analyse this? Let us try to be a little bit coherent. What does this mean?

Two very different situations are evoked here – the patient with his mother, the patient with the analyst.

In the first situation, the subject experiences a satisfaction by means of this spoken exchange. We have no difficulty in distinguishing two planes there, the plane of the symbolic relations, which here are quite indubitably subordinated to, subverted by the imaginary relationship. On the other hand, in analysis, the subject gives himself over to complete surrender, and submits with total good will to the rule. Are we forced to conclude from that that he experiences a satisfaction similar to the primary satisfaction? For many, this step is easily taken – *but of course, that's it*, the subject is seeking out a similar satisfaction. With no hesitation there'll be talk of the compulsion to repeat. And everything else you may want to add. The analyst will pride himself on having detected behind this speech goodness knows what feeling or emotion, which would reveal the presence of a psychological beyond constituted past speech.

But wait a moment, let's think about this! To start off with, the analyst's position is exactly the inverse of the mother's position, he is not at the foot of the bed, but behind, and he is a long way from offering, at least in most instances, the charms of the primary object, and a long way from being party to the same concupiscences. In any case, that is not the way you will be able to draw the analogy.

What I'm saying is downright simple-minded. But it is only by making the structure a bit more explicit, and in saying simple things, that we will be able to learn how to spell out in words of one syllable the elements of the situation in which we act.

What has to be understood is the following – why does a complete transformation of the analytic situation ensue as soon as the relation between the situations has been revealed to the subject? Why do the same words then become effective, and constitute genuine development in the subject's existence? Let us think this over a bit.

Speech as such is instituted within the structure of the semantic world which is that of language. Speech never has one single meaning, nor the word one single use. All speech always possesses a beyond, sustains various functions, encompasses several meanings. Behind what a discourse says, there is what it means [*veut dire*], and behind what it means, there is again another intended meaning [*vouloir-dire*], and nothing will ever be exhausted by that – except that it comes down to this, that speech has a creative function, and that it brings into being the very thing, which is none other than the concept.

Remember what Hegel says about the concept – *The concept is the time of the thing*. To be sure, the concept is not the thing as it is, for the simple reason that the concept is always where the thing isn't, it is there so as to replace the thing, like the elephant that I brought into the room the other day by means of the word *elephant*. If that was so striking for some of you, it was because it was clear that the elephant was really there as soon as we named it. Of the thing, what is it that can be there? Neither its form, nor its reality, since, in the actual state of affairs, all the seats are taken. Hegel puts it with extreme rigour – the concept is what makes the thing be there, while, all the while, it isn't.

This identity in difference, which characterises the relation of the concept to the thing, that is what also makes the thing a thing and the fact⁵ symbolised, as we were told just now. We are talking about things, and not about some eternally unidentifiable I know not what.

Heraclitus tells us – if we introduce absolute mobility in the existence of things such that the flow of the world never comes to pass twice by the same situation, it is precisely because identity in difference is already saturated in the thing. It is from this that Hegel deduces that *the concept is the time of the thing.*

At this point we find ourselves at the heart of the problem that Freud sets up when he says that the unconscious is located outside time. It is true, and it isn't. It is located outside time exactly like the concept, because it is in itself time, the pure time of the thing, and as such it can reproduce the thing within a certain modulation, whose material support can be anything. The compulsion to repeat involves nothing but this. This remark will take us a very long way, indeed well into those problems of time which analytic practice generates.

So let us go back to our example – why does the analysis become transformed the moment the transferential situation is analysed through evoking the old situation, when the subject found himself with an entirely different object, one that cannot be assimilated to the present object? Because present speech, like the old speech, is placed within a parenthesis of time, within a form of time, if I can put it that way. The modulation of time being identical, the speech of the analyst happens to have the same value as the old speech.

This value is the value of speech. There is no feeling, no imaginary projection in it, and Nunberg, who goes out of his way to construct one, thus finds himself in a situation from which he cannot extricate himself.

For Loewenstein, there is no projection, but rather displacement. That is a mythology which has all the hallmarks of a labyrinth. You will only escape from it by recognising that the time-element is a dimension constitutive of the order of speech.

If in actual fact the concept is time, we must analyse speech in stages, to seek in it the multiple meanings between the lines. Is there no end to it? No, it is not without end. Except, what is revealed at the end, the last word, the last meaning, is this temporal form which I am telling you about, and which all by

---

⁵ English in the original.

itself is speech. The final meaning of the speech of the subject before the analyst is his existential relation before the object of his desire.

On this occasion this narcissistic mirage does not take on any particular form, it is nothing other than whatever supports the relation of man to the object of his desire, and always leaves him isolated in what we call fore-pleasure. This relation is a specular one, and here it places speech in a kind of suspension in relation to what indeed amounts to a purely imaginary situation.

There is nothing present, nothing emotional, nothing real in this situation. But, once it has been reached, it changes the meaning of speech, it reveals to the subject that his speech is only what I called in my Rome report *empty speech*, and that it is as such that it is lacking in any effect.

None of this is easy. Are you with me? You must understand that the beyond to which we are referred is always another speech, one that is deeper. As to the ineffable limit of speech, it stems from the fact that speech creates the resonance of all these meanings. In the end, we are referred back to the very act of speech as such. It is the value of this act, here and now, which makes this speech empty or full. What is involved in the analysis of transference is knowing at which point in its presence speech is full.

4

If you find this interpretation a trifle speculative, I am now going to give you a reference, since I am here to comment on Freud's texts, and it isn't an inopportune moment for saying that what I am explaining to you is strictly orthodox.

At what point in Freud's work does the word *Übertragung*, transference, appear? It is not in the Papers on Technique, nor in connection with real, or indeed imaginary, or even symbolic, relations, it doesn't matter which, with the subject. It is not apropos of Dora nor of all the miserable things she did to him, since, supposedly, he did not know how to tell her in good time that she was beginning to feel tenderly towards him. It is in the seventh section, 'The psychology of the dream-processes', of the *Traumdeutung*.

That is a book which I will perhaps give you a commentary on someday soon, one whose sole aim is the demonstration, in the function of the dream, of the superposed significations of a material signifier. Freud shows us how speech, that is the transmission of desire, can get itself recognised through anything, provided that this anything be organised in a symbolic system. There we have the source of what was for so long the indecipherable character of the dream. And it is for the same reason that for a long time no one knew how to understand hieroglyphics – they were not set up in their own symbolic system, all anyone could see was a little human silhouette, which might mean *a man*, but might also represent the sound *man*, and, as such, might be a part of a word by virtue of its being a syllable. The dream is constructed like hieroglyphics. Freud refers, as you know, to the Rosetta Stone.

What does Freud call *Übertragung*? It is, he says, the phenomenon constituted by the fact that it is not possible to give a direct translation, for a given desire repressed by the subject. This desire of the subject is forbidden to his mode of discourse, and cannot get itself recognised. Why? Because amongst the elements of the repression there is something which partakes of the ineffable. There are essential relations which no discourse can express adequately, except in what I called just now the interlineation.

Next time I will tell you about *The Guide of the Perplexed* by Maimonides, which is an esoteric work. You'll see the extent to which he deliberately organises his discourse in such a way that what he wants to say, which is not sayable – it is him who says this – can nonetheless be revealed. He says what cannot or must not be said by means of a certain disorder, certain ruptures, certain intentional discordances. Well, the slips, the holes, the disputes, the repetitions of the subject also express, but here spontaneously, innocently, the manner in which his discourse is organised. And that is what we have to read. We will come back to this, because the texts are worth the trouble of being brought together.

What does Freud say in his initial definition of *Übertragung*? He tells us about the *Tagesreste*, the day-residues, which are, he says, disinvested from the point of view of desire. These are, within the dream, the stray forms which have become, for the subject, of minimal importance – and are emptied of their meaning. So this is a piece of signifying material. The signifying material, be it phonematic, hieroglyphic, etc., is constituted out of forms which have forfeited their own meaning and are taken up again within a new organisation, thanks to which another meaning finds a means of gaining expression. What Freud calls *Übertragung* is exactly that.

The desire which is unconscious, that is to say impossible to express, nonetheless finds a means of expression through the alphabet, the phonematics of day-residues, themselves disinvested of desire. So it is a phenomenon of language as such. That is what Freud calls *Übertragung*, the first time he uses the word.

To be sure, in analysis, in comparison with what happens in dreams, there is this essential supplementary dimension, namely that the other is there. But note also that dreams become more clear, more analysable, as the analysis makes progress. That's because the dream addresses the analyst more and more. The best dreams that Freud puts before us, the richest, the most beautiful, the most complicated are the ones which take place in the course of an analysis, and which tend to address the analyst.

This should in addition clear up for you the true signification of the term acting-out.[6] If, just now, I mentioned the compulsion to repeat, if I mentioned it primarily in relation to language, it is really because every action in the session, acting-out[6] or acting-in,[6] is included in a context of speech. One qualifies as acting-out[6] whatever takes place in the treatment. And not without reason. If so many subjects rush headlong while in analysis into engaging in a host of erotic activities, like getting married for example, it is clearly acting-out.[6] If they act, it is with their analyst in mind.

That is really why one must analyse the acting-out[6] and analyse the transference, that is to say find the meaning of speech in an act. In so far as the point for the subject is to gain recognition, an act is speech.

On this note I will leave you today.

16 June 1954

[6] English in the original.

XX

De locutionis significatione

Following the very interesting contribution our good friend Granoff made, which fitted the shape the previous seminar had taken on like a glove, it was very easy for me to continue with what I was saying, and I was thus led into clarifying something which, up to that point, had been left hanging within the series of questions I raise with you.

This clarification is the following – the function of the transference can only be understood on the symbolic plane. It is around this central point that all the forms in which it becomes apparent to us are organised, and this is true even for the domain of the imaginary.

I couldn't think of a better way to get you to grasp this than to focus on the first definition Freud gave of the transference.

What is fundamentally at issue in transference, is how a discourse that is masked, the discourse of the unconscious, takes a hold of a discourse that is apparent. This discourse takes possession of these emptied-out, available elements, the *Tagesreste*, and of everything else in the preconscious order, which is made available by the smallest investment of this, the subject's fundamental need, which is to gain recognition. It is within this vacuum, within this hollow, with what thus becomes working materials, that the deep, secret discourse gains expression. We see it in the dream, but we also rediscover it in the slip of the tongue and throughout the psychopathology of everyday life.

That is our starting-point for listening to the person who speaks to us. And we only have to refer back to our definition of the discourse of the unconscious, which is that it is the discourse of the other, to understand how it authentically links up again with intersubjectivity in the dialogue, that full realisation of speech.

The fundamental phenomenon revealed by analysis is this relation of one discourse to another, using it as a support. What we discover manifested in it is this fundamental principle of semantics, that every semanteme refers to the whole of the semantic system, to the polyvalence of its usages. Moreover, for everything which properly speaking pertains to language, in as much as it is human, that is to say utilisable in speech, the symbol is never univocal. Every semanteme always has several meanings.

From whence we come upon that truth, which is so absolutely obvious in our experience, and which linguists are well aware of, that every signification only ever refers back [*renvoyer*] to another signification. So linguists have resigned themselves to this, and it is from within this field that from now on they are developing their science.

One should not believe that this is taking place with no ambiguity, and that, for a Ferdinand de Saussure who saw it clearly, perfectly satisfactory definitions had always been available.

The signifier is the audible matter, which, however, does not mean the sound. Not everything belonging to the order of phonetics is on that account included in linguistics as such. It is the phoneme that is the important element, that is to say one sound as opposed to another sound, within a set of oppositions.

When one talks about the signified, one thinks of the thing, whereas in fact signification is what is involved. Nonetheless, each time we talk, we say the thing, the signifiable, by means of the signified. There is a lure here, because it is quite clear that language is not made to designate things. But this lure is structural to human language and, in a sense, the verification of every truth is founded on it.

During a discussion I recently had with the most eminent person in the field in France, someone who can legitimately be qualified as a linguist, M. Benveniste, it was pointed out to me that one thing has never been made clear. It may surprise you, since you are not linguists.

Let us begin with the notion that the signification of a term must be defined by the totality of its possible usages. This can also be extended to groups of terms, and in truth one can't have a theory of language [*langue*] if one doesn't take the usages of groups into account, that is to say, expressions, and syntactical forms as well. But there is a limit, which is – that the sentence, for its part, does not have a usage. So there are two zones of signification.

This remark is of the greatest importance, because these two zones of signification are perhaps something to which we are referring, since it is a way of defining the difference between speech and language.

This discovery was made recently, by a man as eminent as M. Benveniste. It is unpublished, and he imparted it to me as something he is working on at the moment. It is clearly cut out to give us much food for thought.

In fact, Father Beirnaert thought of telling me – *Wouldn't everything that you have been saying on the subject of signification be illustrated in the* Disputatio de locutionis significatione, *which constitutes the first part of the* De magistro? I replied – *That is a splendid idea, what you have just said.* Even what I taught you last time bore traces of what I remember of this text. One must not overlook the fact that the words I despatch to you elicit such responses, indeed such commemorations, as Saint Augustine expresses himself, which, in Latin, is the exact equivalent of recollection [*remémoration*].

Father Beirnaert's recollection is just as much to the point as the articles Granoff introduced. And it is quite telling that the linguists, in as much as we are entitled to make up one large family through the ages bearing this name, *linguists*, have taken fifteen centuries to rediscover, like a sun which has risen anew, like a dawn that is breaking, ideas which are already set out in Saint Augustine's text, which is one of the most glorious one could read. And I treated myself to reading it again for this occasion.

Everything I have been telling you about the signifier and the signified is there, expounded with a sensational lucidity, so sensational that I am afraid that the spiritual commentators who have given themselves over to its exegesis have not always perceived all of its subtlety. They think that the profound Doctor of the Church has strayed off his path into rather futile things. These futile things are nothing other than the latest developments in modern thought on language.

1

FATHER BEIRNAERT: *I only had six or seven hours to venture into this text a little, and I can only give you a short introduction.*[1]

How do you translate *De locutionis significatione?*

BEIRNAERT: *On the signification of speech.*

Undeniably. *Locutio* is speech.

BEIRNAERT: Oratio *is discourse.*

We could say – *On the signifying function of speech*, since a bit further on we come upon a text in which *significatio* itself has exactly this sense. Here *speech* is used in the broad sense, it is language [*langage*] at work in elocution, even eloquence. It is neither full nor empty speech, it is speech in its entirety. Full speech, how would you translate that into Latin?

BEIRNAERT: *There is an expression* – sententia plena. *A full statement is one in which there is not only a verb, but also a subject, a noun.*

---

[1] St Augustine, *De Magistro*, translated as *The Teacher*, in *The Fathers of the Church Vol. 59. Saint Augustine. The Teacher. The Free Choice of the Will. Grace and Free Will*, translated by Robert P. Russell, Washington: The Catholic University of America Press, 1968, pp. 7–61, from which the passages quoted are taken, with certain modifications to accord English and French versions with the Latin text, to be found in: *Corpus Christianorum XXIX Aurelii Augustini Opera, Pars II, 2,* Turnholti, Typographi Brepols Editores Pontificii, 1970, pp. 155–203.

That simply means the complete sentence, that is not speech. There Saint Augustine is trying to prove that all words are nouns. He uses several arguments. He explains that every word in a sentence can be employed as a noun. *If* is a subordinating conjunction. But in the sentence 'I don't like the *if*', the word is used as a noun. Saint Augustine proceeds in as rigorous and analytical a spirit as any modern linguist, and he shows that it is its usage in the sentence which defines what part of speech a word is. Well. Have you thought how to translate full speech into Latin?

BEIRNAERT: *No. Perhaps we will come across it in going over the text. If you will allow me, I am going to supply the context for the dialogue* De Magistro. *It was written by Augustine in 389, some years after his return to Africa. Its title is* On the master, *and it uses two interlocutors – Augustine and his son Adeodatus, who was then sixteen years old. This Adeodatus was very intelligent, so Saint Augustine says, and he assures us that Adeodatus's words were actually spoken by this boy of sixteen, who thus proves himself to be a disputant of the first rank.*

The child of sin.

BEIRNAERT: *– The thematic axis, which determines the direction the entire dialogue takes, is that language transmits the truth from without through words which sound without, but the disciple always sees the truth within.*

Before coming to this conclusion, towards which the discussion is rushing headlong, the dialogue snakes for a long time and proposes a doctrine of language and of speech from which we have much to learn.

There are two large parts – the first is the Disputatio de locutionis significatione, *the discussion of the signification of speech, the second part is entitled* Veritatis magister solus est Christus, *Christ is the sole master of truth.*

The first part is itself divided into two sections. The first is synthetically entitled De signis. *It is poorly translated as – Of the value of words. It is really about something quite different, since one cannot identify* signum *and* verbum. *The second section has as its title* Signa ad discendum nihil valent, *signs are of no use in learning. Let us start off with Of signs.*

Augustine asks his son – What do we want to do, when we speak? Reply – We want to teach or learn, in accordance with the position of master or disciple. Saint Augustine is going to try to show that, even when one wants to learn and when one asks questions so as to learn, one is still teaching. Why? Because one teaches the person one addresses what it is one wants to know. Hence, the general definition – So you see, that through language we do nothing other than teach.

Will you allow me to make a remark? You do realise, don't you, the extent to which we are, right from the start, at the heart of what I have been trying to explain to you here. The question is – what is the difference between communication by signals and the exchange of interhuman speech?

Straightaway Augustine makes for the element of intersubjectivity, since he highlights *docere* and *discere*, which are impossible to distinguish. The entire interrogation is essentially an attempt to make the two speeches agree, which implies that from the first there was agreement between languages [*langages*]. No exchange is possible, except by way of the reciprocal identification of two complete universes of language [*langage*]. That is why speech is already, as such, a teaching. It is not a play of signs, it is to be located, not on the level of information, but on that of truth.

BEIRNAERT: *Adeodatus – I do not think that we wish to teach anything when no one is there to learn.*

Each of these replies is worthy of special attention.

BEIRNAERT: *Having emphasised teaching, he goes on to an excellent method of teaching,* per commemoration, *that is to say, through recalling* [ressouvenir]. *So there are two reasons for speaking. We speak either in order to teach, or in order to induce recollection, either in other people, or in ourselves. Following what is the beginning to the dialogue, Augustine raises the question whether speech exists solely in order to teach or to recall. Here, let us not forget the religious atmosphere which informs the dialogue. The interlocutor replies that there is prayer, after all, in which one enters into a dialogue with God. Can we believe that God is taught or reminded of something by us? Our prayer does not require words, Augustine very precisely states, except when others should know that we are praying. When it comes to God, one does not try to remember or to teach the subject with whom one is in dialogue, but rather alert others to the fact that one is praying. Hence, one only expresses oneself in relation to those people who can see us engaged in this dialogue.*

Prayer here touches on the ineffable. It does not belong in the field of speech.

BEIRNAERT: *That said, teaching is accomplished by means of words. Words are signs. At this point we find a considerable discussion on* verbum *and* signum. *To develop his thought, and render explicit the manner in which he conceives of the relation of the sign to the signifiable, Augustine proposes a verse from the Aeneid to his interlocutor.*

He hasn't defined signifiable yet.

BEIRNAERT: *No, not yet – the point is to signify, but what? We don't know as yet. So he takes a verse from the Aeneid – Book II, line 659 –* Si nihil ex tanta superis placet urbe relinqui. *If it pleases the gods that nothing remain of so great a city. And, through an entire maieutic, he will try to discover this* aliquid *which is signified. He starts by asking his interlocutor.*

> Aug. – *How many words are there in this verse?*
> Ad. – *Eight.*

Aug. – So there are eight signs?

Ad. – That is indeed the case.

Aug. – Do you think you understand this verse?

Ad. – I understand it well enough.

Aug. – Tell me now what each word signifies.

Adeodatus is a bit put out by the si. He has to find an equivalent for it. He doesn't find one.

Aug. – Whatever is signified by this word, do you know at least where it occurs?

Ad. – It seems to me that si signifies doubt. Now, where is doubt to be found, if not in the soul?[2]

It is interesting, because we immediately see that the word refers to something of a spiritual order, to a state of the subject as such.

Are you sure?

BEIRNAERT: *I think so.*

Be that as it may, he is talking there about a localisation.

BEIRNAERT: *Which should not be spatialised. I say* in the soul *in opposition to the material. Then he moves on to the next word. It is* nihil, *that is* nothing. *Adeodatus says – Clearly, this is what does not exist. Saint Augustine makes the objection that what does not exist cannot possibly be something. So the second word is not a sign, because it does not signify something. And it is by mistake that they had agreed that every word is a sign, or that every sign is a sign of something. Adeodatus is perplexed, because if we have nothing to signify, it is madness to speak. So, there must be something to that.*

Aug. – Instead of saying that nihil *signifies something which is nothing, shall we say that this word signifies a certain state in the soul when, failing to perceive a thing the soul nevertheless finds, or thinks it finds, that such a thing does not exist?*

Hence, what is signified here is the state in the soul consequent upon an absence of something which could be there.

The value of this first part lies quite precisely in having shown that it is impossible to deal with language by referring the sign to the thing term by term. It is informative for us, as long as we don't forget that negativity had not been developed in Saint Augustine's time. And you see that, not withstanding, by dint of signs, or of things – we are here to try to find out which it is – he falters on the *nihil* in this beautiful line. It is not an entirely accidental choice. Certainly Freud knew Virgil very well, and this line, which evokes the Troy that has disappeared, has a strange resonance with the fact that, when Freud, in *Civilisation and its Discontents*, wants to define the unconscious, he talks of the

---

[2] *'âme'* in French; *'in animo'* in Latin; 'mind' in English translation.

monuments of the Rome that had once been. Both instances deal with things that disappear in history, but which, at the same time, still remain present, absent.

BEIRNAERT: *Augustine then moves on to the third term, which is ex. Here, his disciple gives him another word to explain what it signifies. It is the word de, a term of separation from a thing in which the object is found, from which it is derived. After which Augustine remarks that he has explained words with words – ex by de, one very well known word by other very well known ones. Then he urges him to move beyond the plane he presently occupies.*

>   Aug. – I would like you to show me, if you can, those very things of which these
>   words are the signs.

He uses rampart[3] as his example.

>   Aug. – Can you point it out to me in such a way that I will see the very thing
>   whose sign this three-syllable word is. You would be showing it to me without
>   the use of words.

Then there's an account of gesture language. Augustine asks his disciple if he has paid attention to the deaf, who communicate with each other by gesture. And he shows that, in this language, it is not only visible things which are shown, but also sounds, tastes, etc.

O. MANNONI: *This reminds me of the little game we played at Guitrancourt, on Sunday. And in the theatre, also, actors make themselves understood and put on plays without speech, with dancing.*

Your allusion is, in fact, very instructive. You're referring to a little game in which one of two teams has to get the other to guess, as quickly as possible, a word supplied in secret by the organiser of the game. Exactly what Saint Augustine is reminding us of in this passage becomes clear in this game. Because what is being talked about here is not so much the dialectic of gesture as the dialectic of pointing. That he uses as his example rampart should not surprise us, since he is going to come up more against the rampart of language than against the real rampart. He thus goes on to remark that it is not only things which can be designated, but also qualities. If every pointing is a sign, it is an ambiguous sign. Because if the rampart is pointed out to you, how are you to know that it really is the rampart, and not, for example, its rough quality, or its green, grey, etc? In the same way, in the little game we played the other day, someone having to express *ivy* went and got some ivy. He was told – *You are cheating.* That was wrong. The person brought three ivy leaves. That could designate the colour green, or the Holy Trinity, and lots of other things.

O. MANNONI: *I was going to say something. I want to say the word chair. If that very word fails me and I hold up a chair to complete my sentence, it is not really the*

---

[3] 'paries'.

thing that I am using, but the word. So it is not possible to speak with a thing, one always speaks with words.

Your example illustrates perfectly how interpretation works in analysis – we always interpret the actual reactions of the subject in as much as they are taken up in the discourse, just like your chair which is a word. When Freud interprets movements, gestures, and supposedly, emotions, that is always what is going on.

BEIRNAERT: *Nothing can be shown without a sign. Yet, Adeodatus will try to show that there are things which can be. Augustine asks him the following question.*

> *Aug. – If I ask you: what is walking? and you, in getting up, accomplish this act: won't you be using the thing itself, in order to teach me, rather than words or any other sign?*
>
> *Ad. – That is the case, I must confess, and I am ashamed at not having seen something so obvious.*
>
> *Aug. – If I were to ask you while you are walking: what is walking? How would you teach it to me?*
>
> *Ad. – I would carry out the same action a bit faster so as to draw your attention after you had asked me by something new, all the time doing nothing more than doing what was to be demonstrated.*

But that is hurrying, which is not the same thing as walking. One would be led to think that ambulare *is* festinare. *Just now, with the* nihil, *we touched on negativity, now, with this example, we come to see that a word like* festinare *can be applied to all sorts of other acts. More precisely, we see that in showing any act whatever in its particular temporality, the subject has no reason, if he does not have words at his disposal, to conceptualise the act itself, because he may think that it is only a question of this particular act at this particular point in time. Again, we come upon* time is the concept. *It is only if the time of the act is taken in itself, separated from the specific act, that the act can be conceptualised as such, that is to say, preserved in a name. Moreover, we are now coming to the dialectic of the name.*

So Adeodatus recognises that we cannot point out a thing without a sign when we are performing the act at the time asked. But, if we are questioned about an act that we can perform, but which we are not performing when being asked, this time we are capable of replying with the thing itself, by setting about and performing this act. In consequence we can show without signs, on condition that we are not in the process of performing the action when questioned about it.

Adeodatus makes an exception of one sole action, that of speaking. The other asks me – *What is speaking? Whatever I say to teach him,* the child says, *I will have to speak. With this starting-point, I would pursue my explanation to the point where I had made it clear what he wanted, without wandering off from the thing which he wanted to have shown him, and without looking for signs outside of this thing itself.* In fact, it is the only action which can demonstrate itself, since it is the action which in its essence is demonstrated by signs. Signification alone is recovered in our call, because signification always refers to signification.

B E I R N A E R T: *Augustine now goes back to all the points which have been touched on in order to go into them more deeply. Let us take up the first point, which is that signs are shown by signs.*

>   *Aug. – Are words the only signs?*
>   *Ad. – No.*
>   *Aug. – So it appears that in speaking, we signify by means of words, either the words themselves, or other signs.*

So Augustine then shows that, using speech, one is able to signify and designate signs other than those of speech, for example gestures, letters, etc.

Examples of two signs which are not *verba* – *gestus* and *littera*. Here, Saint Augustine shows himself to be more sane than our contemporaries, some of whom have come to regard gesture as not pertaining to the symbolic order, but as being located, for instance, at the level of an animal response. The gesture would thus become an objection to our thesis that analysis takes place entirely within speech. *And what about the subject's gestures?* they say. Now, a human gesture does belong with language and not with motor manifestations. That's obvious.

B E I R N A E R T: *I will continue reading.*

>   *Aug. – These signs which are words, to which sense do they pertain?*
>   *Ad. – To hearing.*
>   *Aug. – And gesture.*
>   *Ad. – To sight.*
>   *Aug. – And when we come upon written words? Are these not words, or do they have to be thought of more accurately as signs of words? So that, the word would be what is uttered as a sound of the voice articulated with a signification, which cannot be perceived by any other sense than that of hearing.*

So this written word refers to the word which is addressed to the ear, in such a way that the latter then pertains to the mind. Having said this, Augustine then goes on to pronounce a specific verbum, nomen, *the name.*

>   *Aug. – We do signify something with this* verbum nomen, *since we can signify* Romulus, Roma, fluvius, virtus, *innumerable things – it is only an intermediary. But there really is a difference between this name and the object that it signifies. What is this difference?*
>   *Ad. – Names are signs, and objects are not.*

So, ever on the horizon, always at the limit, are objects which are not signs. It is at this point that the term significabilia *comes up for the first time. We will call those objects signifiable which are susceptible of designation by a sign without themselves being a sign.*

Now we can go a bit faster. The final questions are all concerned with signs which designate themselves. What is required is deeper understanding of the meaning of the verbal sign, associated with the *nomen* and the *verbum* – we have translated *verbum* by *word* [*mot*], whereas Father Tonnard[4] at one point translates it by *speech* [*parole*].

In this connection, I would like to remark that it is possible that an isolated phoneme in language does not designate anything. One can only find this out through usage and use, that is to say through its integration into the system of signification. *Verbum* is used as such, and the argument whether every word may be considered to be a *nomen* turns on this. The question is raised. Even in languages where the substantival use of the verb is extremely rare, as in French, where in everyday language we do not say *le laisser* [the leaving], *le faire* [the doing], *le se trouver* [the finding itself], the distinction between the noun and the verb is more undecided than you may think. What is Augustine's point in wanting to identify *nomen* and *verbum*? And what value do you give to *nomen* in the language of our seminar?

It is precisely what we here call the symbol. The *nomen* is the totality signifier-signified, especially in as much as it makes for recognition, since the pact and the agreement rest upon it. It is the symbol in the sense of pact. The *nomen* is employed on the plane of recognition. This translation conforms to the linguistic essence of Latin, in which there are a fair number of legal usages for the word *nomen*, which can, for example, be used in the sense of 'credit note'.

Hence we may recall Hugo's play on words – it is not necessary to believe that he was a madman – *nomen, numen*. The word *nomen* has indeed an original form connecting it to *numen*, the sacred. To be sure, the linguistic evolution of the word was snatched up by *nocere*, giving rise to such forms as *agnomen*, which is hard not to think comes from a captation of *nomen* by *cognoscere*. But the legal usages are sufficient to show us that we are not wrong in recognising in it a function of recognition, of pact, of interhuman symbol.

BEIRNAERT: *Indeed, Saint Augustine makes it explicit in the passage in which he talks about expressions like* this is called, this is named. *That is accomplished by referring to the idea of intersubjectivity.*

Somewhere else, he sets out a fantastic etymology of *verbum* and *nomen* – *verbum* is the word in so far as it strikes the ear, which corresponds to our idea of verbal materiality, and *nomen* is the word in so far as something is made known by it. Except, what is not to be found in Saint Augustine – because he hadn't read Hegel – is the distinction between knowledge [*connaissance*], *agnoscere*, and recognition [*reconnaissance*]. The dialectic of recognition is essentially a human one, and since he, Saint Augustine that is, is engaged in a dialectic which is not atheistical . . .

4 Père François-Joseph Tonnard, translator of *De Magistro*.

BEIRNAERT: *Nonetheless, when he is dealing with whatever is called, is recalled, and is named, it is recognition which is involved.*

No doubt, but he does not isolate it, because for him, when all is said and done, there is only one recognition, that of Christ. Nonetheless, it is certain that the theme does at least appear. Even the questions which he resolves in a manner different from our own are at least indicated – that is the way of all coherent language [*langage*].

BEIRNAERT: *That, you know, is what is crucial.*

Go on to the second chapter, the one which bears on what you have called the power of language.

BEIRNAERT: *Its title is* – Whether signs are useless for learning. *This time, the issue no longer is the relation of signs to signs, we come instead to the relation of signs to signifiable things.*

From the sign to teaching.

BEIRNAERT: *That's a poor translation, it is rather more like* to the signifiable.

So that is how you translate *dicendum*. Alright, but Saint Augustine tells us on the other hand that *dicere*, which is the essential meaning of speech, is *docere*.

BEIRNAERT: *I will skip two or three pages. Augustine then states that the sign, once heard, directs one's attention to the thing signified. To which he makes an objection that is interesting from the analytic point of view, because one comes across it from time to time. What would you say, he asks Adeodatus, if an interlocutor, in a sort of game, came to the conclusion that if someone talks about a lion, a lion comes out of the mouth of the person who is talking? Adeodatus replies, it is the sign which comes out of the mouth and not the signification, not the concept, but its vehicle. Now, Saint Augustine wants to lead us to the following point, that, in actual fact, knowledge comes from things. Firstly he asks what one should prefer, the thing signified or the sign. In line with a principle that was almost universal at the time, one must esteem the signified things more than the signs, since the signs are imposed on to the things signified, and whatever is imposed on another thing is less noble than whatever it is imposed on. Unless, Saint Augustine says to Adeodatus, you adjudge it otherwise. The other finds an objection.*

> *Ad. – If we say* filth, *this name, in my opinion, is much nobler than the thing signified. Because we like hearing it much better than smelling it.*

This allows him to introduce, between the thing in its materiality and the sign, the knowledge of the thing, namely science. What was the aim, Augustine asks, of those who gave a name to such a shameful and contemptible thing? Their aim was to alert others as to how one should behave towards this thing. One should esteem the knowledge of the thing which the word itself is more highly than the thing.

> *Aug. – The knowledge of filth, in fact, should be held to be superior to the name itself, which in turn is to be preferred to filth itself. Because there is no other reason to prefer knowledge to the sign, except that the latter exists for the sake of the former, and not the former for the latter.*

One speaks so as to know, not the other way round. Another problem – is the knowledge of signs to be preferred to the knowledge of things? Augustine only gives the beginnings of a reply. Finally he winds up the discussion by saying:

> *Aug. – The knowledge of things takes preference over, not the knowledge of signs, but over the signs themselves.*

Then he returns to the problem touched on in the first part.

> *Aug. – Let us examine a little more closely whether there are things which one can show by themselves, without any sign, like speaking, walking, sitting, and other similar things. Are there things which can be shown without signs?*
>
> *Ad. – None, with the exception of speaking.*
>
> *Aug. – Are you that certain of what you are saying?*
>
> *Ad. – No, not at all.*

Augustine uses an example of a thing which doesn't require a sign to show itself, which made me think of the analytic situation.

> *Aug. – Suppose now that someone unfamiliar with the business of snaring birds, which is done with reeds and birdlime, should encounter a bird-catcher fitted out with all his equipment, though he is not snaring birds but simply going on his way. At the sight of him, he quickens his pace and, as is usually the case, reflects and, in amazement, asks himself the meaning of the man's paraphernalia. Suppose, too, that the bird-catcher, aware that the other's attention is fixed upon him, and eager to show off his prowess, releases the reeds and, with his rod and hawk, snares a little bird which he sees nearby which he comes up to and captures. Would he not, I ask you, teach that spectator of his what he was so eager to know, not by any sign, but by the reality itself?*
>
> *Ad. – I am afraid we are confronted here with a situation similar to that where I referred to the man who asks what walking is. Neither do I think that everything about bird-catching has been made known even in the present case.*
>
> *Aug. – It is an easy matter to put your mind at ease. I will make the further qualification, that if the spectator were intelligent enough, he could grasp everything there is to know about the art of bird-catching from what he saw. It is sufficient for our purpose that some men can be taught some things, though not all,[5] without the use of signs.*
>
> *Ad. – I too could further qualify my remarks by saying that if one is really intelligent, he will learn all about walking as soon as someone indicates it to him, by taking a few steps.*
>
> *Aug. – You may make that qualification as far as I am concerned. I not only*

---

[5] The phrase 'though not all', corresponds (loosely) to the Latin *'tametsi'*.

have no objection, but am even favourable to it. You see, in fact, that we have both reached the conclusion that some things can be taught without the use of signs, and that we were wrong in thinking a little while ago that nothing at all can be taught without signs. Actually, these examples bring to mind, not one or two, but thousands of things, which are made known by themselves without having to resort to signs. Quite apart from the numerous plays performed in every theatre by actors who play their part by enacting the events themselves.

To which one could reply that, in any case, whatever can be shown without signs is already significant, since the bird-catcher's actions always take on meaning within a universe within which subjects are already located.

2

What Father Beirnaert has said, with such pertinence, has made it superfluous for me to have to remind you that the bird-catcher's art can only exist in a world already structured by language.[6] There is no need to emphasise it.

What is at the heart of things for Saint Augustine is not the restoration of the hegemony of things over signs, but the casting of doubt on the hegemony of signs in the essentially spoken activity of teaching. This is where the break occurs between *signum* and *verbum*, *nomen*, the instrument of knowing in as much as it is the instrument of speech.

Saint Augustine calls upon the same dimension as we psychologists do. Because psychologists are more spiritual people – in the technical, religious sense of the word – than one might think. They believe, like Saint Augustine, in illumination, in intelligence. That is what they are designating, when they do animal psychology, with the name of instinct, of *Erlebnis* – I say this in passing.

Because Saint Augustine wants to involve us in truth's very own dimension, he abandons the linguist's domain, to take on this lure which I mentioned earlier. As soon as it is established, speech moves in the dimension of truth. Except, speech does not know that it is what makes truth. And Saint Augustine does not know it either, and that is why he tries to meet up with truth as such, through illumination. From whence a total inversion of perspective.

To be sure, he tells us, in the end signs are totally impotent, because we ourselves cannot recognise their value as signs, and we come to know that they are words only when we know what they signify in the language as concretely spoken. From then on, it is easy to make a dialectical about turn, and to say that, in the manipulation of signs which are defined by each other, we never learn anything. Either we already know the truth in question, and it is not, then, the signs which teach it to us, or we do not know it, and we cannot locate the signs which relate to it.

[6] Cf. Wittgenstein, *Philosophical Investigations*, no. 32.

He goes further, and locates admirably well the basis of the dialectic of truth which lies at the heart of the analytic discovery. In the presence of speech which we hear, he says, we find ourselves in extremely paradoxical situations – not knowing if they are true or not, whether or not to stand by their truth, to refute them or accept them, or to put them in doubt. But it is in relation to truth that the signification of everything which is expressed is to be located.

So speech, as much taught as teaching, is located in the register of the mistake, of error, of deception, of the lie. He takes it a long way, since he even places it in the domain of ambiguity, and not only of semantic ambiguity, but of subjective ambiguity. He admits that the very subject who is telling us something very often does not know what he is telling us, and tells us more or less than he means to. He even mentions the slip.

BEIRNAERT: *But he doesn't explicitly say that the slip can mean something.*

He almost does, since he considers it to be significant, but without saying of what. For him it is a slip when the subject signifies something other – *aliud* – than what he means. Another example, a quite striking example of the ambiguity of discourse, the Epicurean. The Epicurean introduces arguments about the function of the truth which he believes to have refuted. But these possess in themselves the virtue of truth in so far as they confirm in the listener a conviction exactly contrary to that which the Epicurean wished to inspire in him. Furthermore, you know the extent to which a masked discourse, a discourse of persecuted speech – as a writer by the name of Leo Strauss calls it – under a politically oppressive regime, for instance, can get things across by pretending to refute arguments which in fact express its true thought.

In short, Saint Augustine orients his entire dialectic around these three poles, error, mistake, ambiguity of speech. Well, it is as a function of this impotence of signs in teaching – simply to take up Father Beirnaert's terms – that next time we will try to get to grips with the founding dialectic of the truth of speech.

In the tripod which I am leaving with you, you will have no difficulty in recognising the three great symptomatic functions that Freud highlighted in his discovery of meaning – *Verneinung, Verdichtung, Verdrängung*. Because what speaks in man goes far beyond speech and penetrates even his dreams, his being and his very organism.

23 June 1954

XXI

Truth emerges from the mistake

FAILED[1] = SUCCESSFUL

SPEECH FROM BEYOND DISCOURSE

THE WORD ESCAPES ME[2]

THE DREAM OF THE BOTANICAL MONOGRAPH

DESIRE

Today, your group, whose fidelity was up to now unfailing, is flagging somewhat. And at the end of the race, it is I who will have had you.

We started with the rules on technique as set out for the first time in Freud's Papers on Technique, formulated as they are both in the most perfect and in the most uncertain fashion. Following a path true to the nature of the subject, we arrived at the central point we have been discussing since the middle of last term – the structure of the transference.

To locate the questions which are tied up with it, one must begin with the central point to which our dialectical investigations have led us, namely that one cannot account for the transference in terms of a dual, imaginary relation, and that the engine of its forward motion is speech.

To bring into play the illusory projection of any one of the subject's fundamental relations with the analytic partner, or again the object relation, the relation between transference and counter-transference, all this, remaining as it does within the limits of a two body psychology,[3] is inadequate. Not only do theoretical arguments show us that, but so in addition does the concrete testimony of authors I have cited. Remember what Balint tells us he notices during what he calls the termination of an analysis – nothing other than a narcissistic relation.

So we have demonstrated the necessity for a third term, which alone allows us to conceptualise the mirror transference, which is speech.

Despite all the effort one can put in to forget speech, or to downgrade it into being just a means, analysis is in itself a technique of speech, and speech is the very milieu in which it moves. It is in relation to the function of speech that the different mainsprings of analysis are to be distinguished from each other, and take on their meaning, their exact position. The whole of the teaching that we will expand upon subsequently will only recast this truth in a thousand different forms.

---

[1] 'Manqué'.   [2] 'Le mot me manque'.   [3] English in the original.

261

1

Last time fortified us with the discussion of a fundamental text from Saint Augustine on the signification of speech.

Saint Augustine's system may be said to be dialectical. It doesn't have a place in the system of sciences as it has been constituted, only over the last few centuries. But neither is it a point of view foreign to our own, which is that of linguistics. On the contrary, we have established that, well before linguistics arose within the modern sciences, someone who meditates on the art of speech, that is to say who talks about it, was led to a problem which lies at the present frontier of this science.

This problem is raised by the question of the relation between speech and signification, what relation the sign bears to what it signifies. In fact, in grasping the function of the sign, one is always referred from one sign to another. Why? Because the system of signs, as they are concretely instituted, *hic et nunc*, by itself forms a whole. That means that it institutes an order from which there is no exit. To be sure, there has to be one, otherwise it would be an order without any meaning.

This blind alley reveals itself only if one considers the entire order of signs. But that is how one really must consider them, as a set, because language cannot be conceived of as the result of a series of shoots, of buds, coming out of each thing. The name is not like the little asparagus tip emerging from the thing. One can only think of language as a network, a net over the entirety of things, over the totality of the real. It inscribes on the plane of the real this other plane, which we here call the plane of the symbolic.

Certainly, comparing is not reasoning,[4] and I am only illustrating what I am in the course of explaining to you.

The result of the blind alley indicated in the second part of the Augustinian argument is that the question of the adequation of the sign, I won't any longer say to the thing, but to what it signifies, leaves us confronted with an enigma. This enigma is none other than that of the truth, and that is where the Augustinian apologetic awaits us.

Meaning, either you've got it or you haven't. When you understand what is expressed in the signs of the language, it is always, in the end, on account of light coming to you from outside of the signs – either through an inner truth which allows you to recognise what is borne by signs, or by the presentation of an object which is correlated, in a repeated and insistent manner, with a sign. And here we have the perspective turned upside down. The truth is outside of the signs, elsewhere. This see-saw of the Augustinian dialectic directs us towards the recognition of the authentic *magister*, of the inner master of truth.

---

[4] *'Comparaison n'est pas raison'* – a French proverb.

We are entitled to pause here for a moment to remark that the very question of the truth is already raised by the dialectical movement itself.

In the same way as, at a certain point in his argument, Saint Augustine forgets that the bird-catcher's technique, this complex technique – a trick, a trap for his object, the bird to be caught – is already structured, instrumentalised by speech – so here, he appears to fail to recognise that the very question of the truth is already included at the heart of his discussion, since it is with speech that he raises the question of speech, and creates the dimension of truth. Every act of speech which is formulated as such brings into the world the novelty of the emergence of meaning. It is not that it is affirmed as truth, but rather that it introduces the dimension of truth into the real.

Saint Augustine argues – speech can be deceiving. Now, the sign, just of itself, can only present and sustain itself in the dimension of the truth. Because, in order to deceive, speech affirms itself as true. That is for the one who listens. For the one who speaks deception itself requires from the beginning the support of the truth that must be dissembled, and, as it unfolds, it presupposes a veritable deepening of the truth to which, if one can put it this way, it replies.

In fact, as the lie is organised, pushes out its tentacles, it requires the correlative control of the truth it encounters at every twist and turn of the way, and which it must avoid. The moralist tradition says it – you must have a good memory when you have lied. You have to know one hell of a lot of things to keep a lie going. There is nothing more difficult than to sustain a lie. Because the lie, in this way, brings about, in its unfolding, the constitution of the truth.

But that is not the real problem. The real problem is that of error, and that is where it has always lain.

It is clear that error is only definable in terms of the truth. But the point is not that there would be no error if there were no truth, as there would be no white if there were no black. There is more to it than that – there is no error which does not present and promulgate itself as truth. In short, error is the habitual incarnation of the truth. And if we wanted to be entirely rigorous, we would say that, as long as the truth isn't entirely revealed, that is to say in all probability until the end of time, its nature will be to propagate itself in the form of error.

You don't have to go much further to see in this a structure constitutive of the revelation of being as such.

On this point, for the moment I wish only to open a small door for you, whose threshold we will someday cross. For today let us keep to the phenomenology of speech.

We have seen that deception, as such, can only be sustained as a function of the truth, and not only of the truth, but of a movement of the truth – that error is the usual manifestation of the truth itself – so that the paths of truth are in essence the paths of error. *So*, you will say to me, *how, from within speech, will error ever be discerned? One needs either the test of experience, the confrontation with the object, or the illumination of this inner truth, the aim of the Augustinian dialectic.*

This objection is not without some force.

The signifier, which is always material and which in Saint Augustine we have recognised in the *verbum*, and the signified are the very foundation of the structure of language. Taken one by one, they appear to have a strictly arbitrary relation. There is no more reason to call the giraffe *giraffe* and the elephant *elephant* than to call the giraffe *elephant* and the elephant *giraffe*. There is no reason not to say that the giraffe has a trunk and the elephant a very long neck. If it is an error in the system as generally accepted, it is not discernible, as Saint Augustine points out, for as long as the definitions are not laid down. And is there anything more difficult than to lay down good definitions?

Nonetheless, if you continue your discourse on the giraffe with a trunk indefinitely, so that everything you say applies perfectly to the elephant, it will be clear that, under the name of the giraffe, you are talking about the elephant. All you have to do is bring your terms into agreement with the generally accepted ones. That is what Saint Augustine demonstrates with respect to the term *perducam*. That is not what we call error.

Error shows itself to be such whenever, at a given moment, it ends in a contradiction. If I started by saying that roses are plants which generally live under water, and if it seems from what follows that for a whole day I remained in the same place as the roses, since it is also quite clear that I cannot remain for a day under water, a contradiction appears in my discourse, demonstrating my error. In other words, in discourse it is contradiction which sorts truth from error.

From whence the Hegelian conception of absolute knowledge. Absolute knowledge is this moment in which the totality of discourse closes in on itself in a perfect non-contradiction up to and including the fact that it posits, explains and justifies itself. We are some way yet from this ideal!

You know only too well the everlasting disputes there are on every theme and on every subject, with greater or lesser ambiguity depending on the zones of interhuman action, and the manifest discordance between the different symbolic systems which prescribe action, the religious, juridical, scientific, political systems. There is neither superposition, nor conjunction of these references – between them there are gaps, faults, rents. That is why we cannot conceive of human discourse as being unitary. Every emission of speech is always, up to a certain point, under an inner necessity to err. So we are led, it would appear, to a historical Pyrronism which suspends the truth-value of everything which the human voice can emit, suspends it in the expectation of a future totalisation.

Is it unthinkable that it might come about? After all, can't the progress of the system of the physical sciences be conceived of as the progress of a single symbolic system, to which things give sustenance and substance? As this system is perfected, in any event we see things being disturbed, decomposing, dissolving under its pressure. The symbolic system is not like a piece of clothing which sticks on to things, it is not lacking in its effects on them and on human life. You can call this upheaval what you will – conquest, rape of nature, transformation of nature, hominisation of the planet.

This symbolic system of the sciences tends towards the *well made language*,[5] which one might consider to be its own language, a language deprived of all reference to a voice. That is also where Augustinian dialectic leads us, by depriving us of reference to this domain of the truth within which its own forward movement nevertheless takes place.

And that is where one cannot but be struck by the Freudian discovery.

2

The Freudian discovery, while being empirical, does not on account of that make any less of a striking contribution, so striking in fact that one gets blinded to its existence, to this question, a question which seems, taken literally, to be a *metaphysical* one.

What is peculiar to the field of psychoanalysis is indeed the presupposition that the subject's discourse normally unfolds – this is a genuine bit of Freud – within the order of error, of misrecognition, even of negation – it is not quite a lie, it is somewhere between an error and a lie. These are the truths of crude common sense. But – this is the novelty – during analysis, within this discourse which unfolds in the register of error, something happens whereby the truth irrupts, and it is not contradiction.

Do analysts have to push the subjects on the road of absolute knowledge, to gain an education in every respect, not only in psychology, so as to have them discover the absurdities whose company they habitually keep, but also in the system of the sciences? Certainly not – we are doing it here because we are analysts, but what if we had to do it to patients!

Nor can we engineer their meeting with the real, since we receive them within the confines of four walls. It is not our function to guide them by the hand through life, that is to say into the consequences of their stupidities. In life, you can see truth catch error from behind. In analysis, truth emerges in the most clearcut representative of the mistake – the slip, the action which one, improperly, calls *manquée* [missed, failed, abortive].

Our abortive actions are actions which succeed, those of our words which come to grief are words which own up. These acts, these words reveal a truth from behind. Within what we call free associations, dream images, symptoms, a word bearing the truth is revealed. If Freud's discovery has any meaning, it is that – truth grabs error by the scruff of the neck in the mistake.

[5] *'langue bien faite'*.

Reread the beginning of the chapter on the dream-work – *a dream*, Freud says, is a sentence, *it is a rebus.*[6] Had it not been explicitly formulated by Freud, fifty pages of *The Interpretation of Dreams* would lead us to this equation just as easily.

It would emerge just as well from the formidable discovery of condensation. You would be wrong to think that condensation simply means the term by term correspondence of a symbol with something. On the contrary, in a given dream, the whole of the dream-thoughts, that is to say the whole of those things signified, the meanings of the dream, is taken as a network, and is represented, not at all term by term, but through a set of interlacings. To demonstrate it to you, all I need do is take one of Freud's dreams, and make a drawing on the blackboard. Read the *Traumdeutung*, and you will see that really is how Freud understands it – the totality of meanings is represented by the totality of whatever is signifying. Each signifying element of the dream, each image, includes a reference to a whole set of things to be signified, and inversely, each thing to be signified is represented in several signifiers.

So the Freudian discovery leads us to hear in discourse this speech which reveals itself through, or even in spite of, the subject.

He tells us this speech not only verbally, but through all his other means of expression. Even through his body, the subject emits a speech, which is, as such, speech of truth, a signifying speech which he does not even know he emits. It is because he always says more than he means to, always more than he thinks he says.

Augustine's main objection to the inclusion of the domain of truth within the domain of signs is, he says, that very often subjects say things which go much further than what they think, and that they are even capable of owning the truth while not adhering to it. The Epicurean who maintains that the soul is mortal quotes his opponents' arguments so as to refute them. But those who have their eyes open can see that that is the true speech, and recognise that the soul is immortal.

The subject, via something whose structure and function as speech we have recognised, testifies to a truer meaning than all he expresses by means of his discourse of error. If that is not how our experience is structured, then it has absolutely no meaning.

The speech that the subject emits goes beyond, without his knowing it, his limits as discoursing subject – all the while remaining, to be sure, within his limits as speaking subject. If you abandon this perspective, what immediately appears is an objection which I am surprised not to hear raised more often – *Why doesn't the discourse, which you detect behind the discourse of mistake, fall prey to the same objection as the latter? If it is a discourse like the other, why isn't it, in just the same way, immersed in error?*

[6] (1900a) GW II/III 283–4; Stud II 280–1; SE IV 277–8.

Every Jungian-style conception, every conception which makes of the unconscious, under the name of archetype, the real locus of another discourse, really does fall prey, in a categorical way, to this objection. These archetypes, these reified symbols which reside in a permanent manner in a basement of the human soul, how are they truer than what is allegedly at the surface? Is what is in the cellar always truer than what is in the attic?

What does Freud mean when he states that the unconscious knows neither contradiction nor time? Does he mean that the unconscious is a truly unthinkable reality? Certainly not, because there is no such thing as an unthinkable reality.

Reality is defined by contradiction. Reality is what makes it so that when I am here, you, my dear lady, cannot be in the same place. It is not clear why the unconscious should escape this type of contradiction. What Freud means when he talks about the suspension of the principle of non-contradiction in the unconscious is that the genuine speech that we are supposed to uncover, not through observation, but through interpretation, in the symptom, in the dream, in the slip, in the *Witz*, obeys laws other than those of discourse, which is subject to the condition of having to move within error up to the moment when it encounters contradiction. Authentic speech has other modes, other means, than everyday speech.

That is what we have to explore in a rigorous fashion if we want to make any progress at all in thinking about what we are doing. Of course, we don't *have* to do so. I will even admit that the majority of human beings quite universally excuse themselves from so doing, and accomplish what they have to in a no less satisfactory fashion. I would go even further – one can push discourse, and even dialectic, extremely far, while avoiding thought entirely. Nonetheless, every step forward in the symbolic world capable of constituting a revelation implies, at least for a brief moment, an effort of thought. Now, an analysis is nothing other than an entire series of revelations particular to each subject. So it is probable that his activity requires the analyst to remain on the alert as to the meaning of what he is doing, and that, from time to time, he devote a moment to thought.

So here we are presented with a question – what is the structure of this speech which is beyond discourse?

The Freudian innovation, in comparison with Saint Augustine, is the revelation, within the phenomenon, of these subjective, experienced moments, in which speech which goes beyond the discoursing subject emerges. An innovation that is so striking that it is only with difficulty that we can believe that it was never previously perceived. No doubt it was necessary for the common run of men to be caught up for some time in a rather perturbed, perhaps even refracted, and in some way inhuman, alienating, discourse for this speech to become manifest with such acuteness, such immediacy, such urgency.

Let us not forget that it made its presence felt in that portion of mankind which suffers, and it was quite clearly in the form of a morbid psychology, of a psychopathology, that the Freudian discovery was made.

3

I will leave you to think about these matters, because now I want to stress the following – it is only in the dialectical movement of speech beyond discourse that the terms we use all the time without giving them a moment's thought, as if they were givens, gain their meaning.

Verdichtung proves to be nothing other than the polyvalence of meanings in language, their encroachments, their criss-crossings, through which the world of things is not recovered by the world of symbols, but is taken up once more as follows – a thousand things correspond to each symbol, and each thing to a thousand symbols.

Verneinung is what shows the negative side of this non-superposition, because one really does have to get the objects into the holes, and since the holes don't fit them, it is the objects which thereby suffer.

The third register, that of *Verdrängung*, can also be remarked in the register of discourse. Because, and make a careful note of this, each time that repression takes place – make note of it in practice, it is an indication, go take a look and you will see – repression in the true sense of the word – because repression is not repetition, repression is not negation – there is always interruption of discourse. The subject says that the word escapes him [*le mot lui manque*].

The word escapes me [*Le mot me manque*] – at what point in literature does such an expression come up? It is Saint Amand who uttered if for the first time – not even written, but said like that one day in the street, and it became part of the innovations introduced into the language by the *Précieux*.[7] Somaize mentions it in his *Dictionnaire des Précieuses* amongst a thousand other forms which are now in current usage but which were not any the less witty plays on words, created in *boudoirs* by this pleasant society, devoted as it entirely was to the perfecting of language [*langage*]. As you see, there is a relation between the map of Tenderness [*la carte du Tendre*][8] and psychoanalytic psychology. *Le mot me manque* – you never would have said a thing like that in the sixteenth century.

You know the famous example of a word which Freud could not find – the name of the painter of the frescos at Orvieto, Signorelli. Why couldn't he find this word? – if not because the preceding conversation had not been brought to a conclusion, a conclusion, which would have been *Herr*, the absolute master,

---

[7] Somaize, *Le Dictionnaire des Précieuses*, nouvelle édition de Ch.-L. Livet, Paris: Jannet, 1856 (orig. published 1661), vol. I, p. 94: 'Je scay bien ce que je veux dire, mais je ne puis m'expliquer comme je voudrois: *Je scay bien ce que je veux dire mais le mot me manque.*'

[8] See p. 213 n5 above.

death. And, after all, there are perhaps internal limits to what can be said, as Mephistopheles, often cited by Freud, says – 'After all, the best of what you know may not be told to boys.'[9] That's repression.

Already, every time the master comes to a halt along the path of his teaching, for reasons pertaining to the nature of his interlocutor, there's repression. And I, who bring you picturesque things, aimed at putting ideas back into place, I am also engaged in repression, but a little less than the usual, for that is of the order of negation.

Take the first dream which Freud discusses in the chapter on condensation, the dream of the botanical monograph, already summarised in the chapter on the material and sources of dreams. It is a wonderful demonstration of everything I am telling you. No doubt, with his own dreams, Freud never gets us to the heart of the matter, but it is not very difficult to guess at it.

So, during the day Freud saw a monograph on the cyclamens, which are his wife's favourite flowers.[10] You get a clear sense that, when he says that many husbands – including him – give their wives flowers less often than they should, he is not unaware what that means. Freud evokes his conversation with Königstein the eye surgeon, who operated on his father anaesthetised with cocaine. Now, you know the famous story about cocaine – Freud never forgave his wife for having made him come to visit her in a hurry, because if he hadn't, he used to say, he would have taken his discovery a lot further, and would have become a famous man. In the associations to the dream, there is also the patient who answers *to the beautiful name Flora*, and Gärtner – which means *gardener* in German – appears at one point with, as if by chance, his wife, whom Freud finds *blühende*, blooming.

Everything is there, implicit. Freud, not having made up his mind to break with his wife, dissembles the fact that he doesn't bring her flowers often enough, also dissembles this complaint, this permanent bitterness of his, at the moment when he is expecting to be elected to an Extraordinary Professorship. Because the struggle he is engaged in to get himself recognised is there, subjacent to what he alludes to from the dialogues with his colleagues, and this is again emphasised by the fact that, in the dream, Prof. Gärtner interrupts him.[11] In the same way one understands why it is these two day-residues, the conversation with the eye-surgeon, and the sight of the monograph, that this dream feeds on. It is because they were the phonematically experienced moments, if I can put it like that, with which the speech which finds expression in the dream is put into motion.

. Do you want me to put it in a formula? To put it crudely, it is – *I no longer love my wife*. Or again, what he refers to in connection with his whimsies and his expensive tastes – *I am not recognised by society, and hampered in my ambitions.*

9 See (1900a) GW II/III 147; Stud II 158; SE IV 142 and 142 n1.
10 (1900a) GW II/III 288–90; Stud II 285–6; SE IV 282–4.
11 GW II/III 177; Stud II 185; SE IV 171.

I am thinking of a colleague of ours, who said in a lecture on Freud – *He was a man without ambitions and without needs*. That is blatantly false, all you have to do is read Freud's biography and be aware of the brutality of his responses to those people who came to him with their hearts of gold, the idealists, and questioned him about his own interests in life. Fifteen years after Freud's death, we really should not fall to the level of hagiography. Happily there's something to be found in his work which somewhat bears witness to his personality.

Let us go back to this famous dream. If there's a dream, that means there is repression, doesn't it? So, what was repressed, here? Haven't I put you in a good enough position to recognise in Freud's very own text that a specific desire was suspended during the day, and that one specific word was not said, could not be said, which went right to the heart of the avowal, to the heart of being?

There I'll leave for today the question – in the present state of relations between human beings, can speech spoken outside of the analytic situation ever be full speech? Interruption is the law of conversation. Everyday speech all the time runs up against failure of recognition [*méconnaissance*], which is the source of *Verneinung*.

If you read the *Traumdeutung*, taking what I teach you as your guide, you will see the extent to which the concepts become clearer and what meaning, ambiguous as it sometimes seems, Freud gives to the word *desire*.

He concedes, which might appear to be a surprising negation, that one has to admit to there being two types of dream, dreams of desire, and punishment-dreams. But if you understand what the issue is, you realise that the repressed desire made manifest in the dream is identified with this register to which I am trying to get you to enter – what is waiting to be revealed is being.

It is this perspective which gives the term desire in Freud its full value. It unifies the domain of the dream, it allows one to understand paradoxical dreams, such as the dream of the poet whose youth was so difficult, who dreams the same dream over and over again, in which he is the insignificant assistant to the tailor.[12] This doesn't so much represent a punishment as a revelation of being. It marks one of the crossings of the threshold of the identification of being, the passage of being into a new stage, a new symbolic incarnation of itself. From whence the value of everything which is of the order of accession, of competition, of the examination, of certification – whose value is not that of testing, of a test, but of an investiture.

On the off chance, I drew this little diamond on the blackboard for you, a dihedron with six faces.

Let us make all its faces similar, one set above, the other below a plane. It is not a regular polyhedron, even though all its faces are identical.

Imagine the median plane, where you'll find the triangle which divides this pyramid into two, to represent the surface of the real, the real just as it is. Nothing here can break out of it, all the seats are taken. But, on the other level, everything has changed. Because words, symbols, introduce a hollow, a hole, thanks to which all manner of crossings are possible. Things become interchangeable.

Depending on the way one envisions it, this hole in the real is called being or nothingness. This being and this nothingness are essentially linked to the phenomenon of speech. It is within the dimension of being that the tripartition of the symbolic, the imaginary and the real is to be found, those elementary categories without which we would be incapable of distinguishing anything within our experience.

It is not for nothing, no doubt, that there are three of them. There must be a minimal law in that, which geometry here only embodies, namely that, if, in the plane of the real, you detach a shutter which moves into a third dimension, the minimum number of shutters you need to construct something solid is two.

Such a schema makes you aware of the following – it is only in the dimension of being, and not in that of the real, that the three fundamental passions can be inscribed – at the junction of the symbolic and imaginary, this fault line, if you will, this ridge line called love – at the junction of the imaginary and the real, hate – and, at the junction of the real and the symbolic, ignorance.

We know that the dimension of transference exists from the start, implicitly, well before analysis begins, before this concubinage, which analysis is, triggers it. Now, these two possibilities of love and hate are never present without the third, which is commonly neglected, and which is not included as one of the primary components of transference – ignorance, as a passion. However, the subject who comes into analysis places himself, as such, in the position of someone who is in ignorance. There is no possible way into analysis without this point of reference – one never says it, one never thinks of it, whereas it is fundamental.

As speech moves forward, the upper pyramid is constructed, corresponding to the working over of the *Verdrängung*, the *Verdichtung* and the *Verneinung*. And being is realised.

At the beginning of the analysis, just as at the beginning of every dialectic, this being, if it does exist implicitly, in a virtual fashion, is not realised. For the naive, for someone who has never entered into any dialectic and believes himself simply to be in the real, being has no presence. The speech included in discourse is revealed thanks to the law of association by which it is put in doubt, in brackets, through suspending the law of non-contradiction. This revelation of speech is the realisation of being.

Analysis is not the reconstitution of the narcissistic image to which it has so often been reduced. If the analysis were only a matter of putting to the test a limited number of minor forms of behaviour, which are more or less well sussed out, more or less cunningly projected, courtesy of the collaboration between the two egos, if we were only concerned with looking out for the emergence of goodness knows what ineffable reality, why should this reality be singled out above all the others? In my schema, the point O moves somewhere to the back and, to the extent that it is symbolised by its speech, is realised in its being.

We will leave it there for today.

Let me immediately urge those of you who have found this discourse interesting, indeed who have been stirred up by it, to ask me questions next time – not too long, since we have only one seminar left – on the basis of which I will try to plan the conclusion, if one may speak of conclusion. This will serve as a knot, with which to broach a new chapter next year.

I am more and more inclined to think that next year I will have to divide this seminar into two if I want, on the one hand, to explain Präsident Schreber and the symbolic world of psychosis to you, and on the other hand to show you, starting off with *Das Ich und das Es*, that ego,[13] super-ego[13] and *Es* are not new names for old psychological entities. I thus hope to make you see that it is in the movement of the dialectic which I have engaged you in this year that the structuration introduced by Freud takes on its true meaning.

30 June 1954

[13] So in the original.

XXII

The concept of analysis

Who has any questions?

MME AUBRY: *I understand that at the conjunction of the imaginary and the real one finds hate, on condition that one takes conjunction in the sense of rupture. What I don't understand quite so well is finding love at the conjunction of the symbolic and the imaginary.*

I am delighted by your question. Perhaps it will enable me to lend to our last meeting of the year the familiar atmosphere which I prefer to the magisterial.

1

Leclaire, surely you must also have things to ask. Last time after the session you said to me something remarkably like a question – *I would have really liked you to have talked about transference, even so.*

They are tough, those *even so*'s – I do nothing but talk to them about it and they're still not satisfied. There are profound reasons why the subject of transference always leaves you craving for more. Nonetheless, we are still going to try today to deal with this subject.

If I wanted to represent the three times of the structuration of speech in search of truth on the model of those allegorical paintings which proliferated in the romantic era, like *virtue pursuing crime, aided by remorse*, I would tell you – *Error taking flight in deception and recaptured by mistake*. I hope you can see that that paints a picture of transference for you, such as I try to get you to grasp it in the moments of suspension which the avowal of speech undergoes.

DR LECLAIRE: *Yes.*

What, in short, are you still craving for? Perhaps for the articulation of what I have been telling you with the usual conception of transference?

DR LECLAIRE: *When one looks at what is written on transference, one always gets the impression that the phenomenon of transference falls in the category of manifestations of an affective order, of emotions, in contrast with other manifestations, of an intellectual order, such as procedures aimed at understanding, for instance. Hence one always finds it a bit difficult to give an account of your view of the transference in the current, ordinary terminology. Definitions of transference always say that it is a question of emotion, of feeling, of an affective phenomenon, which is categorically opposed to everything which, in an analysis, can be called intellectual.*

Yes . . . You see, there are two ways of applying a discipline which is structured as a teaching. There's what you hear, and then what you make of it. These two planes do not overlap, but they can be made to join up in a certain number of secondary signs. It is from this angle that I see the fertility of every truly didactic action. It is not so much a question of transmitting concepts to you, as of explaining them to you leaving you the task, and the responsibility, of filling them in. But something else is perhaps even more imperative, which is to point out to you those concepts which should never be made use of.

If there is something of that order in what I teach you here, it is the following – I urge you, each of you, at the heart of your own search for the truth, to renounce quite radically – if only provisionally, to see if one doesn't gain by dispensing with it – the use of an opposition like that of the affective and the intellectual.

That by using it one gets into a series of blind alleys is only too obvious for it not to be tempting to follow this instruction for a while. This opposition is one of those most contrary to analytic experience and most unenlightening when it comes to understanding it.

You ask me to give an account of what I teach, and the objections that this teaching may encounter. I teach you the meaning and the function of the action of speech, in as much as that is the element of interpretation. Speech is the founding medium of the intersubjective relation, and what retroactively modifies the two subjects. It is speech which, literally, creates what installs them in that dimension of being I try to get you to glimpse.

We are not dealing here with an intellectual dimension. If the intellectual is to be located somewhere, it is at the level of the *ego*-phenomena, in the imaginary projection of the pseudo-neutralised *ego – pseudo* in the sense of lie – that analysis has exposed as a phenomenon of defence and of resistance.

If you are with me, we will be able to go a long way. The question is not so much one of knowing up to what point one should go, the question is more one of knowing if one will be followed. In fact that is an element which allows one to discriminate what one can call reality.

Over the ages, throughout human history, we witness advances which one would be quite wrong to take to be those of circumvolutions. These are the advances of the symbolic order. Follow the history of a science like mathematics. For centuries it stagnated on problems which are now transparent to ten-year old children. And yet these were powerful minds which pondered them. We were stuck on the solution to equations of the second degree for ten centuries too many. The Greeks could have solved it, since they found out cleverer things concerning the problems of maxima and minima. Mathematical progress is not progress in the power of thought of the human being. It comes good the day some man thinks of inventing a sign like this, $\sqrt{}$, or like that, $\int$. That's what mathematics is.

The position we are in is different, more difficult. Because we have to deal with an extremely polyvalent symbol. But it is only to the extent that we succeed in formulating the symbols of our action in an adequate manner that we will take a step forward. This step forward, like every step forward, is also a retroactive step. That is why I would say that we are, in a way, in the middle of building up, to the extent that you follow me, a psychoanalysis. Our step forward in psychoanalysis, is at the same time a return to the aspirations of its origin.

So what is at issue? A more authentic understanding of the phenomenon of transference.

DR LECLAIRE: *I hadn't quite finished. I am asking this question because it is always a little bit in the background for us. It is quite clear that the terms affective and intellectual are no longer common currency in the group we make up.*

A good thing too. What can one do with them?

DR LECLAIRE: *But that's the point, that is one thing which has been left hanging a bit since Rome.*

I believe that I didn't make use of them once in that famous Rome Discourse, except to expunge the term *intellectualised*.

DR LECLAIRE: *Exactly, both this silence, and these direct attacks on the term affective did have an effect.*

I believe that is a term which one must completely expunge from our papers.

DR LECLAIRE: *In asking you this question, I wanted to get rid of something which had been left hanging. Last time, in talking about transference, you introduced three fundamental passions, amongst them ignorance. That is what I wanted to come to.*

2

Last time I wanted to introduce something like a third dimension, the space, or rather the volume, of human relations in the symbolic relation. It is entirely deliberately that it was only last time that I spoke of these ridges of passion. As Mme Aubry clearly underlined with her question, these are junction points,

points of rupture, crests which are located between the different domains over which the interhuman relation extends, the real, the symbolic, the imaginary.

Love is distinct from desire, considered as the limit-relation which is established by every organism with the object which satisfies it. Because its aim is not satisfaction, but being. That is why one can only speak of love where the symbolic relation as such exists.

Now learn to distinguish love as an imaginary passion from the active gift which it constitutes on the symbolic plane. Love, the love of the person who desires to be loved, is essentially an attempt to capture the other in oneself, in oneself as object. The first time that I spoke at length about narcissistic love was, if you remember, as the direct continuation of the dialectic of perversion.

The desire to be loved is the desire that the loving object should be taken as such, caught up, enslaved to the absolute particularity of oneself as object. The person who aspires to be loved is not at all satisfied, as is well known, with being loved for his attributes. He demands to be loved as far as the complete subversion of the subject into a particularity can go, and into whatever may be most opaque, most unthinkable in this particularity. One wants to be loved for everything – not only for one's ego, as Descartes says, but for the colour of one's hair, for one's idiosyncracies, for one's weaknesses, for everything.

But inversely, and I would say correlatively, as a result of exactly that, to love is to love a being beyond what he or she appears to be. The active gift of love is directed at the other, not in his specificity, but in his being.

O. MANNONI: *It was Pascal who said that, not Descartes.*

There is a passage in Descartes on the progressive purification of the ego beyond all its specific qualities. But you aren't wrong, in so far as Pascal tries to take us beyond the creature.

O. MANNONI: *He said it explicitly.*

Yes, but it was a gesture of rejection.

Love, now no longer conceived of as a passion but as an active gift, is always directed, beyond imaginary captivation, towards the being of the loved subject, towards his particularity. That is why it can accept to such a great extent his weaknesses and detours, why it can even admit to his errors, but there is a point at which it comes to a halt, a point which is only located in relation to being – when the loved being goes too far in his betrayal of himself and persists in self-deception, love can follow no longer.

I won't fill out the entire course of this phenomenology, which you can ascertain from experience. I will only remark that love, to the extent that it is one of the three lines of division in which the subject is engaged when he realises himself symbolically in speech, homes in on the being of the other. Without speech, in as much as it affirms being, all there is is *Verliebtheit*,

Dora case, one remains somewhat on the threshold of that, but even so I
ace it for you a little by giving a final reply to the question of the
rence as a whole.

analytic experience is founded on Freud's first discoveries, on the tripod
slip, joke. The symptom is a fourth element, which can serve, not as
, since it is not constructed out of phonemes, but as *signum*, with the
sm as ground – if you can recall the various spheres distinguished in
ine's text. It is within this experience, and with some delay in the
g of the latter – Freud himself says that he was frightened – that he
the phenomenon of the transference. For want of being recognised, the
rence operated as an obstacle to the treatment. Once recognised, it
s the mainstay of the treatment.

ven before he had become aware of the existence of transference, Freud
eady designated it. In the *Traumdeutung*, there is, in effect, already a
n of the *Übertragung* as a function of the double level of speech, as I have
o you. There are parts of the discourse which are disinvested of
tions which another signification, the unconscious signification, will
m behind. Freud demonstrates it with respect to the dream, and I have
it out to you in some striking slips.

pity I have not talked much about the slip this year. Now, that is a
ental dimension, since it is the radical facet of the non-meaning which
ing possesses. There is a point where meaning emerges, and is created.
at this very point, man is very easily capable of feeling that the
is at the same time annihilated, that it is created so as to be
ted. What's a joke? – if not the calculated irruption of non-sense into a
e which seems to make sense.

NONI: *It is the navel of speech.*

In the dream, there is an extremely confused navel. Inversely, the
the joke is perfectly sharp – the *Witz*. And what expresses its most
ssence is non-sense.

we realise this transference is our mainstay.
ed out three senses in which different authors understand it. This
n, which is only didactic, should allow you to get your bearings
he various present-day analytic tendencies – and that is not very
ing.

ant to understand the phenomenon of transference in relation to the
is to say in as much as it is a phenomenon taking place in the present.
s one is making a real breakthrough when one says that every
ust bear on the *hic et nunc*. One thinks one has found something quite
that, one thinks one has taken a bold step forward. On this theme

---

imaginary fascination, but there is no love. There is inflicted love, but not the
active gift of love.

Well, with hate, it is the same thing. There is an imaginary dimension of
hate, in so far as the destruction of the other is one pole of the very structure of
the intersubjective relation. As I've pointed out to you, it is what Hegel
recognises as the impasse for the coexistence of two consciousnesses, from
whence he deduces his myth of the struggle for pure prestige. Even there, the
imaginary dimension is framed by the symbolic relation, and that is why hate is
not satisfied with the disappearance of the adversary. If love aspires to the
unfolding of the being of the other, hate wishes the opposite, namely its
abasement, its deranging, its deviation, its delirium, its detailed denial, its
subversion. That is what makes hate a career with no limit, just as love is.

Perhaps it is more difficult to get you to understand that, for reasons which
may not be such good reasons for rejoicing as one might think, these days we
know less about the feeling of hatred than in times when man was more open to
his destiny.

To be sure, we have seen, not very long ago, manifestations which, within
this genre, weren't bad at all. Nonetheless, these days subjects do not have to
shoulder the burden of the experience of hatred in its most consuming forms.
And why? Because our civilisation is itself sufficiently one of hatred. Isn't the
path for the race to destruction really rather well marked out for us? Hatred is
clothed in our everyday discourse under many guises, it meets with such
extraordinarily easy rationalisations. Perhaps it is this state of the diffuse
flocculation of hatred which saturates the call for the destruction of being in us.
As if the objectivation of the human being in our civilisation corresponded
exactly to what, within the structure of the *ego*, is the pole of hatred.

O. MANNONI: *Western moralism.*

Exactly. Hatred here discovers how to feed on everyday objects. You would be
wrong to think that as a result it is absent from wars, when, for certain
privileged subjects, it is fully realised.

Don't get me wrong. In speaking about love and hate to you, I am showing
you the paths for the realisation of being, not the realisation of being, but only
its paths.

And yet, if the subject commits himself to searching after truth as such, it is
because he places himself in the dimension of ignorance – it doesn't matter
whether he knows it or not. That is one of the elements making up what
analysts call 'readiness to the transference'.[1] There is a readiness to the
transference in the patient solely by virtue of his placing himself in the position
of acknowledging himself in speech, and searching out his truth to the end, the

[1] English in the original.

end which is there, in the analyst. The analyst's ignorance is also worthy of consideration.

The analyst must not fail to recognise what I will call the dimension of ignorance's power of accession to being, since he has to reply to the person who, throughout his discourse, questions him in this dimension. He doesn't have to guide the subject to a *Wissen*, to knowledge, but on to the paths by which access to this knowledge is gained. He must engage him in a dialectical operation, not say to him that he is wrong since he necessarily is in error, but show him that he speaks poorly, that is to say that he speaks without knowing, as one who is ignorant, because what counts are the paths of his error.

Psychoanalysis is a dialectic, what Montaigne, in book III, chapter VIII, calls *an art of conversation*.[2] The art of conversation of Socrates in the *Meno* is to teach the slave to give his own speech its true meaning. And it is the same in Hegel. In other words, the position of the analyst must be that of an *ignorantia docta*, which does not mean knowing [*savante*], but formal, and what is capable of being formative for the subject.

Because it is in the air these days, these days of hatred, there is a great temptation to transform the *ignorantia docta* into what I have called, and this is hardly a novelty, an *ignorantia docens*. If the psychoanalyst thinks he knows something, in psychology for example, then that is already the beginning of his loss, for the simple reason that in psychology nobody knows much, except that psychology is itself an error of perspective on the human being.

I will have to use banal examples to make you understand what the realisation of the being of man is, because in spite of yourselves you put it in an erroneous perspective, that of a false knowledge.

All the same you must have realised that, when a man says *I am*, or *I will be*, even *I will have been* or *I want to be*, there is always a jump, a gap. It is just as extravagant, in relation to reality, to say *I am a psychoanalyst* as *I am king*. Both the one and the other are entirely valid affirmations, which nothing, however, in the order of what one might call the measure of capacities justifies. The symbolic legitimations by virtue of which a man takes on what is conferred on him by others entirely escapes the register of entitlements to office.[3]

When a man refuses to be king, it does not have at all the same value as when he accepts. By the very fact of refusing, he is not king. He is a petit bourgeois – take for example the Duke of Windsor. The man who, just on the brink of being invested with the dignity of the crown, says – *I want to live with the woman I love* – simply because of that remains on this side of the domain of being king.

But when the man says – and in saying it, is it, by virtue of a certain system of symbolic relations – says *I am king* – it is not simply accepting an office. From

[2] *'un art de conférer'*.
[3] *'habilitations capacitaires'*.

---

one minute to the next the meaning of all his psycho
His passions, his plans, even his stupidity take on an
All of these functions become, solely by virtue of th
royal functions. In the register of royalty, his intell
quite different, even his inabilities start to polarise,
of destinies around him, destinies which are found t
the reason that the royal authority will be exercise
person who has been invested with it.

This happens on a small scale every day – a ge
mediocre qualities and who presents all sorts of pr
raised up in to an investiture that is sovereign in so
domain may be, and he changes entirely. All yo
everyday, the significance of his strengths as
transformed, and their relations may well be re

That is also what habilitations, examination
concealed fashion. Why, given the time that has e
clever psychologists, haven't we eliminated th
formerly had the value of initiations, the degre
tions, etc? If we have truly eliminated this va
investiture to the totalisation of the work acquir
the year, or even to a set of tests or examination:
subjects? Why retain this vague archaic charact
protest against these elements of chance and
themselves against the walls of the prison they th
is simply that a competitive examination, in as
with a qualification which is symbolic, cannot b
structure, and cannot just be inserted into t
quantity.

So, when we meet this, we think how clever v
course, let's write a great psychoanalytic article so
of the examination.

This character is obvious. It is fortunate th
unfortunate that the psychoanalyst doesn't alv
partial discovery, which he explains in terms
magical thought, whereas it is the dimen
fundamental here.

3

Who has got other questions to raise?

DR BEJARANO: *I have a concrete example in m*
the different registers are followed out in the c

In the
can p
transf

The
dream
verbur
organi
Augus
foundi
isolate
transfe
become

But e
had al
definiti
put it
significa
take fro
pointed

It's a
fundam
all mean
But eve
meanin
annihila
discours

O. MA

Exactly.
navel of
radical e

Well,

I poin
tripartiti
amidst t
encourag

Some
real, that
One thin
analysis
dazzling i

Ezriel writes some very touching things, breaking down doors which are already open: the transference is there, it is simply a matter of knowing what it is. If we take transference on the plane of the real, that is what it yields – a real which is not real, but illusory. What is real is that the subject is there, telling me about his dealings with his grocer. What is illusory is that in complaining about his grocer, it is me he is bawling out – that is one of Ezriel's examples. So he thereby concludes that one should demonstrate to the subject that there is really no reason for bawling me out because of his grocer.

Thus, starting off from the emotions, from the affective, from abreaction, and from other terms designating a certain number of the partitioned phenomena which indeed come about during analysis, one nonetheless ends up, I'll have you notice, with something essentially intellectual. To proceed along these lines leads in the end to a practice equivalent to the original forms of indoctrination which scandalise us so much in Freud's behaviour with his early cases. One would have to teach the subject how to act in the real, show him that he is behind the times. If that is not education and indoctrination, I wonder what is. In any case it is an entirely superficial way of dealing with the phenomenon.

There is another way of approaching the problem of transference, which is to place it on the level of that imaginary whose importance I do not fail to underline here. The relatively recent development of animal ethology allows us to give it a much clearer structuration than Freud could. But this dimension has certainly been named as such in Freud's text – *imaginare*. How could he have avoided it? You have seen as much this year in 'On narcissism: an introduction', the relation of the living organism to the objects that it desires is linked to the conditions of the *Gestalt* which locate the function of the imaginary as such.

The function of the imaginary is not at all overlooked in analytic theory, but to introduce it only in order to deal with transference is to pull the wool over both eyes, because it is present everywhere, and in particular whenever identification is at issue. Except, one musn't use it without rhyme or reason.

Let us note in this connection that the function of the imaginary is at work in the behaviour of every animal couple.

A dimension of parade appears in every action that is linked up with the moment of pairing of individuals caught up in their cycle of sexual behaviour. In the course of the sexual parade, each of the individuals finds himself captated into a dual situation, in which what is set up, via the go-between of the imaginary relation, is an identification – no doubt only momentarily, on account of its being linked to the instinctual cycle.

Similarly, in the course of the struggle between males, one can see subjects coming to an agreement in an imaginary struggle, in which there is, between the adversaries, a regulation at a distance, transforming the struggle into a dance. And, at a given moment, as in pairing, roles are chosen, one of them is recognised as dominant, without it coming down, I won't say to blows, but to claws, teeth, or prickly spines. One of the partners takes on a passive attitude and submits to the superiority of the other. He gives way to him, adopts one of the roles, quite clearly as a function of the other, that is to say as a function of what the other has made a claim to on the plane of the *Gestalt*. The adversaries avoid a real struggle which would lead to the destruction of one of them – and transpose the conflict on to the imaginary plane. Each takes his bearings on the other's image, what results is a regulation in which the roles are distributed within the situation as a whole, within the dyadic set-up.

In man, the imaginary is reduced, specialised, centred on the specular image, which creates both impasses and the function of the imaginary relation.

The image of the ego – simply because it is an image, the ego is ideal ego – sums up the entire imaginary relation in man. By being produced at a time when the functions are not yet completed, it has a salutary value, expressed well enough in the jubilatory assumption of the mirror phenomenon, but it does not possess any the less of a connection with the vital prematuration and hence with an original deficit, with a gap to which it remains linked in its structure.

The subject will rediscover over and over again that this image of self is the very framework of his categories, of his apprehension of the world – of the object, and he will achieve this through the intermediary of the other. It is in the other that he will always rediscover his ideal ego, from whence develops the dialectic of his relations to the other.

If the other saturates, fills this image, he becomes the object of a narcissistic investment, that of *Verliebtheit*. Recall Werther meeting Charlotte just when she is holding a child in her arms – that hits the bull's-eye of the narcissistic image of the novel's young hero. If, on the contrary, on the same slope, the other manifests himself as frustrating the subject of his ideal and of his own image, it engenders the maximal destructive tension. A mere nothing turns the imaginary relation to the other either this way or that, giving us the key to the questions which Freud raises apropos of the transformation that takes place, in *Verliebtheit*, between love and hate.

This phenomenon of imaginary investment plays a pivotal role in the transference.

If it is true that the transference is established in and through the dimension of speech, it only brings about the revelation of this imaginary relation at certain crucial points in the spoken encounter with the other, that is to say, in this instance, with the analyst. The discourse, stripped of a certain number of its conventions by the so-called fundamental rule, begins to move, more or less freely, in relation to ordinary discourse, and opens up the subject to this fertile mistake through which genuine speech joins up once again with the discourse of error. But also, when speech flees from revelation, from fertile error, and develops into deception – an essential dimension, whose existence precisely forbids us from eliminating the subject as such from our experience, and from reducing that experience[4] to objective terms – what is discovered are those points which, in the subject's history, have not been integrated, taken on, but repressed.

In the discourse of analysis, the subject develops what is his truth, his integration, his history. But there are some holes in this history, where what had been *verworfen* or *verdrängt* took place. *Verdrängt* – come for a moment into discourse and was rejected. *Verworfen* – the rejection is primal. For the present I don't want to talk at any further length about this distinction.

The phenomenon of transference encounters the imaginary crystallisation. It revolves around it and it has to join up with it again.

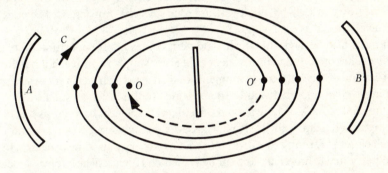

A schema of analysis

At *O*, I place the unconscious notion of the ego of the subject. This unconscious is made up of what the subject essentially fails to recognise in his structuring image, in the image of his ego – namely those captivations by imaginary fixations which were unassimilable to the symbolic development of his history – this means that it was traumatic.

What is involved in analysis? That the subject be able to totalise the various accidents the memory of which is retained in *O*, in a form closed off to him. It only opens up through verbalisation, that is to say through the mediation of the other, that is the analyst. It is through the spoken assumption of his history that the subject becomes committed to the path of bringing into being his truncated imaginary.

This complementation of the imaginary is achieved in the other, in as much as the subject assumes it in his discourse, in so far as he gets the other to hear it.

What is on the side of *O* passes over to the side of *O'*. Everything which is

<hr />

[4] '*de la réduire*' in the original. I have chosen to make it clear in the translation that '*la*' refers to '*l'expérience*', and not to '*le sujet*'.

proffered from *A*, from the side of the subject, makes itself heard in *B*, on the side of the analyst.

The analyst hears it, but, in return, so does the subject. The echo of his discourse is symmetrical to the specularity of the image. This revolving dialogue, which I represent on the schema by a spiral, binds *O'* and *O* more tightly. The progress of the subject in his being must finally bring him to *O*, via a series of points spaced between *A* and *O*.

On this line, the subject, settling down to his labour, over and over again,[5] acknowledging his history in the first person, makes progress into the order of fundamental symbolic relations in which he has to find the time, resolving the halts and the inhibitions which make up the super-ego. You need time for that.

If the echos of the discourse come together too quickly from point *O'* – that is to say if the transference gets too intense – a critical phenomenon takes place, evoking resistance, resistance in the most acute form in which it manifests itself – silence. So you see why, don't you, as Freud says, the transference becomes an obstacle when it is excessive.

It must also be said, that, if this moment comes at an opportune time, the silence takes on its full value as silence – it is not simply negative, but has value as a beyond of speech. Certain moments of silence in the transference represent the most vivid apprehension of the presence of the other as such.

One final remark. Where should the subject be placed, in so far as it is to be distinguished from point *O*? It is necessarily somewhere between *A* and *O* – much closer to *O* than any other point – let us say, so as to come back to it, in *C*.

When you will have left me for holidays which I hope will be happy, I beseech you to reread the precious little technical writings of Freud in the light of these reflections. Reread them, and you will see the extent to which they will take on a new and more vital meaning for you. You will realise that the apparent contradictions regarding transference, simultaneously resistance and motor of the analysis, can only be understood within the dialectic of the imaginary and the symbolic.

Analysts whose teaching is by no means lacking in merit have argued that the most up to date technique of analysis, that which has taken to itself the title of the analysis of resistances, consists in isolating off from the ego of the subject – single out,[6] which is Bibring's term[7] – a certain number of patterns[6] which are manifested as defence mechanisms, in relation to the analyst. That is a radical perversion of the notion of defence as introduced by Freud in his early writings, and reintroduced by him at the time of 'Inhibitions, symptoms and anxiety', one of his most difficult articles and one which has lent itself to most misunderstandings.

---

[5] '*remettant cent fois l'ouvrage sur le métier*' – see p. 187 n1 above.
[6] English in the original.   [7] Bergler in the original.

There's an intellectual operation for you. Because it is no longer a question of analysing the symbolic character of the defences, but of lifting them, in so far as they constitute an obstacle to a beyond, a beyond which is nothing more than a beyond – it doesn't matter what one puts into it. Read Fenichel, you will see that everything can be approached from the point of view of defence. Does the subject give himself over to the confession of tendencies whose sexual or aggressive character is completely acknowledged? From the simple fact of his having told you them, one can very easily set oneself looking for something beyond which is much more neutral. If one qualifies everything which is made manifest at the outset as a defence, everything can be legitimately considered as a mask, behind which something else is hidden. This systematic inversion is the butt of Jean Cocteau's famous jest – if you can tell someone that he dreams of an umbrella for sexual reasons, why not tell him when he dreams of an eagle swooping down on him to savage him that it is on account of his having forgotten his umbrella?

In centring analytic intervention on the dissipation of patterns[8] which hide this beyond, the analyst has no other guide than his own conception of the subject's behaviour. He attempts to normalise it – in accordance with a norm that is coherent with his own *ego*. So this will always be a modelling of one *ego* by another *ego*, hence by a superior *ego* – as everyone knows, the analyst's *ego* is not negligible.

Read Nunberg. What is the essential mainspring of the treatment in his eyes? The good will of the subject's *ego*, which must become the ally of the analyst. What does that mean? – except that the subject's new *ego* is the *ego* of the analyst. And Hoffer is there to tell us that the normal end of the treatment is identification with the *ego* of the analyst.

Of this end, which is none other than the spoken assumption of the ego, the reintegration not of the ideal ego, but of the ego-ideal, Balint gives us a very moving description. The subject enters into a semi-maniacal state, a sort of sublime release, a freedom from a narcissistic image through the world – for which one must allow him a bit of time so he can pull himself together and rediscover all by himself the paths of common sense.

This conception is not entirely false, since there really is a temporal factor in an analysis. And, besides, this is what has always been said, in a confused fashion, to be sure. Every analyst can only grasp it in his experience – there is a certain staggering of the time-for-understanding. Those of you who came to my discussions on the *Wolfman* will see in this a reference. But you will rediscover this time-for-understanding in Freud's Papers on Technique in connection with *Durcharbeiten*.

Is that something like borrowing from psychology? Or is it rather, as I said in

---

[8] English in the original.

what I wrote on empty and full speech, something from the order of discourse, from discourse as labour? Yes, without a shadow of a doubt. The discourse has to be maintained for a long enough time for it to appear as entirely engaged in the construction of the *ego*. From that point on, it may quite suddenly be resolved into the person for whom it was constructed, that is to say the master. By the same token, its own value falls, and now appears just as labour.

Where does this take us? – if not to grant once again that the concept is time. In this sense, one can say that the transference is the very concept of analysis, because it is the time of analysis.

The so-called analysis of resistances is always too much in a hurry to unveil for the subject the patterns[9] of the *ego*, its defences, hideaways, and that is why experience shows us and Freud teaches us in a specific passage in the Papers on Technique – such an analysis won't get the subject to take one more step. Freud says, when this happens, you have to wait.

You have to wait. You have to wait as long as it takes for the subject to realise the dimension at stake on the plane of the symbol, that is to say to disengage from the thing experienced in analysis – from this pursuit, from this brawl, from this tight embrace which the analysis of resistances produces – the appropriate duration of certain repetition-compulsions, which in some way gives them symbolic value.

O. MANNONI: *I think that that is a concrete problem. For example, there are some obsessionals whose lives consist in waiting. They turn their analyses into another waiting. That is exactly what I want to get to grips with – why does this waiting of the analysis reproduce in a certain manner the waiting in life, and change it?*

Exactly, and that is what has been asked of me with respect to the case of Dora. Last year, I developed the dialectic of the *Ratman* around the master-slave relation. What is the obsessional waiting for? The death of the master. What use does this waiting have for him? It is interposed between him and death. When the master is dead, everything will begin. You re-encounter this structure in all its guises.

What is more, he is right, the slave, he is quite right in banking on this waiting. To take up a comment attributed to Tristan Bernard, the day he was arrested to be brought to the Danzig camp – *Up to now we have been living in anxiety, now we are going to live in hope.*[10]

The master, let us get it straight, has a much more abrupt relation to death. The master in the pure state is in a desperate position in this respect, because he has nothing but his own death to wait for, since he expects nothing from the death of his slave, except a little inconvenience. On the other hand, the slave

---

[9] English in the original.
[10] Paul Bernard, usually known as Tristan Bernard, (1866–1947), novelist and playwright.

has a great deal to expect from the master's death. Beyond the death of the master, he really will be obliged to confront death, as every fully realised being has to, and to assume, in the Heideggerian sense, his being-for-death. Now precisely, the obsessional does not assume his being-for-death, he has been reprieved. that is what has to be shown him. That is the function of the image of the master as such.

O. MANNONI: . . . *who is the analyst.*

. . . who is embodied in the analyst. It is only after having sketched out several times the imaginary exits from the master's prison, and done this in accordance with certain scansions, in accordance with a certain timing,[11] it is only then that the obsessional can realise the concept of his obsessions, that is to say what they signify.

In each obsessional case, there necessarily is a certain number of temporal scansions, and even numerical signs. I have already touched on that in an article on 'Logical time'.[12] The subject thinking the thought of the other, sees in the other the image and the sketch of his own movements. Now, each time the other is exactly the same as the subject, there is no other master than the absolute master, death. But the slave requires a certain time to see that.

All because, like everyone else, he is much too happy being a slave.

Jacques Lacan has figurines representing elephants handed out.

7 July 1954

[11] English in the original.
[12] E 197–213.

APPENDIX

A spoken commentary on Freud's *Verneinung*, by Jean Hyppolite*

To start off with, I must thank Dr Lacan for his insisting on my giving you a presentation of this article of Freud's, because it gave me the occasion for a night's work; and of bringing you the fruit of this labour.[1] I hope that it will prove worthy in your eyes. Dr Lacan made sure to send me the German text with the French. That was a wise thing to do, because I don't think I would have understood anything in the French text, if I hadn't had the German.[2]

I wasn't familiar with this text. It has an absolutely extraordinary structure,

* [Originally published as 'Commentaire parlée sur la *Verneinung* de Freud', *La Psychanalyse* 1, 1956, 29–40. Reprinted as Appendice I to Lacan's *Écrits*, pp. 879–87, and also in Jean Hyppolite, *Figures de la pensée philosophique, écrits de Jean Hyppolite*, Paris: P.U.F. 1971, vol. I, pp. 385–96. We would like to thank Presses Universitaires de France for permission to translate this text.

It will be clear from what follows that the task of translating this talk is a peculiarly complicated one, since Hyppolite is sometimes commenting on the German text (in French), sometimes commenting on the French translation of the German text, and English readers will wish to rely upon the English translation of SE. On occasion, Hyppolite's rendition of the German text differs considerably from that of SE; notes will indicate this where necessary. The SE translation has been relied upon and often adapted (see p. 292 n10 below for a major inaccuracy in it).

There is an additional complication owing to the lack of fit between key terms in German, French and English. As Strachey notes, the translation of '*Verneinung*' by 'negation' was chosen to distinguish it from 'denial', which had previously been used to translate '*Verleugnung*', but which SE renders with 'disavowal'. (There is also the third term in this series, '*Verwerfung*', translated in SE by 'repudiation'.) While Hyppolite explicitly recognises the value of translating '*Verneinung*' by '*dénégation*', rather than by '*négation*', he does not appear to hold consistently to this practice; hence, where 'negation' appears in the text, it corresponds to '*dénégation*'; where '*négation*' was used in the original, the French word appears in square brackets afterwards.

Having been translated from the Appendix prepared in 1966 for the *Écrits*, this is the one passage in the Seminar with annotations supplied by Lacan and by the editor of *Écrits*, Jacques-Alain Miller. Notes added for the English edition are to be found in roman square brackets; annotations and additions already present in the body of the French text are to be found in ⟨ ⟩.]

[1] '*Je t'apporte l'enfant d'une nuit d'Idumée.*' (J. L.) ['I bring you the fruit of a night of Idumée' – reference unclear.]

[2] The French translation of Freud's *Verneinung* appeared in volume VII, no. 2 of the official organ of the Société Psychanalytique de Paris, in 1934, under the title *La négation*. The German text first appeared in *Imago* IX, in 1925, and has been reproduced in several collections of Freud's works. It can be found in GW XIV, as the second article, pp. 11–15. [The English translation, entitled 'Negation', is to be found in SE XIX 235–9; the newer German edition is Stud III 373–7.]

and deep down it is extremely enigmatic. Its construction is not at all that of a professor. The text's construction is, I don't want to say dialectical, so as not to abuse the word, but extremely subtle. And it obliged me to give myself over, with both the German text and French text (in which the translation is not very accurate but is, in the end, when compared with others, honest enough) to a genuine interpretation. And this is the interpretation I am going to offer you. I think it is valid, but it is not the only possible one and it is certainly worth talking over.

Freud begins by introducing the title *Die Verneinung*. And I realised, making the same discovery Dr Lacan had already made, that it would be better to translate it by '*la dénégation*'.

In the same way, further on you will find *etwas im Urteil verneinen*, which is not 'the negation of something in the judgement',[3] but a sort of readjudication [*déjugement*].[4] Throughout this text, I think one must distinguish between the negation [*négation*] internal to judgement and the attitude of negation [*négation*]; otherwise it doesn't seem possible to understand it.

The French text doesn't bring out the extremely concrete, almost entertaining style of the examples of negation with which Freud starts off. To start off with, take the following one, which contains a projection whose role you can easily locate given the analyses this seminar has engaged in, in which the patient, let us call him the person being psychoanalysed [*psychanalysé*], says to his analyst: 'Now you'll think I mean to say something insulting, but really I've no such intention.' 'We realise', Freud says, 'that this is a rejection, by projection, of an idea that has just come up.'[5]

'I came to realise that when, in daily life, as frequently happens, we want to say "assuredly I do not want to insult you by saying what I am saying", one should translate this by "I want to insult you." Such an intention is never lacking.'[6]

But this remark leads Freud to a very daring generalisation, through which he will address the problem of negation in so far as it might be the very origin of

---

[3] [SE: 'to negate something in a judgement']

[4] As is sufficiently indicated by the following sentence, in making the *Verurteilung*, that is the condemnation that it designates as the equivalent (*Ersatz* [SE: substitute]) of repression, whose very *no* must be taken as a hall-mark, into a certificate of origin comparable to the *made in Germany* impressed upon an object. (J. L.) [The phrase 'Made in Germany' appears in English in the original German (and in the French), thus highlighting that the hall-mark of repression is written in a foreign language. There is a historical aspect to this: the requirement that German goods display a hall-mark of origin (written in English) was imposed on the governments of Germany and Austria following the First World War (and hence a few years before Freud was writing): the ruling was intended to facilitate discrimination against German goods by stigmatising them. In fact, it had the opposite effect, since goods bearing the stamp 'Made in Germany' thereupon became sought after.]

[5] [SE XIX 235]

[6] [It is not clear why this passage is in quotation marks, since it is not a quotation from Freud's text.]

intelligence. That is how I understand the paper, in all its philosophical density.

In the same way, he gives an example of someone saying: 'You ask who this person in the dream can be. It's *not* my mother.' In which case, the question is settled, we can be sure that it is indeed her.

He goes on to cite a procedure which is useful to the psychoanalyst but in addition, we would say, to anyone, for clarifying what it is that has been repressed in a given situation. 'What would you consider the most unlikely thing in that situation? What do you think was furthest from your mind at that time?' And the patient, or it might just as easily be anyone you happen to be talking to, at a party or over supper, if he lets himself be caught in your trap and indeed tells you what he considers to be the most unbelievable thing, then that is what one has to believe.

So this is an analysis of concrete goings on, generalised until its basis is encountered in a mode of presenting what one is in the mode of not being it. Because that is exactly how it is constituted: 'I am going to tell you what I am not; pay attention, that is exactly what I am.' That is how Freud engages with the function of negation and, in order to do this, he uses a word which I could not but feel at home with, the word *Aufhebung*, which, as you know, has had a variety of destinies; it is not for me to say it . . .

DR LACAN: But if not you, then who else will it fall to?

M. HYPPOLITE: It is Hegel's dialectical word, which means simultaneously to deny, to suppress and to conserve, and fundamentally to raise up. In reality, it might be the *Aufhebung* of a stone, or equally the stopping of my newspaper subscription. At this point Freud tells us: 'negation is already an *Aufhebung* of the repression, though not, of course, an acceptance of what is repressed.'[7]

This is the start of something truly extraordinary in Freud's analysis, whereby what emerges from these anecdotes, which we might well have taken for nothing more than anecdotes, are implications of prodigious philosophical importance, which I will attempt to summarise in a moment.

Presenting one's being in the mode of not being it, that is truly what is at issue in this *Aufhebung* of the repression, which isn't an acceptance of what is repressed. The person speaking says: 'This is what I am not.' It would no longer be repressed, if repression signified unconsciousness, since it is conscious. But in its essentials, the repression persists,[8] in the form of non-acceptance.

Here Freud is going to lead us through an argument of extreme philosophical subtlety, in which it would be a gross lapse of attention to overlook the remark that Freud makes, simply on account of its everyday use which we never reflect on, that 'in this the intellectual function is separated from the affective process'.

---

[7] [SE XIX 235–6]
[8] 'bei Fortbestand des Wesentlichen an der Verdrängung' [GW XIV 12; Stud III 374].

Because, in the manner in which he then goes on to deal with it, there's a truly profound discovery.

Extending my hypothesis, I would say that, in proposing an analysis of the intellectual, he does not show how the intellectual is separated from the affective, but how it, the intellectual, is that sort of suspension of content for which the term, in rather barbaric language, sublimation[9] is not inappropriate. Perhaps what is born here is thought as such; but not before the content has been affected by a negation.

To refer to a philosophical text (which I once again ask you to excuse me for, although Dr Lacan is my surety here with respect to such a necessity), at the end of one of Hegel's chapters, the issue becomes that of substituting genuine negativity for that destructive appetite which takes hold of desire and which is there conceived of in a profoundly mythical rather than psychological manner, substituting, I was saying, for this destructive appetite which takes hold of desire and which is such that in the final outcome of the primordial struggle in which the two combatants confront one another, there would be no one left to remark the victory or the defeat of the one or the other, an ideal negation [*négation*].

The negation which Freud is here talking of clearly shows us, in so far as it is different from the ideal negation [*négation*] in which the intellectual is constituted, the sort of genesis whose vestiges Freud points to, in bringing his text to a conclusion [*moment de conclure*], in the negativism characteristic of certain psychotics.[10] And Freud goes on to give us an account of what differentiates this point from negativity, all the while speaking mythically.

In my view, this is what has to be acknowledged in order to understand what, in this article, is being spoken of, quite properly, under the name of negation, even though it isn't immediately visible. Similarly, one must take cognisance of an asymmetry expressed by two different words in Freud's text – which have been translated by the same word in French – an asymmetry between the emergence of affirmation starting off from the unifying drive [*tendance*] of love, and the genesis, starting off with the destructive drive [*tendance*], of that negation whose true function is that of giving rise to intelligence and the very starting point of thought.

But let us make our way with more care.

We have seen that Freud posits the intellectual as separated from the affective: whatever is yet to be added to this by the desired modification of

---

[9] We intend some day to establish a strict definition for analysis for this term – something which has not yet been done. (J. L. 1955). A promise since kept (1966).

[10] '*Die allgemeine Verneinungslust, der Negativismus mancher Psychotiker, ist wahrscheinlich als Anzeichen der Triebentmischung durch Abzug der libidinosen Komponenten zu verstehen.*' ['The general pleasure in negation, the negativism of many psychotics, is probably to be understood as a sign of a defusion of drives that has taken place through a withdrawal of the libidinal components.' (GW XIV 15; Stud III 376–7; SE XIX 239 – translation modified; amongst other imprecisions, SE gives 'wish to negate' for '*Verneinungslust*')]

analysis, 'the acceptance of what is repressed', repression is not, for all that, suppressed. Let us try to represent the situation.

First stage: this is what I am not. One concludes from that what I am. Repression still subsists in the guise of negation.

Second stage: the psychoanalyst obliges me to accept intellectually what I just denied; and Freud adds, after a dash and without any further explanation – 'the repressive process itself is not yet removed (*aufgehoben*) by this'.

Which seems very profound to me. If the analysand accepts, he renounces his negation, and yet the repression is still there! I conclude from this that one must do what Freud didn't do: call what happens here by a philosophical term – the negation of the negation. Literally, what appears here is intellectual affirmation, which is only intellectual, in so far as it is negation of the negation. These terms are not to be found in Freud, but I think that all we're doing is taking his thought one step further by formulating it in this way. That is what he really means.

At this point (let us be vigilant over a difficult text!) Freud finds himself in a position where he can show how the intellectual separates itself ⟨in action⟩[11] from the affective, to give a formulation of a sort of genesis of judgement, that is, in short, a genesis of thought.

I apologise to the psychologists here, but I do not much like positive psychology in itself; one might take this genesis for a positive psychology. To me its implications seem more profound in belonging to the order of history and of myth. And I think, given the role that Freud has this primordial affectivity play, in so far as it is the progenitor of intelligence, that it should be understood in the way that Dr Lacan teaches: that is to say that the primal form of relation known psychologically as the affective is itself situated within the distinctive field of the human situation, and that, if it engenders intelligence, it is because it already, from its beginnings, brings with it a fundamental historicity. There is no pure affective on the one hand, entirely engaged in the real, and the pure intellectual on the other, which detaches itself from it in order to grasp it once again. In the genesis described here, I see a sort of grand myth. And behind the appearance of Freud's positivity, there's this grand myth sustaining it.

What does that imply? Behind affirmation,[12] what is there? *Vereinigung*, which is Eros. And what is there behind negation (careful – intellectual negation will be something more)? The emergence of a fundamental asymmetrical symbol. Primordial affirmation is nothing more than affirming; but to deny is more than to wish to destroy.

The process which leads to that point, which has been translated by *rejet* [rejection], without Freud having used the term *Verwerfung*,[13] is still yet more forcefully accented, since he uses *Ausstossung*, which means expulsion.

---

[11] Words added. These will be indicated from now on by similar brackets.
[12] *Bejahung.*   [13] [See p. 43 n8 above.]

Here, then, in some way one finds ⟨the formal couple⟩ of two primary forces: the force of attraction[14] and the force of repulsion, both, it appears, under the domination of the pleasure principle, which in this text cannot but strike one.[15]

So, here judgement has its primary history. And at this point Freud distinguishes two types:

In conformity with what everyone learns concerning the elements of philosophy, there is a judgement of attribution and a judgement of existence. 'The function of judgement . . . affirms or disaffirms the possession by a thing of a particular attribute, and it asserts or disputes that a presentation has an existence in reality.'

And Freud then shows what lies behind the judgement of attribution and behind the judgement of existence. It seems to me that in order to understand this paper, one should consider the negation [négation] of the attributive judgement and the negation [négation] of the judgement of existence as being on this side of negation [négation] when it appears in its symbolic function. At bottom, judgement doesn't yet exist in this moment of emergence, rather there is a primary myth of the outside and the inside, and that is what has to be understood.

You can sense the implication of this myth of the formation of the outside and the inside: that of alienation, which is founded in these two terms. What is translated in their formal opposition becomes, beyond, alienation and hostility between the two.

What makes these four or five pages so dense is that, as you see, they put everything in question, and in them one is led from concrete remarks, seemingly so slight and yet so profound in their generality, to something which sweeps away an entire philosophy, by which we should understand an entire structure of thought.

Behind the judgement of attribution, what is there? There is the 'I should like to take in (to myself) [(m')approprier], introject' or the 'I should like to eject.'

In the beginning, Freud seems to be saying, but in the beginning means nothing more than the myth 'once upon a time' . . . Within this history, once upon a time there was an ego (by which we here should understand a subject) for which nothing as yet was alien.

Distinguishing between the alien and itself is an operation, an expelling. Which renders comprehensible a proposition which, having emerged rather abruptly, seems for a moment to be contradictory:

'Das Schlechte, what is bad, das dem Ich Fremde, what is alien to the ego, das Außenbefindliche, what is external, ist ihm zunächst identisch, are, to begin with, identical.'

---

[14] Einbeziehung.
[15] The seminar in which J. L. gave a commentary on Beyond the pleasure principle took place in 1954–55.

Now, just before, Freud had said that one introjects and one ejects, that therefore there is an operation which is the operation of expulsion ⟨without which⟩ the operation of introjection ⟨would have no meaning⟩. So that is the primordial operation upon which the judgement of attribution is founded.

But what lies at the origin of the judgement of existence is the relation between representation and perception. And here it is very difficult to miss the sense in which Freud deepens this relation. What is important is that, 'in the beginning', it is of no importance to know whether something exists or doesn't exist. The subject reproduces its presentation of things from the primitive perception it had of them. Now, when he says that this exists, the question is ⟨not⟩[16] one of knowing whether this presentation still preserves its state in reality but if it can or cannot be refound. Such is the relation which Freud stresses: he founds [the testing] of the presentation by reality in the possibility of its object being refound once again. This emphasis on the source of repetition shows that Freud is working in a more profound dimension than that of Jung, the latter's dimension being more properly that of memory.[17] At this point one must not lose the thread of his analysis. (But it is so difficult and detailed that I am afraid of losing you.)

What was at issue in the judgement of attribution was expelling or introjecting. In the judgement of existence, it is a question of attributing to the ego, or rather to the subject (it is more comprehensive), a presentation to which its object no longer corresponds, although an object had once corresponded to it, through a retracing of its steps. What is here in question is the genesis 'of the external and of the internal'.

Hence this offers us, Freud tells us, 'an insight into the origin' of judgement, 'from the interplay of the primary drive-impulses'. So here there is a sort of 'continuation, along lines of expediency, of the original process by which the ego took things into itself [*appropriation au moi*][18] or expelled them from itself, according to the pleasure principle.'

'*Die Bejahung*, affirmation, Freud tells us, *als Ersatz der Vereinigung*, in so far as it is simply the equivalent of unification, *gehört dem Eros an*, belongs to Eros': this is what lies at the source of affirmation. For example, in the judgement of attribution, there's the fact of introjecting, of taking into ourselves [*nous approprier*] instead of ejecting outside.

[16] Words added by the editor, in line with Freud's text: '*Der erste und nächste Zweck der Realitätsprüfung ist also nicht, ein dem Vorgestellten entsprechendes Objekt in der realen Wahrnehmung zu finden, sondern es wiederzufinden, sich zu überzeugen, daß es noch vorhanden ist.*' [GW XIV 14; Stud III 375] ['The first and immediate aim, therefore, of reality-testing is, not to *find* an object in real perception which corresponds to the one presented, but to *refind* such an object, to convince oneself that it is still there.' (SE XIX 237–8)]
[17] Is the author here referring to Platonic reminiscence? (J. L.)
[18] [The term in the German text at this point is '*Einbeziehung*', earlier rendered as 'attraction', whereas the earlier use of '*approprier*' was a rendering of '*einführen*'; SE renders both '*Einbeziehung*' and '*einführen*' by 'take into'.]

For negation [*négation*], he doesn't employ the word *Ersatz*, but the word *Nachfolge*. But the French translator translates it by the same word as *Ersatz*. The German text gives: affirmation is the *Ersatz* of *Vereinigung*, and negation [*négation*] the *Nachfolge* of expulsion, or more exactly of the instinct of destruction (*Destruktionstrieb*).[19]

As a result this becomes entirely mythical: two instincts which, as it were, are mixed together in this myth which bears the subject: one of unification, the other of destruction. A grand myth, as you see, and one which repeats others. But the little nuance, whereby affirmation in some way only comes to substitute for unification, whereas negation [*négation*] ensues well after expulsion, only this nuance appears to me capable of explaining the sentence which follows, in which it is simply a question of negativism and of the instinct of destruction. In fact this explains how there can be a pleasure in negation, a negativism which results straightforwardly from the suppression[20] of the libidinal components; that is to say what has disappeared in this pleasure in negating (disappeared = repressed) are the libidinal components.

As a consequence, does the instinct of destruction also depend upon ⟨the⟩ pleasure ⟨principle⟩? I think this is very important, crucial for technique.[21]

Except, Freud tells us, 'the performance of the function of judgement is only made possible by *the creation of the symbol of negation*'.[22]

Why doesn't Freud say: the functioning of judgement is rendered possible by affirmation? Because negation [*négation*] has a role to play not as a tendency to destruction, no more than within a form of judgement, but in so far as it is the fundamental attitude of symbolicity rendered explicit.

'The creation of the symbol of negation which has permitted an initial degree of independence in relation to repression and its consequences and, with it, from the compulsion (*Zwang*) of the pleasure principle.'[23]

---

[19] [For this sentence, SE XIX 239 gives: 'Affirmation – as a substitute for uniting – belongs to Eros; negation – the successor to expulsion – belongs to the instinct of destruction.']

[20] The German *Abzug*: deduction, deducting, withholding, docking, 'what is withheld in the pleasure in negating are the libidinal components'. Its possibility is referred to the *Triebentmischung* which is a sort of return to a pure state, a decanting of drives which is commonly – and mediocrely – translated by: '*désintrication des instincts*' [SE: 'defusion of instincts'].

[21] The admirable way in which M. Hyppolite's presentation at this point presses close to the difficulty appears to me all the more important given that I had not as yet produced the theses that I was to develop in the following year in my commentary on *Beyond the Pleasure Principle*, on the death instinct, which is simultaneously both so elusive and so present in this text.

[22] Underlined by Freud. [There is no emphasis of this passage in the German text. Here, the passage is translated directly from the French, since it differs markedly from SE: '*Die Leistung der Urteilsfunktion wird aber erst dadurch ermöglicht, daß die Schöpfung des Verneinungssymbols dem Denken einen ersten Grad von Unabhängigkeit von der Erfolgen der Verdrängung und somit auch vom Zwang des Lustprinzips gestattet hat.*' (GW XIV 15; Stud III 377) 'But the performance of the function of judgement is not made possible until the creation of the symbol of negation has endowed thinking with a first measure of freedom from the consequences of repression and, with it, from the compulsion of the pleasure principle.' (SE XIX 239)]

[23] [See previous note.]

A sentence whose meaning would not have created any problem for me, if I hadn't started off by linking up the tendency to destruction with the pleasure principle.

Because here there is a difficulty. From then on, what does this asymmetry between affirmation and negation [*négation*] signify? It signifies that all of the repressed can once again be taken up and used again in a sort of suspension, and that, in some way, instead of being under the domination of the instincts of attraction and repulsion, a margin of thought can be generated, an appearance of being in the form of non-being, which is generated with negation, that is to say when the symbol of negation [*négation*] is linked up with the concrete attitude of negation.

Because that is how one should understand the text, if one admits its conclusion, which at first seemed so strange to me.

'This view of negation fits in very well with the fact that in analysis we never discover a "no" in the unconscious . . .'

But one certainly finds destruction there. So one must make a clearcut distinction between the instinct of destruction and the form of destruction, otherwise one won't understand what Freud meant. In negation, one should see a concrete attitude at the origin of the explicit symbol of negation [*négation*], which explicit symbol alone makes possible something like the use of the unconscious, all the while maintaining the repression.

Such appears to me to be the meaning of the end of the conclusion cited above: '. . . and that recognition of the unconscious on the part of the ego is expressed in a negative formula'.

That is the summary: in analysis there is no 'no' to be found in the unconscious, but recognition of the unconscious on the part of the ego demonstrates that the ego is always failure to recognise [*méconnaissance*]; even in knowledge [*connaissance*], one always finds, on the part of the ego, in a negative formula, the hall-mark of the possibility of being in possession of the unconscious in refusing it all the while.

'There is no stronger evidence that we have been successful in our effort to uncover the unconscious than when the analysand reacts with the phrase: "I didn't think that", or (even): "I didn't (ever) think of that."'

So, in these four or five pages of Freud's – and I apologise if I myself have demonstrated some difficulty in finding in it what I believe to be its thread – there is, on the one hand, the analysis of that kind of concrete attitude, which emerges simply from observing negation; on the other hand, the possibility of seeing the intellectual dissociate itself ⟨in action⟩ from the affective; finally, and above all, a genesis of everything which occurs on the level of the primal, and in consequence the origin of judgement and of thought itself (in the form of thought as such, since thought is already there before, in the primal, but it does not figure as thought there) – grasped by means of negation.

BIBLIOGRAPHY

The bibliography contains full references to all works cited in the text, including some works that are only alluded to in passing.

Alexander, Franz, 'A metapsychological description of the process of cure', *Int. J. Psa.* 6, 1925, 13–34

    'The logic of emotions and its dynamic background', *Int. J. Psa.* 16, 1935, 399–413

Angelus Silesius, *Selections from The Cherubinic Wanderer*, translated with an introduction by J. E. C. Flitch, London,1932

Augustine, Saint, *De Magistro*, translated as *The Teacher*, in *The Fathers of The Church, Vol 59. Saint Augustine. The Teacher. The Free Choice of the Will. Grace and Free Will*, translated by Robert P. Russell, Washington: The Catholic University of America Press, 1968, pp. 7–61. Latin text in: *Corpus Christianorum XXIX Aurelii Augustini Opera*, Pars II, 2, Turnholti, Typographi Brepols Editores Pontificii, 1970, pp. 155–203

    Le maître, translated by Père François-Joseph Tonnard, Bibliothèque Augustinienne: Oeuvres de Saint Augustin 6.3, 2nd edition, Paris, 1952

Austin, J. L., *How To Do Things With Words*, Oxford: Oxford University Press, 1962

Balint, Alice, 'Love for the mother and mother love' (1939), in Balint, Michael, *Primary Love and Psycho-analytic Technique*

Balint, Michael, *Primary Love and Psycho-analytic Technique*, London: Hogarth Press and the Institute of Psycho-analysis, 1952

Bergman, Paul, 'The germinal cell of Freud's psychoanalytic psychology and therapy', in Sandor Lorand, ed., *The Yearbook of Psychoanalysis* (New York: International Universities Press, 1950) 6, 1950, pp. 51–73

Bibring, E., 'Symposium for the theory of the therapeutic results of psychoanalysis', *Int. J. Psa.* 18, 1937, 170–89

Boileau, *Works*, translated by N. Rowe and others, London, 1711–13

Bühler, Karl, *Sprachtheorie. Die Darstellungsfunktion der Sprache*, Jena: Fischer, 1934

Cusanus, Nicholas, *De Docta Ignorantia (Of Learned Ignorance)* (1440), translated by Germain Heron, introduction by D. J. B. Hawkins, London: Routledge & Kegan Paul, 1954

Ezriel, H., 'The scientific testing of psycho-analytic findings and theory. II The psychoanalytic session as an experimental situation', *Brit. J. Med. Psychol.* 24, 1951, 30–4

Fenichel, Otto, *The Psychoanalytic Theory of the Neuroses*, London: Routledge & Kegan Paul, 1946

Ferenczi, Sandor, 'Stages in the development of the sense of reality' (1913), in *First Contributions to Psycho-analysis*, London: Hogarth Press and the Institute of Psycho-analysis, 1952, chapter 8

Freud, Anna, *The Ego and the Mechanisms of Defence* (1936), London: Hogarth Press and the Institute of Psycho-analysis, 1968 (revised edition)

Freud, Sigmund and Breuer, Josef, (1895d) *Studies on Hysteria*, GW I; SE II

Freud, Sigmund, (1896b) 'Further remarks on the neuro-psychoses of defence', GW I 379–403; SE III 162–85

(1900a) *The Interpretation of Dreams*, GW II/III; Stud II; SE IV & V

(1901b) *The Psychopathology of Everyday Life*, GW IV; SE VI

(1904a) 'Freud's psycho-analytic procedure', GW V 3–10; Stud Erg 101–6; SE VII 249–54

(1905a) 'On psychotherapy', GW V 13–26; Stud Erg 109–19; SE VII 257–68

(1905d) *Three Essays on the Theory of Sexuality*, GW V 29–145; Stud V 43–145; SE VII 130–243

(1910d) 'The future prospects of psycho-analytic therapy', GW VIII 104–115; Stud Erg 123–32; SE XI 141–51

(1910k) '"Wild" psycho-analysis', GW VIII 118–25; Stud Erg 135–41; SE XI 221–27

(1912b) 'The dynamics of transference', GW VIII 364–74; Stud Erg 159–68; SE XII 99–108

(1914a) 'Fausse reconnaissance ("déjà raconté") in psycho-analytic treatment', GW X 116–23; Stud Erg 233–8; SE XIII 201–7

(1914c) 'On narcissism: an introduction', GW X 138–70; Stud III 41–68; SE XIV 73–102

(1915d) 'Repression', GW X 248–61; Stud III 107–118; SE XIV 146–58

(1917d) 'Metapsychological supplement to the theory of dreams', GW X 412–26; Stud III 179–91; SE XIV 222–35

(1918b[1914]) 'From the history of an infantile neurosis', GW XII 29–157; Stud VIII 129–232; SE XVII 7–122

(1919a) 'Lines of advance in psycho-analytic therapy', GW XII 183–94; Stud Erg 241–9; SE XVII 159–68

(1921c) *Group Psychology and the Analysis of the Ego*, GW XIII 73–161; Stud IX 65–134; SE XVIII 69–143

(1923b) *The Ego and the Id*, GW XIII 237–89; Stud III 282–330; SE XIX 12–66

(1927e) 'Fetishism', GW XIV 311–17; Stud III 383–8; Stud XXI 152–7

(1933a) *New Introductory Lectures*, GW XV 3–197; Stud I 448–608; SE XXII 3–182

(1937d) 'Constructions in analysis', GW XVI 43–56; Stud Erg 395–406; SE XXIII 257–69

(1950a) *The Origins of Psycho-analysis*, with 'Project for a scientific psychology' (also in SE I 295–387); London: Hogarth Press and the Institute of Psycho-analysis, 1954

Gracián, Balthasar, *El Criticon* (1651–7), translated as *The Critick*, London: Henry Brome, 1681

Oraculo Manuel y Arte de Prudencia, seceda de los aforismes que se discurren el las obras de Lorenco Gracian (1653), Amsterdam: J. Blaeu, 1659, translated as *L'Homme de*

Cour, Paris, 1684 (the title Lacan gives it); translated as *The Oracle, A Manual of the Art of Discretion*, by L. B. Walton, London: J. M. Dent, 1953

Hartmann, Heinz, 'Technical implications of ego psychology', *Psychoanalytic Quarterly* 20, 1951, 31–43

Hoffer, W., 'Development of the body ego', *Psychoanalytic Study of the Child* 5, 1950, 18–23

Hyppolite, Jean, *Figures de la Pensée Philosophique, Écrits de Jean Hyppolite*, Paris: Presses Universitaires de France, 1971

Janet, Pierre, *Les Obsessions et la Psychasthénie*, Paris: Alcan, 1903

Jones, Ernest, 'The theory of symbolism' (1916), in *Papers on Psycho-analysis*, 2nd edition, London: Baillière, Tindall & Cox, 1918, 129–86

'Early development of female sexuality' (1927), in *Papers on Psycho-analysis*, 5th edition, London: Baillière, Tindall & Cox, 1948, 438–51

Jung, Carl Gustav, *Wandlungen und Symbole der Libido* (1911–12), translated as *The Psychology of the Unconscious*, New York, 1916; revised edition and translation: *Symbols of Transformation*, in *The Collected Works of C. G. Jung*, vol. 5, Princeton: Bollingen, 1953–79

Klein, Melanie, *The Writings of Melanie Klein*, under the general editorship of Roger Money-Kyrle in collaboration with Betty Joseph, Edna O'Shaughnessy and Hanna Segal, 4 vols., London: The Hogarth Press and the Institute of Psycho-analysis, 1975

Kris, Ernst, 'Ego psychology and interpretation in psychoanalytic therapy', *Psychoanalytic Quarterly* 20, 1951, 15–30

Lacan, Jacques, 'La psychiatrie anglaise et la guerre', *L'Évolution Psychiatrique* 1947, 293–312; reprinted in: Jacques Lacan, *Travaux et Interventions*, Paris: Association Régionale de l'Éducation Permanente, 1977 (non-paginated)

'Intervention on transference', E 215–26; translated in Mitchell and Rose, eds., *Feminine Sexuality* 62–73

'The neurotic's individual myth' (1953), *Psychoanalytic Quarterly* 48, 1979, 405–25

Écrits, Paris: Seuil, 1966

Écrits: A Selection, translated by Alan Sheridan, London: Tavistock, 1977

The Four Fundamental Concepts of Psycho-Analysis (Seminar, Book XI, 1964), edited by Jacques-Alain Miller, trans. Alan Sheridan, London: The Hogarth Press and the Institute of Psycho-analysis, 1977.

The Seminar. Book II. The Ego in Freud's Theory and in the Technique of Psychoanalysis. 1954–1955, edited by Jacques-Alain Miller, translated by Sylvana Tomaselli, with notes by John Forrester, Cambridge: Cambridge University Press, 1987

Leuba, John, *Introduction à la Géologie*, Paris: Colin, 1925

Little, Margaret, 'Counter-transference and the patient's response to it', *Int. J. Psa.* 32, 1951, 32–40

Loewenstein, Rudolph M., 'The problem of interpretation', *Psychoanalytic Quarterly* 20, 1951, 1–14

Mallarmé, Stéphane, *Oeuvres Complètes*, Paris: Gallimard, Pléiade, 1945. *The Poems*, translated and introduced by Keith Bosley, Harmondsworth: Penguin, 1977

Mitchell, Juliet and Rose, Jacqueline, editors, *Feminine Sexuality. Jacques Lacan and the École Freudienne*, translated by Jacqueline Rose, London: Macmillan, 1982

Moses Maimonides, *The Guide of the Perplexed*, translated with an introduction and notes by Shlomo Pines, with an introductory essay by Leo Strauss, Chicago: Chicago University Press, 1963

Nunberg, H., 'The theory of the therapeutic results of psychoanalysis', *Int. J. Psa.* 18, 1937, 161–9

'Transference and reality', *Int. J. Psa.* 32, 1951, 1–9

Rado, Sandor, 'The economic principle in psychoanalytic technique', *Int. J. Psa.* 6, 1925, 35–44

Rickman, John, *Selected Contributions to Psycho-analysis*, compiled by W. C. M. Scott, with an introductory memoir by S. M. Payne, London: The Hogarth Press and the Institute of Psycho-analysis, 1957

Rivière, Joan, 'On the genesis of psychical conflict in earliest infancy', *Int. J. Psa.* 17, 1936, 395–422

Sachs, Hanns, 'Metapsychological points of view in technique and theory', *Int. J. Psa.* 6, 1925, pp. 5–12

Sartre, Jean-Paul, *Being and Nothingness* (1943), translated by Hazel E. Barnes, New York: Simon & Schuster, 1956

Schmideberg, Melitta, 'Intellectual inhibition and disturbances in eating', *Int. J. Psa.* 19, 1938, 17–22

Somaize, *Le Dictionnaire des Précieuses*, nouvelle édition de Ch.-L. Livet, Paris: Jannet, 1856

Sterba, Richard, 'Das Schicksal des Ichs im therapeutischen Verfahren', *Int. Ztschr. f. Psa.* 20, 1934, 66–73; 'The fate of the ego in analytic therapy', *Int. J. Psa.* 15, 1934, 117–26

Strachey, James, 'The nature of the therapeutic action of psychoanalysis', *Int. J. Psa.* 15, 1934, 127–59; reprinted in *Int. J. Psa.* 50, 1969, 275–91

Strauss, Leo, *Persecution and the Art of Writing*, Glencoe, Illinois, 1952

Valéry, Paul, *Oeuvres I*, Paris: Gallimard, Pléiade, 1959. *Poems*, translated by David Paul, in *The Collected Works of Paul Valéry*, ed. Jackson Mathews, vol. I, London: Routledge & Kegan Paul, 1971

Wälder, Robert, 'The problem of the genesis of psychical conflict in earliest infancy. Remarks on a paper by Joan Rivière, *Int. J. Psa.* 18, 1937, 406–73

Wiener, Norbert, *Cybernetics, or Control and Communication in the Animal and the Machine*, Paris: Hermann et Cie; New York: John Wiley, 1948

Wittgenstein, *Philosophical Investigations*, translated by G. E. M. Anscombe, Oxford: Basil Blackwell, 1976

INDEX

imaginary fascination, but there is no love. There is inflicted love, but not the active gift of love.

Well, with hate, it is the same thing. There is an imaginary dimension of hate, in so far as the destruction of the other is one pole of the very structure of the intersubjective relation. As I've pointed out to you, it is what Hegel recognises as the impasse for the coexistence of two consciousnesses, from whence he deduces his myth of the struggle for pure prestige. Even there, the imaginary dimension is framed by the symbolic relation, and that is why hate is not satisfied with the disappearance of the adversary. If love aspires to the unfolding of the being of the other, hate wishes the opposite, namely its abasement, its deranging, its deviation, its delirium, its detailed denial, its subversion. That is what makes hate a career with no limit, just as love is.

Perhaps it is more difficult to get you to understand that, for reasons which may not be such good reasons for rejoicing as one might think, these days we know less about the feeling of hatred than in times when man was more open to his destiny.

To be sure, we have seen, not very long ago, manifestations which, within this genre, weren't bad at all. Nonetheless, these days subjects do not have to shoulder the burden of the experience of hatred in its most consuming forms. And why? Because our civilisation is itself sufficiently one of hatred. Isn't the path for the race to destruction really rather well marked out for us? Hatred is clothed in our everyday discourse under many guises, it meets with such extraordinarily easy rationalisations. Perhaps it is this state of the diffuse flocculation of hatred which saturates the call for the destruction of being in us. As if the objectivation of the human being in our civilisation corresponded exactly to what, within the structure of the *ego*, is the pole of hatred.

O. MANNONI: *Western moralism.*

Exactly. Hatred here discovers how to feed on everyday objects. You would be wrong to think that as a result it is absent from wars, when, for certain privileged subjects, it is fully realised.

Don't get me wrong. In speaking about love and hate to you, I am showing you the paths for the realisation of being, not the realisation of being, but only its paths.

And yet, if the subject commits himself to searching after truth as such, it is because he places himself in the dimension of ignorance – it doesn't matter whether he knows it or not. That is one of the elements making up what analysts call 'readiness to the transference'.[1] There is a readiness to the transference in the patient solely by virtue of his placing himself in the position of acknowledging himself in speech, and searching out his truth to the end, the

[1] English in the original.

end which is there, in the analyst. The analyst's ignorance is also worthy of consideration.

The analyst must not fail to recognise what I will call the dimension of ignorance's power of accession to being, since he has to reply to the person who, throughout his discourse, questions him in this dimension. He doesn't have to guide the subject to a *Wissen*, to knowledge, but on to the paths by which access to this knowledge is gained. He must engage him in a dialectical operation, not say to him that he is wrong since he necessarily is in error, but show him that he speaks poorly, that is to say that he speaks without knowing, as one who is ignorant, because what counts are the paths of his error.

Psychoanalysis is a dialectic, what Montaigne, in book III, chapter VIII, calls *an art of conversation*.[2] The art of conversation of Socrates in the *Meno* is to teach the slave to give his own speech its true meaning. And it is the same in Hegel. In other words, the position of the analyst must be that of an *ignorantia docta*, which does not mean knowing [*savante*], but formal, and what is capable of being formative for the subject.

Because it is in the air these days, these days of hatred, there is a great temptation to transform the *ignorantia docta* into what I have called, and this is hardly a novelty, an *ignorantia docens*. If the psychoanalyst thinks he knows something, in psychology for example, then that is already the beginning of his loss, for the simple reason that in psychology nobody knows much, except that psychology is itself an error of perspective on the human being.

I will have to use banal examples to make you understand what the realisation of the being of man is, because in spite of yourselves you put it in an erroneous perspective, that of a false knowledge.

All the same you must have realised that, when a man says *I am*, or *I will be*, even *I will have been* or *I want to be*, there is always a jump, a gap. It is just as extravagant, in relation to reality, to say *I am a psychoanalyst* as *I am king*. Both the one and the other are entirely valid affirmations, which nothing, however, in the order of what one might call the measure of capacities justifies. The symbolic legitimations by virtue of which a man takes on what is conferred on him by others entirely escapes the register of entitlements to office.[3]

When a man refuses to be king, it does not have at all the same value as when he accepts. By the very fact of refusing, he is not king. He is a petit bourgeois – take for example the Duke of Windsor. The man who, just on the brink of being invested with the dignity of the crown, says – *I want to live with the woman I love* – simply because of that remains on this side of the domain of being king.

But when the man says – and in saying it, is it, by virtue of a certain system of symbolic relations – says *I am king* – it is not simply accepting an office. From

---

[2] 'un art de conférer'.
[3] 'habilitations capacitaires'.

one minute to the next the meaning of all his psychological attributes changes. His passions, his plans, even his stupidity take on an entirely different meaning. All of these functions become, solely by virtue of the fact of his being the king, royal functions. In the register of royalty, his intelligence becomes something quite different, even his inabilities start to polarise, to structure an entire series of destinies around him, destinies which are found to be profoundly modified for the reason that the royal authority will be exercised in this or that way by the person who has been invested with it.

This happens on a small scale every day – a gentleman who has decidedly mediocre qualities and who presents all sorts of problems in a low-level job, is raised up in to an investiture that is sovereign in some way, however limited the domain may be, and he changes entirely. All you have to do is observe him everyday, the significance of his strengths as well as his weaknesses is transformed, and their relations may well be reversed.

That is also what habilitations, examinations reveal in an unobtrusive, concealed fashion. Why, given the time that has elapsed since we became such clever psychologists, haven't we eliminated the various milestones which formerly had the value of initiations, the degrees, the competitive examinations, etc? If we have truly eliminated this value, why not pare down the investiture to the totalisation of the work acquired, the notes taken down over the year, or even to a set of tests or examinations measuring the abilities of the subjects? Why retain this vague archaic character for these examinations? We protest against these elements of chance and fortune like people throwing themselves against the walls of the prison they themselves have built. The truth is simply that a competitive examination, in as much as it clothes the subject with a qualification which is symbolic, cannot be given an entirely rationalised structure, and cannot just be inserted into the register of the addition of quantity.

So, when we meet this, we think how clever we are and tell ourselves – *But of course, let's write a great psychoanalytic article so as to show the initiatory character of the examination.*

This character is obvious. It is fortunate that we are aware of it. But it is unfortunate that the psychoanalyst doesn't always explain it very well. His is a partial discovery, which he explains in terms of omnipotence of thoughts, of magical thought, whereas it is the dimension of the symbol which is fundamental here.

3

Who has got other questions to raise?

DR BEJARANO: *I have a concrete example in mind. You should try to show us how the different registers are followed out in the case of Dora.*

In the Dora case, one remains somewhat on the threshold of that, but even so I can place it for you a little by giving a final reply to the question of the transference as a whole.

The analytic experience is founded on Freud's first discoveries, on the tripod dream, slip, joke. The symptom is a fourth element, which can serve, not as *verbum*, since it is not constructed out of phonemes, but as *signum*, with the organism as ground – if you can recall the various spheres distinguished in Augustine's text. It is within this experience, and with some delay in the founding of the latter – Freud himself says that he was frightened – that he isolates the phenomenon of the transference. For want of being recognised, the transference operated as an obstacle to the treatment. Once recognised, it becomes the mainstay of the treatment.

But even before he had become aware of the existence of transference, Freud had already designated it. In the *Traumdeutung*, there is, in effect, already a definition of the *Übertragung* as a function of the double level of speech, as I have put it to you. There are parts of the discourse which are disinvested of significations which another signification, the unconscious signification, will take from behind. Freud demonstrates it with respect to the dream, and I have pointed it out to you in some striking slips.

It's a pity I have not talked much about the slip this year. Now, that is a fundamental dimension, since it is the radical facet of the non-meaning which all meaning possesses. There is a point where meaning emerges, and is created. But even at this very point, man is very easily capable of feeling that the meaning is at the same time annihilated, that it is created so as to be annihilated. What's a joke? – if not the calculated irruption of non-sense into a discourse which seems to make sense.

O. MANNONI: *It is the navel of speech.*

Exactly. In the dream, there is an extremely confused navel. Inversely, the navel of the joke is perfectly sharp – the *Witz*. And what expresses its most radical essence is non-sense.

Well, we realise this transference is our mainstay.

I pointed out three senses in which different authors understand it. This tripartition, which is only didactic, should allow you to get your bearings amidst the various present-day analytic tendencies – and that is not very encouraging.

Some want to understand the phenomenon of transference in relation to the real, that is to say in as much as it is a phenomenon taking place in the present. One thinks one is making a real breakthrough when one says that every analysis must bear on the *hic et nunc*. One thinks one has found something quite dazzling in that, one thinks one has taken a bold step forward. On this theme